2015

Contact details for the Society are on its website
http://www.bedfordshirehrs.org.uk

THE PUBLICATIONS OF THE BEDFORDSHIRE
HISTORICAL RECORD SOCIETY
VOLUME 94

BEDFORD'S MUSICAL SOCIETY

A History of Bedford Choral Society

Michael Benson
With an Introduction by Donald Burrows

Mike Benson

THE BEDFORDSHIRE HISTORICAL RECORD SOCIETY

THE BOYDELL PRESS

First published 2015

A publication of
Bedfordshire Historical Record Society
published by The Boydell Press
an imprint of Boydell & Brewer Ltd
PO Box 9, Woodbridge, Suffolk IP12 3DF, UK
and of Boydell & Brewer Inc.
668 Mt Hope Avenue, Rochester, NY 14620–2371, USA
website: www.boydellandbrewer.com

ISBN 978–0–85155–081–7

ISSN 0067–4826

The Society is most grateful for financial support from the
Simon Whitbread Charitable Trust, Bedford Choral Society and other
donors who have helped make the publication of this volume possible

Details of previous volumes are available from
Boydell and Brewer Ltd

A CIP catalogue record for this book is available
from the British Library

Contents

Illustrations

Cover

Bedford Musical Society's choir accompanied by the Riddick String Orchestra and conducted by Norman Frost in a performance of Mendelssohn's *Elijah,* 22 March 1946. The soloists are Isobel Baillie (second left), Muriel Brunskill, Walter Widdop and Roy Henderson (right).

Plates are between pages 70 and 71

Preface

In 1991, Bedford Choral Society celebrated its 125th anniversary. A year earlier, as part of my degree with the Open University, I had studied the Arts Foundation course, which included units on musical performance during the Victorian period and on provincial music-making. This prompted me to ask questions about the formation of Bedford Choral Society, of which I was a member. To my surprise no-one knew very much about its origins. When I started to investigate, I found that the date chosen to celebrate the anniversary was incorrect: the Society was actually founded very early in 1867. It was a commonly held view that it was founded in 1866.[1]

I set out to write an article about the Society's history for *The Bedfordshire Magazine*, and began research early in 1991 in the local studies section of Bedford Central Library. My article was published around the time of the main celebratory concert in November 1991.[2] Soon after I had started work on the article, I had a fascinating discussion with Kate and Hans Freyhan (both long-term members of the Society) whom many people thought would be able to give me a large amount of background information. They were not as knowledgeable about the history of the Society as I had hoped, perhaps because they had escaped to England, from Germany, just before the Second World War. They did, however, pass on to me many of the Society's early concert programmes, which proved to be enormously helpful.

I soon realised that my article only 'scraped the surface' and decided that I wanted to write a fuller history; this present book is the outcome. Since 1991, the history of Bedford Choral Society has been a constant companion, but as I was elected as general secretary of the Society following retirement in 2002, I was not able to do much work on the book during the six years that I held that post.

Undertaking the research for this book has taken me to places, libraries and archives that I would not otherwise have known about or visited, and this experience has been invaluable. But I also had a lot of luck while working on this history, including finding a second-hand music shop in Hay-on-Wye with a number of musical scores of works which were sung in the Victorian period but which are now seldom, if ever, performed, and obtaining some musical scores that had been used by members of the Society from the late 1890s onwards.[3]

Having sung with the Choral Society for nearly forty years, I am very fortunate to have known a number of the older choir members. Some of them had contacts going back to the turn of the twentieth century. It has been inspiring and humbling to

1 This is stated in Joyce Godber's *History of Bedfordshire 1066–1888* (Bedford, 1969), p. 524. The error probably occurred because of confusion about how each season was numbered.

2 Benson, Mike, 'Bedford Choral Society', *The Bedfordshire Magazine*, vol. 23, no. 179 (Winter 1991), pp. 100–4.

3 These were in the possession of former chorus master, Freddie Stevens, and passed to me by members of his family.

talk to these people and to learn first-hand about the work of the Society over a long period. They have helped to make it possible for me to write this book. The Internet was not available in 1991, and while it has certainly been invaluable in recent years, I might have undertaken my research differently – and not so effectively – had it been accessible when I began.

I would like to especially thank those who have inspired me, but who have not lived to see the finished result: Kate and Hans Freyhan, Sylvia Palmer, Michael Diemer, Joe Pinnock, Tom and Mollie Winter, Ken Wesley (of the Bedford Competitive Music Festival), Bill Knight, Freddie Stevens and Anthony Chapman. I am also very grateful to Deirdre Knight for all the information that she has provided, and to George Thomson, who at the age of ninety-six has been very helpful, especially with information about events that took place in the years before the Second World War. Without exception, all of the above have been very supportive and positive.

I also wish to thank the many other people who have assisted including: Boneventura Bottone, James Collett-White, Antony le Fleming, John Handley, Andrew Morris, Paul Paviour, Michael Rose, John Shayler, Ian Smith, Malcolm Struthers, John Watson and Sir David Willcocks. In addition, I would like to acknowledge the assistance I have received from Bedford Central Library, Bedford Modern School, Bedford School, Bedfordshire and Luton Archives and Records Service, Lancing College, The Royal College of Music, The Royal College of Organists and Sidmouth Library. If I have omitted anyone, I apologise.

I would like to thank my wife, Reiko who has patiently put up with me spending so much time working on this volume and has been unhesitatingly supportive. It was while staying with her relatives in Japan that I wrote some parts of the book.
I am also very grateful to Professor Donald Burrows for writing the Introduction. He wrote some of the Open University course material for the musical sections of the Arts Foundation course and for the other music courses I studied, inspiring my research.

Finally, I would like to thank Richard Wildman for his help and support and other members of the Bedfordshire Historical Record Society (BHRS), for accepting my draft proposal. I am most grateful to BHRS for its interest in my work and undertaking the publishing of this book. In particular, I must thank Nicola Avery, who has spent a great deal of time and done a great deal of work to improve the formatting and accuracy of the book. I have benefited hugely from her expertise and patience, and without her invaluable input, the book, if it had seen the light of day, would be a poor shadow of what she has made it.

Michael Benson
November 2015

Introduction

Donald Burrows

In the following pages Michael Benson traces the history and changing fortunes (and indeed, changing titles) of the musical enterprise that is now Bedford Choral Society. Several historical narratives of parallel institutions in other towns and cities of Britain have been published, many of them less thoroughly researched and less comprehensive than the present work, but all reflect the enthusiasm and determination of the participating musicians. Bedford's society is one of the earliest ones of its type, and its history is both national and local: it exemplifies larger trends in Britain's musical life, but it is also individual because Bedford's geographical and cultural position provided some unique opportunities, enabling more ambitious events to be presented than in other towns of comparable size.

For the origins of the phenomenon of societies in Britain devoted to musical performance, of the type represented by the Bedford Choral Society, we need to look to two strands in the musical life of London in the late decades of the seventeenth century. There was, in the first place, the establishment of musical concerts both public and private. John Banister's public concerts during the 1670s took place in a series of dedicated concert venues, but no less important was the parallel growth of private concerts, often mixing leading professional players and singers with talented amateurs. It was, rather literally, a matter of 'gentlemen and players': it was considered unseemly for young ladies to perform (though not so reprehensible as their appearance in public events), and the amateurs were (as far as the evidence goes) drawn mainly from the professional classes – lawyers, clergy and the like. This is not surprising in view of the costs of musical instruments and music, but the patronage of the concerts was not always so exclusive: one private famous concert series took place in the room above Thomas Britton's coal warehouse in Clerkenwell. In the eighteenth century private concerts burgeoned not only in London but in provincial towns and cities: the musical society at Salisbury was one of the most successful, with concerts every fortnight, including more ambitious ones on full-moon nights when visiting players were able to travel from Bath or Oxford. The cathedral cities were at a particular advantage because they had a pool of resident professional musicians: the organists of the cathedral and the larger churches and the lay clerks of the cathedral choirs. Typically, the evening programmes were in two parts, with an overture, an aria and a concerto in each half: 'concertos' here meaning the classic repertories of works in the Baroque Concerto Grosso style for which famous pieces by Corelli and Handel provided the classic model. Given plentiful local resources (as, for example, at Oxford), the musical society might produce a 'choral night' each month at which more substantial works would be performed, though perhaps spread over two meetings.

The second strand behind the phenomenon of the musical societies was the development of annual music festivals. An early instance was the London celebrations of St Cecilia's Day. These began with the performances of odes for solo singers supported by a (modest) chorus and orchestra; a repertory to which Henry Purcell contributed in 1683 and 1692. Through a curious series of events, this musical style moved into the church, first with a series of state Thanksgiving services at St Paul's Cathedral in the early years of Queen Anne's reign, and then to the annual celebrations in the same building for the Festival of the Sons of the Clergy. The Festival day comprised a dinner at Merchant Taylors' Hall preceded by a church service at the Cathedral; the main income for the charity in support of clergymen's children was the money collected at the service and at the rehearsal of the music a couple of days before. The classic work for the service was Purcell's Te Deum and Jubilate in D Major with orchestra in the early years, supplanted later by Handel's 'Utrecht' and 'Dettingen' settings coupled with new anthems (also sometimes orchestrally accompanied) by Greene and Boyce. As with private concerts, the model provided by the Sons of the Clergy service spread to provincial cities, beginning with the Three Choirs Festival which rotated between the cathedrals of Gloucester, Hereford and Worcester. In some places (again, for example, at Salisbury) the annual festival began as an independent venture, but was subsequently presented as a charity event, for example in aid of a local hospital. (The festival at St Philip's church, Birmingham, began as a charity event of this type from the start.) The festivals gradually grew in scope to become events over two or three days, with evening concerts to supplement the church services. For the concerts the most ambitious programmes were Handel's oratorios, or works of varying dimensions by various composers in similar style.

Circumstances and musical styles changed, but this pattern of public concerts, private music clubs and annual festivals remained relevant well into the nineteenth century. The new grand halls in the large provincial cities – as at Birmingham (1834), Manchester (1854) and Leeds (1858) – were prepared for large choirs and the ever-expanding symphony orchestra, and equipped with organs of commensurate size and power. In London, Exeter Hall and St James's Hall turned out to be preludes to the extravaganza of Crystal Palace, with space for a cast and audience of thousands for the Handel Festivals, but which also had suitable venues for orchestral and chamber concerts. All this, however, would have been irrelevant had there not been an expansion in the numbers of musical performers, professional and – especially – amateur. The educational programmes of the tonic sol-fa movements brought singing to a wider social range of potential performers, but it was not the whole story: in many cases, sol-fa was regarded (and effectively used) as a stepping stone to conventional musical notation. The half-accidental invention of the octavo-size vocal score by Novello and Company in the 1840s rendered the choral classics – particularly Handel's *Messiah* and Haydn's *Creation* – into a cheaper and more portable form. Perhaps the most significant development for the wider social dissemination of music was the manufacture of cheap, modest but generally serviceable upright pianos, which could be bought on the instalment system. Although the extent and velocity is difficult to measure, by the middle of the nineteenth century musical activity had spread down the social spectrum as populations and incomes increased.

With this background we can begin to interpret the early musical activities of the Bedford musicians as outlined here. The initial choral performance in 1812 was clearly of the 'Festival' type and it may have been intended to initiate an annual celebration, but neither the audience nor performing resources were sufficient for that to happen: even a performance of *Messiah* required the assistance of performers from elsewhere, and there was probably much the same experience with another attempt in 1825. Relatively little is known of the activities of the Bedford Harmonic Society because it was more on the private 'music club' model, but it had two essential features that promised some prospect of success: the leadership of a local professional musician (John Nunn) and the support of the headmaster of the Grammar School (John Brereton). The latter probably brought both social and practical prospects of stability – strong connections with the town and a place to rehearse regularly. Twenty-six performers and 118 supporters was not a bad practical basis, especially given the small size of available concert venues, but the venture broke up in somewhat mysterious circumstances at the turn of the year 1859–60. According to a later memoir, politics and sectarianism had 'something to do with it' (In London, the foundation of the Sacred Harmonic Society, which provided the core of the singers for the Crystal Palace Handel Festivals, was a reaction to the exclusion of Dissenters – and women – from the chorus of the 1834 Handel Commemoration performances at Westminster Abbey). Anglican clergy were prominent in the leadership of musical activities and, although many of them were no doubt competent musicians, it is possible to imagine the causes for resentment among nonconformists and the socially less well favoured. There was a structural problem however, in that the posts of organist in Bedford's Anglican principal churches were probably the only fully permanent and professionally paid jobs for performers. Beyond that, Bedford's musicians maintained their trade by teaching (either in the schools or by developing private practices), and eked out their livings with ancillary activities such as selling music and pianos. The Bedford economy could only support a handful of professional musicians. According to the *Post Office Directory of Northamptonshire, Huntingdonshire, Bedfordshire, Buckinghamshire, Berkshire and Oxfordshire 1869*, Bedford had four Organists (Charles Bithrey at St Cuthbert's, Miss Barker at St Mary's, Robert Rose at St Paul's and Philip Diemer at Holy Trinity), four Music and Musical Instrument Sellers (including Rose, who also appears in the list of three Pianoforte Dealers) and five Teachers of Music (Bithrey, Diemer, John Nunn, Rose and Mrs Saunders).[1]

Where the Harmonic Society had failed in 1860, the Bedford Amateur Musical Society succeeded a few years later. The critical difference was probably in the nature of the leadership. Philip Diemer's professional leadership was of a new order. He came from a local family, and had received training at the Royal Academy. The Academy was not a full conservatoire in the modern sense (or as existed then in Paris or Leipzig), but Diemer had the best teachers that were available in Britain – Macfarren and Holmes. His period at the Royal Academy coincided with that of Arthur Sullivan, six years his junior: Diemer probably made out well as a student, but would have been in the shadow of Sullivan, who had been awarded the first

[1] E. R. Kelly, ed., *Post Office Directory of Northamptonshire, Huntingdonshire, Bedfordshire, Buckinghamshire, Berkshire and Oxfordshire 1869* (London, 1869), p. 322ff.

Mendelssohn scholarship to study at the Academy and then in Leipzig. Inevitably, if Diemer was to earn a living in Bedford he had to take posts as an organist, but his professional status probably enabled him to avoid too close an identification with the previous problems of the Harmonic Society and, above all, he seems to have formed a good working relationship with Robert Rose, an established local musician, who presumably accepted his authority and was able to co-operate. Both Diemer and Rose brought with them essential contributions to the success of the Society in the participation of their relatives and pupils.

It is difficult to assess the significance of the fact that two of the founders – Diemer and Steinmetz – were of German origin. The musical influence of Germans in mid-century provincial Britain is a topic that still awaits attention, though the prevalence of German band-masters is well documented. Diemer, although he was professionally (necessarily) attached to the Anglican churches, came from the Moravian community, which had always valued the role of music. (The hymnody of the Wesleys had been influenced by their experience of the Moravians during their visit to Georgia (USA) in the 1730s.) Steinmetz's origins were Lutheran, and he probably carried with him German cultural assumptions about both domestic music-making (hausmusik) and larger-scale musical activity. In Britain, professional musical activity in the 1860s was only just developing alternative centres to London, principally in the cities of the midlands and northern England. In Germany, the honeycomb of courts (the historical result of the absence of the principle of primogeniture) meant that almost anywhere you were not far from an establishment with its own *capella* and chamber musicians, even a modest court orchestra. (Some of these institutions, in various civic forms, survived unification in 1870, and even into the late twentieth century.) Famously, in 1914 a book about 'England' was published in Germany under the title *Das Land ohne Musik* ('the land without music'). By then it was not true, and arguably had never been true of London, but Steinmetz may have thought it quite natural to assist in the promotion of music in the Bedford community in a comparable manner to that he would have known in or around Sachsenhausen. It is fortunate that the Bedford schools had need of a German teacher and thus the Musical Society gained an efficient manager.

In its inception the Society was close to the 'club' model: the concerts in the early years were events for the performing and subscribing members, not for the general public. The participants in the early years had probably the same type of social mix in the membership as we see later, though this is difficult to analyse without a full list of names and occupations. Inevitably, more is known about the people who were in some way locally prominent or institutionally significant – the physicians, lawyers, industrial employers or agents and (for example) policemen. The choruses needed women and men singers, and the names of women appear from time to time in the early years in other roles, as for example piano accompanists. At the start the numbers of participants make an interesting comparison with the earlier figures quoted for the Harmonic Society: an orchestra of eighteen and about one hundred singers, the expansion in the latter probably attributable to Diemer's activity as a teacher. The balance of these numbers, however, already raises a question about the Society's centre of gravity – was it 'musical' or was it 'choral'?

Given performers, an audience, a place to rehearse (courtesy of the Grammar

School headmaster) and a place to perform (though the Assembly Rooms quickly proved inadequate even after the addition of balconies), the next requirement for success was to develop programmes which would retain the momentum that had been achieved at the foundation. The formula of the first concert – a longer work for the first half and then a miscellany of shorter pieces – worked for a time. There was something of a limitation in the availability of half-programme works, though contemporary composers such as van Bree composed for this 'cantata market', and Diemer himself eventually contributed with *Bethany*, which took its place in the repertory published by Novellos in London. It was not long, however, before the situation gravitated towards the attempt at full-length works for the complete programme, beginning, inevitably, with *Messiah*.

Once programmes moved up onto this new plateau, however, the dynamic changed. While the 'Amateur' Society initially prided itself on performing from its own resources, the larger-scale works required help from outside: a string quartet to lead sections of the orchestra, and then fully professional soloists. Diemer once again was a fortunate asset in this situation: his Royal Academy days must have left him with contacts for the necessary professional musicians from London (and elsewhere). Thus, as early December 1868, the performance of Handel's *Judas Maccabaeus* brought to the Society the tenor Edward Lloyd, on his way to a national reputation. (Officially he was called in when a local tenor became unavailable, but this could have been a diplomatic cover when the local singer realised that he was not up to the job.) With a hotline to the best available from London, Diemer brought to Bedford some of the leading performers of the day, and also contemporary composers such as Julius Benedict and Emanuel Aguilar to direct performances of their works; the experience was apparently eccentric when it came to Edmund Chipp. It is not clear whether Sullivan ever really intended to come, but Diemer did justice to the performances of *The Prodigal Son*, *The Martyr of Antioch* and *The Golden Legend*. Old Academy influence is also to be seen in the representation of Sterndale Bennett and Macfarren in the repertory. The mainstream, however, remained with works by Handel, Haydn's *Creation* and Mendelssohn's *Elijah*. The more substantial orchestral scoring of *Elijah*, and the large orchestral element in 'The Hymn of Praise', meant that a rather haphazard local minstrelsy supplemented by harmonium and organ was really insufficient. And, as the repertory moved towards larger works and professional soloists, the choral element inevitably became less dominant. It is not surprising that 'Amateur' was dropped from the title of the Society in 1880: the music of the solo parts for soprano and (especially) tenor in Rossini's *Stabat Mater*, first performed that year, would have been well beyond the capacities of amateur singers. Meanwhile, the opening of the Corn Exchange in 1874 had provided a new home for the Society's concerts, and it is then that there was a definitive move from the 'club' structure towards public concerts. The new venue was, however, not without its own practical problems, and the provision of an organ had to wait nearly a quarter of a century: the latter was, perhaps, not entirely a disadvantage, for it meant that there was little cover for an inadequate orchestra, and indeed orchestral music featured largely in one of the opening concerts for the Corn Exchange.

When Diemer moved into retirement at the turn of the century, the Bedford Musical Society was fortunate to find a comparable successor in Harry Harding.

Inevitably the day-to-day course of Harding's musical activity in Bedford was as an organist and a teacher, but the Society continued to flourish under him partly because, like Diemer, he had suitable professional connections in London. He was recommended for his post in Bedford by Sir Frederick Bridge, organist of Westminster Abbey, and he gained national importance within the music profession as secretary to the Royal College of Organists. He brought Bridge to Bedford to conduct one of his own works, and also similarly Frederic Cowen, Samuel Coleridge-Taylor and Charles Stanford. Among the singers were Agnes Nicholls, Plunkett Greene, Gervase Elwes and Elsie Suddaby; orchestral players brought in included Aubrey Brain and Marie Goosens; miscellaneous programmes included contributions from the leading pianists Backhaus and Busoni.

Harding's taste ran mainly to contemporary, large-scale, romantic-period works, including Parry's *Blest Pair of Sirens* and Brahms's Requiem. There was an experiment with Wagner (needing some additional players from London); Mendelssohn and Gounod stayed in the repertory, but Handel nearly vanished, with only one performance each of *Messiah* and *Israel in Egypt* in the period 1900–13. It was under his direction that the major works of Elgar, requiring a full modern symphony orchestra as well as an exceptionally competent choral contribution, were taken up – *King Olaf*, *The Dream of Gerontius* and *The Apostles*. His surprise resignation in 1923 followed after two performances of *The Apostles*, and it seems plausible that it came because he had fulfilled his ambitions with the Society, and wished to move on instead to other areas, including Bedford's competitive music festival and a more active national role with the Royal College of Organists. (He remained in post as organist of St Paul's church and director of music at Bedford School and Bedford High School.) From the beginning, the Society had relied on Diemer and Rose for its leadership, but with the appointment of Harding, and the fact that multiple facets of his career inevitably took him away from Bedford from time to time, further distribution of responsibility onto chorus masters and accompanists had been required.

The consequences for the Society of Harding's departure were not happy. Two competent local musicians offered themselves as his successor, but they did not have the flair or connections of their predecessors, and attempts to get them to work together did not last long. Under Herbert Colson some good programmes were given. The choral works were mainly repeats of pieces previously performed by the Society, though this period saw the first attempts at works by J. S. Bach and an experiment with a concert version of *Carmen*; an orchestral concert became a regular element in the annual programme. The foundation of the Musical Society had coincided almost exactly with the completion of St Pancras station, and the ease of travel to London should have put Bedford in a beneficial position for the addition of professional players on concert days, had the timetable of the London, Midland and Scottish Railway been more co-operative with evening trains for their return. Singers with national careers, such as Roy Henderson, Parry Jones and Elsie Suddaby once again came as soloists, but local musical politics sapped energy, membership and audiences as other choirs established themselves, in particular the Bedford Choral Society that developed from the Free Church Choral Union. The type of repertory on which the Musical Society was now based required substantial choral and orchestral resources, which could probably only be delivered in a monopolistic situation and without the distraction of local competition. Furthermore, the polarisation of repertory, with works by Handel and Haydn going to the Choral Society, in effect restricted the variety of the Musical Society's offering. There was little motive at that time to challenge the organ-accompanied oratorio performances of the Choral Society with more authentic performances using orchestral accompaniment. Also, there was a tendency to abbreviate the major works: at earlier periods, complaints about the length of *Messiah* or *Elijah* suggest that they were performed uncut. As the works performed gradually required more ambitious resources, particularly in the orchestral contribution, ways had to be found to meet the expenses. Financial security relied considerably on sheer numbers – the quantity of performers, and the paying audience they brought with them. Once in a declining situation, the more concerts that are given, the more money is lost. One response was a reduction in the number of performances. At foundation, the Society's plan was to give four concerts a year; at the changeover from Diemer to Harding this was reduced to three, on a rhythm approximately coincident with the school terms. (The abandonment of the May concert was initially attributed to the loss of performers to the modern craze for cycling: in the last quarter of the twentieth century, late-spring concerts became even more vulnerable to changes in holiday habits and gardening.) In the Colson era, choral concerts went down to two per year, but even so by 1930 the financial outlook of the Musical Society had become uncertain, as had morale and membership numbers. In this increasingly insecure environment, the public concerts of Musical Society died in 1931 with scarcely even a whimper.

The Society revived in the circumstances of the Second World War. This probably could not have been predicted, because the policy in the First World War had been to close things down: the Society's only performances had been of *Messiah* for the troops in November 1914. This time, however, after an initial period of hesitation the emphasis was rather on maintaining national morale by sustaining established social activity, though the Society rather better fitted the description of 'abandoned social activity'. Henry Wood and the Promenade Concerts in London continued after the destruction of the Queen's Hall and Malcolm Sargent dashed around Britain keeping the larger choral societies, as well as the London Philharmonic and the Liverpool Philharmonic orchestras, active when some other prominent British conductors had left the America. The catalyst for Bedford's recovery was the exceptional good fortune that resulted from the relocation of the BBC's musical staff at the end of July 1941, with the personnel of their orchestras, bands and choirs resident (indeed, virtually billeted) in the local community and a number of buildings adapted for permanent studio use. Marshall Palmer, under threat from his post as organist at the magnificent instrument in St Mary's, Woburn, took the initiative to attempt the re-foundation of the Musical Society, and this was successfully accomplished as a choral institution. The Society only rarely participated in broadcasts (the BBC bodies included choral groups), but the resident professional musicians weighed in with their assistance: concerts with substantial programmes of choral and orchestral items were again possible, and the Society's concerts had the assistance of great names such as the violinist Paul Beard and the bassoonist Archie Camden. The Society (which restored the name Bedford Musical Society, but declared its aim to 'perform the major works of the choral repertoire') began with

Handel's *Judas Maccabaeus*, already with one hundred performers (itself remarkable during wartime) and soloists from the BBC singers: subsequently it could muster the forces for works that demanded a full symphony orchestra – Parry's *Blest Pair of Sirens*, Elgar's *Sea Pictures* and *The Music Makers*. When Palmer departed from Bedford in a career move, his role was energetically continued by Norman Frost, who wanted to shift the repertory towards more orchestral music and extend the range of the choral repertory.

The bright sunshine bought by the BBC's presence, through the willing contribution of their musicians and the general level of local interest in music that was generated by the opportunity to attend free broadcast concerts, lasted until the summer of 1945. With *Jesu meine Freude* in December of that year, Norman Frost introduced the first choral work by Johann Sebastian Bach since the Society's foundation, and the performance of Mendelssohn's *Elijah* the following March was a landmark in its re-establishment, with nationally-famous soloists and a large choir, but a rather skimped orchestra based around only eighteen string players. By then, as it happened, problems about orchestral participation, and the broader question of the repertory for which the Society should be responsible, were on the horizon. The chorus was formed, as it always had been, from amateur singers, but it was now fairly well established that, with the exception of a few minor contributions, professional singers would be hired from concert to concert for the solo vocal roles. The orchestra had hitherto been gathered largely from local players, supplemented with others brought in and paid as necessary, according to the demands of particular works and, as noted, the BBC players had been willing to participate. Much depended on keeping definitions of status in the background, and the mixing of 'amateur' and 'professional' players was a matter for local negotiation: those brought in could be impatient or patronising, but sometimes they had the magic touch and made everyone else play better. A rather abrupt movement towards 'professionalization' in music took no account of local situations: vocal soloists now had to be booked through agents rather than personal connections, and rigid unionisation produced its own definition of the orchestral player. In terms of orchestral players who entirely earned their living by performance the defensive move towards a closed shop is understandable, especially since the phasing-out of cinema orchestras had substantially reduced the opportunities for employment. However this drew a rigid line within the music profession, separating full-time players from equally professional musicians who (for example) had received the same training but had taken a different path as teachers, from choice or necessity, and maintained their credibility as teachers by keeping up their playing as local opportunities arose. It also took no account of professionals of the type represented by Philip Diemer and Harry Harding, serving in posts as organists and teachers, but trained as general practitioners with an understanding of musical composition, choir training and orchestration.

Norman Frost, in the Diemer/Harding tradition, fell foul of this situation. In response to the prohibition in the mixing of (so-defined) professional players with others, the concerts in December 1946 and April 1947 employed entire orchestra packages for *Messiah* (the Boyd Neel Orchestra) and a Brahms concert with the *German Requiem* and the second symphony (the New London Orchestra). There followed, however, the demand that these players would not perform except with 'a conductor of national reputation', or their own designated conductor. That Frost had probably proved his competence in recent concerts with professional orchestras apparently counted for nothing: his position was untenable and Clarence Raybould was appointed as the Society's conductor. In the circumstances Raybould was a good choice, as he had become known locally during the BBC period of residence, and indeed continued to live in Bedford until 1950. The orchestral tail wagged the choral dog, however: during the 'Raybould years' (1947–1957) the Musical Society gave as many orchestral as choral concerts. There were some excellent programmes and no doubt some first rate performances. For the singers, much of the value of their experience must have depended on the succession of chorus masters (Daphne Braggins, Charles Farncombe, Freddie Stevens and Kate Freyhan); while there was a gain in the efficiency of the 'on-the-day' professional orchestra, there was no opportunity to evolve a performance over a number of rehearsals with choir and orchestra. In the programmes the choral 'standards' (*Messiah*, *Elijah*, *The Creation*, *Hiawatha's Wedding Feast*) were mixed with ventures into new repertory, including works by Kodály, Holst, Ireland and Vaughan Williams.

Among the innovations were the Society's first performances of the Requiems of Verdi and Fauré. The Kodály/Verdi programme in March 1949 was probably the first time that the Society had performed a work in Latin in the eighty-plus years since its foundation. The early programmes had included Mendelssohn's *Lauda Sion* and Rossini's *Stabat Mater*, but in spite of the Latin titles these would have been sung to English texts as found the Novello vocal scores, in the latter case bearing little relationship to the Latin original. (The word 'mother' does not occur anywhere in the translation.) The Twelfth Mass attributed to Mozart (performed in 1868) and his Requiem Mass (performed in 1885) would similarly have been rendered in the alternative English versions. It took even longer for the choir to come to grips with German texts. Bach's *Jesu meine Freude* (1945 onwards) and *Wachet auf* (1954) would have become 'Jesu priceless treasure' and 'Sleepers awake', though *Herz und Mund und Tat und Leben* (1970) made it into German. Brahms's *Ein Deutches Requiem* had to wait until 1985 for a German performance. The Kempe/Fischer-Dieskau German recording in 1962 had helped to make this work better known in its original language, and a similar awareness arose from recordings of Bach's cantatas, including John Eliot Gardiner's more recent complete cycle of these cantatas.

The Raybould/professional orchestra phase was unsustainable in the long term because it relied on two things: a honeymoon period with Bedford audiences who had developed a taste for orchestral music during the BBC years, and substantial grant funding. When the latter came under threat in 1952, a re-grouping was forced upon the Society. Orchestral concerts continued as before, but the choral concerts had to be performed at slender expense with organ accompaniment; the only exception was a performance of Handel's *Samson* with full orchestra, conducted by Raybould in 1955. By then he was no longer resident in Bedford and the orchestral concerts must have seemed increasingly like visiting engagements. Responsibility for the choral programmes was with Freddie Stevens, the chorus master and the occupant of a new professional post as Bedfordshire's first county music adviser. Stevens made the best of the job by developing the repertory of unaccompanied choral music, including the Society's first performance of Palestrina's *Missa Papæ Marcelli*. Bach's *Christmas Oratorio* (or rather, the first half of it) and *St Matthew*

Passion, and Handel's *Messiah* were performed, but with organ accompaniment: this was not really satisfactory, even though first-rank organists were employed, but the deficiencies were probably not appreciated as they would have been a couple of decades later when the first recordings of performances with 'early-instrument' orchestras revolutionised the aural experience. (The Society's organ-accompanied concerts moved out to St Paul's church: the Corn Exchange organ had been disposed of in 1951.) In 1958, an external proposal relating to orchestral concerts concentrated the minds of the committee, and the Society withdrew from the presentation of orchestral concerts, though orchestral items continued to be included in choral concerts. The Raybould era was over, but it took until 1988 to catch up with the consequences and rename the Bedford Musical Society as the Bedford Choral Society.

Although Stevens, assisted by Kate Freyhan, had worked positively on the programmes within the given limitations, the choir really needed the restoration of opportunities for performances of works with orchestra, and preferably at least one major work of that type each season. The solution came again as a result of good fortune in Bedford's geographical location, this time not from the south (London) but from the east. David Willcocks, recently appointed to King's College, Cambridge, came in to direct a performance of Bach's *St John Passion* with the Jacques Orchestra, involving a manageable cost because the orchestral requirements were less than those of a full symphony orchestra; similar performances of Bach's Mass in B Minor (the Society's first) and the *Christmas Oratorio* (again Parts 1–3 only) followed. Willcocks conducted all of the concerts in the 1959/60 season, including one for which he brought his full orchestra from the Cambridge University Musical Society. This, it turned out, would provide the Society with a way forward. By 1960 the national improvements in instrumental tuition were beginning to work through the school systems and Cambridge University attracted excellent young players, many of them participants in the National Youth Orchestra and some who trained to professional level at the music colleges either before or after their degree studies. By doubling up on performances of major works in Cambridge and Bedford, Willcocks was able to bring his carefully-trained orchestra to the Choral Society's performances, and it was thus that Beethoven's 'Choral' Symphony was performed at the Corn Exchange in 1961, followed by Verdi's Requiem in 1966 and 1972 and Elgar's *The Dream of Gerontius* in 1968. When Willcocks moved from Cambridge to the Royal College of Music, a similarly proficient student orchestra from the College followed on. For works involving an orchestra of less than symphonic proportions, Willcocks could still call upon the Jacques Orchestra, and for another type of concert repertory he brought the Gabrieli Brass Ensemble or the Philip Jones Brass Ensemble.

Willcocks's contribution was essential to the success of the Musical Society not only on account of his ability to provide an affordable orchestra, but also because he presented more modest concerts, including Christmas-season celebrations, in an engaging manner. He had many professional engagements beyond Cambridge/London and Bedford, however, and although he was effectively the principal conductor from 1959 to 1987 it was not practical for him to take on the complete programmes for the seasons. Nor was it diplomatic for him to do so, because the Society faced another new situation. The growth and improvement in the area of musical education was working through to produce a larger number of graduate musicians with practical competence from universities and music colleges. The procession of different names involved with the Society as conductors, chorus masters and accompanists from the 1960s onwards becomes rather fast-moving. Other first-rate musicians (Roy Rimmer, Michael Rose) followed Freddie Stevens as county music adviser, and it was both practical and beneficial for the Society to incorporate them as conductors. Furthermore, under these two men, the orchestral scene in Bedford revived to an extent that there were local alternatives to the Willcocks orchestras. Anthony le Fleming, Rimmer and Rose were all associated both with the Society and with the founding and development of Bedford's orchestras, including the New Bedford Symphony Orchestra, the Bedfordshire Symphony Orchestra, the Bedford Sinfonia and the Bedfordshire Youth Orchestra. Under Michael Rose particular success was achieved on twin tracks: excellent executants were attracted to Bedfordshire as peripatetic teachers, and their pupils combined into one of the country's outstanding youth orchestras. Other talented musicians were also involved, including Deirdre Knight, Michael Smedley and Michael Ashcroft. Diemer and Harding had made all the running for the Society in their days, and their relationship with performers and committees would have been fairly straightforward, but the Society must have been heavily involved for thirty years in the later twentieth century with diplomatic transactions between the alternative talents, though the resulting record of performances is impressive. It was only with the appointment of Ian Smith in 1985 that there followed a return to a single permanent conductor (in 1988).

The following narrative traces the season-by season fortunes of the Society, which has had a continuous history since 1867, apart from a hiatus in the 1930s, and the re-foundation in 1941 was correctly seen at the time in terms of continuity. The Society has been fortunate in the context of a market-town base: although Bedford had no nucleus of professional singers such as would be found in cathedral cities on which to build, the essential personnel and resources were to hand, and connections to London and Cambridge provided essential supplementary musical resources. The schools and churches of Bedford and the surrounding area are part of the enabling background, though there were inevitably recurring problems about venues and finances. The essential part of the story however lies with people – the professional leadership, the membership and the audiences. The documentation from minutes and newspaper reports take us only a certain distance in understanding and recovering the musical experiences that were, and are, the reason for the Society's existence and its value. Well-attended performances that 'go well' are an obvious high point, but there are different satisfactions from different musical repertories, and a successful performance (sometimes against the odds) can take place to a small audience: a perplexing experience for the performers and bad news for the balance sheet. As the activities of the Choral Society developed, a large part of the management necessarily involved solo singers and orchestra, in addition to the local provision of conductors, chorus masters and accompanists, but the morale of the members has ultimately been the most important factor in success and preservation. Choral singing is a social musical activity, requiring discipline and cohesion to a common purpose. There are obvious dangers to the future of the tradition from the fragmentation and atomisation of social practices, but most seriously from the decline in choral experience at school level: this is less tangible (and less measureable) than the threats to instrumental tuition that occasionally hit the headlines on the subject of educational provision. The future of the Choral Society may be at risk as the horizons of many of today's students are limited to *West Side Story* and never reach the Verdi Requiem.

Chapter One

Choral Music in Bedford, c.1800–66

> Catherine was fond of music but only as an expression of her own feelings. For music as music – for a melody of Mozart, for example – that is to say for pure art which is simple beauty, superior to our personality, she did not care. She liked Handel, and there was a choral society in Easthorpe which occasionally performed the 'Messiah'.[1]

Twenty-five years before the formation of the short-lived Bedford Harmonic Society and fifty-five years before the Bedford Amateur Musical Society was established in 1867, Handel's *Messiah* was performed in Bedford, probably for the first time, in October 1812. Before the performance, Samuel Whitbread was asked by one Thomas Revis and others if he felt that there was a need for more good-quality music locally.[2] They wrote: 'It having been the wish of several of the inhabitants of Bedford to have a Music Meeting on an extensive plan in the Town, by the assistance of some of the London and other performers, we take the liberty to apply to you to unite with his Grace the Duke of Bedford in affording us your interest and support.'[3]

The result was a performance of *Messiah*, given with the assistance of some musicians from London and elsewhere. After the event, a Mr Williamson wrote to his son, Edmond, about the performance, which his mother and sisters had also attended: 'went to the Oratorio at Bedford … There was very little Company – Mr. Trevor of Bromham was there and Mrs. Higgins of Turvey and some others. I believe not a hundred. I am afraid the performers will be the losers.'[4] No further regular music meetings appear to have been organised in the immediate months or years following this performance.

In 1825, a music festival was arranged: 'for the benefit of the Bedford Infirmary and for the support of some new established schools in the county.'[5] The programme consisted of a selection from *Messiah*. The concert was performed in St Paul's

1 Mark Rutherford, *Catharine Furze* (London, 1893), p. 137. Mark Rutherford was the *nom de plume* of the author William Hale White (1831–1913), a novelist who was born and grew up in Bedford. He modelled his fictional Easthorpe on the town. By the time he wrote *Catharine Furze* Bedford Musical Society was well established. The first secretary of the Bedford Harmonic Society was a Mr Furze.

2 Samuel Whitbread (1764–1815) was the son of Samuel Whitbread. He was educated at Eton; Christ Church, Oxford; and St John's College, Cambridge. He was Whig MP for Bedford from 1790, supporting Charles Fox and opposing William Pitt and his government. He inherited the house and grounds of Southill Park, Bedfordshire, from his father, and was head of the family brewery company.

3 Margaret McGregor, 'Music in Bedfordshire II', *Bedfordshire Magazine*, vol. 17, no. 130 (Autumn 1979), p. 56.

4 McGregor, 'Music in Bedfordshire II', p. 56.

5 Ibid.

church by visiting musicians, some from the Chapel Royal, Windsor, and some from Kings College, Cambridge. Admission prices ranged from 2s 6d to 10s 6d. Among the patrons was the Rev. Dr John Brereton FSA FRGS, headmaster of the Grammar School in Bedford.

John Brereton (1782–1863) had been appointed headmaster of the Grammar School in 1811, at the age of twenty-nine, following the death of Dr Hook. He had been educated at Winchester and New College, Oxford. He then taught at Blundell's School, Tiverton. John Brereton was headmaster of the Grammar School until 1855, a period of forty-four years. He very adequately fulfilled the mission for which he had been appointed - raising the standard and the standing of the school.[6] The quality of education available in Bedford helped to account for the growth of the town, at least until the establishment of Howard's Britannia Ironworks in the late 1850s.[7]

The next concert in the town, of which there is a record, was held in the Bedford New Rooms (later known as the Assembly Rooms, now the Harpur Suite). The Bedford New Rooms were designed by Thomas Gwyn Elger.[8] Building work started in October 1834 and was completed in June 1836. The concert was organised by John Nunn (1805–81), and was held in July, a month after the building work was completed. John Nunn was the organist of St Paul's church, Bedford, and the borough organist (by virtue of playing at civic services). He took up the latter post in 1836 and retained it for approximately thirty years. The concert had a full programme, and many of the performers came from London. This was before the days of railway transport to Bedford, so travel to the town was comparatively slow and difficult.[9]

The Bedford Harmonic Society was formed six months later, in January 1837.[10] It was not until the Harmonic Society's establishment that regular performances of choral and secular music could be heard in the town. Although John Nunn was the dominant musician, John Brereton deserves much of the credit for the formation and initial success of the Harmonic Society. According to his obituary in the *Bedford Times and Bedfordshire Independent*:

[6] Obituary in the *Bedford Times and Bedfordshire Independent*, 23 September 1862, pp. 4–5. This obituary is more adulatory than Joyce Godber's description of him. She writes: 'But with the years, though he would support local activities such as concerts or the Horticultural Society he became more Olympian.' Joyce Godber, *The Harpur Trust, 1552–1973* (Bedford, 1973), p. 43.

[7] John Howard (1791–1878) established a foundry in Bedford. By the time he retired he was successfully manufacturing a patent plough. His two sons took over the business and established the Britannia Ironworks in 1859. The Britannia Ironworks was to become Bedford's largest employer. Sir Frederick Howard (1827–1915), one of John Howard's sons, was an enthusiastic supporter of the Bedford Musical Society and was its president for many years.

[8] Thomas Gwyn Elger was a Bedford architect. He competed unsuccessfully for the Harpur Trust's new schools in Harpur Street (now the Harpur Shopping Centre), but designed the New Rooms opposite in Greek Doric style. He was elected mayor of Bedford in 1830, 1835 and 1838. His son, Thomas Gwyn Empy Elger, a noted astronomer, was elected mayor in 1878.

[9] The first railway to pass through Bedfordshire was the London to Birmingham railway, which opened in 1838; there was a station at Leighton Buzzard. The first railway to come to Bedford was that from Oxford to Cambridge. St John's Station, Bedford, on this line, was opened in 1846.

[10] A number of other choral societies were established in the 1830s. The Sacred Harmonic Society (London) was founded in 1832, the Huddersfield Choral Society in 1836 and the Choral Harmonic Society (London) in 1837.

> lovers of good music in Bedford, of all classes, owe much to him. Under his patronage the Harmonic Society flourished many years ago, and by his guidance and that of his son, contributed greatly to the formation of that taste which has since been cultivated by others with much success … his own taste was exact and refined by high training and his voice and ear excellent.[11]

Initially, the Harmonic Society had twenty-six performing members and 118 honorary members. Among the membership were representatives of many leading families in Bedford. No known list of members has survived. However, the printed constitution that contains the rules, several programmes 1837–42 and a poster from the end of 1842 are still extant.[12] From the programmes it is known that John Brereton was president of the Society. The names of the other officers were John Nunn, leader; Mr Furze, secretary; and Thomas Barnard, treasurer. Thomas Barnard was the owner of Barnard's Bank, a well-known institution in the town. He lived in Cople, where there is a memorial to him in the church. The committee members were Mr C. Robinson, Mr H. Mayle, Mr Riley, Mr W. Jones and Robert Rose.

The leader, John Nunn, was an active local musician. His brief obituary in the *Bedford Times and Bedfordshire Independent* states:

> For many years Mr Nunn held the appointment of organist to St Paul's Church, Bedford, and was highly appreciated as a teacher of music, having a large and select number of pupils in the town and neighbourhood. He was also conductor of the first Harmonic Society, established here under the presidency of the late Dr. Brereton by whom he was appreciated and held that important position for almost 20 [*sic*] years. Many of his contemporaries who attended the amateur concerts will recollect his energetic leadership, as well as his vocal and instrumental abilities … Mr. Nunn was one of a talented family well known at Bury St Edmunds and by the music profession generally.[13]

The Harmonic Society aimed to put on six concerts a year with programmes that included a mixture of songs, glees and short orchestral pieces, especially overtures by Handel and Mozart. The concerts were held in the Assembly Rooms. The typical format for concerts at this time was short songs interspersed with instrumental or orchestral pieces. Robert Rose, later one of the founding fathers of the Bedford Amateur Musical Society, and its chorus master for many years, was a performer with the Harmonic Society.

11 *Bedford Times and Bedfordshire Independent*, 23 September 1862, pp. 4–5.

12 The programmes of the Bedford Harmonic Society 1837–42 and a poster from 1842 are preserved in the Bedfordshire Heritage Library, Bedford Central Library. The constitution and rules can be found in Bedfordshire and Luton Archives and Record Service (BLARS), X 274/35–7.

13 *Bedfordshire Times and Independent*, 25 June 1881, p. 5. A different light may be shed on John Nunn by a reference in an interview given by Sir Frederick Howard in the *Bedfordshire Times and Independent,* 15 July 1910, p. 7: 'I can never forget the sermon, nor can I ever forget the Bishop's (Wilberforce of Oxford) sad look up into the gallery where the little Bluecoat boys were singing the Te Deum from a simple Gregorian chant, the red-faced organist carelessly blundering and putting the poor little fellows into lamentable confusion. This erratic organist, having passed away years ago, I cannot think of mentioning his name, though he so grievously disturbed the service.' The visit is most likely to have occurred when John Nunn was organist, and he may be the red-faced organist referred to. Samuel Wilberforce was Bishop of Oxford from 1845–68, and is best remembered for leading the attack on Darwinism, especially his debate with Thomas Huxley at the British Association, on Darwin's theory of evolution.

Mr J. T. Brooks of Flitwick, who had supported the Harmonic Society since its inception, recorded in his diary for 20 December 1839 that he: 'went to the concert of the Bedford Harmonic Society, dining at the Witts.'[14] Dr George Witt was another founder member of the Society, and was also a noted collector of scientific objects. His name appears on the plaque commemorating the opening of Bedford Town Bridge without toll in 1837; he was mayor at the time.

There are no known surviving programmes after those for the 1842/43 season, and there are no reports of Harmonic Society concerts in the later 1840s and 1850s in the *Bedford Times*.[15] It is therefore difficult to trace the history of the Harmonic Society between 1843 and its brief revival in the 1850s. That it did survive is suggested by John Brereton's obituary, which refers to his involvement with the Harmonic Society for twenty years.[16] It is possible that there were financial difficulties in the early 1840s, as a local paper reported that concerts were held: 'to liquidate a debt of £24 still pending for the pianoforte belonging to the Society.'[17]

Reports of a number of other concerts that took place in Bedford in the later 1840s and 1850s do survive. [18] John Nunn conducted a Grand Concert on 2 April 1850, and Robert Rose promoted a Grand Annual Concert of Sacred Music in the spring of 1850 and 1851. He played the piano-forte and harmonium on each occasion. Mr Sanderson (who is not mentioned elsewhere) was leader of the band in 1850, while John Nunn was leader in 1851. These are not referred to as Harmonic Society concerts.

One other Bedford concert is significant because it was given by well-known professionals from London. This was Mr Jullien's Grand Concert, held on 17 August 1850. Louis Antoine Jullien was a French composer of dance music and a conductor of a wide range of orchestral music. He conducted the London Promenade Concerts at the English Opera House 1838–59. These were very popular. Despite conducting many concerts and becoming well-known and wealthy, Jullien over-reached himself financially, and he died in poverty. According to the advertisement for the Bedford concert, he was accompanied by the *elite* of his unrivalled band, and Herr Koenig was the principal 'Cornet-a-Piston*ist*' [*sic*]. The review states that:

14 McGregor, 'Music in Bedfordshire II', pp. 57–8.

15 This local newspaper went through a number of name changes over the years, *Bedford Times* (1845–59), *Bedford Times and Bedfordshire Independent* (1859–72), *Bedfordshire Times and Independent* (1872–1939), *The Bedfordshire Times and Bedfordshire Standard* (1939–64), *Bedfordshire Times* (1965–95), *Bedfordshire Times & Citizen* (1995–97), *Times & Citizen* (1997–).

16 *Bedford Times and Bedfordshire Independent*, 23 September 1862, pp. 4–5. However, a letter to the *Bedfordshire Times and Independent*, 20 February 1903, p. 8, states that the Harmonic Society came to an end after John Brereton died (in 1863), ten years before the Bedford Amateur Musical Society was formed. It is possible that the letter writer's memory was inaccurate.

17 McGregor, 'Music in Bedfordshire II', p. 58.

18 Margaret McGregor states that the middle years of the century appear to have been a rather dead period for music and that professional concerts were few. Margaret McGregor, 'Music in Bedfordshire I', *Bedfordshire Magazine*, vol. 17, no.129 (Summer 1979), p. 58. The evidence does not bear this out. As well as the concerts referred to above concerts were also held on the 15 November 1848, at the Wesleyan chapel, with a selection of sacred music from the works of Handel and Mozart with John Nunn as leader and Robert Rose as organist (defraying expenses for the erection of a new organ); and 1 April 1851, a Grand Concert by the Distins, performing on their sax-horns. The Distins were a family of brass instrument manufacturers, musicians and publishers.

> Herr Koenig's solo on the Cornet-a-Piston was encored; but failed to overcome our objections to the monopolizing tones of the instruments as displayed in a small concert room. In this solo however, the tones were moderate when compared with the noise of the brass in some parts of the concerted music. The tones required by the area of the Surrey Zoological Gardens must be out of place in a small room like ours. When will musicians learn that one part of their 'art and mystery' should be to find the proportionate volume of tone for the room in which they play. We should have preferred hearing some of the blasts from the Cornets, on Saturday evening, through some half dozen pairs of good Witney blankets. Or, if given from a boat at Cox's pits, they would, perhaps, have made a pleasing serenade for an audience assembled on the bridge. If this fashion for spoiling music with noisy brass continue, we must have ear-dampers … advertised as 'indispensable for the enjoyment of modern orchestral music'.[19]

At the very end of 1859, an advertisement for a concert of Christmas music, scheduled for 3 January 1860, was placed in the *Bedford Times and Bedfordshire Independent* under the auspices of the Harmonic Society.[20] The advertisement does not refer to John Nunn or John Brereton. Details of the concert are rather obscure, for neither the soloists nor the leader, nor even the organisers, are named. The concert was never held. It is known what happened because Philip Diemer explained this when he addressed the Bedford Musical Society, following a presentation made to him for his long service to that organisation, in May 1905.[21] The following is a report from the *Bedfordshire Times and Independent* of his 1905 speech:

> A Society existed before the present one, and he [Philip Diemer] belonged to it, not as a conductor but as a humble second violinist and also as a vocalist, now and then singing bass solos. But the Society, which was conducted by the Rev. Henry Havergal, met with some success for a time, but unfortunately there were some quarrelsome people in the society.[22] He was told that musical people were very quarrelsome, but he did not think it was true, in his experience. It always took two to make a quarrel, and any way they were not a quarrelsome set in the present Society. The old Society came to a sudden, and, he thought, an inglorious end. There was a great quarrel. Politics had a good deal to do with it. Politics and music never did agree. Sectarianism was also strong in the town and had something to do with it. At any rate, the quarrel ended, he was ashamed to say, in a free fight. The ladies screamed, the boys, of whom there were a few, laughed and enjoyed it, and the next morning appeared a bill that the concert announced for that evening was unavoidably postponed. (laughter) … That concert had never been given … and money was still owing to the subscribers. It was a bad preparation for another Society and made it difficult to get subscribers.[23]

19 *Bedford Times*, 24 August 1850, p. 3. The reference to Surrey Zoological Gardens refers to one of Jullien's 'grande music fetes' with 400 instrumentalists, three distinct choruses and three distinct military bands in May 1849.

20 *Bedford Times and Bedfordshire Independent*, 27 December 1859, p. 1.

21 Philip Henry Diemer (1836–1910) was a founder member of the Bedford Amateur Musical Society (later the Bedford Musical Society) in January 1867. His contribution will be considered in following chapters.

22 The Rev. Henry East Havergal (1820–75) was vicar of Cople, and built an organ for himself in the church there. He also played the trumpet. The *Oxford Dictionary of National Biography* (*ODNB*) refers to the fact that Henry Havergal formed a musical society in Bedford. *ODNB*, vol. 25 (Oxford, 2004), p. 859. His father, W. H. Havergal, and his sister, Frances Havergal (who wrote the hymn "Take my Life and Let it be") are also referenced.

23 *Bedfordshire Times and Independent*, 19 May 1905, p. 5.

In the early 1860s, there was a sudden increase in the number of concerts. John Nunn and Robert Rose feature regularly as does the Rev. C. Brereton, vicar of St Mary's church, Bedford. [24] Philip Diemer appears too, both as accompanist and as conductor. A typical concert was that held in March 1862 at the Working Men's Institute, given for the benefit of Mr Kipps, a pupil of Robert Rose, who was leaving Bedford. The concert was under the direction of Robert Rose, but he was assisted by John Nunn, Philip Diemer and Emily Miller; it was well received. [25]

In 1866, Philip Diemer took a leading part in several concerts, including two concerts in February and one in April in aid of the Holy Trinity Church Enlargement Fund. The latter of these concerts included his *Fantasia for Pianoforte* ('Minnie'). In November, he took part in a Grand Promenade Concert promoted by The Bedford Literary and Scientific Institute and the General Library, and in December, he organised the Grammar School annual school concert, which included his own composition 'The Angel's Song' for solo and chorus. The reviewer writes of the Grammar School concert:

> Ever since Mr. Diemer has had the management of the singing class, this concert has come to be quite an annual institution, and each year have seen him bringing his pupils better and better prepared to undergo their trial of skill before their parents, school fellows and friends ... In the second half, the well-known 'Aldiborontiphoscophornio' was given as an encore.[26]

One of the boys named in the review as taking part was C. Halliley, later to become a prominent solicitor in the town and treasurer of Bedford Musical Society in the early years of the twentieth century.[27]

In addition to the variety of concerts now being held in Bedford, both The Bedford Literary and Scientific Institute and The Working Men's Institute provided educational support to musical activity in the town.[28] The Bedford Literary and Scientific Institute was founded in 1846 and later amalgamated with the Reading

24 John Nunn did not become involved with the - soon to be formed - Bedford Amateur Musical Society. By this time he had retired as organist of St Paul's church, though he was still teaching pianoforte, violin, singing and dancing at 16 The Crescent, Bedford. His advertisements appeared in the *Bedford Times and Bedfordshire Independent* during the 1860s.

25 'The vocal music was pleasingly rendered by the amateurs of the town. Mr. Nunn very much delighted the audience by the effective manner in which he played a solo on his favourite instrument, the violin ... Mr. Diemer gave the *Blue Bells of Scotland*, with his own variations in a truly brilliant style; the audience applauded heartily, and the accomplished pianist was recalled ... It must have been very gratifying to Mr. Rose to have been assisted on this occasion by his old pupil, Mr. Diemer, as well as by Mr. Kipps, his present pupil.' *Bedford Times and Bedfordshire Independent,* 18 March 1862, p. 5.

26 *Bedford Times and Bedfordshire Independent*, 18 December 1866, p. 5. The 'Aldiborontiphoscophornio', a glee for three voices, by John Wall Callcott is a paraphrase of the opening lines of Henry Carey's *Chrononhotonthologos; The Most Tragical Tragedy that was ever Tragedized by any Company of Tragedian* (London, 1777).

27 C. Halliley was the grandfather of the well-known actor John Le Mesurier, best known for playing the part of Sergeant Arthur Wilson in the television comedy *Dad's Army*. John Le Mesurier's actual name was John Elton Halliley. *ODNB*, vol. 33, pp. 324–25.

28 The Bedford Literary and Scientific Institute first considered presenting a concert in 1864 and re-considered the idea a couple of years later. The minutes for 4 September 1866 read: 'The report of the Sub-committee as regards the Promenade Concert was unanimously adopted. Mr. Diemer to receive £25 and to undertake the whole musical arrangement'. Bedford Literary and Scientific Institute, *Minute Book*, BLARS Li/LibB1/1/3.

Room Society and soon after with the General Library.[29] Regular meetings were held, from 1854, in the Assembly Rooms.

The Working Men's Institute, opened in 1855, was to some extent a parallel institution, but possibly less erudite. The building of its large headquarters in Harpur Street, now The Guildhouse, was largely funded by the Rev. Richard William Fitzpatrick, curate and later vicar of Holy Trinity church. His obituary in the *Bedford Times and Bedfordshire Independent* says: 'Witness the establishment, mainly at his own cost, of the Working Men's Institute and of the allotment system in connection with it, which was the result of his earnest desire to benefit the numerous and important class for which it was intended.'[30]

The enlarged Holy Trinity church, of which Philip Diemer was organist, was re-opened on Friday 26 October 1866.[31] The church had been built, and the parish established, in 1841 as a result of a government-funded programme to build new churches and establish new parishes in areas of need. Among the many dignitaries who came for a special sung Holy Communion was the Rev. Sir Frederick Arthur Gore Ouseley, who was professor of music at Oxford from 1855 until his death in 1889 and precentor of Hereford Cathedral for the same period.[32] He was also the founder of the preparatory school, St Michael's College, Tenbury Wells, in 1856, and its main benefactor. Together with the Rev. Sir H. W. Baker and W. H. Monk, Ouseley was one of the original compilers of the first edition of *Hymns Ancient and Modern.*

The churches of the town, as in the country at large, flourished in the 1860s, despite the publication of Charles Darwin's *Origins of Species* in 1859. As well as Holy Trinity's enlargement in 1866, the Howard Congregational church in Mill Street (now a night club) was also significantly enlarged. And a new organ was also installed at St Peter's church.

This expansion of the churches may have helped to provide wider interest and impetus for the formation of The Church Music Society (for the archdeaconry and county of Bedford) in 1865. At The Church Music Society's general meeting held in January 1866, the committee presented a schedule of rules which had been drawn up by the Rev. Havergal.[33] This Society survived for a number of years. Both the secretaries, the Rev. C. Brereton and Mr J. P. Piper, became actively involved in the Bedford Amateur Musical Society.

29 Austin Baker, *The Library Story: Bedford Public Library and its Forerunners 1700–1958* (Bedford, 1989), p. 9ff.

30 *Bedford Times and Bedfordshire Independent*, 10 January 1871, p. 5. There is a copy of *Memorials of R. W. Fitzpatrick* (London, 1878) published by C. F. Timaeus, 90 High Street, Bedford, in the Bedfordshire Heritage Library at Bedford Central Library.

31 A photograph of the Holy Trinity church opening can be seen in Richard Wildman's book *Bedford* (Stroud, 1995), Britain in Old Photographs, p. 56.

32 It is not clear why the Rev. Sir F. A. Gore Ouseley was invited although there are three possible reasons: he had been a university friend of the Rev. Henry Havergal, then vicar of Cople; there was a Thomas Ouseley, who was possibly a relative, living in Alexandra Road, Bedford (Thomas Ouseley's daughter, a violinist, played in the orchestra at the Society's concerts late in the century); the Rev. Sir F. A. Gore Ouseley was by this time prominent in church musical circles and, as noted above, had recently been involved with compiling *Hymns Ancient and Modern.*

33 *Bedford Times and Bedfordshire Independent,* 30 January 1866, p. 5.

The musicians of Bedford had a busy 1866, by the end of which the stage was set for the establishment of the Bedford Amateur Musical Society. At the time, it probably seemed an uncertain move, requiring commitment, dedication and hard work. In retrospect, the formation of the new Society was a very obvious step.

Chapter Two

Formation and Founding Fathers, 1867

> A preliminary meeting was held in the Working Men's Institute, but no one felt very sanguine about the success of the proposed Society except Mr Diemer, the idea being that musical people were a quarrelsome lot and could not hold together for any length of time.[1]

The idea that Philip Diemer should form a new musical society was first suggested by Dr Herbert Barker, several years before the Bedford Amateur Musical Society was actually formed.[2] His proposal is known from Philip Diemer's 1905 speech where he talked about the origins of the Musical Society. His speech, from which the extract below is taken, was reported in full in the *Bedfordshire Times and Independent*:

> There was no Society in existence for some years, but there were private meetings, and there was one held on a Tuesday evening at the house in which the present Secretary (Dr Skelding) was now living, and the gentleman who lived in that house at that time was one of Bedford's greatest worthies, Dr. Herbert Barker (applause). He suggested that they might start another Society. He (Mr. Diemer) talked it over with a few friends, such as Dr Coombs and Mr. Fitzpatrick's father (The Rev. R. W. Fitzpatrick), who was one of his and Bedford's best friends (applause).[3] The meeting to which Mr. W. L. Fitzpatrick had referred was called [in January 1867]. Dr. Coombs was also present, and one to whom the Society would ever owe a great debt.[4]

The meeting at which the Bedford Amateur Musical Society was formed took place on the 16 January 1867 at the Working Men's Institute in Harpur Street. Details of the discussion were minuted in the first of the three minute books from

1 From a letter to the *Bedfordshire Times and Independent,* 20 February 1903, p. 8, signed by 'AN OLD MEMBER'. The writer of this letter gives the date of the meeting as 3 January 1866, a year and several days too early.

2 Herbert Barker lived at 43 Harpur Street (between Dame Alice Street and Lime Street, where the Social Club car park now is). He was very prominent in his work to improve public health both nationally and locally. He faced much opposition in Bedford against improving drainage and providing a regular supply of pure water for the whole population, but before his death in 1865 some of the improvements he advocated had been made. Poignantly, he died of typhoid fever, the disease he had worked so hard overcome. There is a memorial to him in the south aisle of St Paul's church. For fuller information see his obituary in the *Bedford Times and Bedfordshire Independent*, 31 October 1865, p. 4.

3 Mr W. L. Fitzpatrick, who is referred to here, was currently the high sheriff of Bedfordshire, and present at the concert when this speech was given.

4 *Bedfordshire Times and Independent,* 19 May 1905, p. 5.

the Victorian period.[5] The minutes also list those present, who were Philip Diemer; the Rev. R. W. Fitzpatrick, chairman, vicar of Holy Trinity church; the Rev. F. M. Sadler, Mr Fitzpatrick's curate (who later became vicar of St Paul's church); Robert Rose; Mr H. C. Cooper, a music retailer whose premises were at 3 St Paul's Square (Mr Cooper was Philip Diemer's brother-in-law, having recently married one of his sisters, Louisa. He was also an amateur bassoonist); John Day, architect and musician, who was later to become choirmaster at St Paul's church while Robert Rose was still the organist; Mr J. P. Piper, joint secretary of the local Church Music Society; and Mr P. S. Fry. Despite Philip Diemer's reference in his 1905 speech, quoted above, Dr James Coombs was not present at the meeting, according to the minutes.[6]

The main object of the Musical Society, 'the encouragement of a high class of vocal and instrumental music', was spelled out in the introductory statement of the minutes.[7] The name chosen was the Bedford Amateur Musical Society.[8] The five resolutions of that first meeting, set out on the first page of the minute book, were that: such a society should be formed under the name given above; the mayor of Bedford for the time being be requested to be the patron of the society; the Rev. Frederick Fanshawe (headmaster of the Grammar School) be requested to be president; Philip Diemer be conductor and Robert Rose chorus master and organist; and Mr S. Rock be requested to act as treasurer and honorary secretary. The meeting was then adjourned to the following Monday. Other gentlemen thought likely to be interested in the movement were to be invited to attend and several did. Among these were the Rev. C. Brereton, vicar of St Mary's church; Dr James Coombs; Dr Hermann Steinmetz, German teacher at the Grammar School; and Mr Issett.

An advertisement announcing the intended formation of the Musical Society appeared in the *Bedford Times and Bedfordshire Independent* on 26 January 1867 signed by Hermann Steinmetz, the secretary, and dated 22 January 1867, six days after the initial meeting.[9] Would-be performers were asked to meet at the Working Men's Institute on Friday 1 February. Fast work indeed! About fifty people were present at that opening meeting of whom twenty-eight are named in the minute book. The first business was to approve the rules of the Society. These were proposed by Mr Piper and seconded by Hermann Steinmetz (who as secretary had probably written them). The minutes then record the following:

> A committee of 12 'gentlemen', six performers and six non-performers, was formed. Mr. Cooper and Mr. Rose undertook to provide the music for the society, Mr. Fanshawe agreed to allow a room of the Grammar School [which was still in St Paul's Square] while he was Headmaster to be used for rehearsals.

5 Three minute books covering the period 1867–1901 survive and are stored in the Choral Society's archive at the Bedfordshire and Luton Archives and Record Service, BLARS X817/1/1, X817/1/2 and X817/1/3. For the first twenty-five years or so, Dr Hermann Steinmetz was the author.

6 James Coombs's name is on the foundation stone of the Corn Exchange as he was mayor in 1871.

7 *Minute Book 1867–1893*, 16 January 1867, BLARS X817/1/1.

8 'Amateur' did not have the somewhat derogatory meaning that it has today. It then meant doing something not as a profession or occupation but for the love of it – not 'amateurish', i.e., second rate.

9 *Bedford Times and Bedfordshire Independent*, 26 January 1867, p. 4.

> The conductor had to choose the music for each concert and to submit his choice to the approval of the committee.[10]

The new committee met on the following Tuesday and it was agreed that the first concert should take place at the end of April. Philip Diemer submitted part of his proposed programme for the concert; this met with the approval of the committee. The first rehearsal was fixed for Tuesday 12 February. The committee met twice more before the concert. The committee members agreed that a platform should be erected in the concert hall and John Day arranged for this to be constructed by a local carpenter, Mr Freshwater. The cost of erecting the platform amounted to £16 4s 2d. An advertisement appeared in the *Bedford Times and Bedfordshire Independent* on the day of the performance.[11]

The concert started at 8.00p.m., and was given in the Assembly Rooms on Tuesday 30 April 1867, three months after the Musical Society's formation. A description of the scene before the concert started is included in the review:

> There was a large and fashionable company, which included some of the principal families of the town and neighbourhood; the ladies were, as usual, in strong force, and added by their presence very much to the attractions of the scene. The performers, both, vocal and instrumental, were punctual in their attendance to the time appointed, the whole were in their places a few minutes before eight o'clock ready to answer the summons of their energetic conductor, Mr Diemer. When the performers rose in their places at the call of the baton, the orchestra presented a very striking appearance, the males occupying the upper rows of the galleries, and their fair companions, forming the front ranks.[12]

The format of the concert, with a longer work in the first half and a number of short pieces in the second half, was common to many of the Musical Society's concerts in the Victorian period. It started with Mendelssohn's *Lauda Sion* and included extracts from Handel's *Joshua*, *Jeptha*, *Samson,* and *Messiah.* Pieces from Costa's *Naaman* and Rossini's *Moses in Egitto* were also featured. The *Bedford Times and Bedfordshire Independent* review gives a detailed sketch of the concert and was fulsome in its praise:

> All who attended the first concert on Tuesday evening and listened to the wealth of harmony and exquisite melody displayed by the amateurs, will readily admit that the musical element abounds in Bedford, particularly amongst the fair sex, and only required a suitable medium which this admirable society affords for its proper development … The orchestral arrangements were very good indeed, the best being made of the very limited space available for the purpose. The singers occupied the galleries erected on the raised platform, the altos and basses were on the right, the sopranos and tenors on the left and the band in the centre. The singers numbered about 100; the band 18, composed of the following instruments: 3 first violins, 2 second violins, 1 violoncello, 2 flutes, 2 clarionets, 1 bassoon, 2 cornets, 1 trombone, 2 double basses. One of the last-named instruments, a very fine one, belonged to the late Mr. George Bryant (whose memory is still cherished by many musical friends in this town), and was kindly lent for

10 *Minute Book 1867–93*, 1 February 1867, BLARS X817/1/1.
11 *Bedford Times and Bedfordshire Independent*, 30 April 1867, p. 1.
12 *Bedford Times and Bedfordshire Independent*, 7 May 1867, p. 5.

> the occasion by Mr. Frederick Howard, the present owner. Miss Barker presided at the pianoforte, and Mr Rose at the harmonium.[13]

Of the 'Hallelujah Chorus', the reviewer writes: 'We believe it was the opinion of the oldest musician present, that this sublime production of Handel was never given here so correctly and effectively as on this occasion.'[14]

Admission was limited to subscribers, and this remained the case while the Musical Society's concerts were held in the Assembly Rooms (1867–73). The hall was filled, 'to almost positive inconvenience', as a subsequent review put it.[15]

The Musical Society followed its successful first concert with three further concerts, in June, October and December. The June and October 1867 concerts were similar in format to the first concert, with longer works in the first half and shorter pieces in the second half. The December concert comprised one work – *Messiah*. Four concerts each year, at approximately these times, became the norm for most of the Victorian period.

The June 1867 concert included, in the first half, Haydn's cantata *The Tempest* and Locke's 'celebrated' (as the review puts it) music to *Macbeth*.[16] The second half included songs by Rousseau (the philosopher) from his *Le Devin du Village*, described as 'in the style of Handel', a few further short pieces by Handel including 'Shake the Dome' (from *Solomon*), and 'Will He Come?', a song by: 'that rising composer of whom England ought now to be so proud who has done so much, and promises so much more – Arthur Sullivan.'[17] Sullivan was twenty-five years old at the time. This was several years before he met W. S. Gilbert and collaborated with him on the comic operas for which they became so well-known.

The main work in the first half of the October concert was a cantata, *St Cecilia's Day*, by the Dutch composer Johann Bernhard van Bree. This cantata was quite popular at the time and was described in the review as music that throughout was of a pleasing and tuneful character. The second half of the concert included songs by Michael Balfe and Sir Henry Bishop.

The final concert of the year was the Society's first performance of *Messiah*. There is a surprisingly brief review, perhaps because it took place shortly before the Grammar School concert. The review pays tribute to local instrumentalists and also gives details of the five London professional players, noting: 'The Society appears to be very fortunate in being able to balance the four parts well … the choruses "For unto us a child is born", "All we like sheep have gone astray", and "the Hallelujah Chorus" went the best.'[18]

The annual Grammar School concert was held a couple of days after *Messiah*. The concert is significant because the main work was Philip Diemer's *Thoughts of Home*, specially composed for the occasion, using text by Mr Halsted, a master at

13 Ibid.
14 Ibid.
15 *Bedford Times and Bedfordshire Independent*, 29 October 1867, p. 5.
16 It is generally accepted that Matthew Locke did not actually write this music. A more likely composer is the earlier composer, Robert Johnson. See Percy A. Scholes, 'Locke's Music to Macbeth', *The Oxford Companion to Music*, 8th ed. (Oxford, 1950), p. 584.
17 *Bedford Times and Bedfordshire Independent,* 11 June 1867, p. 5.
18 *Bedford Times and Bedfordshire Independent,* 24 December 1867, p. 5.

the school. The cantata started with an overture. This was followed by a spirited and tuneful chorus 'Merry Boys are we', and later by 'We go to our Homes', and the 'Song of the Master': 'which was sung, we might also say in character, by the author, Mr. Halsted, with his usual taste and skill'.[19] Interestingly, there was no mention of Christmas in the music of this concert. However, the room was decorated with evergreens, banners and inscriptions.

At the Musical Society's first annual general meeting, held in February 1868, the financial statement for 1867 was presented. It was reported that all but £5 9s 3d of the total income of £136 8s 1d was used. Annual general meetings continued to be held in February until the 1890s, when the start of the season was moved to September.

It was obvious, even at the first concert in April 1867, that the Assembly Room hall was too small. The review of that concert ends with a long note about this:

> The complaint, often made, that the Assembly Room is insufficient and is, besides, ill-adapted to the requirements of a musical entertainment, was never more manifest on Tuesday evening. The building which sufficed to meet the wants of the town when the population numbered eight or nine thousand, can hardly be considered adequate now, with a population of fifteen thousand: and as it is understood that there is no chance of the building being enlarged a feeling is gaining ground amongst influential inhabitants in favour of a project to erect a musical hall. If the Amateur Musical Society continues to prosper, a much larger room than is at present available will become an absolute necessity; and taking into account the growing importance of the town, it is thought there would be no difficulty in forming a Limited Liability Company to carry out the undertaking.[20]

It is not surprising, therefore, that at the committee meeting that followed the first concert, members discussed the erection of new rooms, and at the annual general meeting in February, the committee was asked to take decisive steps to provide a larger concert room. Provision of a new concert hall remained a recurring theme, especially in reviews. The Musical Society's requirements added weight to other calls for a larger hall.

Bedford Amateur Musical Society had made a big impact in the town during its first year. The three 'wise men' who by their initiative, enthusiasm and energy were responsible for the establishment and the subsequent success of the Society were Philip Diemer, Robert Rose and Hermann Steinmetz.

Philip Henry Diemer (1836–1910)

Philip Diemer's ancestors came originally from Germany to England as members of the Moravian church (or Moravian Brethren as they were known).[21] This branch

19 Ibid. Cecil Higgins is one of the named trebles who took part in Philip Diemer's *Thoughts of Home*. He was also a soloist at the Musical Society's concert in February 1884. Cecil Higgins belonged to a Bedford brewing family and founded an art gallery and museum in Bedford, in what was once the family home. The museum is renowned for its collection of decorative and applied art. See the articles by Halina Grubert in *The Bedfordshire Magazine,* vol.18, no. 143 (Winter 1982), pp. 269–74, and vol.18, no. 144 (Spring 1983), pp. 334–40.

20 *Bedford Times and Bedfordshire Independent,* 7 May 1867, p. 5.

21 Much of the information that follows is from Philip Diemer's obituary in the *Bedfordshire Times and*

of the church originated in the mid-fifteenth century in Prague, but after persecution in their own country, and near extermination in 1620 in their adopted country, Poland, they re-formed in Saxony in the eighteenth century. The Moravian church was characterised by its missionary vigour.

Philip Jacob Diemer (Philip Diemer's great grandfather) was probably the first Diemer to set foot in England, arriving from Ratisbon (now known as Regensberg), situated north of Munich and on the Danube, in 1769. He spent four years in England, marrying his wife Rebecca in 1773. In that same year they went to Jamaica as missionaries, dying relatively young in 1782 from dysentery, a common fate then, as it was not a healthy climate.

Frederic Diemer (1774–1852), Philip Diemer's grandfather, arrived in England and settled in Bedford. His letter of entreaty to join the Moravian church in Bedford still exists in the church archives in Bedfordshire and Luton Archives and Records Service.[22] He was appointed a master at the English School, subsequently the Commercial School.[23] He was also organist of the Moravian church. Philip Diemer received his first music lesson from his grandfather on a four-and-a-half octave pianoforte that had originally been sent to Frederic's own father, Philip Jacob, in Jamaica. Philip Diemer was also taught to sing at an early age by a lady who was the niece of the Scottish poet and hymn-writer, James Montgomery.[24]

Frederic Diemer's son, Joseph Diemer (1798–1875), was a tailor who lived in St Peter's Street, eventually at number thirty-six, just near the junction with St Cuthbert's Street.[25] Philip Diemer was the second of Joseph Diemer's three children by his second wife, Elizabeth; he had two sisters. Philip Diemer also had a half-brother and a half-sister by Joseph's first wife.

Philip Diemer was born in July 1836 and was educated at the Commercial School. He first played the organ for a service at the Moravian church in Bedford at the age of twelve, and a couple of years later played at Cardington parish church on Sundays for a year during the illness of the organist there.[26] At the age of fourteen, he was articled to Robert Rose. Under 'so good a master' (as the *Bedfordshire Times and Independent's* obituary puts it), he had abundant opportunities for study and work. He served seven years' apprenticeship, and then went to the Royal Academy of Music, living in London for two years 1857–58. He worked hard, practising eight hours a day. His music teacher was William Henry Holmes, and he learnt harmony from Sir George Macfarren and singing from Regaldi.[27] Among his fellow students

Independent, 13 May 1910, p. 8. The author is also grateful to Philip Diemer's great grandson, Michael Diemer, who provided additional information.

22 13 January 1795, BLARS MO438.

23 The name changed in 1837 when Latin was introduced and the curriculum broadened - it was eventually changed to 'Modern'.

24 James Montgomery was the son of a pastor and missionary of the Moravian Brethren. Although he was born in Scotland, he was educated in Leeds and settled in Sheffield where he became a newspaper editor. He was a good and philanthropic man, twice imprisoned for publishing political articles. He is best remembered for his hymns, which include "Angels from the Realms of Glory", "Hail to the Lord's Anointed", "Songs of Praise the Angels Sang", "Stand up and Bless the Lord" and "Palms of Glory, Raiment Bright".

25 36 St Peter's Street is currently an Italian Restaurant, 'Mama Mia'.

26 This was before the opening of the Leicester to Hitchin railway in 1857, which would have made it easier for him to travel, using the train from Bedford to Cardington.

27 William Henry Holmes was a pianist, composer and teacher and trained some of the most eminent

was Arthur Sullivan. The principal of the Royal Academy was Ciprianni Potter.[28] Philip Diemer used to relate that when he was leaving the Academy Ciprianni Potter shook hands with him and said: 'Remember, you have shaken hands with a man who has shaken hands with Beethoven.'[29] It is on record that Beethoven thought highly of Ciprianni Potter.[30]

The students at the Academy were brought up on Heller, Dussek and on Potter's own studies which were then held in high regard.[31] Philip Diemer, who sang bass, belonged to the Bach Society. The conductor was William Sterndale Bennett and the secretary was Dr Charles Steggall.[32] According to his obituary, Philip formed his taste for oratorio at performances of the Sacred Harmonic Society and from singing in the Bach Choir. While still studying at the Royal Academy, he undertook the Sunday duties of organist of Holy Trinity church, Bedford, coming home each week-end to fulfil his commitments. He was known as 'the boy organist'.[33] On his return to Bedford in 1858, he immediately took up a post at Holy Trinity church. This was the same year that the Rev. R. W. Fitzpatrick succeeded the Rev. H. B. Worthington as vicar, having been his curate since 1850. By 1867, Philip Diemer was well established as the organist at Holy Trinity and very involved with music making in the town as already described. He was just thirty years old and married to Mary (*née* Herbert). They had a young family.[34]

musicians of the time. He was a founder member of the Bach Society. By the end of his life he was known as 'father of the Academy'. *The New Grove Dictionary of Music and Musicians*, vol. 11 (London, 2001), p. 644. Sir George A. MacFarren studied under Ciprianni Potter. He helped found the Society of British Musicians in 1834 and the Handel Society in 1844. He was a patron of Bedford Musical Society. *New Grove*, vol. 15, pp. 471–2.

28 Ciprianni Potter was a composer, pianist and teacher. He succeeded Dr William Crotch as principal of the Royal Academy of Music in 1832. He was a prolific composer, but largely confined himself to instrumental and orchestral music, completing nine symphonies. He also produced one substantial cantata, *Medora e Corrado*. *New Grove*, vol. 20, pp. 221–2.

29 *Bedfordshire Times and Independent*, 13 May 1910, p. 8.

30 Ibid.

31 Stephen Heller was a Hungarian born pianist and composer. He was a much admired as a pianist and was considered by some critics as even more poetic than his friend Chopin. He was also a friend of Liszt and Berlioz. Lionel Salter, ed., *More Romantic Pieces for the Piano* (London, 1990), p. 12. Jan Ladislav Dussek was a renowned pianist and composer. He was born in what is now the Czech Republic. He lived and performed in many parts of Europe and fled from Paris in 1790, coming to London where he spent eleven years. His piano works were popular in his lifetime, but are not played very much now, except as studies. Howard Allen Craw, 'Dussek', *Grove Music Online,* accessed 4 February 2015, http://www.oxfordmusic online.com/subscriber/article/ grove/music/44229pg2.

32 Sir William Sterndale Bennett was an English composer, pianist and teacher. He entered the Royal Academy of Music in 1826 and was admired by Mendelssohn. A little later he became a friend of Schumann. He founded the Bach Society and became principal of the Royal Academy of Music in 1866. Michael Kennedy, *The Oxford Dictionary of Music* (London, 1985), p. 69. Charles Steggall was an organist and composer. He studied under Sterndale Bennett at the Royal College of Music, who consulted him about the formation of the Bach Society. He was one of the founders of the Royal College of Organists to which he delivered the inaugural lecture in 1864. J. A. Fuller Maitland, ed., *Grove's Dictionary of Music and Musicians*, vol. 3 (London, 1904–1910, repr. 1921), p. 800 and James D. Brown, and Stephen S. Stratton, *British Musical Biography: A Dictionary of Musical Artists, Authors, and Composers born in Britain and its Colonies* (New York, 1971), p. 392.

33 'Some years later he was offered the organ at a larger church but this he refused in loyalty to the church where he was first known as the "boy organist"' (from an account of Miss Diemer). K. M. Westaway, ed., *A History of Bedford High School* (Bedford, 1932), p. 136.

34 Four children were born to Philip Diemer and his wife around the time of the founding of the Society, in 1865, 1867, 1869 and 1870.

The early minutes of the Musical Society and the local newspaper reviews do not refer to Philip Diemer as the founder of the Society, but he seems to have been the driving force that got it up and running. Later, he is described as the founder, for example at a presentation at the start of the tenth season.[35] He was also described as the founder by the writer of the letter quoted at the start of this chapter and by his daughter Miss Diemer.[36]

Robert Rose (1814–98)

Robert Rose was born in Newport Pagnell.[37] His irrepressible love of music showed itself at an early age, and while yet a youth he overcame opposition from his family to follow his musical interests. The pianoforte was the first instrument to which he had access, but he soon obtained permission to practise on a local chapel's organ. His first lessons had to be taken against the wish of practically-minded relatives, who predicted no very bright future for a boy who showed such a passion for music.

He came to Bedford as a young, married man and commenced a professional practice, which in after years extended widely across Bedfordshire and adjoining counties. He was organist at St Peter's church from the late 1830s, remaining in post for fifty years. While there, he was responsible for some of the progress made in musical services. For this he faced much opposition for what would later be thought of as mild innovations, though at the time they aroused much indignation. For some time he was also the principal music teacher in the town. He was not only an excellent musician, but also had a music shop on the corner of St Peter's and the High Street (at 123 High Street). The building still survives.

During his latter twenty-five years at St Peter's church he was also the organist at St Paul's church. He was, at first, assistant to John Nunn, initially playing for the week-day services there, when the Rev. Fitzgerald was vicar. When John Nunn retired in the early 1860s, Robert Rose succeeded him. He was assisted in carrying out his various roles by Miss Rose and by his youngest son, Henry Rose. Afterwards, in association with the Rev. Mr Sadler, he did much to improve the musical part of the service. There had been a choir of charity boys and one of Robert Rose's earliest tasks was to establish another choir. Some years later, the organ was enlarged under his direction. There were so many good points about the instrument, inadequate though it was, that it was decided to have it re-built and enlarged rather than replaced.

35 The framed address read: 'To Mr. P. H. Diemer, Royal Academy of Music – the performing members, about 200 of the Bedford Amateur Musical Society, desire to express to you as its founder and conductor their high appreciation of the zeal and ability with which you have conducted its concerts and practices during the past nine years and as a small and inadequate token of their gratitude for the uniform kindness and consideration you have shown to them as a Musical Class and with the assurance of their cordial esteem and good wishes, beg your acceptance of the accompanying purse of gold.' *Bedfordshire Times and Independent,* 19 February 1876, p. 5.

36 Westaway, *A History of Bedford High School*, p. 136.

37 Based on the obituary of Robert Rose in the *Bedfordshire Times and Independent,* 25 March 1898, p. 7.

Dr Hermann Steinmetz (1826–93)

Hermann Steinmetz was born in the little town of Sachsenhausen in the Principality of Waldeck, south of Hanover.[38] His father was the pastor of Sachenhausen and superintendent of his district - equivalent to being archdeacon. After taking his degree as Doctor of Philosophy at the University of Jena, Hermann Steinmetz was for some time himself a minister of religion, so was rightly 'the Rev. Dr Steinmetz'. Before coming to England, he became interested in the Kindergarten movement and taught in a school conducted by one of Friedrich Froebel's assistants.

Hermann Steinmetz came to Bedford following a proposal by a George Hurst, and seconded by James Coombs, that a German master should be appointed to the Commercial School. In March 1866, he was transferred to the Grammar School, and retained that position to the day of his death.

Soon after arriving in Bedford, he became involved with the Bedford Literary and Scientific Institute. In 1858 he was appointed a member of the committee, and in 1860 he succeeded James Coombs as honorary secretary. He read numerous papers to the Institute, including a paper on Mozart in conjunction with Philip Diemer in 1860. That year he married the daughter of a Mr Samler. In 1869 he published an educational book entitled *A History of Modern Europe from the Invasion of the Barbarians to the Present Day*.[39]

These, then, are the men behind the Bedford Amateur Musical Society's formation; good, capable, educated citizens with considerable expertise and experience in their respective areas. In the next chapter it will be seen how they were able to build on the solidly-laid foundations.

38 Based on the obituary of Dr Hermann Steinmetz in the *Bedfordshire Times and Independent*, 13 May 1893, p. 8.

39 H. Steinmetz, *A History of Modern Europe from the Invasion of the Barbarians to the Present Day (AD 375–1869): A Hand-book for Schools* (London, 1869).

Chapter Three

Eminent Victorians, 1868–1900

> In 1866 [*sic*] I assisted in the formation of the Bedford Musical Society, an institution highly appreciated by all lovers of good music and promising under the able leadership of Mr Diemer and its zealous and genial Secretary, Dr Steinmetz, with the wise counsel of its President, to flourish for the years to come as a source of pure and elevated enjoyment to all who come within the range of its influence.[1]

The early years, 1868–73

The first concert of 1868, held on 28 April, had as the main work Mozart's 'Twelfth Mass'.[2] A mass seems a strange choice of music in Bedford with its strong nonconformist tradition. However, the English words are not really a translation of the Latin, but take the form of prayers and praises with only marginal reference to the original. Perhaps this wording allowed English choirs to think that they were singing an oratorio, rather than a mass.[3] There is a vivid description of the performance in the *Bedford Times and Bedfordshire Independent*:

> The members of this well-organised society gave the first concert of the second season on Tuesday evening, the 28th April, at the Assembly Rooms, the spacious hall being crowded to the very doors. The programme was arduous and attractive, the *piece de resistance* being Mozart's Twelfth Mass (sung in English). The performance of this fine composition was, throughout, eminently satisfactory. The most notable feature to our mind, was the vast power of the choruses. This was especially the case in the passages of the Kyrie.[4]

The soloists, too, were praised.[5] They were all members of the chorus, and the solo passages for each voice were shared between several singers so that they each had a few extracts to sing. The soloists included Miss Brereton, two Mr Breretons,

1 James Coombs, *Recollections Personal and Political: As Read before the Bedford Liberal Club the President Alderman Hawkins JP Mayor in the Chair April 4 1889* (Bedford, 1889), p. 19. The reference to the president is to Mr (later Sir) Frederick Howard. It generally agreed that the Musical Society was founded in 1867.

2 The 'Twelfth Mass' was at one time attributed to Mozart. Koechel, in his catalogue of Mozart's works (1862) recognised it as spurious. It is now generally accepted that the composer was the Austrian Wenzel Muller, a noted conductor and composer of *Singspiel*.

3 It is perhaps worth noting that the first mass in the newly-built presbytery in Brereton Road, Bedford, was celebrated on 31 March 1867. The Catholic church of The Holy Child and St Joseph was opened in April 1874, two weeks after the opening of the Corn Exchange.

4 *Bedford Times and Bedfordshire Independent*, 5 May 1868, p. 5. The melody for the opening Kyrie is now familiar as the most frequently used tune for the hymn "Take my Life and Let it be". The words for this are by Frances Havergal, brother of Henry East Havergal, the vicar of Cople.

5 'The solo passages were, in every instance, effectively rendered and thoroughly enjoyed, evidencing deep care on the part of the talented amateurs entrusted with these prominent parts.' Ibid.

Miss Sirett, Mr Piper, Mr Day and Mr Harrison. The band, which did not include any professional instrumentalists and was similar in size to that of the Musical Society's first concert a year earlier, elicited the only adverse criticism in the review – of being too small.[6] The review finishes thus:

> The town should congratulate itself on having a body of amateurs able to produce these great masterpieces in so effective a manner: and it is not too much to say that the amateurs themselves ought to be proud of having a director like Professor Diemer, whose ability and genius have led an infant organisation to such a remarkable degree of efficiency.[7]

The new balcony in the large Assembly Room hall was completed in the summer of 1868, a little over a year after the Musical Society's first concert – no mean achievement – and was able to accommodate approximately one hundred people. The first of the Musical Society's concerts to be held after the completion of the balcony was given in October 1868. The miscellaneous second half opened with the overture from Philip Diemer's *Thoughts of Home*, the work he had composed for Bedford Grammar School and first performed there in December 1867.

For the final concert of the season, Handel's *Judas Maccabaeus*, four professional instrumentalists were engaged. They were all from the band of the Royal Italian Opera and were Mr F. Folks, first violin; Mr T. Watson, second violin; Mr Burnett, viola; and Mr Petitte, cello. The bass soloist was Alfred Howard, subsequently organist of the Mill Street Baptist church and owner of a music shop in the town. Mr Young, a local man who was to have been the tenor soloist, was unable to sing, and his place was taken by Edward Lloyd, the principal tenor of St Andrew's church, Well Street, London. In 1870, Edward Lloyd sang again with the Musical Society in Haydn's *Creation*. Edward Lloyd joined the Gentlemen of the Chapel Royal in 1869 and went on to have an outstanding career as a concert singer.[8] His first national success was as soloist in Bach's *St Matthew Passion* at the Gloucester (Three Choirs) Festival in 1871. Later in his career, he sang in the first performances of Elgar's *King Olaf* (without taking part in rehearsals), *Caractacus*, and in the rather unsatisfactory performance of *The Dream of Gerontius*.[9]

It may seem strange today, but throughout the Victorian period solos and choruses were applauded during performances, as still happens in opera, and sometimes encored. In *Judas Maccabaeus*, Alfred Howard's rendering of 'Arm, Arm, ye Brave', and the chorus's 'Welcome, Welcome' were both applauded.[10] Sometimes

[6] 'The effectiveness of the instrumental portions was also decisive, although it is in this department we think there is most room for improvement, at least by the accession of other performers.' Ibid.

[7] Ibid.

[8] The following indicates his importance: 'No tenor was ever associated with the production of so many important works in the concert-room.' Fuller Maitland, ed., *Grove's Dictionary of Music and Musicians*, vol. 2, p. 755.

[9] Michael Kennedy, *The Works of Ralph Vaughan Williams* (London, 1964), p. 389. Vaughan Williams was disappointed with the performance of *The Dream of Gerontius* and described the way that Edward Lloyd sang the title part as: 'like a Stainer anthem, in the correct tenor attitude with one foot slightly withdrawn'. Jerrold Northrop Moore also quotes this comment in his biography, *Edward Elgar: A Creative Life* (Oxford, 1984), p. 331.

[10] The reviewer wrote: 'The effect of those passages was decisive, the audience testifying their approval by repeated bursts of applause.' *Bedford Times and Bedfordshire Independent*, 22 December 1868, p. 5.

audiences were chided by reviewers for not applauding sufficiently and therefore seeming cold.

The review of the April 1869 concert includes a vivid description of the concert room with the new balcony. The reviewer was not happy with the lay-out:

> The public hall of the Bedford Rooms, though attractively ornamented and well arranged for meetings, is but ill adapted to musical performances. The effect of solo singing, especially, is to a great degree marred by the construction of the roof ... To obviate as far as possible this unavoidable difficulty, the performers are placed on a semi-circular platform at a considerable height from the floor, so that when the audience are seated underneath there is comparatively little to arrest the uniform expansion of the waves of sound either in a lateral or a longitudinal direction ... a partial homage was done to the Genius of Music by placing in prominent positions ... the busts of Mendelssohn, Beethoven, Mozart, and Rossini.[11]

The concert included Mendelssohn's *Lauda Sion*, which the Musical Society had sung at its first concert two years earlier.[12] The review draws attention to:

> an unwelcome practice which has of late spread amongst a section of the male auditory, of beating time with the foot on the floor. It was extremely indulged in on Tuesday evening, not only during the instrumental portions, but also we regret, during some of the solos ... This should be at once put down at any cost.[13]

Handel's *Alexander's Feast* was performed in June. It is not known who sang the solo parts from the choir because:

> we have, in accordance with a wish intimated by the Hon. Sec., abstained from giving the names of the members on whom the prominent parts devolved, and for the express reason that thereby we are consulting for the interests of the Society by preventing an apple of discord from falling among them.[14]

The reviewer also notes: 'On Tuesday evening, the hall was, as a matter of course, intensely warm, and consideration for the physical exertion which the principals had to go through ought to have suggested the advisability of doing away with encores.'[15]

An extract from Philip Diemer's cantata, *Ivry*, was included in the second half of the miscellaneous concert in October 1869. *Ivry* is based on Thomas Babington Macaulay's stirring poem, *Ivry: A Song of the Hugenots*, which the reviewer thought would be familiar to all readers of the *Bedford Times and Bedfordshire Independent.*[16] The cantata was composed expressly for the concert, and: 'as far as we have

11 *Bedford Times and Bedfordshire Independent,* 20 April 1869, p. 5.

12 The reviewer comments that this piece is: 'justly admired by the lovers of florid ecclesiastical music, especially of that type which has been so popularised on the continent.' Ibid.

13 Ibid.

14 *Bedford Times and Bedfordshire Independent,* 15 June 1869, p. 6. The somewhat convoluted wording probably reflects that used by Hermann Steinmetz.

15 Ibid.

16 *Bedford Times and Bedfordshire Independent*, 26 October 1869, p. 5. Ivry is named after Ivry-la-Bataille (near Evreux) where Henry IV of Navarre, by then the Protestant King of France, famously defeated the Catholic League supported by the Department of Mayenne in 1590.

heard it, a work of no little merit, and it bears throughout the impress of originality and conceptual genius.'[17] The music does not survive.

Mendelssohn's *Elijah* was performed for the first time in December 1869 before a crowded audience. The orchestra was once more augmented by five players from the band of the Royal Italian Opera. Mr Aylward was the cellist in place of Mr Petitte, and this time there was a double bass player, Mr Ould. All the soloists (apart from a Mr Morgan) were members of the Musical Society's chorus. Despite Hermann Steinmetz's veto on naming local soloists earlier in the year, the names of thirteen local soloists are given. Overall, the review was highly favourable.[18] After heaping credit on Philip Diemer the reviewer adds a familiar caveat: 'The only desideratum which the society now required urgently to have supplied to them is a hall adapted for their performance both as regards acoustic properties and the arrangements for the reception of the audience. Until this be procured they must continue to labour under a serious drawback which no temporary alteration can overcome.'[19]

Haydn's *Creation,* which followed in April 1870, was not nearly so well received. This was despite there being three professional soloists, Sofia Vinta (soprano) and Lewis Thomas (bass), both from the Sacred Harmonic Society, and once more, Edward Lloyd (tenor). Four of the five professional instrumentalists who had played in *Elijah* returned for this concert (Mr Ould did not play on this occasion). The problem, in the reviewer's opinion, was that the amateur instrumentalists were under-rehearsed.[20]

The audience came in for criticism, too: 'We must, however, call attention to the reprehensible conduct of some amongst the audience who ought to know better. We noticed some ladies in the body of the hall kept continually discoursing in a loud tone, so as to be very much in the way of enjoyment of the performance by those around them.'[21] The writer hoped that a public chiding would mean that there was no repetition of this behaviour.

The reviewer also reflects on whether a society with the word 'Amateur' in its title should make use of professional players, and considers the problems that amateur musicians have working alongside them. He seems to be in two minds on the subject: 'Even those most opposed to the engagement of professional talent must acknowledge that rarely have the inhabitants of Bedford enjoyed a richer musical treat than that which they were privileged to listen to on this occasion.'[22]

Sterndale Bennett's once popular cantata, *The May Queen*, was the main work in the concert that followed. No vocal or instrumental professionals were engaged. The

[17] Ibid.

[18] 'Considering the magnitude of the undertaking, and the vast amount of trouble and study required before the Society could attempt such a masterpiece of musical composition, we have all the more pleasure now in noting the execution for the work in detail in terms of almost unqualified approbation.' The chorus sang pretty well too: 'the chorus in which Baal is vainly involved by his priests … was thrilling in the extreme.' *Bedford Times and Bedfordshire Independent*, 21 December 1869, p. 5.

[19] Ibid.

[20] 'Could they only realise the many arduous rehearsals, which even the most accomplished artistes of the day go through before a public performance of importance is given, they would appreciate the absolute insuperable difficulty of attempting a great work with only the experience derived from perhaps a few hours' practice in five or six weeks.' *Bedford Times and Bedfordshire Independent*, 3 May 1870, p. 5.

[21] Ibid.

[22] Ibid.

reviewer was highly critical: 'with regard to the performance there was little upon which we can compliment the Society, as it was decidedly not up to their standard of efficiency.'[23] The accompaniment to one of the ballads in *The May Queen*, ''Tis Jolly to Hunt in the Bright Moonlight' drew particular ire: 'A strange feature in connection with the song was the very peculiar manner in which one of the bassoons became erratic.'[24] This, and other criticisms, including that of a trio sung by three ladies in the second part of the concert, was too much for Philip Diemer, whose letter was published the following week:

> In the accompaniment to the song ''Tis jolly to hunt' one of the bassoonists is said to have become erratic, whatever that may be. Now if the object was to say something disagreeable of one of the bassoon players a more unfortunate place could not have been chosen, for the bassoons, except for a bar or two, did not accompany the voice at all, and the few notes they did play were performed in tune and time.[25]

The two bassoonists were Robert Sim Eveleigh, at the time organist of the Moravian church and Mr H. C. Cooper, Philip Diemer's brother-in-law, who had been a member of the Musical Society from the start and was its first librarian.[26] The allegedly 'erratic' trombonist was Mr Cooper. Despite Philip Diemer's robust defence of his two bassoonists, the critic did have some support. One correspondent made the point that the Bedford Amateur Musical Society was not so special.

This review and the subsequent correspondence do, however, underline the danger of placing too much reliance on the critic's judgment, whether complimentary or not. Almost nothing is known about the early reviewers – their names are not revealed – so it is not possible to judge their expertise and musical background. After this outburst future criticisms were more muted.

The October 1870 concert celebrated the centenary of the birth of Beethoven and included a performance of his Symphony No. 1. The long review says a great deal about Beethoven's music but very little about the performance; there is none of the adverse criticism of the last two concerts.[27]

In 1871, three of the four concerts included works by Mendelssohn. The April concert included his setting of Psalm 42, the June concert *The First Walpurgis Night* and the December concert a performance of *St Paul*. Mendelssohn completed *St Paul* when he was twenty-six years old, ten years before *Elijah*. The first performance was in Dusseldorf in May 1836. The first performance in England was given (in English) later in the same year in Liverpool. For the Bedford performance, a professional soprano and a professional bass were engaged. The bass was not able to sing, so a member of the choir – an amateur – was selected to sing in his stead, joining the tenor soloist, another member of the choir. Neither the tenor nor the bass

23 *Bedford Times and Bedfordshire Independent*, 7 June 1870, p. 5.
24 Ibid. The piano accompaniment in the vocal score indicates that the bassoons play briefly three times.
25 *Bedford Times and Bedfordshire Independent*, 14 June 1870, p. 5.
26 Robert Sim Eveleigh was an accountant with offices in Bedford.
27 'Considering the difficulty of the compositions, we may say the whole, more particularly the symphony, was very creditably performed, and we hope the results of the concert will have realised the conductor's wish as expressed by him in his concluding paragraph attached to the book of words, viz, that it might be the means of making some of Beethoven's works better understood and advance the cause of music in the town of Bedford.' *Bedford Times and Bedfordshire Independent*, 1 November 1870, p. 5.

soloist is named, in line with Hermann Steinmetz's diktat. The reviewer was duly complimentary to both of them.[28]

The main work in April 1872 was *Naomi* by Dr Edmund Chipp, then organist of Ely Cathedral.[29] He conducted his own composition. The review is crushing:

> It is our duty to add also that Dr Chipp's mode of conducting had the undesirable effect of concentrating on himself no small share of the attention which ought to have been bestowed on his composition. The unusual demonstrativeness which he exhibited, the excited manner in which he wielded the baton, the variety of grimaces, not to say contortions, in which he felt constrained to indulge, together with the fact that he adapted his voice occasionally to instrumental as well as to vocal portions of the performance, conspired to amuse most of the audience to a degree inconsistent with a proper appreciation of the oratorio … The second half of the concert (miscellaneous pieces) was decidedly the best part of the concert and was under the conductorship of Mr. Diemer, whose manner contrasted favourably with that of the previous holder of the wand.[30]

The concert did not finish until nearly eleven o'clock, and the reviewer concludes: 'whilst congratulating the amateurs, we must regret that the concert was not commenced punctually, a departure from discipline that Mr Diemer has never permitted.'[31]

The Musical Society performed *Elijah* again in December 1872, three years after their first performance. Four professional instrumentalists were engaged including, for the first time, Mr Waud playing the viola.[32] Alice Barnett, the contralto soloist, was referred to as being of the Royal Albert Hall concerts – only eighteen months after the Royal Albert Hall was opened. Of Mr Lander, the bass soloist who sang the part of Elijah, the reviewer comments that he was: 'a basso full of melody and power without the echoing flatness which not infrequently distresses the ear. His voice is one of great compass, we may remark that he was uniformly good and repeatedly applauded.'[33]

The number of performers, choir and orchestra combined are reported to have totalled about 135. The audience gave vent to their feelings by frequent applause – which may be why the concert lasted for three hours, from eight until eleven o'clock! Despite this, no-one is reported to have left early.

After such a glowing review of this second performance of *Elijah*, it must have

28 'And here we would especially say a word of well-deserved praise to the tenor and the bass for the exquisite manner in which they rendered the duets devolved upon them.' *Bedford Times and Bedfordshire Independent*, 26 December 1871, p. 5.

29 Jeremy Dibble, *John Stainer: A Life in Music* (Woodbridge, 2007), p. 7, makes reference to Dr Chipp: 'Stainer may have heard (H.J.) Gauntlett play at the tender age of six, but it is more likely that he heard Edmund Chipp (later organist of Ely Cathedral) who was a celebrated performer of Mendelssohn, and was succeeded by Gauntlett in 1846 [at St. Olave's Church, Southwark].'

30 *Bedford Times and Bedfordshire Independent*, 23 April 1872, p. 5.

31 Ibid.

32 There seem to have been a family of four string-playing Wauds. J. H. (Haydn), J. P., S. J., and W. W., are all listed in Michael Musgrave's *The Musical Life of the Crystal Palace* (Cambridge, 1995), p. 220. W.W. Waud is the only one listed as a viola player, so was probably the performer on this occasion.

33 The review is also complimentary of the choir: 'The choruses were given with almost surprising power and efficiency; indeed, we have it on the best authority that such excellence is rarely or never met with in the provinces and is even equal to some renderings in the great city.' *Bedford Times and Bedfordshire Independent*, 17 December 1872, p. 5.

been galling to be reprimanded, following the March 1873 concert, for having too many repeats.[34] Most of the concert consisted of selections from Handel's works. These had all been performed previously, apart from the 'Dettingham' Te Deum. Gounod's *By Babylon's Wave*, based on Psalm 137, was also a new work. The repeats could, of course, have been included as members of the audience may have wished to hear works again in the only way that was possible at the time, before records and radio broadcasts existed.

Further criticism followed the May concert when Sterndale Bennett's *The May Queen* was repeated three years after the Musical Society had first performed it. In the reviewer's opinion there was no improvement on the original performance. *Judas Maccabaeus*, which had first been performed in 1868, was repeated in December 1873.

Before describing the momentous events of 1874, it is time to pause and say something about how the Musical Society was organised during the early years. At first, weekly rehearsals were held in a large room in the Grammar School (now the old Town Hall). The Rev. Frederick Fanshawe, president of the Musical Society, was headmaster at the time and allowed this arrangement to continue so long as it did not interfere with the running of the school. In fact the arrangement lasted until 1876. Rehearsals were held on Tuesdays, as were concerts. Miss Barker, organist of St Mary's church, Bedford, was the first accompanist, but had to retire due to ill health at the end of 1868. Her place was then taken by Mr T. J. Ford, organist of the Bunyan Meeting church.

Would-be performing members of the chorus had to undergo an examination, usually by the conductor. The committee then had to ratify applications. Trained musicians were exempt from this process. The rules of attendance at rehearsals were quite strict. Anyone absent for three consecutive weeks would not, as Rule 17 (1869) put it: 'be allowed to attend the next concert or would cease to be a member of the Society as the Committee shall determine.'[35] The early minutes have several references to people being excluded for non-attendance, or being re-admitted because they provided sufficient reasons for being absent. The rules also state that it was desirable that those not taking part: 'though unable to sing, should sit in their place on the orchestra [*sic*] instead of in the body of the room.'[36] This included instrumental members as well. It now seems a very extraordinary idea and must have been somewhat disconcerting for the conductor!

The committee met frequently during the early years; in 1870 they met eight times. Committee meetings were held at a variety of places. In the beginning, the meetings were often held at the Grammar School, and sometimes at the homes of members, especially at Philip Diemer's home. After 1875, meetings were regularly held at the Working Men's Institute. At this time the rules did not make any provision for a chairman, so the chairmanship for committee meetings was shared on a rotating system. The committee comprised of seven officers, six performing

34 Of the repeats, the critic rails: 'This is scarcely a proper way in which to treat subscribers; it is not the best mode of advancing the interests of "high-class music"; and certainly it is not the most judicious way of gaining fresh accessions, either to the performing or to the subscribing bodies.' *Bedford Times and Bedfordshire Independent*, 1 April 1873, p. 5.

35 *Minute Book 1867–93*, 8 March 1869, BLARS X817/1/1.

36 Ibid.

members and six non-performing members. Five members formed a quorum at committee meetings, and in the early days there were usually six or seven members at the meetings. The secretary's role included the work of treasurer, and Hermann Steinmetz kept the accounts, booked the halls, dealt with correspondence and took the minutes. His minutes (1867–93) are a superb example of clarity and succinctness, giving outline coverage of discussion and, very importantly, details of resolutions and whether these had been approved.

The minutes of the meeting held immediately before the performance of *Messiah* in December 1870 include details of arrangements for the provision of refreshments at the forthcoming concert:

1. Beer & wine in Gentlemen's Bar room
2. Society purchases provisions for ladies
3. Mrs. Hill to be employed for 3/6 + cost of cups & saucers.
4. Someone be employed to take charge of Cloaks of lady-performers.
5. Charges 2d for tea or coffee + list of prices –
   a plate of sardines 1½d , a glass of Cherry [*sic*] 3d , and for ale or stout.
6. Mr. Smith and Mr. Chamberlain to serve in the Gents bar.
   Refreshments were also provided at rehearsals with tea and coffee available for ladies.[37]

The opening of the Corn Exchange in 1874

The old Corn Exchange, or Floral Hall as it has subsequently been called, was built in 1850, adjacent to the north side of St Paul's church graveyard. By the late 1860s, however, it was already too small for the increased corn trade of Bedfordshire and the surrounding area. Bedford Corporation mooted the idea of building a new Corn Exchange in 1869, but it was not until a means of finance had been determined that local approval was granted in February 1872. The foundation stone of the new Corn Exchange, at the front and to the east of the central window, was laid on 21 April 1872 by the Right Hon. Earl Cowper, KG, Lord Lieutenant of Bedfordshire, assisted by the Duke of Bedford. The new building was designed to be more than a Corn Exchange, and contained offices, cloakrooms, a kitchen, dining rooms and a main hall (100ft by 60ft) suitable for concerts. The formation of the Musical Society in 1867 seems to have been a stimulus to building the new Corn Exchange. At a shareholders' meeting a few years after its completion, one shareholder complained that the hall had been built primarily for use by the Bedford Amateur Musical Society.[38] In the months before the formal opening, the acoustics of the hall were tested: 'There have been various test assemblies, an election meeting, a political dinner, a concert, a campanological entertainment and a Christy Minstrel performance ... on the whole these proved successful when the audience preserved silence, but the slightest disorder was fatal.'[39]

37 *Minute Book 1867–93,* 29 November 1870, BLARS X 817 /1 /1.

38 '(Dr. Coombs) I have taken greater pains than most others and spent more time, at a greater cost to put up this building for you (hear, hear, laughter, and A VOICE: "It was built for the Amateur Musical Society").' *Bedfordshire Times and Independent*, 22 January 1876, p. 5.

39 *Bedfordshire Times and Independent* 18 April 1874, p. 8, quoted in 'Bedford Corn Exchanges' by Mike Benson, *The Bedfordshire Magazine*, vol. 25, no. 194 (Autumn 1995), p. 61.

By January 1874, building work was sufficiently far advanced to enable terms to be discussed with the Musical Society. The fee agreed was £24 for four concerts and four rehearsals.[40] In the months before the opening, the Musical Society successfully advertised for additional new members, as the minutes of early February and early March 1874 show. Ticket prices and seating arrangements were revised because of the different layout of the new hall.

The 1874 season opened in spectacular fashion, following the official opening of the Corn Exchange by the Duke of Bedford on Wednesday 15 April, in the presence of the mayor, George Hurst, the Marquis of Tavistock and the great and the good of Bedford, among them Philip Diemer. The opening included a procession to the Corn Exchange and a dinner there. On the following day the Musical Society put on two concerts, a 'morning' concert, starting at 1.00p.m., and comprising Handel's *Messiah*, and an evening concert, starting at 8.00p.m., consisting of secular music.

The *Messiah* was performed during the day to allow the nobility, gentry and clergy throughout the county the opportunity to attend, to judge the merits of the performers and to see the new hall. There were approximately two hundred musicians. Mr F. Downes photographed members of the Musical Society before the performance.[41] The seating arrangements in the hall are described in the review:

> The vocalists were divided into equal contingents on either side of the platform, seven rows being raised one above the other respectively to a great height so that the sound had full scope. Between these blocks were the instrumentalists, the drums being conspicuous in the rear, while on either side of the conductor, were the piano and the harmonium ... Mr. Diemer's rostrum was immediately in front of the platform, within a draped enclosure, occupied also by the four soloists to the right and the left.[42]

The reviewer was very enthusiastic: 'The choruses were really grand, and fortunately there was an entire absence of the echo which was so painful at the rehearsal on the previous evening when there was no audience.'[43] The soloists were applauded during the performance: Marion Severn (soprano) for 'He Shall Feed his Flock', and Emily Spiller (contralto) for 'How Beautiful are the Feet'. Despite such applause, the reviewer writes that he would have liked to see, 'more enthusiasm by the audience', that is, louder applause. The performance lasted for three and a half hours with one fifteen minute interval. There was an audience of about 400. The names of the most prominent people present are given in the review; these include the Duke and Duchess of Bedford and Mr Samuel Whitbread.

The miscellaneous programme for the evening concert included Beethoven's Symphony No.1 and a variety of songs sung by the soloists. There was not a great deal for the chorus to sing, which was perhaps a good thing after the marathon performance of *Messiah* in the afternoon. The review for the evening concert states: 'the chorus were powerful enough for a larger hall, so if it should become necessary to provide a larger Exchange in a few years, as some sanguine persons predict, the

40 The fee was reduced to £20 in 1884.

41 So far as the author is aware, no copy of this photograph survives.

42 *Bedfordshire Times and Independent* 18 April 1874, p. 8.

43 Ibid.

Society will be equal to the occasion.'[44] The tenors and basses were complimented for their singing of Beethoven's "Chorus of the Dervishes" with appropriate zest. The reviewer only regretted that costumes and movements were lacking! The four soloists who sang in *Messiah* also sang in the evening concert. A 'stringed quintet' from the Royal Italian Opera, led by Mr T. Watson, augmented the orchestra in both concerts.

With the opening of the new Corn Exchange, it was now possible for the Musical Society to reach a wider audience, as the review of the evening concert makes clear:

> On Thursday evening, the occasion was taken advantage of by all classes. Nearly all the chairs were occupied by a fashionable assemblage and the great mass of shilling sittings were full, as were the balconies. The appearance of the hall, with performers and the greater part of the audience in full dress was grand.[45]

All subsequent concerts during the nineteenth century were performed in the Corn Exchange and the Musical Society benefitted financially from performing there as more people were able to attend.

The middle years, 1874–85

The first concert after the opening of the Corn Exchange was Haydn's *Creation*, performed just over a month later in the Musical Society's 'new home'. The costumes worn by the ladies in the chorus struck the reviewer: 'the dresses of the ladies are uniform, but the trebles wore sashes of blue and the ladies of the alto department were distinguished by crimson sashes. The effect of this was extremely pretty.'[46] Henry Guy and Lewis Thomas, who had been soloists in the concerts at the opening of the Corn Exchange, returned to sing once more.

Haydn also featured prominently in the October concert with "Autumn" from *The Seasons* and the first of his *London Symphonies* (No. 93). The review referred to complaints about the chink caused by the counting of door receipts during the concert, and also, from people sitting in the rear seats, about noise made by the stewards: 'ticket collectors [were] moving about during the first part of the concert and one gentlemen in particular displayed a sort of shop day-book and carried it here, there and everywhere in all parts of the room as his customers required him.'[47]

Handel's *Samson*, performed for the first time by the Musical Society, followed in December 1874. One of the soloists, Mr Wadmore, was described in the preview as: 'the eminent baritone, who gained the prize at the Crystal Palace.'[48] He took the part of Samson and Clara Suter, who was to sing at several Musical Society concerts over the next few years, took the part of Delilah. She made a very good first impression, especially with her rendering of 'Let the Bright Seraphim', which: 'shaded all her previous singing, and the marks of approbation she had hitherto received during the progress of the concert were tame compared with the storm of applause she received at the conclusion of this.'[49]

44 Ibid.
45 Ibid.
46 *Bedfordshire Times and Independent*, 23 May 1874, p. 5.
47 *Bedfordshire Times and Independent*, 31 October 1874, p. 5.
48 *Bedfordshire Times and Independent*, 15 December 1874, p. 8.
49 Ibid.

Mendelssohn's Symphony No. 2 ('Hymn of Praise') was performed in full by the Musical Society for the first time in April 1875. Unlike Beethoven's *Choral* Symphony, the Mendelssohn symphony is predominantly choral. Two soprano soloists and one tenor are required. For the Bedford performance, only one professional soprano, Edith Wynne, was engaged. The second soprano solo part, which only consists of singing in the soprano duet, was taken by a member of the choir, Miss Crofts. The reviewer gives her full credit.[50] Already the reviewer criticises the new Corn Exchange, commenting that: 'the defective acoustical properties of the hall were unpleasantly evident.'[51]

There is no review of the October 1875 concert as the reviewer took umbrage at being offered an inferior seat: 'It has been our lot to find representatives of the Press consigned to the cheapest back seats – sans programme, sans civility.'[52] The rest of the short report elaborates on the indignity of being treated in this way. We learn nothing of the programme or the performance. It was most likely to have been a miscellaneous operatic concert.

During the interval of one of the weekly rehearsals in mid-February 1876, a presentation was made by the mayor to Philip Diemer in recognition of his having conducted the Musical Society for nine years. He was presented with a purse of gold and a framed address which read:

> To Mr. P. H. Diemer, Royal Academy of Music: the performing members, about 200 of the Bedford Amateur Musical Society, desire to express to you as its founder and conductor their high appreciation of the zeal and ability with which you have conducted its concerts and practices during a period of 9 years, and as a small and inadequate token of their gratitude for the uniform kindness and consideration you have shown to them as a Musical Class and with the assurance of their cordial esteem and good wishes, beg your acceptance of the accompanying purse of gold. Signed on behalf of the subscribers, J. T. Hobson, Mayor.[53]

In 1876, the committee agreed that classes of study lasting thirteen weeks could be started 'at once'. The classes covered theory and harmony, P. H. Diemer, 4s; vocal music, R. Rose, 4s; and instrumental music, T. J. Ford, 5s.[54] This development would have helped to improve the standard of singers available in Bedford, and Philip Diemer may also have wanted to gauge the demand for musical education in the town. The Musical Society agreed to pay for advertising, but the tutors were expected to meet all other expenses. Philip Diemer subsequently formed the Bedford School of Music at which, in the latter years of the century, his daughters, Norah, Maud and Ethel took a prominent part.[55] The school was later housed at

50 'The ordeal is a severe one for an amateur to sing with an acknowledged prima donna, and Miss Crofts displayed equal courage and ability in sharing the honours with a singer of rare power and artistic skill.' The reviewer was not so complimentary about other aspects of the performance, noting weakness in the tenor line, poor enunciation generally and the organ and piano parts being drowned out by the orchestra. *Bedfordshire Times and Independent*, 24 April 1875, p. 6.
51 Ibid.
52 *Bedfordshire Times and Independent*, 30 October 1875, p. 5.
53 *Bedfordshire Times and Independent*, 19 February 1876, p. 5.
54 Ibid.
55 *Bedfordshire Times and Independent*, 8 February 1901, p. 5 and 15 June 1906, p. 6 (Bedford School of Music concert reviews).

Philip Diemer's house, Marchmont, 25 De Parys Avenue, Bedford. This school must have helped to increase the number of available instrumentalists who could play at concerts and improve the standard of playing. There were also an increasing number of private instrumental teachers at this time, as can be seen from advertisements appearing in the *Bedfordshire Times and Independent*.

The first concert of 1876 included a performance of *St John the Baptist*, composed for the Bristol Festival where it was first performed in 1873 by Sir George Macfarren.[56] Macfarren was a prolific composer, especially of operas. He became secretary of the Handel Society in 1843. Despite becoming totally blind in the 1860s, he continued to be very active and to perform his duties as professor at the Royal Academy. Among his pupils was Philip Diemer, to whom he taught harmony. He was elected professor of music at Cambridge on the death of Sir William Sterndale Bennett in 1875, and appointed principal of the Royal Academy of Music in 1876.[57] Later on he became a patron of the Musical Society.

At the start of the concert, the mayor announced the singing of 'God Bless the Prince of Wales' following the prince's recovery from serious illness. The reviewer felt that the performance of *St John the Baptist* was of a high standard despite the 'scanty' audience.[58]

Concern about how some ladies dressed at concerts was expressed at the November 1876 committee meeting. The minutes state that: 'several ladies omitted wearing scarves at the last concert; it is requested that the by-laws on that subject be strictly adhered to.'[59] The by-laws are presumably the rules of the Musical Society; Hermann Steinmetz, who wrote this minute, sometimes expressed himself in an unusual way.

The first concert in 1877 included a performance Rossini's *Stabat Mater*. The *Stabat Mater* is a mediaeval poem, generally ascribed to Pope Innocent III. The long review in the *Bedfordshire Times and Independent* includes an appraisal of the poem and its origins, and is perhaps surprisingly complimentary given the strong nonconformist traditions in the town. It is not clear whether the work was sung in English or Latin. English would seem more likely, though there is a reference in the review to the 'Cuius Animam' (the second movement) being spoiled for everyone by some people arriving late for the concert, which might suggest otherwise. The soloists included Clara Suter, referred to as an old favourite in Bedford, and Henry Guy, a regular visitor who was by now prominent nationally.[60]

Arthur Sullivan's *On Shore and Sea*, the main work in the second concert of the 1877 season, is set in the sixteenth century on board Genoese and Moorish galleys. However, most of the review of the concert is about the three excerpts from Wagner operas that were included in the second half of the concert. Wagner was, of course,

56 Jeremy Dibble, in his biography *John Stainer*, p. 205, gives the date for Sir George Macfarren's *St John the Baptist* as 1881, four years after this performance.

57 *New Grove*, vol. 15, pp. 471–3.

58 'The quartet "Blessed are they which are persecuted for righteousness' sake" was sustained by the professional vocalists, was an exquisite *morceau*, the merit of the piece being developed with remarkable taste and power.' *Bedfordshire Times and Independent*, 20 May 1876, p. 5.

59 *Minute Book 1867–93,* 20 November 1876, BLARS X817 /1/1.

60 Henry Guy was appointed a Gentleman at the Chapel Royal, St James, in 1876, and in the same year he sang at the Alexander Palace. Two years later he sang at the Worcester Festival. Brown and Stratton, *British Musical Biography*, p. 177.

still alive at this time, and the review anticipates how his music might be perceived in the future:

> It is almost impossible to convey even a faint idea of Wagnerism by three selections performed by so limited an orchestra. Wagner's idea is a noble one, and when some hundreds of years hence musicians will have reached the Wagneresque pitch of development no doubt to us the music of the future will have become the music evermore to be, but for the present it must show the fate of other grand enthusiasms and be not understanded [*sic*] of the people.[61]

The orchestra opened the second half of the concert with Auber's *Fra Diavolo* overture, which prompted the comment by the reviewer: 'to the average English taste, Auber is to Wagner as wine is to vinegar.'[62] Today, the music of Wagner is, of course, very popular and Auber's music is seldom played. The reviewer clearly recognised Wagner as a master, for his 'delicious harmonies and wonderful instrumentation', but considered his music difficult to understand and lacking in melody. Auber, on the other hand: 'was a great melodist, an easy harmonist and an effective orchestrator. His works offered no difficulty to the hearer.'[63]

One of the best known musicians of his time, Sir Julius Benedict, came to Bedford in October 1877 to conduct his own cantata *Undine*.[64] He was born in Germany, but moved to England at the age of thirty. [65] Benedict and was perhaps the most influential musician to settle in the country since Handel, and remained here until his death.[66] He conducted at every Norwich Festival 1845–78 as well as at several other major festivals throughout the country and, from 1859, at the Monday Popular Concerts at St James's Hall, London. A number of professional soloists who sang with the Musical Society over the years were also soloists at the Monday Popular Concerts.

The article in *Grove's Dictionary of Music and Musicians* about Benedict refers to *Undine* as 'beautiful'.[67] The reviewer of the Bedford performance was also complimentary, and considered the cantata to be a *chef d'oeuvre* of the period.[68] The part of Undine was sung by Catherine Penna.

Handel's *Jephtha* was performed in Bedford in December 1878. The reviewer

61 *Bedfordshire Times and Independent*, 2 June 1877, p. 6.

62 Ibid.

63 Scholes, *Oxford Companion to Music*, p. 53.

64 *Undine* was first performed in 1860 at the Norwich Festival. One of the soloists in that first performance was the famous soprano, Clara Novello, making her last public appearance. Undine, the central character, is a water spirit who falls in love with a noble baron who, on proving faithless, is soon made the victim of the wrath of the other water spirits.

65 Sir Julius Benedict was a pupil of Carl Maria von Weber. Weber's influence is evident in his compositions. Before his move to England he held a number of conducting posts and also composed a number of youthful operas. Philip Diemer dedicated his cantata, *Bethany*, to him.

66 This is the opinion of H. Sutherland Edwards who wrote the article on Benedict in *Grove's Dictionary of Music and Musicians*. It was Madame Malibran, the distinguished singer, who originally suggested that Benedict should come to England, when she met him in Paris in 1834. Fuller Maitland, ed., *Grove's Dictionary of Music and Musicians*, vol. 1, pp. 296–7.

67 Ibid.

68 The reviewer comments briefly on the performance of the tenor and the bass soloists. He also notes that the choruses were given with good taste, although there was 'noticeable flatness' in the sopranos. Otherwise, he says little about the performance. *Bedfordshire Times and Independent*, 3 November 1877, p. 6.

thought that *Jephtha* deserved to be better known, as it was not among the small number of Handel's nineteen English oratorios that were then regularly sung. There was a rare mistake in the review: the composer's name was misspelt as 'Handle'. Miss Whittle, a local singer who was to become very prominent in the Musical Society, took the part of an angel, eliciting the comment that: 'She possessed a voice of which any singer might be proud.'[69] Mr Rendle, a first violin of the Royal Italian Opera, led the orchestra as he did several times over the next few years.[70] Although the concert finished punctually, a few members of the audience left during the final chorus causing some disturbance.

The 1879 concert season in Bedford got off to a bad start. At the first concert, Haydn's *Creation,* George Vernon Rigby, the tenor soloist, could not sing as he had a bad cold, and his replacement, Bernard Lane, did not turn up.[71] So Mr Jarman, probably a member of the choir, though this is not specified, sang the tenor solo part at very short notice. According to the reviewer, he was not able to interpret the part adequately. Otherwise there was not a full review because, 'The *Creation* is so well-known'.[72]

For the Musical Society's fiftieth concert, held in May, just twelve years after its formation, the main work was their third performance of Sterndale Bennett's *The May Queen*. The reviewer comments that the band, largely increased by professional artists (nine of them according to the advertisement in the *Bedfordshire Times and Independent*): 'was undoubtedly the best that has assisted at any of the Society's concerts'.[73] The second half of the concert included a minuet and trio by Philip Diemer and Molloy's 'Darby and Joan' sung by Miss Spiller.

A perennial problem, familiar to members of many choral societies today, is highlighted in the review of *Elijah*, performed in December, in the short-lived paper, *The Bedford Bee*:

> With the Oratorio 'Elijah', the last concert of the season, Mr. Diemer had made special efforts to ensure a first class performance. The orchestra had been strengthened, rehearsals increased, and a spirit of enthusiasm had been fairly aroused in every member of the Society. The result was all that could have been desired. The unanimous verdict is that this was the most perfect oratorio performance that has been given in Bedford, and Mr. Diemer is entitled to hearty congratulation. All the choruses, including the final one, were sung with spirit and precision, no slight testimony to this being the fact that the entire audience remained to the end the long programme ... Before now, we have remarked on the loudness of the orchestra during vocal parts and this was occasionally observable last week. It probably arises from the instruments being central and having the wall as a sounding board. If it were borne in mind that an orchestra should only accompany the singers, the effect would be more harmonious.[74]

69 *Bedfordshire Times and Independent*, 21 December 1878, p. 5.

70 The advertisement for the October 1879 concert refers to Mr Rendle as being of 'Her Majesty's Private Band'. *Bedfordshire Times and Independent*, 11 October 1879, p. 1.

71 By this time, George Vernon Rigby was a well-known opera and oratorio singer. Brown and Stratton, *British Musical Biography*, p. 345.

72 *Bedfordshire Times and Independent*, 1 March 1879, p. 5.

73 He goes on to say that their playing was spoilt by the wind portion being complete while the strings were weak in comparison. And he later seems to contradict himself when he writes: 'Throughout the whole cantata, the band was much too loud.' *Bedfordshire Times and Independent*, 17 May 1879, p. 5.

74 *The Bedford Bee*, December 1879, p. 441.

The word 'Amateur' was dropped from the Society's title at the annual general meeting at the start of 1880. For more than a hundred years, until the late 1980s, the Society would be known as The Bedford Musical Society.

The main work in the opening concert of the 1880 season, held in April, was Sullivan's oratorio *The Prodigal Son*, composed for the Worcester Festival in 1869.[75] At nearly the same time as the 1880 Bedford performance, the Gilbert and Sullivan comic opera, *The Pirates of Penzance*, was performed for the first time, and the well-known song 'The Policeman's Lot' heard. The bass soloist at the Musical Society's performance of *The Prodigal Son* was Henry D'Egville, who was somewhat hoarse during the performance and rather coolly received by the audience.[76] The concert also included Rossini's *Stabat Mater*, sung in Bedford for the first time in 1877. It was repeated several times while Philip Diemer was conductor, but not again by the Musical Society until 1980.

In October, Emanuel Aguilar conducted, with limited success, his own cantata *The Bridal of Triermain*, based on a poem by Sir Walter Scott.[77] Aguilar, composer and pianist, was born in London in 1824, the son of a West Indian father of Spanish descent and a Jewish mother. His sister, Grace Aguilar, was a novelist who achieved some success, although she died at a relatively young age. Aguilar was resident in London where he taught and performed, though he also gave concerts in Germany. His compositions included three symphonies and a collection of canons and fugues as preparatory exercises for the playing of Bach. Most of his chamber music was performed at the Musical Artists' Society concerts – an organisation established for the encouragement of British music.[78] The date of *The Bridal of Triermain* in the British Library Catalogue is given as1884, four years after the Bedford performance. In Aguilar's works listed in *The British Musical Biography* the work is described as 'The Bridal of Triermain, Bedford 1880'.[79] It is dedicated to The Bedford Musical Society.

There were problems at this first performance of the work. The music was unfamiliar and: 'with difficulties accompanying manuscript music, great allowance must be made for the unsteadiness of some of the movements.'[80] Also, according to the reviewer, the soloists were not up to the usual standard. In view of the state of the music, they may not have had time to rehearse adequately. The renowned harpist,

75 This was the current way of describing what would now be called The Three Choirs Festival.

76 John Henry d'Egville joined the Carla Rosa Company in 1881. A few years later he toured with the D'Oyly Carte Company in a round of Gilbert and Sullivan operas. Brown and Stratton, *British Musical Biography,* p. 186.

77 There is a short biography of Emanuel Aguilar in Nicolas Slonimsky, *Baker's Biographical Dictionary of Musicians* (Oxford, 1984), p. 25, and a longer one in Brown and Stratton, *British Musical Biography*, p. 3. *The Bedford Mercury*, 1 March 1884, p. 5, has an advertisement that states that Mr Aguilar visits Bedford weekly.

78 The Society was established in 1874 and a series of semi-private concerts was inaugurated at which performances of chamber music were given. The vice-presidents included J. F. Barnett, Sir G. A. Macfarren and Sir Arthur Sullivan. The Society was dissolved in 1899. 'Among the numerous attempts made for the direct encouragement of British music in the latter part of the 19th century, those for which this Society holds no small place.' Fuller Maitland, ed., *Grove's Dictionary of Music and Musicians*, vol. 3, p. 335.

79 Brown and Stratton, *British Musical Biography*, p. 3.

80 *Bedfordshire Times and Independent*, 30 October 1880, p. 5.

Herr Charles Oberthür, performed at the concert.[81] He played in the cantata and he also played *Martha* for solo harp (probably a solo piece from Friedrich von Flotow's opera of the same name) in the second half of the concert. The reviewer thoroughly approved of his playing, but did not approve of the inclusion of 'Rataplan' among the shorter songs – possibly because it was thought to be too populist.[82]

The soprano soloist in the December 1880 performance of Handel's *Israel in Egypt* was Clara Samuell, singing for the first time with the Musical Society. She was born in Manchester in 1856, and studied at the Royal Academy of Music where she was a winner of the Parepa-Rosa scholarship.[83] She married Henry Rose, Robert Rose's son, so had strong connections with Bedford. Henry Rose had been appointed organist of St Pancras church in London in 1879, succeeding Henry Smart.[84] Clara Samuell was to sing with the Musical Society many times during the next twenty years and became very popular with Bedford audiences. Both she and Henry Rose became professors at the Royal Academy of Music. Although they lived in London, Clara Samuell became a regular visitor to Bedford to give music lessons.[85]

Of her first performance, the reviewer writes: 'Miss Samuell's singing, in fine voice and with beautifully clear enunciation was a rich treat and highly appreciated by all.'[86] In the duet, 'The Lord is my Strength', she was joined by Miss Whittle, the local singer who had been a soloist in *Jephtha* a couple of years earlier. The duet was loudly applauded, but the length of the oratorio prevented repetition.

The printed programme for this performance of *Israel in Egypt* is the earliest Musical Society programme that survives. Clara Samuell heads the list of soloists. The programme states that the chorus, as well as the band, was reinforced with outside help. It was unusual for the chorus to receive additional support. However, this work has a lot of double choruses, with each voice part split in two, meaning that, in effect, there are two choirs. The classes of ticket shown on the programme were complicated:

> TERMS OF SUBSCRIPTION TO FOUR CONCERTS
> Block A, Reserved and Numbered, 15s each. Family Tickets, to admit five £3 2s. 0d. Block B, Reserved & Numbered, 12s.6d each. Family tickets, to admit five, £2 12s. 6d. Admission to ONE CONCERT: Block A , 5s ; Block B, 4s ; Block C, 2s ; Block D, 1s. Balconies ; Front seats, 3s ; Back seats, 2s.
> Schools are admitted at Half-price in Blocks A and B (if there is room).
> The Committee do not guarantee Seats in Block D.
> Tickets at Mr. Porter's, 7, High Street, or at the Doors.[87]

81 Charles Oberthür had a distinguished career on the Continent before settling in London in 1848. He became harp professor at the London Academy of Music, founded in 1861, and was widely known as a teacher. He was a prolific composer. *New Grove*, vol. 18, pp. 255–6.
82 Rataplan is an onomatopoeic word mimicking the sound of a drum. It occurs as the title for solo and ensemble arias in operas by Donizetti, Meyerbeer and Verdi.
83 Musgrave, *The Musical Life of the Crystal Palace*, p. 95.
84 Some of Henry Smart's hymn tunes are well-known, including those used for 'God of Mercy, God of Grace' and 'Light's Abode, Celestial Salem'.
85 She advertised in the *Bedfordshire Times and Independent* regularly. The advertisement in the paper of 12 June 1903, p. 7, reads: 'Mme Clara Samuell, F.R.A.M. … visits Bedford Weekly to give lessons in Singing and Voice production. For terms &c. apply at 123 High Street, Bedford or to 3 Gordon Place, Gordon Sq., London.'
86 *Bedfordshire Times and Independent*, 18 December 1880, p. 5.
87 *Concert Programme,* December 1880, BLARS X817/3/1.

A performance of *Messiah* was given a week later by the Musical Society without any professional assistance. The orchestra included some players who no longer played regularly at the Society's concerts. All the soloists were members of the choir. The performance lasted three and a half hours, but despite this hardly anyone in the audience left before the end.

The most significant event for the Musical Society in 1881 was the completion and performance of a new work by Philip Diemer, his cantata *Bethany*. This was composed for the opening of a new organ in the new hall at Bedford Modern School where the first performance was given.[88] The organ was built by Messrs Trustam & Sons of Bedford, and detailed specifications of the organ are given at the start of the review of the performance. The text of *Bethany* comes from chapter eleven of St John's gospel and tells of the death and raising of Lazarus by Jesus. It was arranged by the Rev. R. B. Poole, headmaster of Bedford Modern School, and dedicated to Sir Julius Benedict.

There were approximately 150 performers in this first performance, mostly from the Modern School and from the Musical Society. The soloists, Miss Whittle, Miss Armstrong, Mr A. H. Allen and William Kingston, were all singers with the Society.[89] No instrumentalists came from London. The only person taking a prominent part who was not from Bedford was the narrator, the Rev. C. H. Murphy of Ely Cathedral, and he was a former curate of St Paul's church, Bedford. The reviewer felt that the performers had been well-rehearsed and that the performance was very successful.[90] *Bethany* was subsequently performed by the Musical Society as an additional Grand Complimentary Concert in November 1881, between Barnett's *The Building of the Ship* and Handel's *Judas Maccabaeus*. For this performance, the band was increased substantially by eminent 'London Artistes' (according to the *Bedfordshire Times and Independent's* advertisement) and the soloists included Clara Samuell. There was a packed audience and the soloists were encored.[91]

The reviewer felt that certain sections of the work were notably original, especially those commencing 'Full of Grace are His Lips' and 'Like a Father Pitieth his own Children'. He hoped that *Bethany* would make Philip Diemer better known and, as he put it: 'would be performed wherever good music is performed'.[92]

Despite the compliments paid to Philip Diemer when he was presented with a testimonial a week later, and the critic's view that *Bethany* deserved to become widely known, the work was only performed once more by the Musical Society two and a half years later. However, 'Brother, Thou Art Gone Before Us' was regularly

88 Philip Diemer was professor of music at the Modern School as well as at the Grammar School at this time.

89 Mr A. H. Allen was clerk and receiver to the Harpur Trust 1876–1922.

90 'The favourable opinion entertained by the audience was continually expressed and culminated in loud and prolonged applause at the close of the last chorus.' *Bedfordshire Times and Independent*, 16 July 1881, p. 5. The author has the score that Philip Diemer gave to his son Herbert on the day of the first performance. This has his handwritten inscription which says: 'Herbert Diemer with his father's love. P. H. Diemer. July 13th 1881 the date of the first performance of "Bethany"'.

91 'The trio (unaccompanied) sung by Miss Samuell, Miss Damian and Miss Eveleigh, contains some very sweet music and was rendered so well that the audience demanded an encore. The hymn "Brother, thou art gone before us", sung by the four principal soloists is very touching.' *Bedfordshire Times and Independent*, 26 November 1881, p. 8.

92 Ibid.

sung by the Society after prominent members had died.[93] *Bethany* was published by Novello, and is one of many works listed at the back of the choral music scores published by the company in the late nineteenth and early twentieth centuries.

The 1882 season opened in February with a second performance of Sir George Macfarren's *St John the Baptist*. The reviewer noted some unsteadiness in the performance, explaining that there had been insufficient rehearsal time. He also makes the comment that nearly all the singers had joined the Musical Society since the earlier performance in 1876 – a fact that seems somewhat improbable. Mr T. J. Ford, organist at the Bunyan Meeting church, accompanist at the Musical Society's rehearsals and pianist at the concerts is reported to have: 'had charge of no less than five instruments, viz., pianoforte, harmonium, big drum, cymbals and tambourine, all of which he very skilfully handled.'[94]

The leader of the orchestra, Mr Rendle, made his last appearance in May 1882 when he played in *The Erl King's Daughter* by the Danish composer Neils Gade.[95] In October, Ada Batley and William Kingston sang solo parts in a ballad concert, returning in December to appear in Mendelssohn's *Elijah*. They later married and were both to become prominent members of the Musical Society.[96]

Edward Halfpenny, the London professional player who was to lead the Society's orchestra for many years, led the orchestra for the first time in February 1883.[97] The concert included Gade's *Spring Message* and also Mendelssohn's *The First Walpurgis Night*. The reviewer thought that there were not really enough first violins, but pays tribute to Edward Halfpenny's playing.[98] Messrs Woolhouse and Waud, the professionals playing the violoncello and the double-bass respectively, also went on to play at Musical Society concerts for many years.

Alfred R. Gaul was a prolific composer from the Midlands.[99] He composed *The Holy City* for the 1882 Birmingham Festival and it was the main work at the May 1883 concert. The reviewer thought that the solemnity and gravity of the words were not reflected in the light and secular character of the music.[100] In this, the

93 In his book, *And the Glory – A History in Commemoration of the 150th of Huddersfield Choral Society 1836–1986* (Leeds, 1985), p. 86, R. A. Edwards refers to that Society singing 'Brother, Thou Art Gone Before Us' in memory of Ben Stocks in 1911 (Ben Stocks was a prominent member of the Society). They did not sing Philip Diemer's setting, but an unaccompanied setting by Sullivan, from his cantata *The Martyr of Antioch*. The author is grateful to Malcolm Hinchcliffe of the Huddersfield Choral Society who confirmed this and sent him a copy of the review from the *Huddersfield Examiner*, 4 March 1911, p. 5.

94 *Bedfordshire Times and Independent*, 25 February 1882, p. 5.

95 *The Erl King's Daughter* is based on a German (or Danish) mythical story which is given in the review, which also praises the: 'exceptionally well trained chorus, assisted by thoroughly competent soloists.' *Bedfordshire Times and Independent*, 27 May 1882, p. 5.

96 The review for *Elijah* is quite short. The choir and the soloists seem to have been fine, but the reviewer was not too happy with the orchestra, which does not seem to have played as well as it did at the previous performance of this popular work.

97 When he first played at Musical Society concerts, Edward Halfpenny was playing with the Richter Orchestra. He subsequently moved to the London Philharmonic Orchestra.

98 'The leader, Mr. Halfpenny, exerted himself to the utmost to make good the deficiencies, and his powerful and telling tone rendered admirable service.' *Bedfordshire Times and Independent*, 10 February 1883, p. 5.

99 The 1921 Novello edition of *Stabat Mater* by Rossini has a page full page advertising the published works of A. R. Gaul.

100 Having said that, he actually quite liked the work. Of the choir he wrote: 'The balance between the tenors and the basses in the chorus was better preserved than has sometimes been the case … It may be

reviewer chimes with the view later expressed in *Grove's Dictionary of Music and Musicians* that Gaul's compositions had a: 'superficial fluency [which] won them a wide popularity.'[101] The concert also included Gounod's *By Babylon's Wave*, first performed in March 1869.[102]

Spohr's *The Last Judgment* was performed early in December. There does not appear to be a review for this concert, perhaps because there was an extra performance of *Messiah* nine days later. Between these two concerts the Musical Society held a sale of 'Useful and Ornamental Articles' in the Assembly Rooms.

The second performance of *Bethany* was given towards the end of February 1884. The reviewer wrote: 'The cantata was very successfully treated throughout ... At the conclusion of his composition, Mr. Diemer was accorded a magnificent ovation.'[103] Most of the soloists were local, Miss Whittle, Marion Eveleigh, Mrs Kingston (née Batley), Cecil Higgins and William Kingston. The twenty-eight year-old Cecil Higgins (baritone) was by this time working in Bedford with his brother Lawrence, manager of the family brewery. Of him, the reviewer wrote that his voice was somewhat light for the air 'I am the Resurrection', but he was loudly applauded. He sang several times more as a soloist at Musical Society concerts.

The concert also included Rossini's *Stabat Mater*, performed for the third time by the Society. Mr Kenningham, the tenor soloist, was probably Alfred Kenningham, a member of the choir at St Andrew's, Well Street, London, who at the time of the concert was assistant vicar choral of St Paul's Cathedral, and in 1888 vicar choral.[104] The reviewer was most impressed with his rich tenor voice. Edward Halfpenny led the first violins and Mr Inwards the seconds. Among the other named – presumably professional – instrumentalists, Mr Kilby (viola) and Mr Adcock (violoncello) were, unusually, from Leicester.

The main work in the May concert was Frederic Cowen's *The Rose Maiden*. Cowen who was then thirty-two, had showed extraordinary talent from a very young age and performed in public before he was in his teens.[105] Cowen went on to become a well-known conductor and composer. His music is very rarely heard now. Of the Bedford performance the critic writes: 'It says much for the Society that for an adequate performance of a somewhat difficult new work, it was only necessary to augment the orchestra with five performers and to engage two vocalists.'[106]

well on the other hand to call attention to the lack of force on the part of the contraltos, whose feebleness occasionally reduced the choruses in effect to trios.' *Bedfordshire Times and Independent*, 12 May 1883, p. 8.

101 Fuller Maitland, ed., *Grove's Dictionary of Music and Musicians*, vol. 2, p.148.

102 This was described as: 'a pompous and brilliant, if somewhat demonstrative arrangement of words so frequently treated by musicians, and none more successfully than our own Dr. Boyce.' Ibid.

103 *Bedfordshire Times and Independent*, 1 March 1884, p. 5.

104 Brown and Stratton, *British Musical Biography*, p. 229. There are also details of a Charles Kenningham, but it seems more likely that it was the older Alfred Kenningham who sang at the Bedford concert as the *British Musical Biography* reference states that he sang in London and provincial concerts.

105 He had also composed from an early age. Cowen studied in Leipzig and Berlin where his abilities as a conductor were first evident. In 1869 his Symphony in C and Piano Concerto in A Minor were performed in St James's Hall, London. *The Rose Maiden* was composed a year later. It uses a poem translated from the German.

106 There do not seem to have been any professional players in the wind section. Some difficulties were encountered by the local amateurs, though overall they managed well. The two local soloists, soprano and baritone, were, once more, Miss Eveleigh and Cecil Higgins. The reviewer considered that the performance was fairly successful and that the 'always efficient' chorus deserved to be awarded the

As might be expected, the Musical Society celebrated the bi-centenary of Handel's birth (23 February 1685) with a concert on Tuesday 24 February 1885. This concert must have been difficult to organise, with very limited rehearsal time. There were excerpts from nine of Handel's choral works.[107] The reviewer expected that choruses such as the 'Hallelujah Chorus' would be successful, but was pleasantly surprised that the double choruses were so well sung. One of these choruses was the 'Hailstone Chorus' (from *Israel in Egypt*). Another was 'Shake the Dome' (from *Solomon*). Five London professional instrumentalists played at this concert.

At the May 1885 miscellaneous concert, Edward Halfpenny was the soloist in movements from de Bériot's seventh, and last, violin concerto.[108] Edward Halfpenny was, by this time, well-known to Bedford audiences as an orchestral player and teacher of the violin, but this was the first time he took on the role of soloist in the town. The reviewer states that he fully established his position as an admirable violinist both in technique and feeling. The second half of the concert included two new works, one of them a part song by Mr E. Bandey, who had recently taken over as the Musical Society's accompanist in place of Mr T. J. Ford.

The main work at the October concert was another cantata by Philip Diemer, *Alcestis*. *Alcestis* is based on the fourth play in a tetralogy by Euripides. It was originally composed for the twenty-fifth concert put on by Bedford Grammar School where it was first performed in December 1884. With the original performers in mind it was not a technically difficult work. For the Musical Society performance, Philip Diemer provided more elaborate orchestration. Two professional soloists were employed, Catherine Penna (of the Crystal Palace Concerts) and Sinclair Dunn (the celebrated Scottish tenor). Two local soloists also took a prominent part, William Kingston and Cecil Higgins.[109] The reviewer was not that enthusiastic about *Alcestis* writing: 'it is not characterised by any great pretension and originality'.[110] The Bedford public were not enthusiastic about it either; there was only a 'very moderate' audience. They may have preferred works using more familiar texts based on Biblical stories. For whatever reason, *Alcestis* was not repeated, and Philip Diemer did not write any more cantatas. Maybe he was too busy. Maybe he was not asked again. Or maybe he felt discouraged. Subsequently, he confined himself to songs and short piano works.

Mozart's Requiem was performed by the Musical Society for the first time in December 1885. Before the start of the concert, Hermann Steinmetz announced that one of the soloists, Madam Avigliana, was unwell so not able to sing. Her

place of honour. He only regretted that there were not more people in the audience. *Bedfordshire Times and Independent*, 17 May 1884, p. 8.

107 Novello's Octavo Choruses, individual choruses from many of Handel's and other composers' oratorios, had been published some years before this date, so full scores would not have had to be ordered. Approximately two hundred choruses by Handel were published separately, the majority for 1d. or 1½d.

108 Charles-Auguste de Bériot was a Belgian composer and one of the great violinists of the nineteenth century.

109 'Mr. Cecil Higgins sang with care and finish, but was overpowered by the instrumental accompaniment in the chorus and scene "Ah, he is gone"' *Bedfordshire Times and Independent*, 24 October 1885, p. 5.

110 Ibid. This review contains a printing error which was unusual. Writing of the orchestration, the review states 'employing all possible resources including a liberal use of trap and percussion instruments.' 'Trap' should be 'harp'; the harpist is named in the concert advertisement.

place was taken by Miss Larkcom. Soloists seem to have been indisposed more often during this period than they are today, probably because modern medicines are more effective, the atmosphere is cleaner, fewer people smoke and people are generally healthier.

In the review there is a little information about the earliest performances of the work.[111] The reviewer comments on the voices of the soloists, but not on the performance of the Requiem itself. The audience was not large and there were hardly any demonstrations of appreciation during the performance. In contrast, the second half of the concert consisted of selections from *Messiah*, which were heartily applauded.

The Sullivan years, 1886–89

The main work in the October 1886 concert was a performance of Sullivan's cantata *On Shore and Sea*, first performed by the Musical Society in 1877. The 1886 performance started the pattern of including a major Sullivan work for the next four seasons. There is no specific mention of the comic operas in any of the reviews, though the preview of *The Martyr of Antioch*, the second Sullivan work to be performed in Bedford, refers to Sullivan's fame: 'doubtless the Corn Exchange will be filled with persons anxious to become acquainted with this fine example of the genius of our most popular living composer to be given for the first time in this town.'[112]

Gilbert and Sullivan had a run of nine successful comic operas, mostly performed for the first time at the Savoy Theatre in London 1878–89.[113] The Musical Society's run of works by Sullivan in the second half of the 1880s occurred as the following comic operas were being given, or were about to be given, their first performance runs: October 1886, *On Shore and Sea* (*The Mikado* from March 1885); March 1887, *The Martyr of Antioch* (*Ruddigore* from January 1887); December 1888, *The Light of the World* (*The Yeoman of the Guard* from October 1888); October 1889, *The Golden Legend* (*The Gondoliers* from December 1889).[114]

After 1889 Sullivan did not compose further large choral works. There was also a drop in the number of Sullivan's works performed by the Musical Society, though *The Golden Legend*, the most popular of his choral works, was repeated several times in the 1890s and in 1901.

On Shore and Sea includes the call to prayer, "Alla hu Akbar", which the reviewer of the Bedford performance found, 'a very weird and strange composition'.[115] There seems to have been a shortage of basses in the Bedford performance, and those who sang encountered technical difficulties.

The story of *The Martyr of Antioch* concerns Margarita, the daughter of a priest of Apollo whose conversion to Christianity results in the loss of her lover and her

[111] There follows an unattributed description of the Requiem: 'It is the true and legitimate expression of his artistic nature at its highest point of finish – his imperishable monument.' There is nothing about Sussmayr's contribution in the review, which the reviewer might have noted. *Bedfordshire Times and Independent*, 12 December 1885, p. 6.

[112] *Bedfordshire Times and Independent*, 12 March 1887, p. 8.

[113] This was the first theatre to have been lighted with electricity.

[114] *The Mikado* had a run of 672 performances, so overlapped with the Bedford performance of *On Shore and Sea*.

[115] *Bedfordshire Times and Independent*, 23 October 1888, p. 8.

friends, and ultimately her martyrdom. The reviewer comments: 'Most of the music is exceedingly beautiful, although it can hardly be appreciated at a single hearing; much of it is solemn, and some of it weird.'[116] This work includes Sullivan's unaccompanied chorus 'Brother, Thou Art Gone Before Us'.

The third major Sullivan work was his 'splendid' – the reviewer's words – oratorio *The Light of the World*. The subject matter is described in the review in some detail before the specific comments about the Bedford performance.[117] The scene about the raising of Lazarus at Bethany was omitted due to the length of the work, though the fact that Philip Diemer's *Bethany* had covered this topic might also have influenced the decision. The performance was definitely a success; the reviewer thought – again – that is was one of the most successful concerts that the Musical Society had ever held. Mrs Hutchinson, of the Birmingham Festival and of 'principal London concerts', was the soprano soloist. The baritone and bass were non-professionals, respectively, Cecil Higgins and William Kingston.[118]

William Kingston was born in Bedford. He was educated at Bedford Modern School, and on leaving school joined the auction firm of Messrs Stafford and Son (later to become Stafford and Rogers), remaining with them for the rest of his working life. For considerably over thirty years he conducted stock sales at Bedford Cattle Market and at other venues in the surrounding area. As noted in his obituary: 'he was gifted with a fine bass voice, which not only well qualified him for his business, but also stood him in good stead as a vocalist.'[119]

The last in this one-a-season run of performances of Sullivan's choral works was *The Golden Legend*. This was written for the Leeds Festival, of which Sullivan was then conductor. It was first performed there in October 1886 and became hugely popular. In common with a number of other English composers around this time, Sullivan turned to the American poet Henry Wadsworth Longfellow and used his rewriting of the famous medieval legend.[120] In his introduction to the poem, Longfellow writes: 'it seems to me to surpass all other legends in beauty and significance.'[121] The story of *The Golden Legend*, summarised in an essay in the Novello score, is Victorian melodrama on an epic scale.

At the Musical Society's annual general meeting in January 1889 Philip Diemer spoke about his preparations for the performance, and this was reported in the *Bedfordshire Times and Independent*:

116 *Bedfordshire Times and Independent*, 19 March 1887, p. 6.

117 '*The Light of the World* aims to set forth the human aspect of the life of the Saviour on earth, exemplified by some of the incidents of his career, which bear specially upon his attributes of preacher, healer and prophet ... The most remarkable portion of the oratorio is that which depicts the way to Jerusalem, and it is here that that orchestra appeared to great effect. The descriptive instrumentation was very fine, and the choruses that followed are masterpieces of construction and effect.' *Bedfordshire Times and Independent*, 8 December 1888, p. 6.

118 Cecil Higgins sang the rather long solo 'Daughters of Jerusalem' and sang it 'exceedingly well' according to the reviewer. William Kingston: 'maintained his good reputation. He gave a satisfactory interpretation of the solo "Blessed art thou" and in concert with others, his powerful bass proved very useful.' Ibid.

119 *Bedfordshire Times and Independent*, 18 June 1915, p. 5.

120 Longfellow's verse is also used by Elgar, *The Saga of King Olaf*, 1896; Coleridge-Taylor, *The Song of Hiawatha*, 1898–1900 and *The Blind Girl of Castel-Cuille*, 1901; and J. F. Barnett, *The Building of the Ship*, 1876. The words for Parry's famous song, 'Excelsior', are also by Longfellow.

121 *The Poetical Works of Longfellow* (London, undated), p. 160.

> Mr. Diemer stated that at one of the concerts during the year, Sir Arthur Sullivan's 'Golden Legend' would be performed, and on account of the unusual expense that this performance would entail, the Committee recommended that no 1s. tickets be issued but that the lowest price of admission be 2s. If this proposal were not carried out, the Committee would have to ask for a guarantee fund to be formed to secure them from loss.[122] The cost of producing this wonderful work would be from £50 to £100. They had the permission of Sir Arthur Sullivan to use the work and for kindly reasons, Sir Arthur had forgone his fee (applause). He (*Mr. Diemer*) called at Sir Arthur Sullivan's house the other day, and that eminent composer expressed his satisfaction with the arrangements as to the vocalists and the *personnel* of the Band, and there was a possibility that Sir Arthur would attend to conduct the concert, but that entirely depended upon the state of his health, although a date had been fixed in October to suit his convenience. Sir Arthur spoke well of the Bedford Society, and said that although he had not heard their performance, he was acquainted with what they had done. The production of the 'Golden Legend' was an expensive affair. There was a peal of bells, the property of Sir Arthur Sullivan, that it was necessary to obtain. In the Albert Hall, where ordinarily there were 1s. seats, 4s. was the lowest price of admission to entertainments of this character. The 'Golden Legend' was a popular production, for the publishers informed him (*Philip Diemer*) that there were to be no less than sixty performances of it before next May.[123]

The Golden Legend was performed on Tuesday 22 October 1889. Sir Arthur Sullivan did not, in the event, come to conduct. The soloists were Mrs Hutchinson (Elsie); Miss Morgan (Ursula), standing in for Hilda Wilson who had met with an accident; Mr Hirwen Jones (Prince Henry); William Kingston (the Forester); and Mr W. H. Brereton (Lucifer).[124] Twenty-six professional instrumentalists were engaged and they are named, as are nine of the most prominent local instrumentalists. Altogether, there were approximately fifty orchestral players.[125] The professionals also ensured that a good performance of Schubert's 'Unfinished' Symphony, with which the concert opened, was given.

The Golden Legend opens with the chiming of bells followed by a prologue in which, as the reviewer wrote of the Bedford performance: 'Mr Brereton distinguished himself as "the arch enemy of mankind" trying to pull down the cross of Strasburg Cathedral.'[126] The performance as a whole was considered a great success and was very much appreciated by the audience.[127] The reviewer noted that: 'It was half-past ten, and St Paul's-square was more crowded with carriages than probably

122 Interestingly, the Musical Society had declined to do Gounod's *The Redemption* a year earlier because of the cost.

123 *Bedfordshire Times and Independent*, 26 January 1889, p. 6.

124 W. H. Brereton was the son of the Rev. Charles Brereton, rector of St Mary's church, Bedford, and grandson of the Rev. John Brereton, headmaster of Bedford Grammar School and the driving force behind the formation and initial success of the Bedford Harmonic Society.

125 It is not possible to give an accurate number. The review names the professionals and adds for the string sections the number of amateurs. The names of some of the numerous other instrumentalists of some reputation are given, but not all.

126 *Bedfordshire Times and Independent*, 26 October 1889, p. 7.

127 'The choruses were sung well, the most successful, judged by the applause, being the evening hymn "O, Gladsome Light" and the Epilogue chorus "God sent his messenger the rain". The duet, "We are alone" was enthusiastically applauded and there was an attempt to obtain a repetition, but without success.' Ibid.

it had ever been before in the memory of man.'[128] The Musical Society repeated *The Golden Legend* in 1891, 1896 and in 1901, when it was one of the first works to be performed after Dr Harry Harding's appointment.[129]

Edward Halfpenny did not play in the first three concerts of 1886. Mr Haydn Inwards, a scholar of the Royal College of Music, led the orchestra instead. It is also not clear if Edward Halfpenny played the Mozart Requiem in December 1885. There is no reference to him leading the orchestra in the programme (which survives) or in the review.

There were several other significant concerts 1886–90 apart from the 'Sullivan concerts'. The May 1886 concert included Sir John Stainer's *Daughter of Jairus*.[130] This is the only performance of a major work by Stainer by the Musical Society in the Victorian period, despite the fact that he was such an eminent musician. Towards the end of *Daughter of Jairus* there is a duet, which is a more elaborate version of the familiar hymn 'Love Divine, All Love Excelling', used nowadays, sometimes, at weddings.

The names of all the orchestral players are given in the review of *Elijah*, performed (once again) in November 1886.[131] This is the earliest record of the names of all the instrumental players in the orchestra. The professional players are included without being differentiated. There are several local musicians worthy of note who have not been mentioned before including Frederick John Nutter, Harry Thody, Norah Diemer, Mary Chetham, Amy Crommelin and Florence Ouseley.[132] Frederick Nutter, the principal violinist (after Edward Halfpenny), and Harry Thody, a viola player, were prominent townsmen. Frederick Nutter was chairman of the Board of Governors of the County Hospital. He was also a JP.[133] Harry Thody was a senior police officer.[134] From the latter part of the 1890s, the names of members of the orchestra were included in programmes.

Mr W. H. Brereton and his wife Sarah (who is referred to by her professional name, Miss Ambler, and also by her married name) both sang solo parts. Mr Brereton

128 Ibid.

129 For the 1901 performance there were seventy-six orchestral players, additional violinists largely accounting for this.

130 *Bedfordshire Times and Independent*, 15 May 1886, p. 8.

131 Names of the players: 1st violins, Mr E. Halfpenny*, Mr Nutter (principals), Mr Craddock, Mr Stokes, Mr Williamson, Miss Chetham, Miss A. Crommelin, Miss Diemer, Miss Ouseley, Miss Windhurst; 2nd violins, Mr J. Haines, (principal), Mr Ball, Mr Blackshaw, Mr J. Bucklow, Mr Chetham, Mr Hughes, Mr Norman, Mr Sydall and Miss Head; violas, Mr Thody, Rev. F. W. Mozley, Rev. V. W. Popham; violoncello, Mr E. Woolhouse* (principal), Mr A. E. Anthony, Miss Crommelin, Mr H. G. Gotch, Mr C. L. Hall, Rev. G. O. Wray DD; contrabasses, Mr Taylor, Mr Ball; flutes, Mr Lauder, Mr Foster; oboes, Mr Statham, Mr Ouseley; clarionets, Mr Short, Mr Routledge; horns, Mr Mann, Mr P. Godfrey; bassoons, Mr Cooper, Mr Eveleigh; trumpets, Mr Morrow*, Mr Tate; trombones, Mr Whitworth, Mr Carter, Mr Crawley; drums, Mr Rich; organ harmonium, Mr Rose; orchestral harmonium, Mr Bandey. Only three London professionals appear to have been playing. They are identified in the above list by an asterisk (*). *Bedfordshire Times and Independent*, 4 December 1886, p. 8.

132 These four ladies performed as a violin quartet in a ballad concert in October 1890.

133 There is a window dedicated to his memory in the south aisle of St Andrew's church, Bedford.

134 In the review of the Musical Society's 100th concert, he is referred to as an old and active member of the Society as well as being the Chief Constable. *Bedfordshire Times and Independent*, 12 December 1891, p. 7. Harry Thody died on 30 December 1925. There is an obituary in the *Bedford Record*, 5 January 1926, p. 2. There is also an account of the funeral in the *Bedfordshire Times and Independent*, 8 January 1926, p. 8.

was by this time well-established nationally as a bass soloist. In addition to her own part, Mrs Brereton sang the sections that should have been sung by Master Perkins, the boy treble, who was unable to sing because he had a cold.

In May 1887 there was a Grand Concert to celebrate Queen Victoria's Golden Jubilee. The main work was Stanford's *The Revenge*. But the programme also included Handel's *Zadok the Priest*, Arne's 'Rule Britannia' and a choral ode *Sing People, Sing* by Philip Diemer, composed for the occasion. The next concert, a ballad concert in October 1887, included the Rev. Vyvian W. Popham's *Hymn to Peace* which he himself conducted.[135] He also took most of the rehearsals because Philip Diemer was ill with an unspecified illness. Philip Diemer recovered sufficiently to be able to conduct other works in the concert.[136]

At the performance of *Messiah* in December, the 'Dead March' from Handel's *Saul* was played in memory of Sir George Macfarren, one of Philip Diemer's teachers at the Royal Academy of Music, later professor of music at Cambridge and patron of the Bedford Musical Society. He died at the end of October.

The penultimate concert of 1888 included a selection from Wallace's opera *Maritana*, composed in the 1840s. It had, as the reviewer put it: 'enjoyed such a long-standing popularity that it is unnecessary to refer to it here.'[137] Clara Samuell was once more the soloist, and her performance was reported to have exceeded expectations. *Maritana* contains some very attractive and memorable songs. As well as *Maritana*, a *Grande Concertante* for voice, harp, violin and pianoforte by Gustavus Holst was performed.[138]

Gade's cantata, *The Crusaders*, performed in May 1889, did not impress the reviewer. He thought that the selection in the second half of the concert was much more interesting and wrote that Clara Samuell, 'quite brought the house down' with Rossini's *Non Piu Mesta*.[139] The last movement of Schubert's 'Trout' Quintet was also included in the concert, with Philip Diemer playing the piano. He was joined by some of the London professional players.

The closing years, 1890–1900

Throughout 1867–89, the three key officers, conductor, chorus master and secretary, remained the same. This was possibly one of the strengths of the Musical Society during these formative years. Robert Rose, chorus master and organist at concerts, was the first of the key officers to tender his resignation, which he did at the committee meeting of 2 January 1890. He was then seventy-five. By this time

135 The Rev. Vyvian Popham (1833–96), sometime curate of Ravensden, was a well-known local musician. A number of his compositions are listed in the *British Library Music Catalogue*. His composition *Early Spring* is included in the 1 March 1908 list of Novello's Original Octavo Editions at the back of Henry Smart's *The Bride of Dunkerron*.

136 Philip Diemer conducted at every concert April 1867-May 1900.

137 *Bedfordshire Times and Independent*, 13 October 1888, p. 6.

138 The *Grande Concertante* was brilliantly executed according to the reviewer, who also notes of the instrumentation that: 'such a combination may be somewhat unusual but it produced a remarkably melodious effect.' Ibid. Gustavus von Holst (grandfather of Gustav Host) wrote a number of music 'salon' works for combinations of instruments, including the harp, and had been for many years a peripatetic harp teacher, travelling around Britain. Information provided by The Holst Birthplace Museum, Cheltenham.

139 *Bedfordshire Times and Independent*, 29 May 1889, p. 8.

he had retired as organist of St Peter's and St Paul's churches. He had also retired as borough organist (in 1887) because of increasing deafness. 'On his final retirement, the Vicar, Church-wardens and congregation [of St Paul's church] presented him with a silver tray, an illuminated address, and purse of money, as a mark of esteem, respect and gratitude for the efficient manner in which for nearly a quarter of a century hc had discharged his duties as organist.'[140] As it says in his obituary:

> He loved the organ and it was a bitter trial when, owning to an infirmity of deafness, he yielded to the persuasions of his relatives and gave up the services at St. Paul's. Mr. Rose has been called 'The Father of Music in Bedford'. Associated with Mr. F. [*sic*] Diemer, the late Mr. Day, Mr. (now Sir) Frederick Howard, the late Dr. Steinmetz, and others, he was one of the founders of the Bedford Musical Society.[141]

On his resignation from the Musical Society, Robert Rose was elected an honorary member. He lived for another eight years and died on 21 March 1898 in his eighty-fourth year. The obituary to him in the *Bedfordshire Times and Independent* pays generous tribute:

> In spite of his advanced age, his geniality, activity, and youthfulness never forsook him. He was out and about on Saturday fortnight and up to then personally managed his business, kept his books in admirable order, and directed the movements of his assistants. In their welfare he took a personal interest, and by them he was regarded with affection … Mr. Rose was twice married, and in all there have been twelve children, of whom five survive. Three of the sons are in America, Miss Rose was living with her father, and the youngest son is Mr. Henry Rose, who has been the pride of his father's life. His appointment some years ago as organist at St. Pancras, in succession to Henry Smart was probably the proudest gratification in the life of our lamented townsman. That sense of satisfaction must have been well sustained since by the honourable career of the son as a professor at the Royal Academy … [Mr Rose] was a good man of business, exceedingly methodical in his habits, very observant, interested in all that he saw, buoyant in spirits and, clear of intellect … The same determination and persevering industry characterised him throughout his life. These and other sterling business qualities, which developed themselves in after years, were the admiration of his many friends.[142]

His grave, which still survives, though damaged, is in the old Bedford Cemetery.[143]

Robert Rose's successor as the Musical Society's organist was Mr T. J. Ford, who had been the Society's accompanist at rehearsals and pianist at concerts for many years. Mr Ford took over the role of organist, but not that of chorus master. Robert Rose's immediate successor as organist of St Paul's was Mr J. H. Righton, who had been organist of Holy Trinity, Dorchester (Dorset) before his appointment to Bedford. He was organist of St Paul's for less than two years.[144] He was succeeded there by Harry Harding early in 1889.

140 *Bedfordshire Times and Independent*, 25 March 1898, p. 7.

141 Ibid.

142 Ibid.

143 There is a cart that belonged to Robert Rose's business in Bedford Museum.

144 This information comes from an article on eighteenth and nineteenth century organists at St Paul's church, Bedford, in *The Bedfordshire Times and Bedfordshire Standard,* 16 February 1940, p. 10.

Three major works were performed in 1890. The first was Mendelssohn's 'Hymn of Praise'. For this work, a prominent member of the Musical Society, Miss Whittle (soprano), joined professionals Mary Davies (soprano) and Mr Gawthrop (tenor), a Gentleman of Her Majesty's Chapel Royal. Berlioz's *Faust* – its full title was not used in the *Bedfordshire Times and Independent's* advertisements or by the reviewer – was performed in May. This is the only time that the Musical Society has performed a major work by Berlioz at one of its own concerts, and the fact that it was able to do so is evidence of the high standard of the Society at the time. Indeed, the reviewer makes this very point: 'Not many towns in England can boast of a Musical Society which would, or a Conductor who dare, attempt a performance of this very elaborate work which, let us say at once, was not only attempted but most successfully accomplished.'[145] Clara Samuell, the Bedford favourite, was Margaret, one of the principal characters. Mr W. H. Brereton was Mephistopheles who: 'not only sang the music, but made us feel that he was for the time the character he impersonated.'[146] Durward Lely took the part of Faust. He was a singer with the D'Oyly Carte company, and had taken part in the original performances of several Gilbert and Sullivan comic operas including *Patience* (1881), *Iolanthe* (1882) and *The Mikado* (1885) in which he sang the part of Nanki-Poo.[147] There is no reference to this in the review, possibly because the writer assumed that his readers would know it.

According to the reviewer, the chorus sang well. The tenors and basses especially were complimented: 'right heartily did they enter into the spirit of the work, singing with great gusto the Drinking Chorus.'[148] There was a large audience with many, apparently, coming from great distances to hear the work, which the reviewer hoped would soon be repeated. At the end of the concert, Robert Rose was presented with an illuminated address and a 'valuable gift' from members of the Society on his retirement.

The Golden Legend was repeated in May 1891, eighteen months after the first performance. This time, Clara Leighton, late *prima donna* of the Carla Rosa Opera, took the part of Elsie. Mary Morgan, who sang in the 1889 performance, was again Ursula. Durward Lely was Prince Henry. The parts of the Forester and Lucifer were taken respectively by William Kingston and Mr W. H. Brereton as they had been in 1889. Mr Brereton had been Lucifer in *Faust*, so this was the third time that he had sung the part of Satan in Bedford. The reviewer, noting that Mr Brereton had received especial commendation from Sir Arthur Sullivan, adds: 'It is to be hoped that the ancient enemy will always sing as pleasantly as Mr. Brereton does.'[149]

There were eighteen professional instrumentalists out of a total of fifty-five orchestral players in this second performance – a substantial proportion. Beethoven's Symphony No. 5 was performed in the second half of the concert followed by Rossini's *William Tell* overture. The concert did not finish until 10.25p.m., and many

145 *Bedfordshire Times and Independent*, 17 May 1890, p. 8.

146 Ibid.

147 The advertisement for the Bedford concert states that Durward Lely was a tenor with the Carla Rosa Opera. *The Bedfordshire Times and Independent*, 3 May 1890, p. 4. Durward Lely returned to Bedford to sing in the performance of Handel's *Judas Maccabaeus* in December 1890.

148 *Bedfordshire Times and Independent*, 17 May 1890, p. 8.

149 *Bedfordshire Times and Independent*, 16 May 1891, p. 6.

people left before or during the Rossini, resulting in a somewhat undignified ending to the evening.

The main items in the miscellaneous concert, held towards the end of October, were Stanford's *The Revenge* and a selection of music from Sullivan's latest opera, *Ivanhoe*. Sir George Grove, author of the article on Sullivan in the first *Grove's Dictionary of Music and Musicians*, published in four volumes 1878–89, had expressed the hope that Sullivan would work on a more serious production as it was generally felt that he had devoted too much time and energy to light music.[150] *Ivanhoe* could be said to be the result, and was Sullivan's most significant attempt to write a serious opera. Richard D'Oyly Carte opened the Royal English Opera House in Cambridge Circus, London, in January 1891 with a production of the work. It was *not* a resounding success, despite the fact that it ran for 160 performances.[151]

Ivanhoe had almost certainly closed by the time the music was heard in Bedford. Despite its failure as an opera, the extracts went down well when the Society performed the concert version. Clara Samuell, the principal soloist, created a *furore* (according to the reviewer) with her splendid singing of the recitative and prayer 'Lord of Our Chosen Race'. Among other pieces performed at the concert were some gipsy songs by the still relatively unknown Antonin Dvořák (misspelt 'Dvorah' in the review), sung by Clara Samuell and accompanied by her husband, Henry Rose. The reviewer thought that William Kingston, the other principal soloist, could, with credit, take his place in the professional world, describing him as the *primo basso* of the Musical Society. It was probably his singing of solos from *Ivanhoe* that prompted the very complimentary remarks in the review.[152]

The Musical Society's hundredth concert was held on 8 December 1891, and consisted of the seventh performance of *Elijah*, for which: 'Neither pains not expense were spared and the very best professional assistance, vocal and instrumental, were requisitioned. Nor was the enthusiasm limited to members … the Exchange being on Tuesday evening densely packed.'[153] The soloists included Edith Morton (soprano), a pupil of Philip Diemer's; Miss Whittle, that stalwart member of the Society; and Lizzie Neal, gold medallist at the Royal Academy of Music. According to the reviewer, the *chef d'oeuvre* was Lizzie Neal's exquisite interpretation of the beautiful aria 'O, Rest in the Lord'. Had time permitted, the audience would gladly have listened to a repetition. But the only redemand allowed was the trio 'Lift thine Eyes', where Miss Whittle and Miss Neal were joined by Miss McFarlowe. The performance lasted for nearly three and a half hours, finishing at 10.55p.m.

150 The article on Sullivan in the second edition of *Grove's Dictionary of Music and Musicians*, published in 1904, quotes substantial parts of the original article in the first edition. Fuller Maitland, ed., *Grove's Dictionary of Music and Musicians*, vol. 5, pp. 743–7.

151 The music was considered uneven – too much 'Savoy' for serious opera. It was also too demanding for a single cast to perform six nights a week, so two casts were employed, but not in a very systematic way. As a result, it was never clear which principal singers would be singing on any given night. But after another, non-English opera – André Messeger's *Basoche* – ran at the Royal English Opera House for a few months, the Opera House was deemed to have been a failure and was transformed into the Palace Theatre of Varieties and given over to music hall. It was renamed the Palace Theatre in 1910.

152 *Bedfordshire Times and Independent*, 24 October 1891, p. 8.

153 *Bedfordshire Times and Independent*, 12 December 1891, p. 7.

In the interval, Philip Diemer and Hermann Steinmetz were both presented with silver salvers as a token of the esteem in which they were held by the Society and by the musical public of Bedford.[154] The review of the concert begins by noting that twenty-five years ago the Musical Society started on the lowest rung of the ladder, had passed through storm and sunshine and was now more virile and healthy than ever.[155] Throughout the Musical Society's history, there were regular complimentary remarks about Philip Diemer and how much he had done for its advancement. Less frequently remarked upon was appreciation for Hermann Steinmetz, the secretary. Philip Diemer said, following the presentations to them both, that: 'His own work had been an exhibition and he had been to the front, but Dr Steinmetz had been in the background and had done all the work (applause).'[156] The review ends with a note stating that the idea of the silver salvers originated with Harry Thody, the chief constable, an old and active member of the Musical Society and one of the two leading viola players.[157]

In the 1892/93 and 93/94 seasons there were four miscellaneous concerts, two ballad concerts, one operatic concert and one concert of sacred music.The first of these miscellaneous concerts, an operatic one in February 1892, rather surprisingly featured the Begum Ahmadee, a princess of the royal house of Delhi. She is described as having a beautiful mezzo-soprano voice, and the reviewer seems to have taken something of a shine to her. He writes: 'To her considerable personal charms this lady adds great musical gifts … there was naturally a great desire to see and hear so happy a combination of graces and talents … gifted with a refined type of Oriental loveliness … opera glasses were in great request, and eyes seemed more interested than ears.'[158] She had studied from the age of sixteen in Milan and afterwards in Paris. Among the songs she sang was a Neapolitan air in which she accompanied herself on the harp.

Gounod's *The Redemption* was performed early in April 1892, shortly before Holy Week. Gounod completed this for the Birmingham Festival in 1882, although he had sketched it some years earlier. In his twenties Gounod had studied for the priesthood, and although he abandoned this idea later in life he: 'plunged into religious mysticism and devoted himself to the composition of great sacred works, especially adapted to the taste of a large section of the English public.'[159] Gounod's choral music was especially popular in the 1890s, just as Sullivan's was on the wane. Of Gounod's religious works, the writer of the article in *Grove's Dictionary of Music and Musicians,* M. Gustave Chouquet, notes that: 'He [Gounod] has made simplicity an absolute rule … incessant reiterations of the same chords; these impart a monotony and heaviness to the work which must weary the best audience.'[160]

Chouquet's criticisms are reflected in the review: 'The oratorio may present difficulties no greater than others that the Society has already successfully overcome, but

154 Sadly the salver was stolen from the home of Philip Diemer's great-grandson, Michael Diemer, in the autumn of 1991.
155 *Bedfordshire Times and Independent,* 12 December 1891, p. 7.
156 Ibid.
157 Ibid.
158 *Bedfordshire Times and Independent*, 27 February 1892, p. 6.
159 Fuller Maitland, ed., *Grove's Dictionary of Music and Musicians*, vol. 2, p. 210.
160 Ibid.

its length and tediousness are trifles that only lovers of music for its own sake can afford to laugh at … The choruses for the most part were recurrences of the original theme, but were full of emotional expression and the sacredness of the theme was most marked.'[161] The professional soloists included Mr W. H. Brereton, and they were joined once more by Bedford's *primo basso*, William Kingston.

The December 1892 performance of Handel's *Samson* was: 'wretchedly attended, because the weather was the worst imaginable.'[162] The cold weather seems to have suited the choir for the reviewer observed: 'The choruses were as near perfection as possible. The attack of the tenors, and particularly the basses was fine in the extreme.'[163] The tenor soloist, who had been booked, telegrammed to say that he was voiceless. The 'popular' Welsh tenor, Dyved Lewis came in his place.

The concert held on 16 May 1893 started on a sad note. The long-serving secretary and treasurer of the Musical Society, Hermann Steinmetz, had died a week earlier, on Tuesday 9 May. At the start of the concert, the chorale from Philip Diemer's cantata *Bethany*, 'Brother, Thou Art Gone Before Us', was sung by the full chorus, accompanied by the band, in his memory. The ladies of the choir each wore a small black rosette and black gloves instead of the usual red and blue sashes. The gentlemen wore black ties.

The concert itself consisted of a 'grand concert recital', as the review puts it, of Gounod's *Faust*.[164] The hall was not full but attendance was, 'rather superior to a good average'. *Faust*, the opera that brought Gounod real fame, was first performed in March 1859 and has remained his most popular work. But as Percy Scholes noted, those who love Goethe do not love Gounod.[165] The two main tenor parts of the Bedford performance, Faust and Valentine, were sung respectively by Joseph O'Mara of The Royal English & Italian Opera, and Emeric Beaman of the Carla Rosa Opera Company. Once more, Mr W. H. Brereton took the part of Mephistopheles, while William Kingston sang the small part of Wagner. The reviewer notes: 'Mr. Brereton's voice was in fine form and was well adapted to the character that he has personated before.'[166] The choruses were more successful than might have been expected, 'especially the Chorus of the Soldiers in which the male voices blended with rich effect.'[167]

Hermann Steinmetz's obituary appeared in the *Bedfordshire Times and Independent* before the concert:

> A painful feeling of loss was the common sentiment of Bedford townspeople on Wednesday when it became known that their popular fellow-citizen, Dr. Hermann Steinmetz was no more. His demise was not unexpected. For sometime he had been in broken health, and when, during the last week or two, his indisposition was complicated by heart troubles, the worst was feared. It was

161 *Bedfordshire Times and Independent*, 9 April 1892, p. 8.
162 *Bedfordshire Times and Independent*, 10 December 1892, p. 7.
163 Ibid. In *The Bousfield Diaries: A Middle-class Family in Late Victorian Bedford* edited by Dr Richard Smart (Bedford 2007), plate 9 shows people skating on the frozen Great Ouse at Bedford. Dr Smart gives the date as either 1890 or 1892. The reviewer's comments suggest that it was 1892.
164 *Bedfordshire Times and Independent*, 20 May 1893, p. 7.
165 See Percy Scholes's article on Gounod in the *Oxford Companion to Music*, p. 374. He makes the same point about Gounod's opera *Romeo and Juliet*, 'Those who love Shakespeare do not love Gounod.'
166 *Bedfordshire Times and Independent*, 20 May 1893, p. 7.
167 Ibid.

> announced by Mr. Diemer at the rehearsal of the Musical Society on Tuesday that the Doctor was still in a precarious condition. At about ten o'clock the same evening Dr. Steinmetz breathed his last at his residence in Ashburnham-road. His age was 67, and he leaves a widow, four sons, and a daughter. Two of the sons are teachers in Switzerland, and another is at the Britannia Iron Works ... the continued existence of the present Musical Society, which is now in its twenty-sixth year, is a speaking testimony to the persevering efforts of Dr. Steinmetz, who has been its Honorary Secretary through sunshine and rain from the beginning.[168]

Hermann Steinmetz's funeral took place on Friday 13 May at Holy Trinity church, where he had been churchwarden. He was buried in Bedford Cemetery in Foster Hill Road. The committee sent a resolution to his family and held an appeal to raise money for a gravestone in his memory.[169] A paragraph asking for donations was inserted in local papers. The gravestone, which still stands, was put up later in the year.[170] Inserted into the *Minute Book* is a moving 'thank you' letter from Mrs Steinmetz, following her visit to the memorial stone.[171]

Hermann Steinmetz's position as secretary was taken, after some months, by Dr Henry Skelding, who at the time was in his early thirties. He came to Bedford in 1887 as house surgeon to Bedford Hospital after completing his medical training. He had a pleasant tenor voice, and was a member of the Musical Society for many years, according to his obituary.[172] He was secretary 1894–99, and his minutes are brief and succinct like those of his predecessor. He also took a leading part in the Bedford Operatic Society.

The ballad concert in October 1893, included Parry's *Blest Pair of Sirens*, completed in 1887. The reviewer describes this as: 'a rather high-class composition best appreciated by musicians of very cultivated taste.'[173] Mr E. Bandey, the Society's accompanist, also conducted his own choral work *Fishwife's Cradle Song* at the concert.

In December, at a performance of Mendelssohn's *St Paul*, there was a problem with poor lighting in the Corn Exchange: 'Bedford gas being as bad as it could be … oil lamps had to be brought into requisition as an auxiliary to the gas jets.'[174]

168 *Bedfordshire Times and Independent*, 13 May 1893, p. 8.

169 The resolution said: 'The Committee of the Bedford Musical Society desire to assure the family of the late Dr. Steinmetz of their sincere sympathy with them in the irreparable loss which has recently befallen them, a loss which will be also long and deeply felt not only by this Society, but by other public Institutions of this Town.' *Minute Book 1867–93*, 25 May 1893, BLARS X817/1/1. Hermann Steinmetz was also secretary of the Bedford Literary and Scientific Institute, the Whist Club and the Horticultural Society. *Bedfordshire Times and Independent*, 13 May 1893, p. 8.

170 The inscription reads: 'To the Memory of Herman F. L. C. Steinmetz Ph. D. who was born at Mandern: Germany October 3 1825 and Died at Bedford May 9 1893 "A man greatly beloved" Erected by the Bedford Musical Society of which he was for 26 years Honorary Secretary. Treu und Fest.'

171 Mrs. Steinmetz wrote: 'This afternoon I had the sad pleasure of visiting the Cemetery to view the monument which your Society has raised over the last resting place of my lamented husband. I now hasten to express ... to the members of the Musical Society the sentiments of grateful and appreciative admiration ... regarding the very chaste and appropriate memorial thus erected to the beloved memory of my husband.' *Minute Book 1867–93*, 16 January 1894, BLARS X817/1/1.

172 *Bedfordshire Times and Independent*, 21 October 1932, p. 9.

173 *Bedfordshire Times and Independent*, 21 October 1893, p. 6. Unusually a Gilbert and Sullivan ballad – 'Poor Wandering One' –from *The Pirates of Penzance* was included.

174 *Bedfordshire Times and Independent*, 16 December 1893, p. 6

The choir was weakened by absenteeism at this concert, mostly due to illness.[175] The reviewer still considered that the performance was another brilliant success.

During 1894–1900, the Musical Society performed few newly-composed compositions and few compositions that they had not previously performed. The two recently-composed works that they did undertake were by the young Scottish composer Hamish MacCunn. They repeated two Sullivan works, *The Prodigal Son* and *The Golden Legend*. And they also repeated Parry's *Blest Pair of Sirens*, Barnett's *The Ancient Mariner* and Sterndale Bennett's *The May Queen*, the latter two of which were probably, by this time, rather out of fashion.[176] Many of the 'evergreens', *Messiah*, *Creation* and *Elijah*, were performed again. And there was at least one miscellaneous concert in each season. A special Diamond Jubilee concert was held in 1897.

MacCunn's *Lord Ullin's Daughter* was performed in a miscellaneous concert in May 1894. MacCunn was born in Greenock in March 1868 and won a scholarship to the Royal College of Music in 1883, the year the college opened. He was a pupil of Parry. The orchestral work by which he is still best known, *The Land of the Mountain and the Flood*, was performed at the Crystal Palace in 1887. *Lord Ullin's Daughter* was first performed at the Crystal Palace almost a year later, just before his twentieth birthday. At the Bedford performance, the principal soloists were Clara Samuell and Joseph Layland, a pupil of Sims Reeves.[177] The reviewer notes that Clara Samuell had the distinction of having been engaged for the Handel Festival at the Crystal Palace the following month. There is very little about *Lord Ullin's Daughter* in the review, apart from the comment that the theme of a 'Scotch' melody runs through it – which is hardly surprising![178]

The main work at the December concert seems an odd choice, as the reviewer pointed out: 'Sir Michael Costa's grand oratorio *Eli*, a work which has apparently gone out of favour with the public and it is not performed so frequently as it deserves to be.'[179] *Eli* was composed in 1855 for the Birmingham Festival of which Costa was then conductor.[180] Philip Diemer may have heard Costa conduct *Eli* while he was studying in London, as Costa was also conductor of the Sacred Harmonic Society, a post he held for many years. Costa also conducted the Handel Festival concerts

[175] 'The well-trained chorus contributed largely to the striking effect of the numbers that fell to their share, but the chorus was somewhat weakened by the absence of several members who were suffering from colds.' Ibid.

[176] Parry composed three oratorios that the Musical Society might have sung, *Judith* (1888), *De Profundis* (1891) and *Job* (1892). For some reason none them were performed.

[177] Sims Reeves was a very well-known tenor. He made his name in opera, but his greatest triumph was as soloist at the Handel Festivals at the Crystal Palace, especially that of 1857.

[178] *Bedfordshire Times and Independent*, 12 May 1894, p. 7.

[179] *Bedfordshire Times and Independent*, 8 December 1894, p. 6.

[180] Costa was conductor of the Philharmonic Society 1846–54. He was succeeded as conductor (for one year) by Wagner, who wrote of the orchestra to his wife Minna: 'A magnificent orchestra as far as the principal members go. Superb tone – the leaders had the finest instruments I ever heard – a strong Esperit de corps – but no distinct style'. Fuller Maitland, ed., *Grove's Dictionary of Music and Musicians*, vol. 5, p. 403. Wagner, of all people, went on to complain that the orchestra and audience consumed more music than they could possibly digest and that it was impossible to do justice to the monster programmes!

at the Crystal Palace 1857–80. Philip Diemer formed his taste in oratorio when he heard performances of the Sacred Harmonic Society.[181]

The review of the Bedford performance of *Eli* is quite short. The chorus seems to have found it quite difficult to sing. The band part was not difficult in comparison, though the reviewer commented that the orchestration was peculiar and often original. Edward Halfpenny is the only professional instrumentalist named as playing. Among the soloists was Mr A. Beagley, who seems to have taken over from William Kingston as the member of the Musical Society most able to sing bass solos.[182] He 'personated' Phineas (as the review puts it). *Eli* is a long work and the reviewer felt unable to mention: 'a tithe of the many solos and airs which were equally well sung.'[183] However, he does single out Samuel's 'Evening Prayer' as a masterpiece, sung by Mr Gawthrop, a regular singer with the Society.

The Bride of Dunkerron by Henry Smart was performed in May 1895.[184] Like Costa's *Eli*, it dates from earlier in the century, having been composed in 1864, and also seems an odd choice for the Musical Society. It was composed for, and first performed at, the Birmingham Music Festival of 1861, and is based on an Irish folk story. Henry Smart was organist of St Pancras church in Euston Road, London, for many years. He died in 1879 and, as already noted, his successor was Henry Rose. This could have been why the work was chosen, though neither Henry Rose nor his wife, Clara Samuell, took part in the performance. The soprano soloist, Eugenia Morgan, was from the Crystal Palace Saturday concerts. The tenor and bass were, respectively, Charles Ellison and W. H. Burgon, both late principals with the Carla Rosa Opera. Edward Halfpenny led the orchestra and Mr Woolhouse was the principal cello. Members of the Bedford Professional String Band augmented the orchestra, replacing the professional players who usually came from London.[185] The reviewer comments: 'To one who has not previously heard the piece, the orchestration is, in the opening passage, to say the least of it, bewildering, but the noisy strains gradually die away … The band was excellent; each instrument was used with just sufficient power.'[186]

The third major work not previously performed by the Musical Society was Handel's *Joshua*, given in December 1897.[187] *Joshua* tells of an Old Testament char-

181 Referred to in Philip Diemer's obituary in the *Bedfordshire Times and Independent,* 13 May 1910, p. 8.

182 Mr Beagley sang the part of the Forester in *The Golden Legend* in December 1897. William Kingston sang this part in the previous two performances.

183 *Bedfordshire Times and Independent*, 8 December 1894, p. 6.

184 Henry Smart is now best remembered for several fine hymn tunes, including those used for 'Blessed City, Heavenly Salem', 'God of Mercy, God of Grace' and 'Just as I am Without One Plea'.

185 There is a photograph of Bedford Professional String Band in *Bedford in Times Past* by A. E. Baker and N. C. Wilde (Chorley, 1980), p. 18. The note about the band states that it was founded in the 1880s and they played in Charlie Keith's circus in the winter of 1892–93, moving to Gloucester in the spring. When the circus came to grief, the string band returned to Bedford and performed in the High Street by day and in residential areas and at private functions by night wearing either a uniform or the bowlers and dark suits as seen in the photograph. Despite the name, the five performers shown are playing bugle, clarinet, violin, harp and double bass. It looks as though the photograph was taken in the south of the Market Square.

186 *Bedfordshire Times and Independent*, 25 May 1895, p. 7.

187 The author has a score of *Joshua* which originally belonged to Mary Whitchurch, sister of J. Arnold Whitchurch, president of the Society 1941–53. This was printed in September 1895, and was probably used by her in the Musical Society's performance.

acter, as *Eli* and the 'evergreen' *Elijah* also do. *Joshua* is a late oratorio by Handel composed in 1747 between *Judas Maccabaeus* and *Solomon*. It is rarely performed now, perhaps because of the sensitivity of the subject matter (the violent displacement of people and what might be described as ethnic cleansing). The soloists at the Bedford performance included Reginald Brophy as Joshua who was said to be, 'well and favourably known to Bedford audiences', although this seems to be the only occasion that he sang with the Musical Society, and Mr Sam Heath as Caleb, who had been a silver medallist at the Royal Academy of Music and subsequently gave weekly singing lessons in Bedford.[188] Although *Joshua* was new to Bedford audiences, one of the choruses would have been familiar, 'See, the Conqu'ring Hero Comes'. Ebenezer Prout points out in the Novello score's introduction to *Joshua* that this chorus was originally composed for *Joshua* and was subsequently inserted into *Judas Maccabaeus*.[189]

In the 1898/99 season there were only three concerts. The minutes of the annual general meeting explain why: 'Reduction in the number of concerts from 4 to 3. Mr. Diemer stated that the concert usually held in May was not so well attended as it used to be, before the cycling rage came in. Everything had to give way to cycling.'[190]

At the first concert of the season in November 1898, the twenty-six year-old Clara Butt was the main soloist in the miscellaneous concert. She dominated the programme, as is demonstrated by the newspaper headline and the comment that followed: 'MISS CLARA BUTT IN BEDFORD … That, rather than the familiar heading "THE BEDFORD MUSICAL SOCIETY" seems the fit description of Tuesday's concert. No-one who then heard Miss Clara Butt for the first time will ever forget the impression produced on the crowded audience by her glorious singing.'[191]

After studying at the Royal College of Music, Clara Butt made her debut at the Albert Hall as Ursula in *The Golden Legend* in December 1892, and three days later sang the part of Orpheus in Gluck's opera *Orfeo ed Euridice* at the Lyceum Theatre. Despite her success there, she made her career on the concert platform. Her first two festival engagements were in 1893 at Hanley (Stoke on Trent) and Bristol. She sang in *Israel in Egypt* at the Handel Festival at the Crystal Palace, as did Clara Samuell, in June 1894.[192] In 1897, Clara Butt was one of the soloists in the Diamond Jubilee performance of *Elijah* at the Crystal Palace.

188 See advertisement in *The Bedfordshire Times and Independent,* 5 June 1903, p. 7.

189 The author is grateful to Dr Donald Burrows for confirming that Ebenezer Prout's account is correct. 'See the Conqu'ring Hero Comes' was composed in 1747, and first performed in 1748. The first performances of *Judas Maccabaeus,* earlier in 1747, therefore did not include it; it was transferred for the revivals of that oratorio in either 1748 or 1750, and stayed there thereafter. Donald Burrows, *Handel* (New York, 2012), The Master Musicians; Master Musicians Series, pp. 388–9 and 422.

190 *Minute Book 1893–1900*, 5 February 1895, BLARS X817/1/ 2.

191 *Bedfordshire Times and Independent*, 25 November 1898, p. 5. The programme survives and it is included in a book of Bedford Musical Society's programmes 1893–1904 in the Bedfordshire Heritage Library in Bedford Central Library. The signatures of many of the soloists who sang during this period are included in the book, among them, Clara Butt's very flamboyant signature.

192 Mary Whitchurch attended this concert on 29 June and wrote details of the music performed and the performers in the front of her copy of the programme. Clara Samuell is one of the named sopranos. The anthem "Lamentations of the Israelites for the Death of Joseph" was sung following the assassination of President Carnot of France.

Her visit to Bedford in 1898 was one of the highlights for the Musical Society during the last few years of the nineteenth century. The reviewer could hardly contain himself: 'It is not only a marvellous voice, however, but the charm of style, the perfect expression, the dramatic interpretation of whatever she sings that, in our opinion, makes Miss Clara Butt the great singer that she is.'[193] She sang six songs at the Bedford concert including an excerpt from *Orfeo ed Euridice*; 'The Silver Ring' by Cecile Chaminade, a female French composer; a hymn; a ballad; a cradle song; and 'When you Return' by another woman composer, Maud Valerie White, who was English. The audience was hugely animated: 'After each appearance, they recalled the singer again and again, and for a Bedford audience became uproariously enthusiastic.'[194]

Clara Butt gave the first performance of Elgar's *Sea Pictures* in Norwich in October 1899, less than a year after the Bedford concert. She married Kennerley Rumford, a baritone singer, in 1900. She sang again in Bedford in November 1922. This was not at a Musical Society concert, however.

Fanny Chetham, a local soprano, made her *debut* with the Musical Society in the performance of *Elijah* that followed the Clara Butt concert, in December 1898: 'One of the most interesting things about the concert was the debut of Miss Fanny Chetham as a vocalist. She took the soprano music throughout and the Society have a right to be proud that from their own ranks so promising a singer should have sprung. Miss Chetham's singing was a little uneven.'[195] The reviewer said that he expected a singer making her debut to be nervous, especially when facing a familiar audience, but he noted that she soon overcame this.

The first concert in 1899, early in April, was a repeat of *Lord Ullin's Daughter*. Another new work by Hamish MacCunn, *The Cameronian's Dream*, was included in the October concert. The reviewer thought that the music was beautiful, but that it was under-rehearsed and that members ought to do more in support of the Society.[196]

The Musical Society ended the year, and indeed the century, with a performance of *Messiah*, early in December. This prompted the reviewer to comment that the need for an organ was made painfully apparent by the: 'hurdy-gurdy of a harmonium which even Mr. Ford could not coerce into tunefulness!'[197] Clara Samuell sang for the last time with the Musical Society at this concert.

The first concert of the new century, a sacred musical concert, held in March 1900, was something of a watershed. It was the last concert for which Philip Diemer was the chief conductor. Among the orchestral players at this concert were Mr Eveleigh on the bassoon, and Mr T. J. Ford on the organ (presumably still playing that hurdy-gurdy instrument!), who had both performed with the Musical Society from its earliest days. Agnes Nicholls, the soprano soloist, sang with the Musical

193 *Bedfordshire Times and Independent*, 25 November 1898, p. 5.

194 Ibid.

195 *Bedfordshire Times and Independent*, 16 December 1898, p. 6.

196 'With the exception of the baritones, who really sang conscientiously, the chorus was altogether feeble and hesitating.' And he ends with an admonition: 'It is never pleasant to find fault, and of course, it would be absurd to apply too high a standard of criticism to an amateur society, but we cannot help feeling that there is an abundance of talent in Bedford to make a really strong Society, and that members might themselves do much more than they do at present to second and support Mr. Diemer's laudable efforts.' *Bedfordshire Times and Independent*, 20 October 1899, p. 7.

197 *Bedfordshire Times and Independent*, 8 December 1899, p. 5.

Society for first time, and was to sing regularly with it over the next few years, as Clara Samuell had done in the 1880s and 1890s.[198]

In the opening remarks, the reviewer alludes to the grim news from South Africa: 'It was a courageous venture to hold the concert at all under the circumstances … when the public mind is alternately torn with anguish and elated with success.'[199] Mendelssohn's 'Hymn of Praise' occupied the first half of the concert, and was the best performance yet, according to the review. Miss Whittle sang the duet 'I Waited for the Lord' with Agnes Nicholls. In the second half of the concert, Beethoven's Symphony No.5, Mendelssohn's Psalm 43, 'Judge Me, O Lord' for unaccompanied voices, and 'The Heavens are Telling', from Haydn's *Creation* were performed. All the orchestral players' names – there were fifty of them – are given in the review. This was Philip Diemer's last concert as the Musical Society's chief conductor and the last for which he would take rehearsals.

The Corn Exchange organ

Despite the optimism that members of the Musical Society felt when the new Corn Exchange was opened in 1874, the Society as a whole did not find the building quite as satisfactory as had been initially hoped. There were doubts about whether the hall was big enough and about the acoustics, but the main concern was the lack of a fitted organ.[200] The Society had to hire an organ for concerts as they had had to before the Corn Exchange was opened.

In January 1878, Philip Diemer raised the subject of erecting an organ at the annual general meeting. Two years later, at the annual general meeting in February 1880, the chairman, Frederick Howard, proposed that consent should be sought from Bedford Corporation to allow the placing of an organ in the Corn Exchange. He advised that the Musical Society should present the organ to the town and the Bedford Corporation, who would then be responsible for its maintenance and repair. The Corporation were willing to allow the organ to be built, and the Musical Society launched an appeal in 1882. The Duke of Bedford gave a donation of £50, regular bazaars were held, and an extra performance of *Messiah* was given in December 1882.[201] £640 was placed at Barnard's Bank for the organ fund in September 1883, and by June 1884 the fund had grown to £790.

Over the next three years, however, the fund hardly grew at all. One possible reason for this is that some members of the Musical Society felt that the Corn

198 Agnes Nicholls really belongs to the next chapter, so information about her background is included there.

199 *Bedfordshire Times and Independent*, 30 March 1900, p. 6. The news related to the South African War, which had seen the Boers gain impressive victories at Stormberg, Magersfontein and Colenso in mid-December 1899 (called 'Black Week' in Britain) and Spioenkop in January 1900. But by late February things had begun to change with the British relief of Kimberley and Ladysmith.

200 As early as April 1880, in a brief note about a very good company of comedians in the *Bedfordshire Times and Independent* (in the 'Local Notes' column), it was noted that: 'the very excellence of the playing only throws into a greater and more painful relief the annoyingly bad acoustic properties of the Exchange. Shall we ever have a room which will be really suitable for music and drama?' *Bedfordshire Times and Independent,* 10 April 1880, p. 5.

201 For the bazaar held in June 1883, it is recorded in the *Minute Book* that: 'The Mayor was asked to be present with the Corporation at the Bazaar, Mr. Preston was to be asked to provide an omnibus to fetch and take home the ladies who hold stalls. Police attendance to be requested.' *Minute Book 1867–93,* 7 June 1883, BLARS X817/1/1.

Exchange was not suitable for concerts because it was not big enough and had inadequate acoustics. Members of the committee began to consider the possibility of building a new concert hall. By 1885 this was being seriously discussed.[202] In due course, a site in Midland Road was chosen as being most suitable.[203]

Hermann Steinmetz explained the current situation at the 1889 annual general meeting when he said that: 'They had nearly enough money for a new organ … but the difficulty had been to find a suitable place to put the organ in when they had got it. They had been treating for such a site, but there were too many difficulties in the way and they were forced to withdraw from it. It was a great disappointment to them. When they had a suitable building, he hoped the usefulness of the Society would be greater than it had hitherto been.'[204]

As well as the Musical Society not having what it considered to be a suitable hall for performances, when the time came to take measurements for a new organ in the Corn Exchange it was found that the platform was not wide enough for the instrument to be placed there. The Society also had concerns about the risk to a valuable instrument in a building where there were such extremes of heat and cold. It was therefore thought to be wise to wait until there was a 'Town Hall' worthy of the town.

There was no further progress towards installing the organ for several more years. The Musical Society considered, but discounted as unsuitable, the use of an opera house planned by Carl Milberg St Amory, which the Bedford architects Mallows and Grocock had been commissioned to design in 1895. This was to have been built on the corner of St Cuthbert's Street and Lurke Street (where Gaston House, now a dental surgery, stands).[205]

In March 1896 the committee finally decided that, after all, they should place their organ in the Corn Exchange, with the suggestion that the north end of the building be enlarged to allow space for fixing the instrument.[206] But it was not until 14 June 1899 that the following recommendation was put to the Bedford Corporation by the Estates Committee: 'That the Bedford Musical Society be allowed to erect an organ in the Corn Exchange in accordance with the plan produced. The terms and conditions of the placing of such an organ to be drawn up by the Committee and to be

202 'Proposed discussion about building a new Concert Hall - Dr Coombs and Mr. J. W. Hill [were] requested to make enquires of a piece of ground at the corner of the Kimbolton and Goldington Roads.' At the following meeting, it was reported that: 'This land was not in the market, but Dr Coombs and Mr Hill [were] requested to make enquires regards another piece of land in Midland Road.' *Minute Book 1867–93,* 10 September 1885, BLARS X817/1/1.

203 Other sites subsequently suggested at committee meetings were a piece of land in De Parys Avenue, September 1886; some ground on The Embankment belonging to the Duke of Bedford, December 1886; and the spot where the old alms-houses adjoined the prison in St Loyes, June 1888. *Minute Book 1867–93,* BLARS, X817/1/1.

204 *Bedfordshire Times and Independent*, 26 January 1889, p. 6.

205 Carl St. Amory drew up another plan for an opera house early in 1898, but despite a prospectus for the sale of seven thousand £1 shares being printed, this scheme failed, as it became obvious to St. Amory's backers that his amateur productions could never make this scheme pay. Richard Wildman writes: 'I last saw the C. E. Mallows designs for the Bedford opera house at the RIBA Drawings Collection … The opera house site was cramped, being that of Carl St Amory's house on the north corner of Lurke Street and St Cuthbert's Street … The rear garden was much bigger in 1898. I think the idea was to have lock-up shops on the Lurke Street frontage, to provide an alternative source of income.' Personal communication from Richard Wildman to the author.

206 *Minute Book 1893–1900*, 26 March 1896, BLARS X817/1/2.

submitted to the Council at a future meeting.'[207] Just before the organ was installed, the secretary was asked to obtain the assurance of the borough surveyor that the beams were of sufficient strength to bear the weight of the instrument. This seems rather late in the day, but was a very valid concern, as will be seen.

The organ was built by Messrs. W. Hill and Son of York Road, Islington, at a total cost of £1,334.[208] Hill and Son also built two other organs for Bedford churches, St Paul's and Mill Street Baptist and, notably, had built organs for Westminster Abbey and Birmingham Town Hall.

The report in the *Bedfordshire Times and Independent* of 12 October 1900, a day after the opening ceremony, gives detailed specifications of the instrument and an account of the event.[209] Mrs Guy Pym, recently elected as president of the Musical Society (in succession to Sir Frederick Howard), was the main celebrity at the ceremony. After the National Anthem in Costa's arrangement had been sung, Philip Diemer made a speech, summarised in the *Bedfordshire Times and Independent* report: 'he said that as founder of the Musical Society and its conductor for 33 years, it was thought fitting that he should speak on this occasion.[210] He confessed that it had been "the dream of his life" to see a good organ erected in a public hall in the town … Mr. Diemer humorously asked the Town Council to remember three things in their care of the instrument and to try to preserve it from Dust, from Sun and from Mice (laughter and applause).'[211] The report goes on: 'The President, Mrs. G. Pym, then (metaphorically!) presented the organ to the Mayor and Corporation and the Mayor gave appropriate thanks to the Society and also made reference to the fact that the Borough Organist would give free recitals in the winter months. The opening ceremony was followed by a recital by Mr Henry Rose, FRAM, organist of St Pancras church, and a selection of music was performed by the Musical Society's band and chorus, with Fanny Chetham as soloist. She included among her solos

207 The reports of the meeting, in the *Bedfordshire Times and Independent,* 16 June 1899, p. 6 and in *The Bedford Mercury*, 16 June 1899, p. 5, make amusing reading. The proposition was carried by twelve votes to three, according to *The Bedford Mercury* and thirteen to two according to the *Bedfordshire Times*. The proposer of the motion, Ald. Moulton said that: 'if they shelved it, the Society would probably look for another place in which to put the organ.'

208 Messrs. W. Hill wrote to the Musical Society in August asking for payment of £750 to be paid on account of the organ contract, and this was approved by the committee who agreed to sell £800 in library bonds and deposit the balance of £50 in the London-County Bank. *Minute Book 1893–1900*, 13 August 1900, BLARS X817/1/2.

209 The report describes the organ thus: 'The organ stands on the incommodious platform at the north end of the hall, towering up into the roof, with a width of 24 feet and a depth of 7ft. 6 ins. In its case of stained pine with many rich cornices and mouldings, the instrument has a massive and noble appearance.' The organ pipes were at first in one case in the centre of the north wall. Subsequently, it was rebuilt and the pipes were placed in two separate cases with some space and the clock in the centre of the north wall between them. 'Hill's patent pneumatic action is used throughout and nearly four miles of tubing have been used. We understand that the tubes, pneumatic and otherwise concealed in the penetralia of the instrument would, if stretched at full length, reach from Bedford to Cotton End. The console is on the right side. There are three rows of keys and an extensive array of stops.' Detailed particulars of the Great, Swell, Choir and Pedal organs are also included. *Bedfordshire Times and Independent*, 12 October 1900, p. 8.

210 This is the first and only reference that the author has come across where Philip Diemer actually refers to himself as the founder of the Musical Society.

211 *Bedfordshire Times and Independent*, 12 October 1900, p. 8.

Mendelssohn's "O, for the Wings of a Dove".'[212] Sadly, the organ survived for only a little over fifty years. Its fate is described in chapter nine.

Sir Frederick Howard and Philip Diemer both announced their retirement at the June 1900 annual general meeting, shortly before the opening of the new organ in the Corn Exchange. Their announcements seem to have come as something of a surprise to members of the Society. Sir Frederick Howard, head of Howard Engineering at the Britannia Works, had been president for eighteen years, having been elected in 1882. He had expressed his support for the establishment of the Musical Society when the advertisement announcing its proposed formation was placed in the *Bedford Times and Bedfordshire Independent* in 1867, and had served on the committee from the early years. Apart from a two-year break in the 1870s, he was on the committee until his resignation in 1900. He always took an active interest in the affairs of the Society and regularly attended annual general meetings and committee meetings. His guiding hand and sound judgement were clearly felt by the members, as is evident in the minutes. He was, as much as anyone else, responsible for providing the impetus to raise funds for the organ and ensuring its eventual installation. The Musical Society owed a very great deal to him. He resigned due to ill health, but lived for another fifteen years, and died early in January 1915 at the age of eighty-seven.[213] Philip Diemer's resignation is described in detail in the minutes:

> Mr. Diemer announced that on account of failing health, the time was approaching when he must, in accordance with the advice of his medical attendant, resign the office of Conductor. He would do this with the greatest reluctance, and, instead of wholly severing his connexion with the Society, hoped that it would be possible to secure the appointment of a co-conductor in the person of Dr. Harding.[214]

Philip Diemer had conducted at all the Musical Society's concerts from 1867 to the summer of 1900, only standing aside to enable composers to conduct their own works, for example, Dr Chipp in 1872 and Sir Julius Benedict in 1877. He had received a number of testimonials for his work, including those of 1876 and 1891.[215] After his resignation, at the May 1905 concert, he was presented with a framed, illuminated address and a casket containing 110 guineas.[216]

The Musical Society's achievements throughout the Victorian period were largely the result of Philip Diemer's inspired leadership, although he was very well

212 Ibid. What the report does not say is that the organ was water powered. Anyone who has heard a water powered organ will know that the sound of running water is clearly audible. This information was given to the author by Sylvia Palmer, wife of H. Marshall Palmer whose influence was crucial for the Musical Society in the early 1940s.

213 In his obituary in the *Bedfordshire Times and Independent*, 8 January 1915, p. 5 there is a brief account of how he tried to buy the old St Paul's organ on which the tune 'Bedford' is said to have been composed, but the person whom he had asked to bid failed to turn up to the auction. The organ was sold to someone else and ended up in the Moravian church in Bedford.

214 *Minute Book 1900–04*, 26 June 1900, BLARS X817/1/3.

215 In 1891 he was presented with a conductor's desk. This, by very good chance, came into the possession of Joan Parkin, who was a long-standing member of the choir. She still has it.

216 *Bedfordshire Times and Independent*, 19 May 1905, p. 5. The full text of the address is quoted. Unusually, there is a misprint. He was presented with a copy of the address and a purse of gold, which is called a 'purpose of gold' in the report.

supported. He was highly regarded in Bedford and more widely. He died in May 1910, and his obituary is very complimentary:

> the long series of brilliant achievements during the next thirty years [after the formation of the Society] is the best proof of the vitality of the Society and of the loyalty of the members, so long and ably led by Mr. Diemer. Throughout his long career he was a musical educationalist and his literary and historical notes on the works performed went far to awaken the interest of the tyro and enhance the charm of the music.[217]

The obituary also refers to his 'tact and unvarying geniality' and to his being: 'an admirable conductor … while ruling his flock with a firm hand, he retained the loyalty and confidence of the members during many years, and was regarded by them with esteem and affection.'[218] The obituary goes on to say that he had a stirring partiality for the old masters.[219]

As well as being conductor of the Musical Society and organist of Holy Trinity church (a post he held for forty-seven years, retiring at Easter 1905), Philip Diemer taught singing classes for a great many years at the Grammar School, Bedford Modern School and the High School, as well as at other private schools. He prepared three concerts a year at the boys' schools and at least one concert a year at the girls' High School. He founded the Bedford School of Music, which he and his three daughters ran for many years.

After 1900, Philip Diemer occasionally conducted some parts of Musical Society concerts. He conducted a large part of the first half of *Elijah* in May 1907.[220] According to his obituary, he last 'officiated' at a Musical Society concert in May 1908 when he conducted the overture to *Messiah*, though the review from the *Bedfordshire Times and Independent* states that: 'Dr. Harding conducted the whole of the work with unfailing touch and unflagging energy.'[221]

Philip Diemer died at about five o'clock on Saturday 7 May 1910, aged seventy-three. As his obituary says, 'Mr. Diemer had been in failing health for a considerable time and had suffered attacks of paralysis, but his last illness only confined him to his room for about a fortnight.'[222] His funeral took place at Holy Trinity church

217 *Bedfordshire Times and Independent*, 13 May 1910, p. 8.

218 Ibid.

219 None of the major Bach choral works were sung during this period by the Musical Society, though Philip Diemer did sing in the Bach Society under Sterndale Bennett in the 1850s when he was a student in London. In a letter to the *Bedfordshire Times and Independent*, 12 February 1881, p. 8, a Mr S. John Cottingham writes: 'In reference to the musical interest of this town, I wish to allude to the fact of the satisfactory recital of the Matthew Passion at Trinity Church last year. I venture to hope that some effort will be made to give a more complete rendering of it at the fitting season and that the Musical Society, under the guidance of Mr. Diemer will establish it firmly among us. It is to be regretted that Handel is still regarded as on equality with Bach, that the time is not far distant when it will be seen that whereas Handel is only an able adapter, Bach is a creator of musical ideas.' 'A Musical Student' replied that he was at one with Mr Cottingham in wishing Bach's Passion music may again take place in Bedford in church – in its proper context. But he condemns the 'odious' comparison between Bach and Handel, *Bedfordshire Times and Independent*, 26 February 1881, p. 8.

220 Henry Barfoot, the writer of an article 'Forty Years of Music in Bedford' in *Bedford Music – A Year Book 1947* (Bedford, 1947), pp. 14–17, was referring to this performance when he wrote, 'The first thing I did was to join the Musical Society, and was just in time to sing under dear old Mr. Diemer's baton when he conducted half the programme. It was his last appearance as a conductor.'

221 *Bedfordshire Times and Independent*, 15 May 1908, p. 7.

222 *Bedfordshire Times and Independent*, 13 May 1910, p. 8.

where he had been organist and choirmaster for so many years. There was a large congregation, and his own composition 'Brother, Thou Art Gone Before Us' was sung by the church choir. The Musical Society sent a floral tribute with a message, 'In affectionate memory, from Bedford Musical Society'. There were a number of tributes from people including a rather touching one from Mr and Mrs H. W. Robinson which read: 'He has moved a little nearer to the Master of all music, to the Master of all singing.'[223] He was buried in the eastern extremity of the old part of the cemetery – on the low level, not very far from the boundary with Bedford Park. His gravestone, which still stands, bears the inscription: 'The Music of his life is nowise stilled but blended now with songs around the throne of God.'

223 *Bedfordshire Times and Independent*, 20 May 1910, p. 7.

Plate 1. John Brereton (1782–1863) headmaster of Bedford Grammar School and founder member of Bedford Harmonic Society (The original painting of 1835 by Charles Turner, after Samuel Lane, was destroyed in the 1979 fire at the school. A copy was painted in 1981 by Mrs Bowker)
(By kind permission of Bedford School)

Plate 2. Philip Henry Diemer (1836–1910) founder member of Bedford Amateur Musical Society and conductor 1867–1900
(Blake and Edgar)

Plate 3. Dr Hermann Steinmetz (1826–93) and the masters of Bedford Grammar School, 1878 (Hermann Steinmetz, back row, first left). Dr Steinmetz was a founder member of Bedford Amateur Musical Society and secretary 1867–93 (By kind permission of Bedford School)

Plate 4. Clara Samuell (1856–1920) soprano and popular local performer. She married Henry Rose, Robert Rose's son and had strong links with Bedford (© Royal College of Music/ArenaPAL)

Plate 5. Bedford Musical Society *Book of Words* 27 November 1906, front and back covers. Brothers J. and A. Beagley were enthusiastic members of the Bedford Musical Society and served in various committee roles as well as undertaking solo parts in concerts (By kind permission of Bedford Choral Society)

Plate 6. Harry Alfred Harding (1855–1930) conductor of Bedford Musical Society 1900–1923 (Langfrier)

Plate 7. Agnes Nicholls (1876–1959) Bedford educated soprano, performer of opera and singer of oratorios and cantatas in many regional music festivals (© Royal College of Music/ ArenaPAL)

Plate 8. Herbert J. Colson (1891–1951) conductor of Bedford Musical Society 1923–33. Cartoon by Mr E. S. Volz, art master at the Modern School from *The Eagle*, vol. 27, no. 3, p.167 (By kind permission of Bedford Modern School Archives)

Plate 9. Henry Marshall Palmer (1906–94) and the Mary Palmer Choir c. 1930 (H. Marshall Palmer is standing on the extreme right of the group) (By kind permission of the Times & Citizen)

Plate 10. BBC Symphony Orchestra (c.1941–45) in Bedford Corn Exchange showing the organ, which was dismantled and sold in 1951 (By kind permission of the Times & Citizen)

Plate 11. Clarence Raybould (1886–1972) conductor of Bedford Musical Society 1947–58 (left) pictured with Tom Winter secretary to Bedford Musical Society 1955–65 (centre) and Arthur Leavins leader of the orchestra (right) December 1956 (By kind permission of the Times & Citizen)

Plate 12. Kate (1909–98) and Hans Freyhan (1909–96). Kate Freyhan was assistant chorus master 1948–74. Hans Freyhan acted briefly as the Society's accompanist, but is mostly known for his erudite concert reviews in the *Bedfordshire Times* 1969–96 (By kind permission of the Times & Citizen)

Plate 13. Frederick E. Stevens (1912–2014) chorus master of the Bedford Musical Society 1952–65 (By kind permission of Mark Stevens)

Plate 14. David Willcocks (1919–2015) conductor of Bedford Musical Society 1959–87 rehearsing the choir at Pilgrim School in March 1974 (By kind permission of the Times & Citizen)

Plate 15. Michael Rose (b.1934) conductor of Bedford Musical Society 1973 to date (By kind permission of Simon Richardson)

Plate 16. Ian Smith (b.1951) conductor of Bedford Choral Society 1988 to date (By kind permission of Ian Smith)

Chapter Four

'Ere Armageddon came' and after, 1900–23

> May 29th. To the Corn Exchange, Bedford, it being rehearsal night for the Musical Society ... At this rehearsal both singers and players did strive to please the worthy doctor, save that a few of the ladies would not look at him, which troubled him very much. And, indeed, they might have looked at him, for he had a pretty buttonhole. Yet on the whole they did please him.
> May 30th. In the evening, I to the Corn Exchange once more, a bad place for sound and plaguey full of draughts so I did admire at the lack of a proper concert hall. There I found many more than before and they did sing and play even more loudly, yet very well.[1]

Dr Harry Alfred Harding (1855–1930)

Although Philip Diemer announced his resignation in June 1900, he remained as joint-conductor. Harry Harding was appointed fellow joint-conductor, but took on all the responsibilities of conductor, including taking the rehearsals, committee work and programme planning.

Harry Alfred Harding was born at Salisbury on 25 July 1855. His early ambition was to become a concert pianist, and he retained throughout his life a particularly delicate pianoforte 'touch' acquired in his youth. The first organ he practised on was a curious instrument with pedals that radiated inwards. While still in his 'teens he became organist at the parish church of Fisherton-de-la-Mere, near Salisbury, where the organ had only one manual and no pedals. He was also accompanist to a travelling pantomime company by the time he was fourteen. In 1873, at the age of seventeen, he was appointed organist and choirmaster of Sidmouth Parish Church.[2]

Harry Harding was instrumental in the formation of the Sidmouth Choral Society in 1874, not long after his arrival there. The Society's activities are faithfully recorded in the local newspapers.[3] There had been earlier attempts to form a choral society in Sidmouth, the first of note being in 1856, but none of these had been successful. The Society that Harry Harding formed gave its first concert at the Assembly Rooms of the London Hotel, Sidmouth, on Wednesday 8 April 1874. The programme consisted of twenty short pieces, including overtures, duets and part-songs. The subsequent review in the local paper stated:

> This much-anticipated performance took place as announced ... and was in every respect remarkably successful. No such concert has been given in Sidmouth for many years, the social position and influence of most of the amateurs giving a

1 From a parody based on Samuel Pepys's diary in the *Bedfordshire Times and Independent*, 2 June 1911, p. 8. The work being performed was Brahms's *German Requiem*. The parody appeared immediately below the review of the concert.

2 Obituary of Harry Harding, *Bedfordshire Times and Independent*, 31 October 1930, p. 9.

3 On microfilm in the Sidmouth Library.

> personal and family interest to the affair, which would ordinarily be lacking in a purely professional engagement ... But it was an excellent concert, reflecting credit on Mr. Harding, the Conductor, who by untiring previous training, as well as by the cool and methodical way in which he led, showed that as some men were said to be born to command, he is evidently one of that number where there is vocal or instrumental music to be performed.[4]

The second concert was held in December 1874, and the format of the first concert was repeated. A year later Haydn's *Creation* was performed, and after that the Sidmouth Choral Society held concerts regularly. Harry Harding also conducted the Sidmouth Volunteer Brass Band and an orchestra in Sidmouth, giving him an intimate knowledge of orchestral scores and valuable experience of the capacities of the different instruments.

In 1875 he passed the examination for the Fellowship of the Royal College of Organists. In 1877, at the age of twenty-two, he took a music degree at Oxford. For this he composed an oratorio about St Thomas: 'How many hundred pupils have been shown with pride that bulky full score, page after page of firm, clear notation?' writes his obituarist in the *Bedfordshire Times and Independent*.[5] He took his doctorate in 1882 as soon as he was eligible to do so, and added the Diploma of Licentiate of the Royal Academy of Music (for organ playing) to his academic distinctions in 1895.

Harry Harding was very popular during his time at Sidmouth and made a great impression. When he left to come to Bedford, he was presented with £200 and a piece of silver plate (a coffee pot) with the engraving: 'Presented to H. A. Harding, Mus. Doc. Oxon, together with £200 in token of the regard and esteem which he has won from all classes in Sidmouth during 16 years of residence and work amongst them. March 28th 1889.'[6]

Of his appointment to St Paul's church, the *Sidmouth Observer* report states: 'Dr. H. A. Harding ... left Sidmouth yesterday to take up the important post of choirmaster and organist of St. Paul's, Bedford, a church capable of seating nearly 1500 persons. Dr. Harding, it will be remembered, first anticipated going to America, then the idea was abandoned in favour of Eastbourne, and finally this in turn gave way to Bedford, Dr. Bridge (of Westminster Abbty [*sic*]) being strongly in favour of the doctor accepting the latter position.'[7]

Harry Harding succeeded Mr Righton as organist of St Paul's church. J. H. Righton had succeeded Robert Rose in 1887, but was organist at St Paul's for less than two years. Immediately following his appointment to St Paul's, Harry Harding advertised himself as a music teacher in the *Bedfordshire Times and Independent.* There soon followed a brief report of a recital given by, 'THE NEW ORGANIST OF ST. PAUL'S.'[8]

4 He was only eighteen at the time. *The Sidmouth Journal & Directory,* 1 May 1874, p. 6.

5 *Bedfordshire Times and Independent,* 31 October 1930, p. 9.

6 *Sidmouth Observer,* 3 April 1889, p. 3.

7 Ibid. One book about the history of Sidmouth includes a reference to the choral society there, but states that Harry Harding moved to Oxford. As recently as a month before his move to Bedford, it was reported in a review of his final concert in Sidmouth that his departure was for All Saints' church, Eastbourne. Anna Sutton, *A Story of Sidmouth* (Sidmouth, 1953), p. 101.

8 *Bedfordshire Times and Independent,* 27 April 1889, p. 8.

He was still looking for suitable accommodation in Bedford and advertised accordingly: 'WANTED immediately, an UNFURNISHED HOUSE, in pleasant situation, containing three Sitting-rooms, five or six Bedrooms, and Bathroom: no basement – Address, Dr. HARDING, Post Office, Bedford.[9] He eventually moved to 42 De Parys Avenue, Bedford, and lived there until after the First World War, when he moved to Hill House in Crofton Close, just off Kimbolton Road, which he had purpose-built.

As organist of St Paul's church he would have had a heavy workload, as the following notice shows, although the organist would not of course have played at all these services.

> ST PAUL'S CHURCH. – Holy Eucharist at 7, 8 and 12. Matins (Matin in F) at 11, Preacher – The Vicar. Holy Baptism at 2. Litany at 5.15, Children's Service at 2.15. Men's Service at 3. Preacher – The Rev. C. E. Smith. Evensong (Lloyd in E flat) at 6.30.[10]

He soon established himself in the town. Within a few years he had formed his own Orchestral Society. He was sometimes piano accompanist at concerts promoted by other organisations in the Corn Exchange. And he sometimes conducted the local opera company that existed in Bedford in the mid-1890s.[11] A year before his appointment as conductor of the Bedford Musical Society, he was appointed director of music at Bedford Grammar School. Soon afterwards, he was appointed to a similar post at the High School for Girls.[12]

The first time Harry Harding is mentioned in connection with the Musical Society is in the minutes of the 1900 annual general meeting, when Philip Diemer said that he hoped it would be possible to secure his appointment as co-conductor. Philip Diemer had already consulted Harry Harding prior to the meeting and learnt that he would be pleased to co-operate in the manner suggested. The annual general meeting was adjourned to enable the committee to meet him, which they did a few days later. Philip Diemer also agreed in discussions that Harry Harding's own Orchestral Society should merge with the Bedford Musical Society.[13] The annual general meeting was reconvened later, and Harry Harding was duly elected. Although joint-conductor, he was to make his mark very quickly on the Society. Among the initial proposals he put forward were the creation of the post of treasurer as distinct from that of secretary, the appointment of Arthur. F. Parris as deputy organist and the holding of a grand performance of Mendelssohn's *Elijah* in November.[14]

9 *Bedfordshire Times and Independent,* 13 April 1889, p. 5.

10 *Bedfordshire Times and Independent,* 3 April 1898, p. 5.

11 E.g. an advertisement in the *Bedfordshire Times and Independent,* 10 March 1894, p. 5, and also the review of *Cavalleria Rusticana*, one of the operas being performed, in the *Bedfordshire Times and Independent,* 2 June 1894, p. 7.

12 *Bedfordshire Times and Independent,* 31 October 1930, p. 9.

13 This resulted in thirty-five new orchestral players for the Musical Society. In addition, some fifty new vocalists joined. It is not clear where they came from. The extra instrumentalists and vocalists are referred to at the end of the *Bedfordshire Times and Independent's* review of the concert played on the new organ in the Corn Exchange by Henry Rose. *Bedfordshire Times and Independent*, 19 October 1900, p. 6.

14 Rule 4 was amended to read 'joint-conductors' at the annual general meeting. *Minute Book 1893–1900*, 26 June 1900, BLARS X817/1/2.

Bedford Musical Society concerts, 1900–10

The first concert Harry Harding conducted after his appointment was the performance of *Elijah* that he had proposed. This was held towards the end of November 1900, a month after the opening of the Corn Exchange organ. Philip Diemer conducted the first half, and Harry Harding conducted the second half. Harry Harding had taken all the rehearsals of both choir and orchestra. The reviewer thought he had had a positive effect on the choir.[15]

Mr A. Beagley, the very talented amateur baritone, was one of the local singers who joined the professional soloists in the double quartet 'For He Shall Give His Angels'. Mr Beagley and his brother were proprietors of J. & A. Beagley, 'Tailors etc, and specialists in dress wear', a well-known shop in the town. They were both enthusiastic members of the Musical Society and served on the committee for a number of years.[16]

Among the instrumentalists was the professional double-bass player, Mr E. Carrodus. His father was the well-known violin teacher J. T. Carrodus, author of *How to Play the Violin: Chats with Violinists*, published in 1895.[17] Despite some reservations about the orchestra, the performance was an auspicious start for the new conductor: 'There were little hitches and wanderings in the instruments occasionally, but this will probably soon be remedied with renewed united practice. We could not help specially noting the first violins, with their talented leader, Mr. Halfpenny. They did splendidly throughout and never failed at critical moments. The 'cello, oboe and flute accompaniments were most admirably given and the brass were effective *when not too boisterous or unsteady*.'[18]

The second concert in which Harry Harding participated was in February 1901. This included Parry's magnificent eight part setting of John Milton's well-known ode *Blest Pair of Sirens* and Mendelssohn's Symphony No. 3, or 'Scotch Symphony'

15 'The performance of Mendelssohn's grand oratorio (Elijah) was worthy of the occasion. The choir and orchestra have been largely augmented, and great pains have been taken to raise their work to a standard of excellence. In the opening chorus 'Help, Lord' the first burst of choral harmony showed improvement in the choir. There was more precision and spontaneity, and a much fuller tone than formerly ... In the first part, the best chorus was 'Thanks be to God' and this was splendidly rendered and roused the enthusiasm of the audience. Mr. Diemer had all his forces admirably in hand throughout this chorus and well merited was the loud applause that followed.' Of Dr Harding's conducting, the reviewer notes: 'Dr. Harding ... took the Chorus at the change of tempo, unusually quickly, and it was surprising that the singers kept up the pace. Other choruses especially deserving note were 'He, watching over Israel' (certainly one of the gems of the evening), 'Holy, Holy, Holy' and 'Then did Elijah', though this last ran rather riotously and vaguely in the 'whirlwind'.' *Bedfordshire Times and Independent,* 30 November 1900, p. 6

16 Mr A. Beagley was presented with a Sheffield plate coffee tray, with the congratulations of his fellow members on the completion of forty years loyal and efficient membership of the Musical Society at the last practice of the1922/23 season. The presentation was made by the honorary conductor who thanked him for all he had done for the Society. Details of this are included in the secretary's report of the 1923 annual general meeting. *Bedfordshire Times and Independent*, 6 July 1923, p. 8.

17 J. T. Carrodus died in 1895, a few months before the book was published. In the preface, written by Henry Saint-George, there is a reference to Mr Carrodus's legacy: 'We have one thing to be thankful for out his large family, five sons are active members of the musical profession. Two are violinists and the other three are, respectively, a 'cellist, a contrabassist and a flautist.' The contra-bassist referred to is Mr E. Carrodus, who played with the Bedford Musical Society throughout the years that Harry Harding was conductor. He presumably was a London professional. J. T. Carrodus's book, *How to Play the Violin: Chats with Violinists* (London, 1895) was published by The Strad Library.

18 *Bedfordshire Times and Independent,* 30 November 1900, p. 6.

(as both the *Bedfordshire Times and Independent* and *The Bedfordshire Standard* call it).[19] Other works included Professor Stanford's *The Last Post* – Stanford was not knighted until the following year. This was played in memory of Queen Victoria, who had died a month earlier on 22 January. The reviewer had no reservations about the orchestra's playing at this concert.[20]

Harry Harding's ability as a very capable choral trainer was also noted in this review: '[he] knows what effects he wants, and is able to get them from his loyal players and singers. There is a unity in the work of the Society, an alert and intelligent unity, which speaks volumes for the work done at rehearsals and the sympathy established between the members and the conductor.'[21] The reviewer's comments of the next concert, *The Golden Legend*, in May 1901 were very much in the same vein.[22]

Harry Harding rehearsed with the Musical Society twice a week, once with the chorus and once with the orchestra. Rehearsals for the chorus were held on Tuesday evenings at the Working Men's Institute (now the Guildhouse) in Harpur Street throughout this period. Additional Wednesday rehearsals were held in the daytime for those living outside Bedford. Harry Harding took rehearsals himself. A final full rehearsal was always held the evening before the concert.

The first performance in Bedford of a choral work by Elgar, aged forty-four at the time, was at the Musical Society's November 1901 concert, when *The Banner of St George* was sung. This short cantata had been composed for the Diamond Jubilee of Queen Victoria in 1897. The words of the ballad were by a Mr Shapcott Wensley of Bristol.[23] The reviewer comments that: 'Under the able conductorship of Dr. Harding, this highly artistic piece of work was excellently performed from beginning to end.'[24] A month later, Elgar's *Caractacus* was performed in Bedford's Corn Exchange at the 'Second Musical Festival'. It was conducted by Henry Tiltman, organist at St Martin's church.[25] The singers were local, but Fransellas' Select Orchestra came from London. The Musical Society was not involved with this performance. Albert Mallinson's *Tegner's Drapa* was also performed, and for this work the composer played the organ.[26]

The main work in May 1902 was the twenty-six year-old Coleridge-Taylor's *The Blind Girl of Castél-Cuillé*, a setting of Henry Wadsworth Longfellow's poem.

19 Parry's *Blest Pair of Sirens* was conducted by Philip Diemer.

20 'It was undoubtedly the orchestra's night … and they made the most of their opportunity. From Dr. Harding down to the drums they revelled in the music so happily selected … Mr. Halfpenny, who, of course led the violins, was evidently enjoying himself.' *Bedfordshire Times and Independent,* 19 February 1901, p. 5.

21 Ibid.

22 'Even to the casual listener, the results of his hard work must have been apparent many a time – in the exquisitely sung chorus 'O pure heart' … and the triumphal choral epilogue … it seemed to us that the chorus improved as the work progressed. The sopranos were weak, decidedly weak, in the Prologue.' *Bedfordshire Times and Independent*, 24 May 1901, p. 6.

23 Northrop Moore, *Edward Elgar,* p. 219.

24 *Bedfordshire Times and Independent,* 22 November 1901, p. 5.

25 *Bedfordshire Times and Independent,* 27 December 1901, p. 5.

26 James Albert Mallinson was born in Leeds. He was an organist and composer, and from 1904 was organist at the English church in Dresden.

Agnes Nicholls was to have been one of the soloists but was unwell.[27] The concert ended with Dr Elgar's (as he then was) *Pomp and Circumstance.*

Arthur Parris was appointed as accompanist for rehearsals in September 1902 on the recommendation of Harry Harding, taking over from Mr E. Bandey. Arthur Parris was, for many years, organist at the chapel of the Bedford County Hospital (now known as South Wing). He was also organist of St Leonard's church in Victoria Road (near the hospital) and subsequently organist of St John's church, Bedford.[28] He was to become a prominent musician in the town in the 1920s, and he had a very important role in the events described in the chapter five.

In the review of the performance of Mascagni's *Cavalleria Rusticana* and Elgar's *Coronation Ode* in November 1902, the reviewer comments: 'there was a marked improvement in the general work of the Society since last season.'[29] 'Improvement' was a word used regularly in reviews at this time, but it is questionable how far real improvement occurred. The orchestra for this concert was also complimented: 'this orchestra has perhaps never been heard to do better.'[30]

The first of a number of prominent composers who came to conduct their own works during Harry Harding's period as conductor was Sir Frederick Bridge. He was organist of Westminster Abbey 1882–1918, and was popularly known as 'Westminster Bridge'.[31] He was a very prominent musician and musicologist of the period. His first visit to Bedford was in February 1903 to conduct his composition *The Forging of the Anchor,* which was based on Samuel Ferguson's poem – his best known – of the same name. Bridge had composed this for the 1901 Gloucester Musical Festival (the Three Choirs Festival). The reviewer, who refers to Bridge by his nickname, writes of the performance: 'it is vigorous, picturesque and thoroughly dramatic. Both band and chorus rose to the occasion and entered into the spirit of the music admirably … As a result, the enthusiastic reception given to the composer when he appeared to conduct his work was quite outdone by the ovation accorded to him at its close.'[32]

At the final rehearsal for the performance of Mendelssohn's *St Paul* in May 1903, there was a near disaster. A new chorus platform had been constructed following the installation of the organ in the Corn Exchange three and a half years earlier. The combined weight of the organ and the new platform eventually proved too much for the supporting beams in the Corn Exchange. The report in the *Bedfordshire Times and Independent* is quite dramatic:

> On Tuesday afternoon, about 4.30, the Secretary of the Bedford Musical Society (Mr. Pacey) was told by the Borough Surveyor's Assistant that he had been

27 Later that year she sang in a performance of *The Dream of Gerontius* at Sheffield. Jerrold Northrop Moore writes: 'a young soprano who made a deep impression, was Agnes Nicholls.' Northrop Moore, *Edward Elgar*, p. 502.

28 Both the old hospital chapel and St Leonard's church have now been demolished.

29 *Bedfordshire Times and Independent,* 14 November 1901, p. 5.

30 Ibid.

31 Bridge's predecessor, James Turle, was organist of Westminster Abbey 1831–78, though was released from active duty in 1875 when Bridge, who was his assistant, effectively took over. On the death of Turle in 1882, Bridge succeeded to the full title. He retired in 1918. 'He [Bridge] was a notoriously indifferent organist, but for 20 years he had the advantage of an outstandingly brilliant assistant, Walter G. Alcock.' *New Grove*, vol. 4, p. 349.

32 *Bedfordshire Times and Independent,* 29 February 1903, p. 6.

examining the beams in the room beneath the platform and considered them unsafe. The night before at the full rehearsal, when the orchestra were present some of the beams gave ¾ inch. Mr. Pacey consulted Dr. Harding, who was on the spot, and he immediately decided that the platform must be shored up with timbers. Messrs. Freshwater's men were set to work, and by the time of the opening of the hall at 7 p.m., it was safe to proceed with the concert. It seems probable that the sagging is in great part due to the placing of the organ (weighing about 11 tons) on the platform without providing any additional support. What might have been a very grave catastrophe was averted by the prompt action taken by Dr. Harding.[33]

The performance of *St Paul* does not seem to have been up to scratch.[34]

Harry Harding's own composition, the unattractively named *Mucius Scaevola*, for male voices, soloists and orchestra, was performed in February 1904. It was repeated two years later. Mr J. Beagley was a soloist in both performances. Of the latter performance, the critic noted that he sang the music that the Herald sings on the discovery of Mucius in Porsenna's camp with great success.[35]

Later in the year, in November, the Musical Society performed Sir Alexander Mackenzie's *The Dream of Jubal*. Mackenzie was a major composer in the last years of the nineteenth century, though his works are largely forgotten now. He was appointed principal of the Royal Academy of Music on the death of Sir George Macfarren in 1888 and conductor of the Philharmonic Society in 1892. He numbered Hans von Bülow and Franz Liszt amongst his friends. The *Dream of Jubal* conflates two mythical accounts of the origin of the invention of the lyre and the pipe. Hermes invented the lyre using a tortoise shell and the pipe from reeds.[36] The Biblical account in chapter four of Genesis, from which the cantata gets its title, states that Jubal: 'was the father of all those who play the lyre and pipe'.[37] In the cantata Jubal sees the future development of his art and hears a variety of forms of music. When he awakes, he dedicates his shell to God, calling on future generations, 'to invoke with sounding praise this holy art.' Even the *Bedfordshire Times and Independent's* reviewer seems to have had problems understanding how the Greek myth and the biblical story are fused. The lyricist of *The Dream of Jubal* was Joseph Bennett, a well-known critic and *litterateur* of the time.

Samuel Coleridge-Taylor, also a prominent composer, conducted the Musical Society in February 1905. The subsequent review says:

The place of honour on Tuesday night was given to Mr. S. Coleridge-Taylor who came to Bedford for the first time, and conducted both his *Three Choral*

33 *Bedfordshire Times and Independent*, 15 May 1903, p. 5.

34 'The chorus were occasionally halting and feeble in their attack and the volume of sound from the sopranos was nothing like what it should have been from so large a number of singers. Do they all really sing? That the Society can do well was shown again and again on Tuesday night, but their performance was very unequal.' Ibid. On the positive side, Mr Chetham, from a prominent Bedford musical family, is singled out for his excellent flute obbligato playing in this performance.

35 *Bedfordshire Times and Independent*, 23 February 1906, p. 6. For other references to Mr A. Beagley see reviews in the *Bedfordshire Times and Independent* 30 November 1900, p. 6; 12 February 1904, p. 6; and 17 May 1907, p. 7.

36 The myth of the invention by Hermes of the tortoise-shell lyre is retold by Robert Graves, *The Greek Myths*, vol. 1 (London, 1955), pp. 63–5.

37 Genesis 4:21, Revised Standard Version. The Authorised (King James) Version calls the pipe an organ.

> *Ballads* [*sic*] and his *Four Characteristic Waltzes*. The latter were composed by him when he was only 21. He is but 30 now, and his record is an extraordinary one for so young a man ... Mr. Coleridge-Taylor wields the conductor's baton as gracefully and effectively as the composer's pen, which is more than can be said of all composers. He was thus able to get the uttermost out of both chorus and orchestra.[38]

The May 1905 concert seems to have been a great success. The first half was given over to a complete performance of Mendelssohn's Symphony No. 2, 'The Hymn of Praise', of which the last movement, following Beethoven's precedent in his Symphony No. 9, is a choral cantata, longer than all the other three movements put together. After the extended interval there was only time for two of the five movements of Moszkowski's *Suite from Foreign Parts*. Agnes Nicholls was the soloist in both the 'Hymn of Praise' and in the Moszkowski. Of her performance in the former the reviewer wrote: 'anyone who heard the way in which Madame Agnes Nicholls sang "The night is departing, departing" and the majestic chorus that followed: It was the climax of the best concert that the Musical Society have ever given, in our experience.'[39]

Agnes Nicholls had been a boarder at Bedford High School, as had her sister, Elsie. Agnes had singing lessons from Harry Harding at the school and she also studied violin playing.[40] Elsie was a visiting mistress in elocution from 1911 until her early death after a long illness in 1924.

At this concert there was a presentation to Philip Diemer, and he used the occasion to speak about the origins of the Musical Society. The presentation began with Miss Whittle giving Mrs Diemer a handsome bouquet.[41] The high sheriff then made a speech and presented Philip Diemer with a testimonial and a casket containing one hundred and ten guineas. The photograph taken at the presentation shows well-known members of the Musical Society in the centre of the stage, including a relatively youthful looking Harry Harding (then aged forty-eight), Mr and Mrs Diemer, Dr Skelding and Mr C. E. Halliley.[42] There are also a number of local celebrities including Mr W. L. Fitzpatrick, the high sheriff, whose father was vicar of Holy Trinity church when the Society was founded; the mayor and mayoress; and Mr Guy Pym, MP. Oddly, there is no mention of Mrs Pym, the Musical Society's president.[43] The organ is shown in its original position, with the organ pipes in one block in the centre. Later the pipes were divided into two separate blocks with a gap in between.

38 *Bedfordshire Times and Independent*, 3 March 1905, p. 5.

39 *Bedfordshire Times and Independent*, 19 May 1905, p. 5.

40 K. M. Westaway recounts a story about Agnes Nicholls while at school: 'I remember ... when Miss E. Roberts came out of the hall into the little staff-room saying "Have you heard Helen Nicholls' voice? You must come and listen: she is in the front row of the singing class". There she stood, I can see her now, so young and fresh and smiling – she was a new girl then and called "Helen" not "Agnes" at school. How little we knew the really great artist she was to become.' Westaway, *A History of Bedford High School*, p. 35.

41 *Bedfordshire Times and Independent*, 19 May 1905, p. 5.

42 BLARS Z160/932.

43 Mrs Guy Pym was elected president of the Society at the same time that Harry Harding was appointed conductor. She did not take such an active part in the work of the Musical Society as her predecessor, Sir Frederick Howard, or her successor, Mr W. H. Allen, did. The fact that the committee remained all-male until 1913 is one possible reason that may have had a bearing on this.

The next concert, in November 1905, was a performance of Elgar's *King Olaf*, for which there were approximately 250 performers of whom sixty-nine were orchestral players. It is interesting to consider how all these performers managed to fit on the platform. The first performance of this early Elgar work had taken place nine years before, at the North Staffordshire Festival in Hanley, Stoke on Trent. The story is about the triumph of the Christian faith over the old religion of Norway; the gods Thor and Odin are overcome with force. The soloists at the performance included Fanny Chetham, a local singer. The critic commended the conductor for his work with the chorus, which resulted in such a good a performance of a very difficult work and was obviously very taken with the chorus 'A Little Bird in the Air'.[44]

Frederic Cowen, the well-known conductor and composer, came to conduct his own work, *John Gilpin*, in May 1906. The *Bedfordshire Times and Independent's* review opens thus:

> Dr. Cowen was in a way the hero of the evening at the Bedford Musical Society's concert on Tuesday. There is evidently a great desire to see the composer of so many well-known songs, cantatas, operas, etc. ... He received a warm welcome and at once settled down to conduct his orchestral suite *In Fairyland*, which begins with a 'March of the Giants' grotesquely pompous and ponderous ... the performance was an extremely interesting one and the orchestra did brilliantly. '*John Gilpin*' is familiar to us all and most of us were curious to see what Dr. Cowen had made of Cowper's ballad. Once again, the ingenuity of his orchestral effects was manifested ... moving wheels, rattling stones and a cracking whip ... The humour and the cleverness of the music were most spiritedly brought out by the orchestra and it was probably in comparison with their excellence that the singing of the Chorus seemed a little lacking in vigour and 'go'.[45]

The generous review also included praise of the soloist, Frederica Richardson.[46]

The *Bedfordshire Times and Independent's* report of the June 1906 annual general meeting, in which future concerts are previewed, contains errors in the secretary's report in reference to one of the soloists engaged for the concert in November that year: 'For the November concert they were departing from the usual procedure and had engaged Bacchus, the great violinist, at considerable expense and, he added, "you must back us up (laughter)".'[47] Bedford was not to be blessed with the god of wine, but by Wilhelm Backhaus, then a twenty-two year-old German pianist. This error, which seems rather comical today, probably occurred because the reporter would have been familiar with Henry Bacchus, the Bedford High Street ironmonger, whose shop survived, roughly where Wilkinson's store now is, until the 1960s.

[44] For this concert, Mr W. T. Baker, Stationer and Printer (St Mary's Printing Works), St Mary's Street, Bedford, organised the tickets and seating arrangements. Mr Baker also printed the concert programmes and (at his own risk) the books of words.

[45] *Bedfordshire Times and Independent,* 18 May 1906, p. 6.

[46] 'One of the greatest pleasures of a very pleasant evening was the singing of Miss Frederica Richardson who has a voice of beautiful tone and of most sympathetic quality. She knows exactly what she can do and is artist enough to restrain herself within those limits ... the mystic vagueness of *For a Dream's sake*, the dainty playfulness of *Snowflakes* (these two being Dr. Cowen's songs, accompanied most beautifully by the composer) all made an encore inevitable.' Ibid.

[47] *Bedfordshire Times and Independent,* 22 June 1906, p. 8.

The concert included only two choral works, Brahms's *Song of Destiny* and Sullivan's part-song 'Evening Hymn'. Backhaus played solo works, which included Rachmaninoff's Prelude in C Sharp Minor – not C Minor, the reviewer points out, as erroneously stated in the book of words. He also played Liszt's *La Campanella*, Handel's 'The Harmonious Blacksmith', Mendelssohn's *Rondo Capriccioso* and several pieces by Chopin: 'each was the performance of a master – that of a veritable giant among contemporary players: his technique and clearness of expression, combined with a perfect touch, entitle him to the highest place in his art.'[48] Two other soloists also performed: 'Herr Sebald, who is probably the greatest Paganini player of the day and Miss Lhombino, the Norwegian soprano.'[49]

Agnes Nicholls sang again with the Musical Society in a miscellaneous concert in February 1907, a few months after she had sung the part of Mary, the role that Elgar created for her, in the first performance of *The Kingdom*.[50] The reviewer wrote enthusiastically about her performance in the Bedford concert noting the 'silver purity of tone'.[51]

Before the start of *Elijah*, in May 1907, the new president, William Henry Allen, presented Edward Halfpenny with a silver bowl to celebrate his twenty-five years as leader of the orchestra.[52] Aubrey Brain, father of the well-known horn player Dennis Brain, played in this performance, and at a number of subsequent Musical Society concerts.[53] The performance received a somewhat ambivalent review, although the bass singer, Charles Knowles, was praised.[54]

48 *Bedfordshire Times and Independent*, 30 November 1906, p. 5.

49 Ibid.

50 Northrop Moore, wrote: 'The singing of Agnes Nicholls, who was to create the role at Birmingham, could soar effortlessly over scoring that would rival the magnificence of the orchestral Prelude to this oratorio, as she sang: "The Gospel of the Kingdom shall be preached in the whole world".' Northrop Moore, *Edward Elgar*, p. 502. The first performance of *The Kingdom* took place in Birmingham Town Hall on 4 October 1906.

51 'After the first overture came the heroine of the evening, Miss Agnes Nicholls, and on this and at her every appearance, she was most warmly welcomed. Despite a cold, she was in splendid voice, and Mozart's beautiful air, *Non mi dir* was perfectly sung. The ease with which the florid passages were taken, the silver purity of tone, the admirable expression, all marked the great singer. For most of those present, perhaps, the solo parts of Mendelssohn's *Hear my prayer* were still more enjoyable.' *Bedfordshire Times and Independent*, 17 May 1907, p. 7.

52 The bowl had the following inscription: 'Presented to Edward Halfpenny by the members of the Bedford Musical Society as a token of their appreciation of his valuable professional services rendered during the last 25 years.' *Bedfordshire Times and Independent*, 17 May 1907, p. 7. At the 1907 annual general meeting, it was stated that W. H. Allen had been elected at the start of the season in place of Mrs Guy Pym, who at the great regret of the committee had resigned after many years. William Allen was more actively involved with the Society than Mrs Guy Pym had been.

53 '[Aubrey] Brain had an astonishing mastery of the horn, an exceptionally fine tone and a restrained and pure style ... While with the BBC SO he appeared frequently as a soloist and made several notable recordings, that of Mozart's Concerto K447 being particularly fine.' Brain was professor of horn at the Royal Academy of Music from 1923 until his death. *New Grove*, vol. 4, p. 230.

54 The reviewer wrote: 'Of course, as Elijah, he [Mr Charles Knowles] had the most work to do and he did it very energetically and with fine, strong dramatic effect. The more vigorous the music, the better he sang. It was in the quieter passages that a slight vocal roughness appeared, but "Is not his word like a fire?" and all the Mount Carmel music was extremely well rendered.' And of the performance: 'We still look on the chorus as marvellously improved in recent years, particularly in the sopranos and tenors. The basses and contraltos retain their fine tone and quality and the other parts have immensely improved. They did excellently on Tuesday, but frequently, it was hard and sometimes impossible to catch the leads and there was a certain amount of raggedness at times.' *Bedfordshire Times and Independent*, 17 May 1907, p. 7.

The president, W. H. Allen (1844–1926), was the founder of the engineering company that bore his name and whose works used to overlook Bedford railway station. At the 1907 annual general meeting, Harry Harding said of him:

> In musical matters, they had a sympathetic President, and in talking to him on musical subjects … he understood what they were talking about … With Mr. Allen at the helm, they had no trouble in respect of finance and his liberality had been very marked, but in musical and other matters they had a President who took the greatest interest in the Society and he had taken that interest ever since he lived in Bedford. Mr. Allen said it was a very great pleasure to belong to the society. His life had been mixed up with music ever since he was child. Everybody knew that music was part of the life of every Welshman. He was brought up among the collieries of Carmarthenshire, where men, instead of drinking, spent their time in getting out musical scores and no music hall songs ever entered their minds. Choirs were got up for the purpose of contending in the Eisteddfod, and there was not a child in that village who could not sing the Messiah music. It had also been his lot to live near the Abbey and hear a great deal of music through his friend Dr. Bridge, who was a great admirer of Dr. Harding'[55]

And at the annual general meeting two years later, in 1909, Harry Harding said that William Allen was an ideal president. He was always so practical and so sympathetic with music. And he was no mean musician, as those who had heard him rolling out the tones of his beautiful organ at Bromham would testify.[56] William Allen replied, saying that he had heard nearly all the choral societies of the big towns of England and did not think that any of them gave greater pleasure than that of Bedford.[57] He was appreciative, and much appreciated, and remained president of the Musical Society until 1922.

Parry's *The Pied Piper of Hamelin* was performed at the next concert, in November 1907. Parry had composed much of this setting of Robert Browning's humorous ballad in the early 1890s, but withdrew it when a pupil, Richard Walthew, used the same text and his composition enjoyed some success. Parry unearthed his own setting in 1905, and with A. J. Jaeger's support and encouragement it was published in time for performance at the Norwich Festival in October of the same year.[58] It subsequently became quite popular and remained so until the 1930s when, like so many Victorian and Edwardian choral works, it went out of favour.[59] It was, therefore, a very new work when the Musical Society performed it.

The chorus narrate the story. The Pied Piper is represented by a tenor soloist and the mayor by a bass. The long and erudite *Bedfordshire Times and Independent's* review analyses Parry's use of Browning's ballad from which ninety lines, approximately one third, are omitted. Then there is a description of: 'the most striking touches of the musician's humour – melodic, harmonic and instrumental.'[60]

55 *Bedfordshire Times and Independent,* 28 June 1907, p. 8.
56 A photograph of William Allen playing the organ in the hall of Bromham House in 1903 is held by Bedfordshire and Luton Archives and Records Service. BLARS Z50/21/27.
57 *Bedfordshire Times and Independent,* 25 June 1909, p. 7.
58 A. J Jaeger, who worked for Novello's, is best remembered for his work as Elgar's publisher. He is immortalised as Nimrod in Elgar's *Enigma Variations*.
59 Jeremy Dibble, *C. Hubert H. Parry: His Life and Music* (Oxford, 1992), p. 407.
60 *Bedfordshire Times and Independent*, 22 November 1907, p. 6.

The reviewer is, perhaps, surprised that the solid and sometimes scholarly British composer is able to compose humorously. But there is nothing in the review about the Bedford performance – its strengths and weaknesses – or of the soloists' performances. The other work in the concert, also analysed at some length, was *Finlandia*, by the then forty-two year-old Sibelius.

In November 1908, two years after Wilhelm Backhaus's visit to Bedford, the well-known pianist and composer, Ferruccio Benvenuto Busoni performed with the Musical Society. His performance in Bedford is not given prominence in the review. This extract comes towards the end of the report: 'The special engagement of the great pianist, Signor Busoni, lent additional distinction to the evening and every solo he gave – with encores, these came to a generous number of eight – was rapturously applauded, and he was recalled again and again.'[61]

This concert was otherwise mainly orchestral. It included what the reviewer calls Sibelius's 'weird' waltz, the *Valse Triste* from *Kuolema,* and part of Bruch's Violin Concerto No.1.[62] The choir sang two Brahms's part-songs, "In Silent Night' and "Love, Fare Thee Well', and Parry's *Blest Pair of Sirens*.

There is some vivid, descriptive writing in the review of Handel's *Israel in Egypt*, performed in May 1909. The contralto, singing for the first time in Bedford, had to sing about some 'nasty details' in one of the arias: 'Miss Effie Martyn … had a trying ordeal to endure. She is a London professional but lives in Bedford and this was her first public appearance in the town. The situation was not rendered more easy by the music which fell to her at the beginning of a trying recitative, and the air "Their land brought forth frogs" which degenerates into nasty details about the "blotches" and "blains" that fell upon the Egyptian men and beasts ... she won the warm applause of the audience. She has a true contralto voice beautifully trained and perfectly managed.'[63]

Sir Charles Villiers Stanford came to conduct some of his own music in Bedford in February 1910.[64] By this time, Elgar and a number of younger English composers (several of whom had been Stanford's pupils at the Royal College of Music) were preferred to Stanford, whose music was rather going out of fashion. His Symphony No. 6, for example, which was premiered in 1905, received only one more performance before succumbing to eighty years of oblivion. However, some of Stanford's other music, notably his choral works, *Songs of the Sea* and *Songs of the Fleet*,

[61] It continues: 'He gave Bach's and his own *Fugue in D*; Chopin's *Scherzo Polonaise in A flat* (etc); and Liszt's *St. Francis preaching the birds* and *St Francis walking on the water*. Of faultless technique, his playing was also distinguished by a firm attack, combined with a delicacy and sensitiveness that was particularly marked in the rendering of tender passages. He seemed to caress the music from the keys. *Bedfordshire Times and Independent*, 27 November 1908, p. 5.

[62] The *Valse Triste* was originally composed in 1903 for string orchestra as one of six items of incidental music for a play *Kuolema* (Death), and revised for full orchestra in 1904. Only the *Valse Triste* is now commonly played.

[63] *Bedfordshire Times and Independent,* 21 May 1909, p. 8.

[64] In his biography of Stanford, Jeremy Dibble writes: 'Visits to the provinces were now a rarer event. Apart from invitations to conduct at the Three Choirs Festival, he made one visit to Birmingham in March 1908 and another to Liverpool in March 1909 to conduct his Irish Symphony. The following year, he was invited to conduct "Ode to Discord" at the rapidly expanding Brighton Festival and as a guest at the Dover Music Festival to direct a revival of "The Battle of the Baltic". However, with more established works, Stanford was content to attend performances of his music rather than take the baton.' Jeremy Dibble, *Charles Villiers Stanford: Man and Musician* (Oxford 2002), p. 386.

remained popular. And his church music – especially his settings of the canticles and some of his anthems – continued to be some of the finest written for the Anglican church. They are still regularly sung in English cathedrals and some parish churches. There is a slip-up in the review when Stanford (who was knighted in 1901) was referred to as Mr Charles Stanford.

The Bedford concert included *Songs of the Sea* and two of Stanford's Irish songs in the first half, 'The Fairy Lough' and 'The Alarm', sung by the bass soloist Harry Plunket Greene. In the second half, Stanford's *Irish Rhapsody No.1* was included. An Irish air, 'When She Answered Me', and 'Trotting to the Fair' (these last two arranged and orchestrated by Stanford) were the final items.[65] Plunket Greene was Parry's son-in-law and was a well-known singer in his day.[66] After some early operatic performances he had confined himself to oratorio and songs. Of this, his first visit to Bedford, the reviewer wrote: 'Mr. Greene is nothing but a genius. There may be singers with better voices but none who can excel him in dramatic force and artistic finish. He sings with complete absorption in the music. He sees the sense, he thrills with the passion he depicts. He is the thing he sings about. It is the gift of the supreme artist.'[67] Stanford was 'enthusiastically received', but the most rapturous applause was reserved for Harry Plunket Greene who seems to have upstaged him. At the end of the concert Plunket Greene was encored twice, at the risk of losing the last train back to London.

Organisation and administration, 1900–10

Harry Harding usually took the chair at the committee meetings for which there is a record 1900–04. Mrs Guy Pym, the president during this period, does not seem to have taken a very active part in the running of the Society.

The honorary secretary and treasurer in 1900 was Henry Pacey, and the minutes in the *Minute Book 1900–04* were written mostly by him.[68] His minutes are long and detailed, but lack the succinctness of earlier secretaries. A substantial proportion of the *Minute Book* is taken up with the names of applicants for membership, successful applicants and financial statements following concerts. The *Bedfordshire Times and Independent* reports of annual general meetings continued to be pasted into the *Minute Book*, as had happened in the 1890s, in place of the handwritten minutes of the secretary. The final committee report in the *Minute Book* for this period is for a meeting held in May 1904, a month before the 1904 annual general meeting. The *Minute Books* 1904–41 do not survive.[69]

In 1900, the secretary's role was split, as Harry Harding had suggested on his appointment. Mr C. Elton Halliley, a prominent solicitor in the town, was appointed

65 *Bedfordshire Times and Independent*, 11 February 1910, p. 5.

66 Harry Plunket Greene wrote the outstanding work about song recitals, entitled *Interpretation in Song* (London, 1912). He was the original bass soloist in the first performance of *The Dream of Gerontius*, which the Bedford Musical Society was shortly to perform.

67 *Bedfordshire Times and Independent*, 11 February 1910, p. 5.

68 *Minute Book 1900–04*, BLARS X817/1/3.

69 A possible explanation of why the *Minute Books* were lost is that when the Musical Society was disbanded, the then secretary, Harvey Goldsmith, took them with him when he moved to the East Coast. He died in Aldeburgh in 1940.

treasurer and held the post until 1912. Mr C. E. Halliley was for some years church warden of St Peter's church, Bedford.[70]

Dr George Harvey Goldsmith, the secretary 1904–32, was an ophthalmic surgeon and practised in Harpur Street. He later moved to another address in Harpur Street, number twenty-three on the east side of (lower) Harpur Street.[71] Harvey Goldsmith was churchwarden at St Paul's church for many years, where, of course, Harry Harding was organist.

Annual general meetings were held in June or July and were usually reported in full in the *Bedfordshire Times and Independent*. However, in 1902 there was only a very brief report, and in 1911 there was no report of the meeting, as the news was dominated by the coronation of King George V. The Musical Society's financial position was given much prominence in the newspaper reports, for example, in June 1906, when details of annual income and expenditure were presented by Mr C. E. Halliley:

> notwithstanding a record year for subscriptions for seats and tickets sold and money taken at doors, there was a loss of £19 16s. 4d. on the concerts of the season. Of the total income of £240, subscriptions for seats amounted to £135 7s., and tickets, etc. sold £96 17s. 6d. The concert expenditure totalled £259 11s. 2d., of which £150 18s. 6d. was for professional assistance, £16 for erecting platform and £25 4s. 3d. for hire of music and performing rights. On the general account appeared a credit balance of £35 0s. 4d.[72]

The surplus (balance in hand) of £35 was typical. Over the next three years, the balance in hand went from £30 11s 2d in 1907 to £7 10s 9d in 1909.

The unsatisfactory nature of the Corn Exchange, despite the installation of the organ, was also regularly discussed at annual general meetings. In 1906, for example, Philip Diemer stated that: 'soon they would have to face the question of a better room. It had been wanted in the town for many years, and now that the Society had become so large, the whole hall would soon be taken up by the performers. Dr. Harding had done such wonders, and he (Mr. Diemer) was proud to feel that their little Society which began in that room with half-a-dozen members, had now grown to such dimensions that the Corn Exchange could not hold it.'[73] In 1908, Harvey Goldsmith lamented that many of those desirous of becoming performing members were refused admittance, owing to lack of seating accommodation on the platform. Criticism was not confined to annual general meetings. The reviewer of the Mendelssohn centenary concert in February 1909 – a big occasion – also refers to the problem in a forthright manner:

[70] Mr C. E. Halliley is one of the named singers at the Grammar School concert that Philip Diemer conducted in 1867, referred to in chapter two. His name appears on a few of the peal boards in the ringing chamber at St Peter's church, Bedford, as the names of the current incumbent and of the churchwardens are nearly always given on these.

[71] Joe Pinnock, who sang with the Musical Society until approximately 2000, remembered seeing Harvey Goldsmith as a patient who gave him his first prescription for spectacles in the early 1920s. Joe Pinnock, *Reminiscences*, 4 November 1989, letter in author's collection. See also Harvey Goldsmith's obituary in *The Bedfordshire Times and Bedfordshire Standard*, 24 May 1940, p. 7

[72] *Bedfordshire Times and Independent*, 22 June 1906, p. 8.

[73] Ibid.

> Never, perhaps was Bedford's need of a suitable Concert Hall felt more than on Tuesday night. Probably if there had been double the accommodation it would have been taken. Some days ago, all the seats were booked. On Tuesday, at the back of the reserved seats, there was a close band of people content to stand through the concert and for a long while beforehand. How many had to be turned away no one knows, exactly. There were some Town Councillors present and perhaps they will take the suggestion offered by this state of things and ponder it well in connection with the Castle Close proposal. Sooner or later, Bedford must have a proper Concert Hall. Where is this site to be found?[74]

Concerts 1910–14, the middle years

The year 1910 marks a turning point for the Musical Society as it was their first performance of one the great Elgar oratorios, *The Dream of Gerontius*. In the years immediately after the war, these big Elgar works were to be a significant part of the Society's musical output, and the performances for which Harry Harding was perhaps best remembered. The standard of the chorus must have been good for them to be able to tackle *The Dream of Gerontius*. Elgar completed this work in 1900, and the first performance (which went very badly) was given that same year in Birmingham City Hall.[75] Harry Harding had originally proposed that the Musical Society should perform the work in 1901, but it had been felt to be too ambitious. He did not pursue the idea, and *The Golden Legend* was performed instead. By 1910 the Musical Society was ready, and *The Dream of Gerontius* was performed in June. Harry Harding seems to have found his forte in conducting these great works of Elgar, thus enriching the Society's repertoire. There were, in fact, two performances of *The Dream of Gerontius* on successive days, one in the afternoon and one in the evening. The choir was supplemented by a semi-chorus of boys, tenors and basses from St Peter's, Eaton Square, London.

The review as a whole is a superb piece of writing. The reviewer was fulsome in his praise: 'Let it be said at once that *The Dream of Gerontius* received a worthy rendering by all the forces under the control of Dr. Harding. He and they girded themselves for a great effort, and they achieved a great triumph. We have never heard the Musical Society do anything like this … the "demon" music was wonderfully sung, while the mass and quality of the tone in the mighty hymn "Praise to the Holiest in the Height" was most inspiring and majestic … It was a magnificent performance.'[76] Gervase Elwes (tenor) sang the part of Gerontius in both performances, and of him the reviewer wrote: 'Mr Gervase Elwes, we are told, has made the part of Gerontius his own. That we can understand after hearing him. The intensity of feeling he puts into it is amazing, from beginning to end. It is the spiritual force of his singing which arrests us more than anything ... when Mr. Elwes sang his confession of faith, or "My soul is in my hand: I have no fear", he sang it with his whole being.'[77]

74 *Bedfordshire Times and Independent*, 19 February 1909, p. 6. Cecil Higgins sold his Castle Close house in 1910. It seems likely that an area adjoining the Castle Close site (in front of the castle mound) was the proposed site for the new concert hall, but this site was used instead for a new roller-skating rink, which was built in 1909. For Castle Close, see Wildman, *Bedford*, p. 85.

75 For a detailed account of that first performance, see Northrop Moore, *Edward Elgar*, pp. 328–35.

76 *Bedfordshire Times and Independent,* 17 June 1910, p. 7. This review covered both concerts.

77 Ibid.

At the end of the 1909/10 season, there was a substantial financial deficit of £199 16s 5d. This was, in part, due to poor ticket sales for the afternoon performance of *The Dream of Gerontius*, resulting in a big loss. Ticket sales amounted to £77, whereas £128 would have been netted had the hall been filled. The second reason for the deficit was that the Musical Society had had to spend £100 on new instruments, owing to an alteration in the pitch of the organ.[78]

Between the *The Dream of Gerontius* and the next major work, Brahms's *German Requiem* in May 1911, there were two less demanding concerts. The first, in November 1910, was selections from parts two and three of the *Song of Hiawatha* – the *Death of Minnehaha* and *Hiawatha's Departure*. And in March 1911 there was a miscellaneous concert, which included a Scherzo and Trio by H. K. St. John Saunderson. St. John Saunderson was a local amateur musician who had provided Bedford Grammar School with several songs and the 'Harper' Waltzes under the pseudonym 'S'. The concert also included Rubinstein's Piano Concerto No. 4.

Brahms's *German Requiem* was performed at the end of May 1911. It was about this performance that the spoof preview, quoted at the beginning of the chapter, was written. The reviewer was deeply impressed by the Requiem itself and by the Musical Society's ability to perform a work of this stature.[79]

Sir Frederick Bridge conducted the Musical Society again in December 1911, when his *A Song of the English* was performed. The concert also included several short orchestral pieces. *A Song of the English* uses a poem by Kipling, 'stirring words' in the view of the reviewer. Earlier in the year, Bridge had arranged the music for the coronation of King George V, as he had in August 1902 for that of King Edward VII.

For six nights in February 1912 Cavaliere Castellano's Italian Grand Opera Company from Drury Lane Theatre, London, performed at Bedford's Royal County Theatre and Opera House (now Mount Zion Pentecostal Church). There was a different opera each night.[80] On 13 February, when *The Barber of Seville* was performed, the Musical Society performed *Elijah*. There is no reference in the review to the size of the audience and no suggestion that it was smaller than usual or that it was affected by the presence of opera in the town. Overall, the review is very favourable: 'We have never heard in Bedford so strong and virile a reading of the music.'[81]

Special augmentation was required for the Wagner concert which was given in May 1912: 'The orchestra was, of course, greatly strengthened for the occasion. There were 4 horns, 3 trumpets and 3 trombones, all we believe, members of the

78 *Bedfordshire Times and Independent*, 29 July 1910, p. 7.

79 Of the chorus's part, the reviewer writes: 'All the parts of the chorus did well, and the tenors were again and again conspicuous. It must be a very difficult work and there were signs of the strains now and again, but it was a great performance and the Society have probably never done better than on Tuesday. They sang, as Dr. Harding conducted, with an intensity of feeling which gave dignity and strength to their efforts.' *Bedfordshire Times and Independent*, 2 June 1910, p. 8.

80 The programme was as follows: Monday, *Faust*; Tuesday, *The Barber of Seville*; Wednesday, *Cavalleria Rusticana* and *I Pagliacci*; Thursday, *Rigoletto*; Friday, *Maritana*; Saturday, *Il Trovatore*.

81 *Bedfordshire Times and Independent*, 16 February 1912, p. 8.

London Symphony Orchestra, and well they played their parts.'[82] The reviewer was very complimentary about the chorus.[83]

The Musical Society's rules were changed at the 1912 annual general meeting to allow for the performance of only two concerts in the 1912/13 season. This was because Lent was very early in 1913.[84] Only two concerts were performed in 1913/14, and this pattern continued after the war. Mr C. E. Halliley stood down as treasurer in 1912, and Mr W. T. Baker was elected in his place.[85] Also at the 1912 annual general meeting, Mrs Wells proposed that three ladies be elected, after the nine performing members (all gentlemen) had been proposed. Until then, serving members of the committee had all been men. The rationale for not electing any ladies at this stage was eventually suggested by Harry Harding who deprecated turning out any of the nine existing members while the number could not be enlarged without altering the rules. At the annual general meeting the following year, the rules were amended and the committee was enlarged from nine to twelve performing members; after some good humoured discussion it was agreed that at least three members *may* (rather than *must*) be ladies. Mrs Wells, Miss Whittle and Miss Gutteridge were the first ladies duly elected to the committee.[86] Miss Gutteridge went on to become, as Harry Harding said at the 1923 annual general meeting, the Society's, 'very able Hon. Assistant Secretary'.[87]

None of the concerts for the 1912/13 and 1913/14 seasons were on as grand a scale as *The Dream of Gerontius* or the *German Requiem*. Harry Harding mooted the idea of performing another large scale work, Bach's Mass in B Minor, at the 1912 annual general meeting, but nothing came of his suggestion.

A Tale of Old Japan was performed in December 1912, three months after Coleridge-Taylor's death at the age of thirty-seven. He died from pneumonia, said to have been brought about by overwork.[88] The Bedford recital was one of the earliest performances of this work. The preview notes: 'It is a delightful work, and it is sure to be delightfully rendered. The chorus and orchestra have greatly enjoyed the rehearsals and it will be given a fine performance. Two of the soloists are those who took the solos at the first performance at Queen's Hall, when Mr Coleridge-Taylor conducted. We refer to Miss Effie Martyn (contralto) and Leah Fellissa ... This will be Miss Martyn's third appearance at a Musical Society's concert and her many friends in Bedford, which is her home, will be charmed to hear her again.'[89] The

82 *Bedfordshire Times and Independent*, 24 May 1912, p. 8.
83 'One of the most effective and attractive items of the evening was "The Spinning Chorus" from the *Flying Dutchman*. The ladies sang this brilliantly and the audience would evidently have been glad to hear it again. The tenors and basses in their turn rose gallantly to the rousing male voice chorus from *Rienzi* – "Romans, Arise"' *Bedfordshire Times and Independent*, 24 May 1912, p. 8.
84 *Bedfordshire Times and Independent,* 19 July 1912, p. 7. Easter was on 23 March. It has only been earlier once in the last 200 years – in 1818 – when it was on 22 March.
85 A number of members of the Baker family were active in the Musical Society from its earliest days. The family owned W. T. Baker's printing and stationery shop and the Post Office in St Mary's Street, Bedford.
86 *Bedfordshire Times and Independent,* 27 July 1913, p. 8.
87 *Bedfordshire Times and Independent,* 6 July 1923, p. 8.
88 *New Grove*, vol. 6, pp.101–4.
89 *Bedfordshire Times and Independent*, 6 December 1912, p. 10. Effie Martyn's previous performances in Bedford were in *Israel in Egypt* in May 1909 and *Elijah* in February 1912.

libretto for *A Tale of Old Japan* is taken from the *Collected Poems* of Alfred Noyes and is reminiscent of *Madam Butterfly*.[90] The review was fulsome in its praise.[91]

Other concerts were sometimes held in Bedford independently of the Musical Society and one of these deserves particular mention. In February 1913, Dame Nellie Melba sang not in the Corn Exchange but at the roller-skating rink.[92] The preview in the *Bedfordshire Times and Independent* explains why: 'Of all great singers, none outshine the illustrious artist who is to appear at the Castle Rink, Bedford on Tuesday evening, February 4th. For several years, Mr. A. St. V. Bannister has been endeavouring to arrange for a visit to Bedford of Madam Melba ... The reason that the Rink has been selected for the concert is that it provides seating accommodation for 3,000 people whereas the Corn Exchange has seating for only 600.'[93] The concert appears to have been a great success and, according to the review: 'Madam Melba expressed her delight at the Bedford audience.'[94] It was estimated that there were about 2,000 people present. This use of the roller-skating rink as a concert hall seems to have been a one-off.

Nina Samuell-Rose, the daughter of Clara Samuell and Henry Rose, sang at the Musical Society's March 1913 concert. This included Gounod's motet *Gallia* in which she sang the soprano part, as well as Stanford's *Songs of the Fleet*. She was a worthy successor to her mother in the opinion of the reviewer.[95]

At the end of the 1911/12 season there had been an outstanding debt of £171. It would have been more had there not been a number of donations. In November 1912, a *Cafe Chantant* was held, raising £132 10s. Together with earnings and donations, including a donation of £32 10s from the president, the Musical Society was nearly out of the red by the time of the 1913 annual general meeting. The balance still owing to the bank was only £22 14s 6d.

Another composition by Samuel Coleridge-Taylor, *Kubla Khan*, was performed in December 1913. The opening lines are some of the best known in all English poetry: 'In Xanadu did Kubla Khan, A stately pleasure-dome decree'. Samuel Taylor Coleridge claimed that he 'wrote' the poem while in a deep sleep and estimated it was not less than 200 to 300 lines altogether. But when he woke, he was at once

90 The story is about a young girl, Kimi, whose artist lover, Sawara, goes away for three years to study, and by the time he comes back he has married someone else. Kimi, meanwhile, has spurned the advances of another suitor as she was waiting for Sawara.

91 'It was a very fine performance. The chorus and orchestra entered heart and soul into the spirit of the music, and revelled in the purple passages ... The chorus was strong and well balanced with a fine round body of sound from each part.' *Bedfordshire Times and Independent*, 13 December 1912, p. 10. *The Concise Oxford Dictionary* definition of a 'purple passage' is nothing worse than an ornate or elaborate passage in a literary composition.

92 The roller-skating rink had quite a short life. The building was later divided, half being rebuilt as the Plaza Cinema (in its last few years it was known as The Nite Spot) while the other, eastern half, was first used as a garage and later as Bedford Museum. The whole building was demolished in 1982, leaving an open space between the river and the Castle Mound. See Wildman, *Bedford*, p. 73 and p. 76.

93 *Bedfordshire Times and Independent*, 24 January 1913, p. 9.

94 *Bedfordshire Times and Independent*, 7 February 1913, p. 8.

95 'Miss Nina Samuell-Rose, the gifted young soprano ... sang the lovely air "Zion's ways do languish" with great delicacy and restraint.' *Bedfordshire Times and Independent*, 28 March 1913, p. 9. Nina Samuell-Rose sang again in Mendelssohn's *St Paul* in March 1914 and in the performances of *Messiah* primarily for the troops in November 1914, shortly after the outbreak of the First World War. She is not heard of again until after the end of the war.

called out on business and did not return for more than an hour. By this time, he could not recall very much of the poem of his dream.[96]

The reviewer describes Coleridge-Taylor's *Kubla Khan* as a beautiful work, attuned to the words. It opens with an orchestral prelude, which sets the scene for the opening chorus with its famous opening line. There is a vivid description of the work with regular quotations from the original poem, and illustrations of how Coleridge-Taylor uses the orchestra and chorus to colour this. [97] The soprano soloist was Phyllis Lett who, the reviewer notes, 'delighted everybody'. The reviewer, stated, once more, that this was one of the most enjoyable and successful concerts in the long history of the Musical Society. He hoped that *Kubla Khan* would be repeated. It was – but not until after the horrors of the First World War.

The final concert before the war was a further performance of Mendelssohn's *St Paul* in March 1914. The reviewer, who is masterly, comments first on the work as a whole, then on various aspects of the performance by the chorus and orchestra and, finally, on the performance of the soloists. Mr Thorpe-Bates, the bass, is mentioned first and commended for his great fervour and expression. He sang the duet early in the work with Mr A. Beagley, the local amateur bass member of the choir. The soprano was: 'Miss Nina Samuell-Rose [who] had a great deal to do, and was fully equal to it ... she sang throughout expressively and artistically.'[98] The tenor, Mr Ripley, also had a lot to do, but by contrast the contralto, Miss Effie Martin, was not stretched. There is a final reference to the concert arrangements, which adds a touch of humour: 'As usual, Messrs. J. Bull's seating arrangements afforded satisfaction to all, except, perhaps, those who had to stand at the back.'[99]

At the annual general meeting in the middle of June, works for the next season were discussed. Harry Harding said that they could not afford to do *The Dream of Gerontius* again, though this would have been a popular choice. Other works suggested included Bantock's *Rubaiyat of Omar Khayyam* and *The Wilderness*, and Cowen's *The Rose Maiden*, none of which were thought to be suitable.[100] In the end it was agreed that the committee should decide. Who, of the committee, could have thought then that, apart from *Messiah* performed for the troops in November 1914, the next 'normal' concert would not be for another five years.

The First World War years, 1914–18

The only report of any performances by the Musical Society during the war years is of three performances of *Messiah* given on Wednesday 11, Friday 13 and Sunday

96 Samuel Taylor Coleridge, *The Works of Samuel Taylor Coleridge,* (Ware, 1994), pp. 295–7.

97 'In Phyllis Lett's first solo, the weirdness of the music was wonderfully brought out by the singer and by the accompaniment on muted strings. One could hear the "woman wailing for her demon lover" and see the chasm "with ceaseless turmoil seething" so vividly suggestive were the extraordinary chromatic passages of the orchestra ... The solo voice followed with a vision of a 'damsel with a dulcimer', while the violins sustained a pizzicato accompaniment.' The music reaches a loud climax, chorus, orchestra and soloist joined by the 'rolling thunder' or the organ and drums as the last lines of the poem are reached: 'For he on honey-dew hath fed, And drink the milk of Paradise.' *Bedfordshire Times and Independent*, 5 December 1913, p. 7.

98 *Bedfordshire Times and Independent*, 27 March 1914, p. 8.

99 Ibid.

100 Granville Bantock was a prolific composer. His music was fashionable and was widely performed in the first quarter of the twentieth century, but has subsequently fallen out of favour.

15 November 1914. The *Bedfordshire Times and Independent* records that these performances were:

> to an audience composed entirely of soldiers in khaki and kilts. There was also khaki on the platform, not only among the basses but among the soloists, for Pte Francis Blake of the 4th Camerons, sang the bass solos in uniform, an unusual and fine sight ... He had a great voice and controlled it admirably in the difficult passages of 'For he is like a refiner's fire' and 'Why do the nations so furiously rage together?'. It was strikingly appropriate at the present time to hear this magnificent air sung by a soldier in uniform.[101]

These three performances of *Messiah* were given without charge to the troops. One feature which would seem very strange to us today is that smoking was allowed: 'The Society could not do otherwise than give the work a fine rendering, in spite of the clouds of tobacco smoke which must have tried the singers somewhat.[102]

After this the Musical Society seems to have gone into hibernation. Harry Harding gave free weekly recitals on the organ in the Corn Exchange, and these are regularly reviewed in the *Bedfordshire Times and Independent*. But of the Musical Society there is not a word. Two post-war reviews make it clear that there were no other wartime performances until those of the peace celebration concert in July 1919: 'It was good to see the Musical Society back in all its glory.'[103] With the January 1920 performance of *A Tale of Old Japan*: 'The Musical Society [was], on its feet again after the long interruption of the war.'[104] The Musical Society did, however, continue to number its seasons throughout the war years – 1913/14 was the forty-seventh season and 1920/21 was referred to as the fifty-fourth season – suggesting that some activity had occurred. It is possible that the members continued to meet to sing together without giving any public concerts, but there is no evidence of this.

Concerts 1919–23

The Musical Society returned to the platform at a peace celebration concert, held on 18 July 1919. The soprano soloist was to have been Agnes Nicholls, but she must have withdrawn shortly before the concert (unless the secretary made a mistake on the earlier advertisements) and Carrie Tubb was soloist on the day.[105] The *Bedfordshire Times and Independent's* report states:

101 *Bedfordshire Times and Independent*, 13 November 1914, p. 6.

102 Ibid.

103 *Bedfordshire Times and Independent*, 25 July 1919, p. 6.

104 *Bedfordshire Times and Independent*, 30 January 1920, p. 5.

105 The advertisement for the concert in *The Bedfordshire Times and Independent*, 11 July 1919, p.1, names Agnes Nicholls as soloist. A week later, on the day of the concert, the advertisement in the paper names Carrie Tubb. *Bedfordshire Times and Independent*, 18 July 1919, p. 1. Carrie Tubb became well-known in the 1920s and 1930s, mainly as an oratorio singer, though she also undertook some operatic roles at Covent Garden with the Beecham company. She taught at Bedford High School for a short while and there is a paragraph about her, written by Patricia Burnaby in Westaway, *A History of Bedford High School*, p. 151: 'For a little while the solo singing was taught by Miss Carrie Tubb, who for many years had been well known to the School Guides as she had often been a visitor to the School camps with her great friend Miss Edith Baron; how many times, I wonder, did their caravan rest in the corner of the School's camp site. Camp fires were memorable when she was present – her rendering of "The Trampling of the Lilies" is to me quite unforgettable. Her short connection with the School was a great

> no more fitting occasion could have been chosen than the eve of Peace Celebration Day. War called leaders and members alike to other work, and they were scattered, some far afield. But happily Peace has brought the majority of them back and everything seemed just as of old in the Corn Exchange on Friday. Certainly there was a crowded audience to welcome the Society's revival ... The numbers were good and probably nobody was more pleased to welcome the many new-comers in both chorus and orchestra than the old members themselves. Dr. Harding has rallied his forces splendidly, and the very fine program [*sic*] at the first concert since the war makes one look forward to good things in the winter.[106]

The number of performers given in the concert programme was similar to that for pre-war concerts. Edward Halfpenny led the orchestra, but this seems to have been the last of the Musical Society's concerts at which he played. The opening choral work was *Vanguard 1914* by Arthur Somervell. It is inscribed: 'to the first seven Divisions, the fallen, the prisoners, the disabled and those still fighting.' The words were by Beatrice Brice. Carrie Tubb's singing of the solo parts was very beautiful according to the reviewer, especially in the closing portion (the 'Last Post'). The choral movement of Mendelssohn's Symphony No. 2, the 'Hymn of Praise', was the main work. The second half of the concert included a number of miscellaneous items including solos by Carrie Tubb and John Booth, the tenor soloist. The orchestral works played at the concert were German's *Henry VIII Suite*, Harry Harding's *Egyptian Dances*, from the incidental music to *Rhodopis,* and Sibelius's *Finlandia.* The concert ended with the 'Hallelujah Chorus'.

Nearly all the main works in the 1920/21 and 1921/22 seasons were repeats of works that had been performed before the war, *A Tale of Old Japan, Elijah, Mucius Scaevola*, *The Dream of Gerontius* and *Kubla Khan*. Possibly this was because they were familiar works, and performing them again would both help to get the chorus back in trim and attract an audience. But it might also reflect something about the conductor, Harry Harding, who was by then in his mid-sixties.

The review of the Musical Society's first 'normal' concert, in January 1920, *A Tale of Old Japan*, opens with a delightful comment: 'Coleridge-Taylor might himself have learned the art of using wonderful colours in the school of Yoichi Tenko, the painter; for he has in this work painted with masterly strokes, now hard, now soft, a glowing picture of old Japan, with its flowers and butterflies and willow-trees, and rose-white temples. With this as a background the sad tale of little Kimi, pale as a drifting blossom, is told.'[107] Arthur Parris undertook most of the preparation of the chorus, while Herbert Colson rehearsed the orchestra. The reviewer was complimentary about the chorus, although somewhat critical of the orchestra because of a lack of balance. But he was especially critical of the soprano soloist, Gwladys Naish, who gave the impression that she was far from familiar with her part. The harpist in the miscellaneous second part of the concert was Marie Goossens.[108]

inspiration and we shall ever be grateful for her generosity in the giving of a singing scholarship when she left Bedford in 1946.' Carrie Tubb lived until 1976, just reaching her hundredth birthday.

106 *Bedfordshire Times and Independent*, 25 July 1919, p. 6.

107 *Bedfordshire Times and Independent*, 30 January 1920, p. 5.

108 Marie Goossens OBE was from a musical family. Her grandfather, father and one of her elder

Elijah was performed in May 1920. The reviewer thought that there was a striking difference in the playing of the orchestra at this and at the previous concert. Of Agnes Nicholls, again one of the soloists, he wrote: 'No finer singer could have been found for the soprano part, nor could it have been sung with more uplifting effect ... Madame Nicholls gave unreservedly of her best throughout and the sense of intimacy between herself and the audience because of her being an old High School girl, added a touch of warmth to the enthusiasm with which she would have been greeted for her singing alone.'[109]

Aubrey Brain and his brother Alfred Brain, both horn players and father and uncle respectively of the more famous horn player Dennis Brain, are listed in the programme for the December 1920 performance of *Mucius Scaevola*. At this same concert, one of the violoncellos was Mr G. B. Barbirolli, in due course to be the internationally renowned conductor, Sir John Barbirolli. Mr De Choisy, a teacher at Bedford Modern School, was the principal cellist and he, rather than Mr Barbirolli, played in the Schumann Quintet movement that was included in the programme.

The Musical Society returned to the large scale works of Elgar in May 1921 with *The Dream of Gerontius*. As in 1910, there were two performances on successive nights. The advertisement states that there were 320 performers, which included the principal vocalists, band and chorus. It is hard to imagine how this number of performers managed to fit on the Corn Exchange stage, especially as some space was taken up by the organ! A large orchestra was required, and the local orchestra had to be augmented by engaging a considerable number of London professionals. A full orchestra of over fifty players was thus formed and: 'all the parts required by the composer's complicated and richly coloured orchestration were represented.'[110] The reviewer, after an imaginative, almost theological introduction, roundly applauded the performers.[111] The conductor is especially commended: 'All that has been said ... is part of the very high tribute due to Dr. Harding, whose reception by both the Society and the audience was eloquent of the esteem and affection in which he is held in Bedford. Dr. Harding was naturally the central figure and source of inspiration of both performances, and although one would imagine they were a big physical and emotional strain upon him, there was never lacking in his conducting that masterly grip and musicianly control and inspiration which obviously ensure the complete success of the day and made both performances an intellectual and spiritual experience of a deeply impressive character.'[112]

Gervase Elwes was due to sing the part of Gerontius as he had in 1910, but sadly

brothers, all called Eugene Goossens, were conductors. Her brother Leon was an eminent oboist and another brother, Adlophe, was a gifted French horn player. Her sister, Sidonie, was also a well-known harpist. Marie was principal harpist with a number of London orchestras. She taught at the Royal College of Music 1954–67. *New Grove*, vol. 10, p. 151.

109 *Bedfordshire Times and Independent*, 21 May 1920, p. 7.

110 *Bedfordshire Times and Independent*, 27 May 1921, p. 7.

111 'In everything hitherto described and also what must be left undescribed, the chorus did splendidly. Not for many years have the Musical Society chorus sung with such conviction, sureness, responsiveness to their conductor: and fine tone and attack in soft and loud passages alike. The majestic volume of the chorus and orchestra in the great rolling chorus "Go Forth", the confident vigour and convincing spirit of the Demons Chorus and the full blown hymning of 'Praise to the Holiest', with many beautiful gradations of tone, were unforgettable and obviously the result of constant, thorough and musicianly rehearsal.' Ibid.

112 Ibid.

he had been killed in a railway accident not long before the Bedford concert.[113] His place was taken by John Adams who, the reviewer comments, would have been approved of by Mr Elwes. The other soloists were Dilys Jones who sang the angel music, 'with a purity and a depth of feeling', and Captain Heyner who took the part of the priest. The choir of St Peter's, Eaton Square, London, also took part, as they had in 1910, and they sang "The Chorus of Angelicals".

Among the unpublished memoirs of H. Marshall Palmer, who subsequently played such a pivotal role in the Musical Society, is his account of attending both performances:

> 1921 was memorable in Bedford, for Dr. Harding had decided to introduce Elgar's great masterpiece *The Dream of Gerontius* to the musical public. He spent many months rehearsing the Bedford Musical Society (which included my parents and my brother Will) for an afternoon and an evening performance in the Corn Exchange. I went to both performances and was overwhelmed by the harmonics, particularly the early Angel's Song in Part II, with its haunting Alleluias, even more than the later Angel's Farewell. All the great music I had heard until then, like *Messiah*, and Sullivan's *In Memoriam* paled into insignificance when compared with these rich melodies and harmonies. I came home and spent hours learning all the leitmotivs, their names and uses, playing them endlessly on the piano. I recall a photograph, taken by Mr. Paige Stewart, the excellent Beds. Times photographer, of the whole platform full of choir, orchestra and soloists on the Corn Exchange platform, with Dr. Harding's tubby figure standing on the rostrum facing the audience. I believe it was taken after the matinee.[114]

The photograph referred to by H. Marshall Palmer was published in the *Bedfordshire Times and Independent* on 3 June 1921.[115] This concert lost money, but this had been anticipated. [116] A *Cafe Chantant* was arranged and raised £170. This cleared most of the debt.

In May 1922, the Musical Society performed another of Elgar's great choral works, *The Apostles*. The orchestra was extensively augmented as it had been the year before. Elsie Suddaby, the soprano soloist, took the part of the Angel and the Blessed Virgin, while John Adams returned as the tenor soloist, though he did not

113 Gervase Elwes was killed in a railway accident in Boston, Massachusetts, early in 1921. A fund established in 1921 in memory of him following his untimely death led to the formation of the Musicians' Benevolent Fund. J. A. Fuller Maitland and H. C. Colles, 'Elwes, Gervase', *Grove Music Online*, accessed 13 March 2015, http://www.oxfordmusiconline.com/subscriber/article/grove/music/08761.

114 H. Marshall Palmer, *Memoirs*. These were kindly copied for the author by his late wife, Sylvia Palmer.

115 *Bedfordshire Times and Independent*, 3 June 1921, p. 8.

116 This concert is also remembered by Elinor Bevan, *A Bedford Childhood: The Early Life (from 1908–1925) of Francis Charles Victor Brightman (1904–2004)* (Edinburgh, 2006), p. 27, and published privately. She states that her great-aunt, Agnes Brightman, sang soprano. Her father, Victor Brightman, went to the concert, but was only thirteen at the time so did not take part himself. In 2004, the author sent Elinor Bevan a copy of the review of this performance of *The Dream of Gerontius*, which she showed to her father before he died. He spoke of the memories that the review brought back to him. He remembered Beagley the shirt maker, a frequent visitor at his family's house and a prominent member of the Musical Society. Elinor Bevan also wrote: 'my grandfather (Charles Thomas Brightman) took part in the performance. He actually learned how to play the French Horn while a member of the society, and I suppose it is just possible he took part in the "Dream …", with the orchestra and not the choir! He was very proud, my father told me, at having played when one of the Brain family had come to Bedford to take part in a concert, as a soloist, I suppose.'

have as much to do as when he had sung the part of Gerontius. The reviewer recognised that performing this work was a worthy challenge, but was somewhat critical, nevertheless.[117] He was more equivocal about the performance of *The Apostles* than about that of *The Dream of Gerontius* in 1921: 'It must be remembered that *The Apostles* is rarely performed in England, partly because of the complexity of its scoring and the great demand it places upon the resources, musical and financial, of any Society that undertakes it. We are fortunate, therefore, in having in our midst a Society and its conductor capable and courageous enough to attempt an interpretation of one of the foremost modern choral works by one of the greatest living composers, if not the greatest.'[118] Elsie Suddaby made a great impression.[119] The orchestral playing prompted very favourable comment too.[120]

The critical comments in the review were discussed at the annual general meeting, which was held just over a month later. Harry Harding said that he had thought at first that they might have taken on too much, but it had been a tremendous effort and was a wonderful performance which retained the sympathetic attention of the audience. He felt that the newspaper report contained remarks gravely reflecting on the chorus which no-one capable of judging would think of as fair criticism - the chorus had sung perfectly in tune and the tone of the choruses had been one of the best features of the performance. There always would some little blemishes in a work of such complexity, but they were big enough to rise above discouraging remarks. A large majority of members voted in favour of repeating *The Apostles* the following year. So, in May 1923, *The Apostles* was again performed in Bedford, with Elsie Suddaby and John Adams once more as soloists and the orchestra augmented as it had been in 1922. The reviewer gave a mixed account, for which he apologised in advance.[121]

117 'In undertaking a performance of Sir Edward Elgar's elaborate and impressive oratorio, *The Apostles*, Bedford Musical Society had submitted to a very severe test of their capabilities. It is no doubt the most complex and difficult work which they have undertaken, at any rate in recent years.' The reviewer also considered that there were technical blemishes, chiefly poor attack in the choral part and occasional raggedness. Also, tone and pitch were not always what they might have been, though there were beautiful moments and lapses were overshadowed by such notable choral passages as 'It is a good thing to give thanks unto the Lord'. *Bedfordshire Times and Independent*, 26 May 1922, p. 8.

118 Ibid.

119 'The purity of her tone and the ease of her production and articulation were just what both parts required, and her ringing upper notes in the parts for soloists and chorus had a great effect.' Ibid. Freddie E. Stevens, chorus master 1952–65, remembers meeting Elsie Suddaby at an exclusive music festival at Grygynog in central Wales, and accompanying her, with one or two other people, in a rowing boat, in 1933 or 1934. Elsie Suddaby was one of the original sixteen singers in the first performance of Vaughan Williams's *Serenade to Music*.

120 'It certainly was a wonderful orchestra and Dr. Harding obtained throughout the performance a most satisfactory balance both within the orchestra and between voices and instruments.' Ibid.

121 In his opening remarks, the reviewer explains why the Musical Society had decided to perform the work again and complimented them on this and, initially, on the performance which he called 'excellent'. Then he qualifies his opening remarks and apologises in advance for any possible misunderstanding, lamenting the unhappy lot of the critic: 'one of the minor miseries of a critic's life is the fact that ninety-nine pieces of praise which he prints are completely forgotten on the day which he prints his one piece of dispraise.' He continued: 'the choral singing as a whole was very good; and of the orchestral work, we would hazard the opinion that none better has been achieved under the capable and genial directorship of Dr. Harding.' Then comes the criticism, complaining of the chorus's lack of variety in dynamics: 'The final chorus itself was a true outburst: but how much more thrilling it would have been if, after the great sustained B flat for the sopranos, led royally by Miss Elsie Suddaby, it had toned down in the last pages to *piano* or *pianissimo* as marked. Over and over again the force of the contrast was lost from the time

In his report to the 1923 annual general meeting, Harvey Goldsmith, the honorary secretary, was, however, positive about the performance.[122] The chorus and orchestra had risen to the occasion and the splendid result achieved more than justified the decision. But there was a surprise announcement at the end of his report: 'The Turpeian [*sic*] Rock is hard by the Capitol and while the Committee in common with all members of the Society were congratulating themselves on the glories of the "Apostles" concert, they were distressed to receive a letter from their beloved Hon. Conductor tendering his resignation in very definite terms.[123] They met at once to consider the position. The reason for Dr. Harding's resignation was that the calls upon his time, both locally and in connection with the Royal College of Organists, had so enormously increased that he felt he could no longer cope with the great and incessant work entailed by the conductorship of such a Society as ours.'[124]

Harry Harding's letter of resignation was read at the meeting. It stated that during term-time he was seldom able to get to bed before 1.00 or 2.00a.m. He had other reasons for giving up besides work – medical reasons – but he did not wish to elaborate on this subject. A few people at the meeting tried to dissuade him from resigning, but his resignation was eventually accepted and he was elected conductor emeritus. The committee was criticised for 'allowing' notification of his resignation to appear in the local press before the members had been informed. There were other ructions as will be detailed in the next chapter.

There was a presentation to Harry Harding at the December 1923 concert. As the *Bedfordshire Times and Independent* reports:

> After a long and honourable conductorship of twenty three years Dr. Harding sat for the first time among the audience … It was sad to realise that the time – inevitable in every career – had come for Dr. Harding to resign his leadership. But there was thankfulness too. He had brought the Society probably to the highest pitch of efficiency it had attained in all its fifty seven years' existence … When the interval arrived, Dr. and Mrs. Harding were escorted to the platform by Mr. R. W Allen, C.B.E., President of the Society, Mr Allen said they all sympathised with Dr. Harding and it was difficult to find words to express their gratitude to so great a man 'He was a character unto his own – most human and at the same time extraordinarily funny. (laughter). The audience stood while Mr. Allen read the testimonial to Dr Harding.[125]

when on a very early page 'a garland of ashes' and 'oil of joy' were taken at almost identical strength ... Apart from this, the choral singing was very good.' *Bedfordshire Times and Independent,* 25 May 1923, p. 8.

122 Ibid.

123 Tarpeia was a Roman goddess. The Tarpeian Rock was at the south-west corner of the Capitoline Hill in Rome, from which prisoners sentenced to death were hurled.

124 *Bedfordshire Times and Independent*, 6 July 1923, p. 8.

125 *Bedfordshire Times and Independent*, 21 December 1923, p. 9. The testimonial and Harry Harding's reply are quoted in the report: 'Dear Dr. Harding, – On behalf of the members of, and subscribers to, the Bedford Musical Society, whose names are appended, we ask you to accept this Address and accompanying Cheque as a permanent expression of our gratitude to you for the Twenty-three Years of devoted and unremitting services you have rendered to this Society as it Honorary Conductor. During that long period, you have not only freely given your time to the Society, but also you have ever striven - and most successfully - to raise the status of music in Bedford, your cheery and inspiring influence being freely extended to every member. To them the Society became a veritable Home of Musical Instruction, for which, all of them are deeply grateful. The signatures which follow are those of the President, Hon. Treasurer and Hon. Secretary. With the album is an envelope containing a cheque for £100.' Dr Harding replied: 'I ought to feel at home on this platform. Everything is very familiar. Here are all my friends

Harry Harding's later years and his achievements

Harry Harding remained organist and choirmaster of St Paul's church – and borough organist – until his death in 1930, having held the post for forty-one years. During that time he maintained the musical services at St Paul's to a high level of both efficiency and reverence.[126] His organ recitals after Sunday evening services were greatly enjoyed by large congregations over many years. He was director of music at both Bedford School and Bedford High School for twenty-seven years, until his resignation in 1926.

He held the post of honorary secretary of the Royal College of Organists for twenty-two years, from 1908 until his death. At the Royal College, he got to know the leading cathedral organists of the day and was in regular contact with those who were council members. Among the vice-presidents were a number of well-known musicians whose church music is still in regular use today.[127]

In late 1919, the 'Bedford Eisteddfod', as the Bedford Festival of Music, Speech and Drama used to be known, was established. The first Bedford Eisteddfod was held in the Bromham Road Wesleyan chapel (now hidden behind business premises and used as a warehouse) on Saturday 10 January 1920.[128] It was originally a musical competition organised between four Nonconformist churches in the town. In 1920, Harry Harding became involved. He was responsible for the promotion and establishment of the Bedford Festival as a national event from 1921. Its growth was phenomenal and within two or three years it had developed into one of the largest festivals in the country.[129] He worked incredibly hard and was not content to devolve detailed work on others and leave it at that: he would make himself personally responsible for the test pieces and innumerable points of detail and, of course, his contact with the larger musical world was invaluable in securing the services of eminent musicians as adjudicators, including Sir Walford Davies, Sir Frederic Cowen and Sir Granville Bantock. His three daughters, Joyce, Barbara and Nancy were all closely involved with the Bedford Festival from its earliest days.[130]

and I am glad to see you all again … Probably you would never know how much I value this wonderful proof of your esteem and respect. My heart is really too full to say more than to thank you all again for your great kindness.'

126 At a presentation to Harry Harding in 1911, Canon Woodard, then Vicar of St Paul's said: 'At St. Paul's they always tried to have the very best. Their bells were supposed to be the best in the Midlands and their choir the best of any parish church in England.' *Bedfordshire Times and Independent*, 30 June 1911, p. 8.

127 Vice-presidents of the Royal College of Organists while Harry Harding was honorary secretary include Sir Hubert Parry, Sir Frederick Bridge, Sir Alexander Mackenzie, Sir Walter Parratt, Sir Charles Villiers Stanford, and Granville Bantock. Council members included H. Walford Davies, Percy Buck, Sir Hugh Allen, Sir Frederick Cowen, Sir Edward Elgar, Sir Henry Wood, Donald Tovey, Ralph Vaughn Williams, Sir Ivor Atkins, Edward Bairstow, Harold Darke, Sir Walford Davies, Alan Gray, Sidney Nicolson, Sir R. R. Terry, and H. Davon Wetton.

128 *Bedfordshire Times and Independent*, 23 January 1920, p. 9.

129 See leaflet by an unnamed author *A Short History of the Festival* (Bedford, c.1980). A silver 'Harding Memorial Bowl' was given in memory by his family, and is the most coveted trophy for choral singing. The competition for this bowl is the concluding item of the festival and the bowl is always presented immediately after the contest. Mr G. H. Thomas, joint honorary secretary of the festival1930–32, and secretary until after the Second World War, was a soloist at the Musical Society's concert in February 1910. He sang "Onaway" (from *Hiawatha's Wedding Feast*); the reviewer complimented him and wrote that his upper register was particularly good.

130 'Harry Alfred Harding', *The Musical Times*, vol. 71, no. 1054 (December 1930), pp. 1084–5.

Harry Harding composed a number of works, mostly to be sung in church. These included a morning service in D, evening services in C, D and F, a communion service in F, a litany of the Sacred Heart and four chorales. He also composed *Two Egyptian Dances*, a number of songs and the dramatic cantata, *Mucius Scaevola.* The last of these was originally composed for the Eglesfield Musical Society of Queen's College, Oxford, but was performed twice by the Musical Society, as has been noted. He was the author of a number of text books including: *Musical Ornaments with Questions and Exercises*; *Score Reading Exercises written specially for Candidates preparing for the Royal College of Organists' Examinations, etc.*(for organists); *5000 Scale and Arpeggio Tests Arranged in Irregular Order in Every Key;* and *Analysis of Form: As Displayed in Beethoven's Thirty-two Pianoforte Sonatas*. He also edited the complete collection of *Bedford School Songs*, which was published in 1929.[131]

'The Doctor', as he was affectionately known, died suddenly at his home, Hill House, Crofton Close, Bedford, on Wednesday 29 October 1930, having collapsed at a meeting of the finance committee of the Bedford Festival the previous evening. There was a very full obituary in the *Bedfordshire Times and Independent* and quite a long obituary in *The Musical Times*.[132] A moving tribute by Dr K. M. Westaway, headmistress of Bedford High School, concludes *The Musical Times* obituary:

> Beyond the wide circle of musicians who now mourn the loss of Dr. Harding, there is a very great company who, as pupils, both boys and girls, during a period of over forty years, have owned him as a master of unsurpassable inspiration. Many, better qualified than I, will commemorate him as composer, organist, pianist, accompanist, examiner, organiser; in all these he was greatly gifted. But as I knew him best, as a teacher of choral singing, his was nothing short of genius. He would have a chorus of two hundred or three hundred boys or girls and put them through part-singing of the most exacting intricacy, and have them singing and thinking as with a single mind. He insisted on work of a meticulous accuracy, and spared neither himself nor his pupils in his pursuit of it, and many memories will be stirring now of thrilling rehearsals that bore witness to this. He had an immense scorn of the sentimental, and he was almost shy in expressing his own love of the beautiful, but it was part of his genius as a teacher that he communicated both these things to his pupils without much talking about either. Among many choirs in the schools and towns [*sic*] of Bedford, he leaves a memory of powerful personality and a mind full of lovely things.[133]

Harry Harding was buried in Bedford cemetery, quite near the east end of the chapel of remembrance. A very modest gravestone marks the spot; the lettering on this has now become indistinct. There is a memorial inscription to him engraved on the north side of the choir stalls in St Paul's church, Bedford. The main memorial

131 H. A. Harding: *Musical Ornaments with Questions and Exercises* (London, c.1912); *Score Reading Exercises Written Specially for Candidates preparing for the Royal College of Organists' Examinations, etc.* (London, c1912); *5000 Scale and Arpeggio Tests Arranged in Irregular Order in Every Key (unknown); Analysis of Form: As Displayed in Beethoven's Thirty-two Pianoforte Sonatas* (London, n.d.); *Bedford School Songs* (Bedford, 1929).

132 *Bedfordshire Times and Independent,* 31 October 1930, p. 9 and *The Musical Times*, vol. 71, no. 1054 (December 1930), pp. 1084–5.

133 *The Musical Times*, vol. 71, no. 1054 (December 1930), pp. 1084–5. The obituary notes that a Harding Prize was established in January 1930 to be awarded in connection with the Royal College's written examinations.

in St Paul's is, however, part of the stained glass in the great west window of the church. Three lights had been placed in the window in February 1930 in memory of the late Canon Lambert Woodard (vicar of the parish 1886–1913), these having as their subject the Te Deum.[134] The remaining light was completed as a memorial to Harry Harding and unveiled on Sunday 22 May 1932. A preview to the unveiling was printed in the *Bedfordshire Times and Independent* two days earlier: 'In the new side light on the right-hand side has been introduced the figure of St. Cecilia, patron saint of music, and other figures are those of Sir William Harper and St. Etheldreda. In the left-hand light appears the patron saint of the diocese, St Alban. The tracery is made up of coloured glazing, portions of which represent the crests of St. Albans and Ely, of the college of the late Canon Woodard, and of the Royal College of Organists of which Dr. Harding was Hon. Secretary. At the bottom of the left-hand light has been placed an inscription indicating that the window has been completed in memory of the Church's late organist.'[135] The work was carried out by Messrs Burlison and Grylls, of London.

The window was unveiled by Harvey Goldsmith, a member of St Paul's church choir, churchwarden and secretary to the Musical Society 1904–32. The music played by Herbert Colson included 'Praise to the Holiest …' from Elgar's *Dream of Gerontius*, a favourite work of Harry Harding.[136] The report of the unveiling notes: 'As the curtains fell apart, a burst of sunshine, which although not directly falling on the window, served to show its striking colours.'[137] A month before the unveiling of the window occurred, the activities of the Musical Society were curtailed.

134 The Rev. Lambert Woodard, born 1848, was the fourth son of Nathaniel Woodard who founded the Woodard group of public schools, which include Lancing College (the flagship school, founded in 1848), Abbotts Bromley School for Girls, Hurstspierpoint College and Worksop College. The author is grateful to Mrs Lesley Edwards, archivist at Lancing College for providing this information.

135 *Bedfordshire Times and Independent*, 20 May 1932, p. 7.

136 Harry Harding's life span matched Elgar's very closely. He was born two years before Elgar and died three years before him.

137 *Bedfordshire Times and Independent,* 27 May 1932, p. 7.

Chapter Five

Decline and Fall, 1923–33

> I was also in the South Wing hospital choir with A. F. Parris and when my voice broke and I started to sing tenor, he immediately insisted that I joined the Bedford Musical Society with its marvellous number of "250" [performers]. A. F. Parris took the choir at practices and H. J. Colson took the orchestra and usually the Doctor, organist at St. Paul's conducted the whole outfit. Owing to ill health, Mr. Parris had to give up most of his conducting for a time and then when Captain Percy Burke left and Mr. Parris had improved, he took over the Bedford Choral Society, so, of course, I joined that fine Society as well.[1]

> In conversation, Mr. Colson outlined the history of modern choral music … There was a decline, he said, in the Victorian period and we were just emerging from that decline.[2]

The joint conductorship

As detailed in the previous chapter, Harry Harding's resignation, after the memorable 1923 performance of *The Apostles*, came as a shock to members of the Musical Society. The committee set about appointing a successor immediately rather than waiting until they had consulted members or until the annual general meeting. The committee interviewed Arthur Parris and Herbert Colson.

Herbert Colson was asked whether, if he was not elected as conductor, he would be prepared to work with Arthur Parris or whoever was appointed. He said deliberately that he would not. When Arthur Parris was asked the same question, he replied: 'My heart and soul are in the Society. I have belonged to the Society for a great many years past and am quite prepared, because I love the Society, to act under anybody in any position to which you may appoint me.'[3] On the strength of their comments, the committee elected Arthur Parris by an overwhelming majority, and announced their decision to the press before notifying the members.

Technically the committee's action in appointing a new conductor was correct. Rule four stated: 'The officers of the Society shall be a President, Vice-President, Secretary and Treasurer. Conductors, Organists, Pianist and Librarian to be elected annually by the Committee at their first meeting. Vacancies, as they occur, shall be filled up by the Committee.'[4] But the committee's action was inept, carried out so soon before the annual general meeting where members would have had the oppor-

1 Extracts from a personal letter, from Bill Stephens, now in the author's possession, written following Bedford Choral Society's appearance on 12 March 1989 on *Highway*, the ITV religious programme hosted by Sir Harry Secombe.

2 *Bedfordshire Times and Independent*, 17 November 1933, p. 10.

3 *Bedfordshire Times and Independent*, 27 July 1923, p. 8.

4 *Bedfordshire Times and Independent*, 6 July 1923, p. 8.

tunity to have their say. And the committee, having failed to consult the membership about the appointment, then compounded the problem by not notifying members of the action that they had taken, instead, 'allowing' them to find out through reports in the local press. The committee's actions caused serious ructions.

Harry Harding managed to hold together what was a very fractious annual general meeting on the 3 July. As the *Bedfordshire Times and Independent* put it: 'The fact that Dr. Harding himself presided and handled the situation skilfully probably saved the attack from developing into a vote of censure [of the committee].'[5] The meeting was adjourned after a sub-committee had been appointed to review what had happened. Members of the sub-committee then met with Harry Harding. Initially they hoped to persuade him to reconsider his decision. This he would not do, so they sought his advice on a successor. He recommended a dual conductorship. If that was not possible, he recommended that Arthur Parris should be appointed, otherwise the Musical Society should be disbanded. This suggests that he had doubts about Herbert Colson.

A special meeting was reconvened three weeks later to try to resolve matters. A motion that Messrs Colson and Parris should be asked to become joint conductors was carried without dissent. The chairman, Rowland Hill, remarked optimistically that: 'once again there is harmony in the Musical Society'.[6]

Arthur Parris, Harry Harding's preferred choice as successor, had, since the turn of the century, been accompanist to the Musical Society at rehearsals. In addition, he played the organ at concerts, and had been chorus master since the end of the First World War. He was also organist at the County Hospital (South Wing), a post he had held since the 1890s. He remained there until his retirement in 1947. A picture of the old hospital chapel, now in the present hospital chapel, was presented to him by the choir-men on his retirement. At the same time, he was also organist of St Leonard's church and later organist of St John's church. H. Marshall Palmer (generally known as Marshall Palmer, and referred to as such from this point on) in his unpublished *Memoirs* gives a pen-portrait of him as follows:

> He was a smiling, relaxed little man with a curious face, one that I often drew in profile – a vertical semi-circle from forehead to receding chin, with a short curved nose and black moustache and spectacles. He was a competent pianist but not a good conductor … At rehearsals, Arthur Parris would always hold his arms out, wait a minute, smile happily and say ''ere we go'. I used to watch with infinite glee, hidden, I hope, by an impassive face, his conducting of the Pastoral Symphony in *Messiah*, when he would beat all 12 quavers in a series of jerks and spasms.[7]

Herbert Colson was born at Sharnbrook, north of Bedford, and attended Bedford School for two years 1906–08. He was assistant organist to Harry Harding at St Paul's church in 1908, probably before going on to university. He was music master at Bedford School 1912–13. After the First World War, he resumed this appointment and held it from 1919 until he was appointed director of music at Bedford

5 *Bedfordshire Times and Independent*, 27 July 1923, p. 8.
6 *Bedfordshire Times and Independent*, 27 July 1923, p. 8.
7 H. Marshall Palmer, *Memoirs*. Most people would appear 'little' from Marshall's point of view. He was 6ft 5ins tall.

Modern School (in succession to Mr A. J. Meyrick) in 1923. This was the same year in which he was elected to the joint-conductorship of the Musical Society. His enthusiasm and drive stand out, not only in newspaper reports, but also in how people remember him. He would make his choir boys sing over and over again until they almost knew what they were singing by heart. He clearly did a lot for music at Bedford Modern School, and is remembered as an inspiring teacher. There were many notable choral concerts during his years at the school.[8] In 1930, Herbert Colson was appointed organist of St Paul's church, in succession to Harry Harding. Bedford Modern School was, at the time, situated near to the church, and provided choirboys for services. One such choirboy was Joe Pinnock. Joe Pinnock remembers Herbert Colson as a great character, and an able and inspiring music teacher who was able to instil into his pupils a real love of music.[9] Fred Rawlins, who was later assistant organist and choirmaster at St Paul's church under Herbert Colson, and subsequently succeeded him, said that he drummed the music into the boys by repetition.[10]

Only three concerts were held under the joint conductorship 1923–24, and only the first two were conducted jointly by Arthur Parris and Herbert Colson. The main choral works performed at the concerts were Vaughan Williams's *Toward the Unknown Region,* Dvořák's *The Spectre's Bride* and Elgar's *King Olaf.*

The December 1923 concert, at which the presentation to Dr and Mrs Harding was made, consisted of two main works, Bach's Double Violin Concerto and *Toward the Unknown Region*. The *Bedfordshire Times and Independent's* reviewer heaped praise on the performance of the Bach, which was conducted by Herbert Colson, calling it 'refined, musicianly, imaginative and virile'.[11] The reviewer was not so happy with *Toward the Unknown Region*, Vaughan Williams's setting of a poem by Walt Whitman, conducted by Arthur Parris in the second half.[12] The soprano soloist, Dorothy Silk, however, made a big impression on the reviewer.

The Spectre's Bride was performed at the end of March 1924. The reservations of the reviewer, William E. Palmer (brother of Marshall Palmer), were primarily

[8] Herbert Colson's obituary, *The Bedfordshire Times and Bedfordshire Standard*, 16 November 1951, p. 7. This says, inaccurately, that he was honorary conductor of the Bedford Musical Society 'for about 12 years'. See also the Bedford Modern School Magazine on Herbert Colson's retirement, *The Eagle*, vol. 27, no. 3 (Summer 1949), pp. 166–7.

[9] Joe Pinnock, *Reminiscences*, 4 November 1989, letter in author's collection. His father was also active in the Society. Joe Pinnock was a second bass in the Musical / Choral Society until 2000 when he was eighty-three years-old. He died in March 2010.

[10] Personal interview with Fred Rawlings by the author.

[11] 'The finest music and the finest performance of the evening were in Bach's Concerto in D minor for two violins and small string orchestra. It was sheer joy from beginning to end. The principals were Mr. H. Wessely, the distinguished Professor of the Royal Academy of Music and his former pupil, Mr. Alfred de Reyghere (otherwise the leader of the orchestra). They were supported by double string quartet of local players.' The local players were: 1st violins, Mrs Robinson and Miss Willetts; 2nd violins, Miss Peck and Mrs Leader; violas, Mrs Ozanne and Mrs Partridge; celli, Mr Maney and M de Choisy. *Bedfordshire Times and Independent*, 21 December 1923, p. 9.

[12] 'The technical difficulties are considerable, particularly in the choral parts. The chorus gets very little lead from the orchestra: time and time again, entries have to be made with no help from the orchestral context, and all the time there are awkward intervals, tricky rhythms and long phrases to be dealt with. On the whole, the chorus did its work courageously. The sopranos, especially, and more especially still some of their leaders, were really valiant. There was, unfortunately, no pianissimo where we most looked for it.' Ibid.

about the work itself: 'The only value of the work lies in the music and even some passages of that might well have been drawn from comic opera.'[13] William Palmer also noted an imbalance between the women's voices and the men's voices.[14] Most praise is reserved for the soprano soloist: 'The most outstanding memory of the performance is the singing of Miss Doris Vane who has a voice of rich and beautiful quality, and of wide range and considerable tonal variety, whose technique is most fluent and cultured.'[15] Webster Millar, described as 'a singer of distinction' by William Palmer, stood in for Walter Widdop who was to have sung the tenor part, but who was unable to do so at the last moment.[16] Walter Widdop is 'WW' in Vaughan Williams's *Serenade to Music*.[17]

The first half of the work was conducted by Herbert Colson and the second half by Arthur Parris. This had occasionally happened when Harry Harding had asked Philip Diemer to conduct part of a work as a gesture of good will. It was unusual, however, and raises speculation about how they managed with rehearsals and how far their interpretations differed. William Palmer does not mention any untoward consequences, but some disquiet about having two conductors for *The Spectre's Bride* was expressed at the annual general meeting in June 1924, and it was agreed that although both conductors should be re-appointed, they should be asked to take the sole direction of one concert each. They replied that they were working well together.

At the annual general meeting, a plan was put forward for the main concert of the year to be undertaken in December 1924; this was to be a performance of the whole of *Hiawatha*. The other work proposed was Mendelssohn's 'Hymn of Praise'. It was later announced that the December concert would be Elgar's *King Olaf*.[18] It is not known why there was such a change to the planned programme. Herbert Colson conducted the whole of *King Olaf*.

Arthur Parris may have been ill when *King Olaf* was performed. Three weeks later, he resigned as joint-conductor and, early in 1925, was appointed conductor of the Bedford Choral Society so putting an end to the joint conductorship.

It seems clear from the programmes of concerts held over the next few years that

[13] He continues: 'That the performance rose to no great heights was the fault of the work rather than that of the performers, who on the whole survived the quite formidable difficulties remarkably well and contrived to hold our interest for the most part.' *Bedfordshire Times and Independent*, 4 April 1924, p. 10. This review was identical to the review in the *Bedford Record*, 1 April 1924, p. 1 and it is this copy which is included in H. Marshall Palmer's unpublished *Memoirs*. He attributes the authorship to his brother, William E. Palmer.

[14] 'The sopranos were splendid, singing with confidence and good clear tone. The altos were as good as ever, but the basses were less good. In fact a little more "foundation" was needed in both chorus and orchestra. The tenors were a gallant few, who sang with as good effect as twice the number could have hoped to obtain, except, of course, for the tonal difference which added numbers would have made … The chorus really deserve high praise … They had to face considerable technical difficulties – awkward entries and intervals and so forth and the way in which they did it showed once more that they are as keen and capable as they should be.' *Bedfordshire Times and Independent*, 4 April 1924, p. 10.

[15] Ibid.

[16] The *Oxford Dictionary of Music* says Walter Widdop was a: 'Fine oratorio singer but better-known for Wagner roles such as Siegmund and Lohengrin.' Kennedy, *Oxford Dictionary of Music*, p.789.

[17] This was composed in honour of Sir Henry Wood's jubilee as a conductor in 1938. It was originally composed for sixteen solo voices and orchestra. The initials of the original sixteen soloists are printed in copies of the work.

[18] *Bedfordshire Times and Independent*, 3 October 1924, p. 10.

Herbert Colson preferred recent and more complex works, while Arthur Parris was happier with more traditional works from the choral repertoire, especially Handel.

The Bedford Choral Society (Free Church Choral Union)

Arthur Parris's appointment as conductor occurred only a few months after the Free Church Choral Union changed its name to The Bedford Choral Society. The idea of Bedford's Free Church choirs combining to form a larger choir was first mooted at the Peace Thanksgiving Service at the Bunyan Meeting church in the early summer of 1919. The choirmasters and organists of the Free Churches then met in December 1919, at the instigation of Bedford Free Church Council, and agreed to hold united musical services in the Corn Exchange on periodical Sunday evenings throughout the year. The quality of the four Free Church choirs that took part in the first Bedford Eisteddfod in January 1920 demonstrated that these four choirs alone had the nucleus of a fine chorus, and gave the impetus to establishing a more fully integrated choir. A correspondent wrote in 'Musical Notes' in the *Bedfordshire Times and Independent* following the Eisteddfod: 'I have noticed in more than one quarter the suggestion that these choirs should amalgamate for an hour's musical service occasionally after the ordinary evening services. It is suggested that they might even combine to give the "Messiah" and similar works in future. The idea is excellent and happily not original on the part of those giving expression to it. It was first made early last summer, after the United Choirs' unrehearsed but very impressive rendering of the "Hallelujah Chorus" at the Peace Thanksgiving Service in Bunyan Meeting.'[19]

The first Bedford Eisteddfod – the Free Church Eisteddfod – which took place on Friday 9 and Saturday 10 January 1920, is described in a full report in the *Bedfordshire Times and Independent*.[20] On the Friday evening there were competitions in recitation, solo and class singing and, for Bromham Road Sunday School only, needlework. The choir competition was the main event on the Saturday evening. The choirs that competed were from Howard Congregational church (considered the best), Mill Street Baptist, Bromham Road Wesleyan and Park Road Primitive Methodist. The test piece was Sullivan's song 'The Long Day Closes'. At the end of the competition, all the choirs sang the test piece together: 'When the four choirs got together at the conclusion of the programme and, conducted by Capt. Burke, sang *The long day closes*, the result was very fine indeed, especially where the increased volume gave strength to the crescendo effect.'[21]

The formation of the Free Church Choral Union was finalised at, 'a particularly enthusiastic little gathering' at the end of February, a little over a month after the Bedford Eisteddfod: 'After previous discussions, formal and informal, the organists and choirmasters of the Free Churches in Bedford on Saturday completed their arrangements for the formation of the Bedford Free Church Choral Union, which hopes to show its quality with a rendering of "Messiah" on Thursday, April 22. Captain Percy Burke has accepted the position of Conductor, by unanimous

19 *Bedfordshire Times and Independent*, 23 January 1920, p. 9.

20 *Bedfordshire Times and Independent*, 16 January 1920, p. 8. The originator, Mr F. E. Smith, is described there as 'energetic'. The adjudicators in 1920 were Percy Burke and Arthur Parris.

21 Ibid.

request.'[22] By the middle of March, progress had been considerable: 'Much enthusiasm has marked the inauguration of this Union, the chorus of which now numbers 230. There was an attendance of 213 at the last rehearsal, and it was remarked how particularly fine the tone and attack were.'[23] There were only seven rehearsals for this, their first concert.[24]

The review of *Messiah* reiterates the original purpose of forming the Free Church Choral Union: 'for the purpose of using to the full the fine material known to be existent in the Free Church Choirs of the town, and for giving the members of those choirs opportunities of singing together in the best oratorios and other great works.'[25] The new Choral Union's future seemed bright: 'The particularly fine performance of the "Messiah" in Bedford Corn Exchange last week fully justified the Union's existence and gave every promise of good times in the future.'[26]

Two hundred and fifty performers took part in the performance. The choir was generally praised by the reviewer, and the *adagio* that ends the chorus 'All we, like Sheep have Gone Astray' was apparently so impressive, and the applause so insistent, that the *adagio* was repeated. [27] Laura Evans-Williams was the soprano soloist. One of the gems of the evening was said to be her singing of 'Come unto Him'. Of Effie Martyn, who had sung with the Bedford Musical Society before the war, the reviewer wrote that her rendering of 'He was Despised' was very moving and that the rich quality of her voice was very noticeable. The organist was William Palmer.

The reviewer also complimented the conductor, Percy Burke, enthusiastically: 'without a capable and enthusiastic Conductor, no Musical Society can prosper, and it is safe to say that the whole-hearted enthusiasm and genial personality of Capt. Percy Burke were the biggest factors in making the Free Church Choral Union what it was. His singers say that he "just makes us sing".'[28] Marshall Palmer wrote of Captain Burke in his memoirs:

> Another of the Bedford musical men was a certain Captain Percy Burke, whose rank was a bit of a mystery, though I think his uniform was naval. He had worked at Cardington aerodrome just outside Bedford. He conducted the first 'Messiah' I had ever heard live in Bedford School Hall. I do not remember much of the performance but recall this bald-headed man in naval uniform as a most energetic conductor ... He had big swathes of white and coloured mutton cloth (or so it seemed) all round his rostrum, behind which he kept a large towel and would mop up vigorously in between items, for he perspired mightily. He was not a good conductor; far from elegant gestures, but his vigour and enthusiasm

[22] *Bedford Record,* 2 March 1920, p.1.

[23] *Bedfordshire Times and Independent,* 19 March 1920, p. 9.

[24] *Bedfordshire Times and Independent*, 30 April 1920, p. 6. This is stated in 'An Appreciation' that follows the review.

[25] *Bedfordshire Times and Independent*, 30 April 1920, p. 6. At the end of the review it is stated that a fuller account appeared in Tuesday's 'Record' (27 April 1920).

[26] Ibid.

[27] 'The sopranos were extraordinarily fresh and clear, and the tenors were quite above the average, while the contraltos and basses were thoroughly sound and rich in quality.' The reviewer's only criticism was for 'over enthusiasm'. Ibid.

[28] Ibid.

ensured lively performances. He also produced some lovely soft singing now and then.[29]

The Choral Union's second concert was a performance of *Judas Maccabaeus* in December 1920.[30] The reviewer notes that: 'it was the singing of the chorus which was the outstanding feature of the evening.'[31] There were, again, 250 performers. In the reviewer's opinion: 'The sopranos take the palm. They are strong in numbers, most of them young, fresh and buoyant in tone, and a sheer delight to listen to ... the Choral Union owes them much.'[32] Immediately after these comments the reviewer makes an interesting reference to the Corn Exchange organ pitch being unusually high, suggesting that the sopranos benefitted from this. The 'efficient orchestra' was largely made up of members of the Musical Society, whose generous co-operation was noted with pleasure in the review. The 'cello accompaniment of M. de Choisy, Commander Muir's flute obbligato, Frank James on the trumpet and especially Herbert Colson's drums in "Sound the Alarm", were all highlighted.'

Members of the Choral Union sang at the annual meeting of the Free Church Council in January 1921: 'A large united choir, conducted by Captain Burke, gave fine renderings of two oratorio choruses, the first of which was "All we like sheep" from "The Messiah" and the second "We will never bow down" from Judas Maccabeus". Mrs Partridge was at the organ.'[33]

Before the Choral Union's next performance, the modest Bedford Eisteddfod that had taken place in 1920 was re-launched in 1921 as the Bedford Eisteddfod Competitive Music Festival. Planning for this started quite soon after the original 1920 Eisteddfod; a meeting was held on Saturday 28 February 1920 (the same day that the meeting to establish the Free Church Choral Union was held). A number of musicians in the town attended, and the meeting was chaired by Harry Harding who devoted much of his energy to the Bedford Festival over the next few years. There is an amusing report of the meeting in the *Bedford and County Record*. The scope of the new Bedford Festival and its name were discussed: 'The Chairman declared and demonstrated his utter inability to pronounce the Welsh word … and arranged to visit Mr Parris for private rehearsal of the correct pronunciation.'[34] One suggestion at the meeting was that only clergy who might be termed musicians should be eligible (for the post of vice-president). Much amusement was caused by the thought of Harry Harding having to test them to see whether they qualified! Dates for the next Bedford Festival were discussed: the 13 and 14 October 1920 were initially chosen. The Bedford Festival was eventually held early in March 1921 with 4000 competitors taking part.[35] It has been held at around that time ever since, apart from during Second World War.

29 H. Marshall Palmer, *Memoirs*.

30 Beside the advertisement for this concert in the *Bedfordshire Times and Independent*, 26 November 1920, p. 9, are advertisements for a Clara Butt concert on 2 December and the Musical Society's concert on 7 December, at which the main work was Harry Harding's *Mucius Scaevola*.

31 *Bedfordshire Times and Independent*, 3 December 1920, p. 9.

32 Ibid.

33 *Bedfordshire Times and Independent,* 21 January 1921, p. 9.

34 *Bedford and County Record*, 2 March 1920, p. 1.

35 There were very full reports in the local press of the 1921 Bedford Festival. See *Bedfordshire Times*

Also in March 1921, the Bedford Ladies' Choral Society, whose thirty or so members were also members of the Choral Union, sang at the London Music Festival in Central Hall, Westminster, winning some trophies. Percy Burke was their conductor too. The *Bedfordshire Times and Independent* includes a personal account by one of the ladies in the choir entitled, 'How we went to London'. It is a delightful and perceptive account including the journey by train to St Pancras and then on to Westminster on the No.77 bus.[36] A picture of the ladies was included in the subsequent edition.

This edition also carried a report, under the heading 'Bedford Free Church Choral Union', of *Messiah*, 'Another fine performance.'[37] This second performance seems to have been just as successful as the one a year earlier, but with a larger and more efficient orchestra than at the Choral Union's previous two concerts. The reviewer thought that the only chorus which did not go really well was "He Trusted in God", because the rhythm was a little unsteady and there were some wrong notes. But he wrote: 'Capt. Burke's handling of all his forces was as usual wonderfully sure and inspiring. He dominated without being predominant, and his influence over the chorus especially was more complete than ever.'[38]

Hiawatha, that old stalwart, followed six weeks later, at the beginning of May.[39] This was another successful performance for which the Corn Exchange was filled: 'The enthusiasm of the members (of the chorus) is obvious to any observer. They take their work seriously and Captain Burke knows how to make full use of their willingness. Another feature worthy of notice is that, we believe, with one exception, both chorus and orchestra on Thursday were composed of Bedford residents.'[40]

Before the next major concert, there were two significant events for the Choral Union. The first was a garden party on 30 June 1921 at which there was a presentation to Captain and Mrs Burke. The garden party was hosted by Mr G. H. Barford, and was at his home, 'St Kilda', 34 Shakespeare Road, Bedford. Mr Barford was a prominent townsman, and was subsequently elected mayor of Bedford (1922–26 and 1928). There was morris dancing by students from the Kindergarten Training College, 'by kind permission of Miss Walmsley' and a singing competition. This event was a noteworthy social occasion, and was reported in the *Bedfordshire Times and Independent* with photographs of members of the chorus and of Captain and Mrs Burke holding the gifts that had been presented to them.[41]

There was also an extra concert given by the Choral Union in October, when members sang excerpts from *Judas Maccabaeus*. This concert was in aid of Bedford

and Independent, 18 February 1921, pp. 7–8 and 25 February 1921, p. 7. There were also reports also in the *Bedford and County Record*, 15 February 1921, p. 1 and 22 February 1921, p. 1.

36 *Bedfordshire Times and Independent*, 18 March 1921, p. 11.

37 *Bedfordshire Times and Independent*, 25 March 1921, p. 9.

38 Ibid.

39 The advertisement states that there was a chorus and orchestra of 250. *Bedfordshire Times and Independent*, 29 April 1921, p. 9. For the Musical Society's performance of *The Dream of Gerontius* at the end of the month, the programme states that there was a band and chorus of 300 performers. There must have been a great many musicians in Bedford at the time.

40 *Bedford and County Record*, 10 May 1921, p. 1. The reviewer thought that the orchestra was a bit under rehearsed. He also notes that: 'Walter Glynn sang "Onaway, awake" with such restrained fervour and beauty of voice that the audience broke the rule against applause until the conclusion of each part.'

41 *Bedfordshire Times and Independent*, 8 July 1921, p. 8.

County Hospital, and was held in the Bunyan Meeting church after the Sunday evening service. J. Arnold Whitchurch, then chairman of the Board of Management at the County Hospital, made an appeal, which was followed by a silver collection. Within a few years he was to become involved with the Bedford Choral Society and later on with Bedford Musical Society.[42]

Handel's *Samson* was performed at the end of November. The choir seemed to be going from strength to strength, the reviewer wrote: 'We believe they could now attempt anything in the way of choral music.'[43] The weakness of the performance seems to have been the orchestra:

> The Choral Union has hitherto had to rely on the generous assistance of what we may call without disrespect a scratch orchestra, some members of which are very good, but others are not. It is inevitable in the circumstances that the orchestral work they undertake should be less satisfactory than the choral … To be frank, there were some quite unpleasant moments on Thursday evening, not withstanding the capable work of leading by Mrs. Ozanne and the good work done by individuals … If the Choral Union is to present such works the orchestral part of them must be treated much more seriously and prepared for far more thoroughly.[44]

The Choral Union sang a selection from *Samson* in the Bunyan Meeting church after the evening service on Sunday 26 March 1922, as they had of *Judas Maccabaeus* in the preceding October.

Before the Choral Union's performance of *Messiah* on Good Friday, Percy Burke tendered his resignation as conductor. According to the report in the *Bedford and County Record*, he gave his reasons to the committee, but these are not given in the report, and it is now not possible to know what was in his mind. [45] He was asked to withdraw his resignation at least until after the rendering of Handel's *Israel in Egypt* in November for which rehearsals had been in progress for some time, and he consented to this.

Of the 1922 Good Friday performance of *Messiah* in St Paul's Wesleyan church, the reviewer wrote that: '[it] was not their best performance of this work. This was only natural in the circumstances, since they were smaller in numbers than usual and divided into two portions, besides being considerably hemmed in by the congregation. However, it was mostly good choral singing.'[46] The soprano soloist was Mary Palmer (Marshall and William Palmer's mother). Her choir was to become prominent in Bedford in the 1930s.

By the time that *Israel in Egypt* was performed, at the end of November, Percy Burke seems to have abandoned the idea of resigning. The reviewer is very complimentary about the performance, particularly of the chorus, though he observes that

42 *Bedfordshire Times and Independent*, 28 October 1921, p. 10.
43 *Bedfordshire Times and Independent*, Supplement, 9 December 1921, p. 1.
44 Ibid.
45 *Bedford and County Record*, 28 March 1922, p. 1. The report refers to an announcement in the previous week's *Bedfordshire Times and Independent* (24 March 1922). This announcement was, in fact, only two or three lines long. No reason for the announcement is given in either paper. The same issue of the *Bedfordshire Times and Independent* has an advertisement stating that Percy Burke is now able to take pupils for singing lessons. *Bedfordshire Times and Independent*, 24 March 1922, p. 1.
46 *Bedford and County Record*, 18 April 1922, p. 1.

they began somewhat timidly.[47] He wrote that the conductor had masterly control of both chorus and orchestra, and that the orchestra played better than it had in *Samson* a year earlier.[48] The soprano soloist failed to turn up at the last moment, which marred the performance, because the opening bars of each part are for soprano solo.

The Choral Union performed *Hiawatha* for the second time in March 1923. The main weakness of this performance was that it was given without woodwind or brass. Their parts were played by the organ, making it hard for the organist, William Palmer. Despite this, the reviewer thought that: 'the result was often quite curiously good. The orchestra had tuned up to the organ (which is not always the case in the Corn Exchange) and the organ held it together and often supplied the missing parts with success.'[49]

One of the highlights for the Choral Union during its short existence was when it combined with the Luton Free Church choirs in February 1924 to sing *Elijah*, first in Luton and then in Bedford. The Luton performance took place on 13 February and was conducted by James Congreve. The review, which covers both performances, gives only qualified approval to the Luton performance. This was because the orchestra was lamentably inadequate, there was no organ and, especially, because there had been no full rehearsal with all the performers. Also, there was nothing approaching *pianissimo,* or even *piano* which was not blurred and heavy.

The Bedford performance, given a day later, was conducted by Percy Burke, and, according to the reviewer, was better than the Luton performance. As he put it, the Luton performance was, in effect, a full rehearsal for the Bedford one.[50] A photograph of the Luton concert appeared alongside the extended report of the Bedford concert in the *Bedfordshire Times and Independent*.

Despite seeming to be very successful, by mid-1924 the Choral Union had some difficulties. The gist of the problem seems to have been that members of the Free Church Council felt that the Choral Union was not co-operating sufficiently with them and that the Choral Union wanted more independence. The issue was thrashed

47 'the Chorus was just magnificent. It is a very great achievement for a local body of singers, possibly busy people in every-day life and with only weekly practices, to give so big and exacting a choral work as *Israel in Egypt* in the way they did.' Because there are a lot of double choruses in *Israel in Egypt* the chorus was split into two choirs, and the reviewer notes the difference in tone and volume between the first and second sopranos which adversely affected the performance. Of the basses the reviewer wrote: 'A few voices in over-excess of enthusiasm tended to "shout" rather than sing once or twice, but mostly the tone in this department was excellent.' *Bedfordshire Times and Independent*, 24 November 1922, p. 7.

48 'The orchestra, as usual, consisted of "musical friends" and Mrs. Ozanne again led with wonderful skill and precision, and was quite well supported. The second violins were weak at times both in intonation and execution. The trumpet part by Mr. Sharpe, and the drums played with distinction as usual by Mr. H. J. Colson, call for special mention.' Ibid.

49 *Bedfordshire Times and Independent*, 30 March 1923, p. 8.

50 'Much of the improvement was due to the personality of the conductor, and part of it was effected by the addition of the organ … The orchestra was better than it was at Luton, but again inadequate in many of the solo accompaniments in spite of the skill of its leader, Mrs. R. T. Ozanne … the choir's tone was full and deep and bright … This may be said of the basses with particular emphasis, for they were really great. The sopranos' tone was clear and ringing and that of the altos rich and deep. The tenors were numerous and worked well and valiantly but they were often blatant in the upper registers … Captain Burke was no more successful than Mr Congreve in obtaining the *pianissimo* effects which such a choir ought to have produced.' *Bedfordshire Times and Independent*, 15 February 1924, p. 7 and 22 February 1924, p. 8.

out at the Choral Union's annual general meeting on Saturday 31 May, where this was the only topic discussed:

> Mr. Warsell referred to attempts which had been made by the Free Church Council to secure representation of the Choral Union on their Committee, and vice-versa, in order to obviate frequent clashes of dates. But the efforts to secure closer co-operation had been futile, and when, after the Choral Union had promised to sing on the occasion of the Rev. F. C. Spurr's last visit only about twenty members had turned up, and he thought it was not playing the game. He suggested that they discuss whether they were going to use the name or cut themselves off.[51]

Later in the meeting William Palmer put forward three options: retain official connection, with the Free Church Council providing financial as well as moral support; retain the existing title, but sever any formal connection with the Free Church Council, though be willing to help; become the Bedford Choral Union and specialise in choral music like the Glasgow Orpheus Choir.[52]

The annual general meeting was then adjourned and a special meeting reconvened early in October. It was agreed at the special meeting to adopt the third option put forward by William Palmer, but that the term 'Society', rather than 'Union', should be used. So the Bedford Choral Society came into being. A significant reason for dropping the close link with the Free Churches was to bring outsiders in. The announcement about the change of name and the report of the special meeting appeared under the headline 'BEDFORD CHORAL SOCIETY' in the *Bedfordshire Times and Independent*.[53] William Palmer resigned as organist, but proposed that his brother should replace him. The first rehearsal for the re-named Choral Society's performance of Handel's *Acis and Galatea* was also announced – Saturday 11 October – but the date for the concert was not specified.

Before the performance of *Acis and Galatea*, Bedford Wembley Choir put on a concert in the Corn Exchange early in December 1924 with organ accompaniment by Marshall Palmer. The report in the *Bedford Record* notes the origins of the Bedford Wembley Choir: 'It was on the initiative of Captain Percy Burke that the Bedford Wembley Choir was formed with the Bedford Choral Society as its nucleus and he is to be congratulated on the fine qualities of the singing on Wednesday night.'[54] The performers are complimented: 'Bedford's contingent of the Imperial Choir of 10,000 singers gave a concert which consisted mainly of the choruses which were sung in the stadium at Wembley on "Mendelssohn Day" [19th July 1924] at the Empire Exhibition.[55] The audience, poor in numbers but rich in enthusiasm, enjoyed a feast of pure choral music as it is rarely provided in Bedford.'[56]

51 *Bedfordshire Times and Independent*, 6 June 1924, p. 13.
52 Ibid. There was a 'Full Report' of the meeting in the *Bedford Record,* 3 June 1924, p. 1.
53 See *The Bedfordshire Times and Independent*, 10 October 1924, p. 8, for the long report of the special meeting of the Choral Society. There is also an advertisement (on page 9) about the first rehearsal, scheduled for the following day, Saturday 11 October at 8.00p.m.
54 *Bedfordshire Times and Independent*, 19 December 1924, p. 9.
55 In the aftermath of the First World War the British government sought to encourage imperial solidarity as part of its strategy for recovery. Events included the Empire Exhibition at Wembley (1924–25).
56 *Bedfordshire Times and Independent*, 19 December 1924, p. 9.

Percy Burke had conducted all the Choral Union concerts, and from the start these had been hugely successful, with a large body of able singers and, reportedly, some very fine performances for which he was given due credit. He resigned suddenly and inexplicably as conductor of the Choral Society less than a month after the Bedford Wembley Choir concert, and before the Choral Society's first performance, under its new name, of *Acis and Galatea*. As when he tendered his resignation in March 1922, the reason or reasons for his sudden resignation are not stated in the brief newspaper reports in either the *Bedford Record* or the *Bedfordshire Times and Independent*. The *Bedford Record* report reads: 'At the rehearsal of this Society on Saturday it was announced that Capt. Percy Burke had resigned the conductorship and that the Committee has accepted his resignation. Mr. O. Elias conducted Saturday's rehearsal and efforts are being made to find a successor to Capt. Burke.'[57]

The fact that Percy Burke had tendered his resignation less than two years previously suggests that there may have been problems for some time. Alternatively, his resignation may have been to do with his work, which meant that he had little spare time to concentrate on conducting.[58] Or it may have been to do with the pressures of organising and conducting concerts with more than two hundred singers, or because of the clashes with the Free Church Council. Whatever the reason, the committee of the Choral Society accepted Percy Burke's resignation and, although he had been so prominent, he drops out of the scene for a few years.

The committee of the Choral Society, as has been noted, appointed Arthur Parris. His appointment was reported in both the *Bedfordshire Times and Independent* and the *Bedford Record* at the start of 1925: 'We were informed officially yesterday that the Committee decided to invite Mr. Parris to conduct ... Mr. Parris has accepted the invitation.'[59] By accepting this appointment, Arthur Parris *ipso facto* severed his connections with the Musical Society. The eighteen month dual conductorship ended, leaving Herbert Colson in sole charge.

Musical Society concerts, 1924–33

Under Herbert Colson, the Musical Society's programmes were conventional; most works were from the nineteenth and early twentieth centuries. The exception was that they did not perform any of Handel's choral works. The Choral Society made up for this. The only major contemporary works were by Granville Bantock – *A Pageant of Human Life* and *The Pilgrim's Progress*. Two concerts – three if the December 1924 performance of *King Olaf* is counted - included works by Elgar.

Despite Herbert Colson's criticism of the Victorian choral tradition at the start of the this chapter, he reverted to the nineteenth century practice of performing the main work in the first part of the concert, with shorter pieces sung by the choir and soloists in the second half. He also introduced a major innovation, and a very positive one, of an annual orchestral concert, usually in February. The first of these was

57 *Bedford Record*, 6 January 1925, p.1 (see also *Bedfordshire Times and Independent*, 9 January 1925, p. 7 where Arthur Parris's appointment is anticipated).

58 A report included at the end of this chapter says that Captain Burke resigned because he had taken a lecturing post at Wandsworth College of Further Education in London.

59 *Bedfordshire Times and Independent*, 16 January 1925, p. 14.

in February 1925 when the programme included Beethoven's Symphony No. 5. One surprise was a concert performance of Bizet's opera, *Carmen*.

Of the December 1924 performance of *King Olaf*, the reviewer wrote: 'Mr. Colson had his forces well under his control and the bite and vigour of both singing and playing were in keeping with the subject.' *King Olaf* was the fourth performance of an Elgar work by the Musical Society within four years. This belies the belief today that public appreciation of Elgar was now declining.[60] The National Anthem and Tchaikovsky's *Capriccio Italien* preceded *King Olaf*. The reviewer (possibly William Palmer) hardly commented on the Tchaikovsky, but was disappointed by the performance of the Elgar.[61]

The soloists in *King Olaf* were particularly notable. The part of King Olaf was sung: 'by a newcomer, Mr. Roy Henderson, whose baritone voice is clear and resonant and who sings with authority and considerable dramatic feeling … it was a pleasure to hear.'[62] John Adams, the tenor: 'sang the narrative of Olaf's acceptance of the challenge with good delivery and variation of tone, and many of his upper notes were of fine quality.'[63] Doris Vane, previously complimented for her part in *The Spectre's Bride*, was again the soprano soloist.

The orchestra was small by today's standards, and the Musical Society had to engage several London professionals while Herbert Colson was conductor to strengthen it. This happened at the performance of *King Olaf*, but as often happened around this time, the London visitors had to leave early: 'Time was short, however, and even that saving *(no applause)* was not enough to prevent the very fine epilogue being spoiled by the London visitors hurrying away in the middle of it to catch their train. An earlier start seems to be the remedy for the future.'[64]

The first Musical Society concert, given when Herbert Colson officially become the sole conductor, was early in February 1925. This was an orchestral concert at which the main work was Beethoven's Symphony No. 5. The review is generally complimentary about the orchestra and the conductor: 'Mr. Colson wisely did not

60 'His [Elgar's] period of old age was a sad one. The death of his wife (in 1920) left him without zest for work and he had the depressing feeling that public appreciation, which had for so long been widespread and keen, was now weakening.' Percy A. Scholes, *Oxford Companion to Music*, 9th ed. (London, 1956), plate 52. Bedford seems to have been something of an exception, for Elgar's choral works were performed by the Musical Society throughout the 1920s.

61 He felt that the performance was technically adequate and occasionally very good but that: 'the vital breath of dramatic instinct and poetic insight and imagination was absent. The pictures were presented faithfully but they did not live.' He was not wholly complimentary about the choir: 'The sopranos, with the confidence of numbers, did as much as anybody in the way of dramatic effect and sang with good round tone and unflagging energy. Often they were a joy to hear. The chorus as a whole was at its best in the passages where broad sustained tone was required and that tone was full and satisfying.' But of the *Epilogue* he writes: 'The chorus sang the lovely "As torrents in summer" in simple and straightforward manner, but did not rise to the sublime passages following it. The absence of breadth and dignity was felt and the "strain of music" that ends the tale was slipshod and heavy where, if only it had been breathed softly with slow pulsating rhythm and had just faded into silence, it would have made an exquisite ending.' *Bedfordshire Times and Independent*, 19 December 1924, p. 10.

62 Roy Henderson was another of the original singers in Vaughan Williams's *Serenade to Music* and, when much more famous in the 1940s, he returned to Bedford to sing several times with the Musical Society. He was one of the few people who were born in the nineteenth century and who lived until the twenty-first century. See his obituary in *The Guardian*, 17 March 2000, p. 26.

63 *Bedfordshire Times and Independent*, 19 December 1924, p. 10.

64 Ibid.

attempt too much: a straightforward musicianly rendering was evidently his intention, and he achieved it without fuss or excitement or sentimentality.'[65]

A flyer advertised both the February orchestral concert and the choral concert scheduled for 7 April. The choral concert did not actually take place until 14 May. The most likely explanation for the change of date is insufficient rehearsal time. This might have been because the Bedford Eisteddfod Competitive Music Festival, which took place early in March, disrupted rehearsals.[66] The *Bedfordshire Times and Independent* of 13 March has an extensive report of the event, including photographs of many of the officials involved. These include prominent musicians, among them Granville Bantock and Ivor Atkins (organist of Worcester Cathedral), and a number of local musicians, including Harry Harding and Arthur Parris. The following week, Harry Plunket Greene's photograph was included with a caption referring to his annual visits to the Bedford Festival.

The main work in the May concert was Granville Bantock's *A Pageant of Human Life,* but the programme also included Bach's Suite in B Minor for Flute and Strings, Parry's *English Suite*, Elgar's *The Snow* and Brahms's *Death of Trenar*. *A Pageant of Human Life* is based on what the review calls: 'Sir Thomas More's little pageant – childhood, resolute adulthood, love, old age, stark and awesome death, fame and time, and so into illimitable spaces of eternity.'[67] The reviewer noted that more men were needed to bring their parts up to the standard of the sopranos and contraltos. The soloist was the well-known opera singer, Edith Furmedge, who had a 'grand voice'. She was currently taking part in the Covent Garden opera season.

The second of the Musical Society's orchestral concerts was given in November 1925; the main work was Dvořák's *New World* Symphony. Alfred de Reyghere and Mr Wessely were once again soloists in the Bach Concerto in D Minor, as they had been in December 1923. Although it was normal for the orchestra to be augmented by up to a dozen London professionals, for this concert all the first violins were local players. There was, surprisingly, only a small audience.

In early December, the Musical Society gave a concert performance of *Carmen*. When Herbert Colson originally proposed this at the annual general meeting earlier in the year there had been some resistance to the idea. Some members thought that grand opera lost much of its effect when performed without costumes. Herbert Colson responded by saying that they had been doing sacred oratorios for some time past and he thought it would be best to give the public a change.

The performance was augmented by a choir of about twenty boys from Bedford Modern School.[68] Their chorus 'When will Soldiers Mount on Guard' was sung with, 'a capital fast rhythm' and had to be repeated – evidence that *encores* during

65 'There was an efficient and well-balanced orchestra of fifty three players with Mr. Alfred de Reyghere as Principal and with about a dozen London players strengthening the lower string, wood-wind and brass departments. The brass was not the best we have had, either in tone or technique but the woodwind was delightfully clean and refreshing and the strings, particularly the first violins and 'cellos played with fine resilience and unity.' *Bedfordshire Times and Independent*, 13 February 1925, p. 9.

66 Bedford Choral Society also seems to have been affected in 1925 by the Music Festival.

67 *Bedfordshire Times and Independent*, 22 May 1925, p. 11.

68 There is only a short comment about the chorus in the review: 'The chorus did not have much to do but on the whole did it well. It is not easy for a chorus to sing music which is often in short "snatchy" phrases and full of accidentals. The sopranos were much better than on some recent occasions and their high notes were fresh and clear.' *Bedfordshire Times and Independent*, 18 December 1925, p. 9.

performance still occurred at this time. Several members of the string section of the orchestra were absent because they were ill. Four local singers, Ethel Gedge, Mrs P. S. Hudson, Mr G. H. Thomas and Mr G. Fitch, took smaller parts.[69] One of the professional soloists, Rosa Alba, had a cold, though was still able to sing. Parry Jones, a well-known tenor, was much praised.'[70] The review ends with a paragraph about the London performers again having to leave early: 'it has got to be more than a nuisance to see the London singers and players scramble out before the concert finishes. The whole concert, in fact, under these conditions becomes a desperate race against time.'[71] The reviewer hoped that the railway company would put on a later train back to London.

Herbert Colson normally took rehearsals himself, but he did not do so for the February 1926 concert, in which the main work was Elgar's *The Black Knight*.[72] This is based on Longfellow's translation of a poem by the German poet Uhland, which tells how the Black Knight came to the Pentecost Feast in the town of Hofburgh and had a devastating effect on the king's family.[73] Herbert Colson conducted the performance, which was judged a distinct success: 'a considerable part of the credit for this – as Mr. Colson would himself admit – is due to Mr. Cyril Gell, who, in the absence from the town of the Hon. Conductor, undertook the training of the chorus at all but the last two or three practices … Mr. Colson took advantage of his singers' greater confidence and responsiveness by widening the range of tone and volume and by obtaining rhythmic vitality and reality of interpretation.'[74] The reviewer was not impressed with the orchestral *ensemble* and blamed this on the fact that the London players and the local players only had one combined rehearsal. The whole assembly stood during the performance of the final item, Maurice Besly's very beautiful song 'The Night is Come', in memory of Mr W. T. Baker who had died a month earlier, aged seventy-five. For many years Mr Baker was the Musical Society's treasurer and librarian. His son, also W. T. (Tom) Baker, took over his mantle.

The next choral concert did not take place until December 1926. After the opening National Anthem, the assembly stood during Sullivan's Overture in C, 'In Memoriam', as a tribute to the memory of William Allen, the late president, who had recently died. The main work, performed in the second half of the concert, was Sullivan's *The Golden Legend*. There was also some Christmas music at the concert,

[69] Mr G. H. Thomas was later to be closely involved with the Bedford Festival. He was a very long serving member of St Paul's church choir. His photograph, along with those of three other long serving choirmen of St Paul's, appeared in *The Bedfordshire Times and Bedfordshire Standard*, 6 June 1952, p. 6. The report below the photograph has biographical notes about each of the four men.

[70] 'The most striking feature of Mr. Parry Jones's singing was his apparently inexhaustible reserve of power of dramatic expression. He gave a most convincing picture of Don Jose.' *Bedfordshire Times and Independent*, 18 December 1925, p. 9.

[71] Ibid.

[72] Elgar's *The Black Knight* is an early work, written in the 1890s, before he became well-known.

[73] It is quite a grim tale, summarised by the reviewer: 'In the play of spears, (the Black Knight) throws the King's son; at the ball, he dances a measure weird and dark ... with the King's daughter; at the banquet he offers both children a cool draught of golden wine and the 'fear-struck father' then beholds his children die.' *Bedfordshire Times and Independent*, 19 February 1926, p. 11.

[74] Ibid.

probably after *The Golden Legend*.[75] The reviewer did not consider this to be the 'grand performance' that the programme had promised, but comments somewhat grudgingly that it was: 'a sufficiently good performance of a difficult work'.[76] There was, for a change, a 'gratifyingly large audience'.

During the epilogue of *The Golden Legend* the London visitors began to leave, disrupting the whole concert. The reviewer comments:

> Never has the effect of that early last train been worse, and something really will have to be done to avoid spoiling the end of a performance like this. During the final duet between Elsie and Prince Lucifer, the visitors in the orchestra were hastily packing their instruments and stealing one by one from the platform, and in the Epilogue, poor Mr. Colson had to conduct a more or less skeleton orchestra and a chorus obviously distracted by the last minute dash of the soloists. It was altogether too exasperating.[77]

The reviewer suggested that the concerts should begin earlier, or that the London people should be entertained for the night in Bedford or be sent home by road. The Musical Society and its supporters needed to face up to the problem without further delay.

The problem was resolved before the next concert – *Elijah*. This was performed early in March 1927. The resolution of the problem received favourable comment from the reviewer: 'The new arrangement of sending the visiting professionals back to town by road enabled us to hear the concert to the end without distraction, and a vast difference it made. May it be continued.'[78] There was a crowded audience for this performance and many people were apparently unable to obtain admission. The reviewer felt disappointed that the high standard of the opening chorus, "Help, Lord", was not consistently maintained, and wrote that closer attention should have been given to the conductor's beat. But he complimented the local singers who sang the trio and the quartet.[79] The professional soloists included Elsie Suddaby and Frank Phillips. Elsie Suddaby's singing was praised as being: 'artistic from the highest point of climax to the slightest detail', but a: 'relaxed throat persistently hampered Mr. Frank Phillips's vocal production.'[80]

75 The order that works were performed at this concert is not clear from the review. Clearly, *The Golden Legend* was near to the end, rather than in the first half, because the London professionals left early while it was still being performed. Some Christmas music seems to have been sung after they had gone, but it is not clear what was performed in the first half of the concert.

76 *Bedfordshire Times and Independent*, 10 December 1926, p. 11. He writes of the chorus: 'The ladies showed discrimination in the interpretation of two opposing roles, first that of the Powers of the Air in the wild and stormy prologue, then that of angels singing delightfully ethereal "Amens". The gentlemen, as monks and pilgrims, sang their Gregorian chant and Hymn of St. Hildebert with satisfying solidity. Together, the whole chorus, representing the villagers, gave a singularly happy version of the familiar evening hymn "O Gladsome Light" … Pleasant, too, as the delicate singing of the lovely little passage "O pure in heart".' Ibid.

77 Ibid.

78 *Bedfordshire Times and Independent*, 1 April 1927, p. 11.

79 'It was a happy thought to leave the trio "Lift their eyes" and the quartet "Cast thy burden" entirely to local singers. The singing of the trio by Miss Gedge, Miss Howe and Miss Hartley was in its way the loveliest music of the evening – three beautiful voices in perfect blend and balance and unanimity of expression. The quartet was only one degree less well sung by Miss Howe, Mrs. Coltman, Mr. Barnes and Mr. Walker. Some of the same singers joined the soloists in "For he shall give His angels" and "Holy, Holy".' Ibid.

80 Ibid.

The main work at the December 1927 concert was a Bach motet. This was the first time that a significant choral work by J. S. Bach was performed by the Musical Society. For this concert there was organ and piano accompaniment only. The lack of orchestra highlighted the chorus's reliance on the orchestra:

> The obvious risk of making a habit of performing works with orchestral accompaniment is that the chorus (whatever the conductor's efforts to the contrary) tend to rely unduly on the orchestra for shelter and support when the difficult passages arrive ... Hesitant entries, weak rhythmic impulse and uncertain phrasing all told the same tale. People today hear so much choral singing of high quality broadcast and reproduced by gramophone records that no Society with a reputation to uphold can afford to be careless about the finer points of technique and interpretation.[81] This does not mean that the performances were bad, but they might have been much better, judged by the standard of the Society's own capacity.[82]

The reviewer was impressed with the chorus at the next choral concert, a performance of Coleridge-Taylor's *A Tale of Old Japan* in March 1928, for which there was a large audience.[83] It was evident that rehearsals had been thorough, and that the chorus and their conductor were putting heart and imagination into the work.[84] Gladys Knight was the contralto soloist.[85] The reviewer thought that her voice and reading of the contralto part did not fit into the scheme of things at all well. The orchestra: 'was to some extend handicapped by illness, no less than six of the strings being absent. The remainder, however, led by Mr. Alfred de Reyghere, were well able to preserve the balance.'[86] The review draws attention to the fact that: 'A distinguished member of the orchestra was Miss Marie Goossens, whose playing of the harp added many happy touches to the performance.'[87]

At the July 1928 annual general meeting, Herbert Colson proposed Elgar's *Caractacus* as the main work, and third concert, of the 1928/29 season. He suggested a lighter concert for December. In fact, Elgar's *The Music Makers* was performed in November, and Brahms's *German Requiem* at the end of the following March.

The Music Makers seems to have been a considerable challenge for the Musical Society: 'Considering all the circumstances, the comparatively few rehearsals, the

81 This comment was written five years after the first BBC broadcast when fewer than 20% of the population would have had access to a wireless.

82 *Bedfordshire Times and Independent*, 9 December 1927, p. 20. The chorus was also notably short of tenors: 'Probably the general effect would have been improved if the two sections of the choir had not been so widely separated and if the connecting link had been stronger than a line of eight valiant tenors.' The separation referred to was probably caused by the organ, which was still placed in the middle of the rear wall in the Corn Exchange. Later it was rearranged, so that there were two separate blocks of pipes, with a gap in the middle.

83 'The chorus sang as they have not sung for a year or two. They were well together, sure in attack (and only less so in release), clear and true in tone and intonation. Their phrasing and gradation were flexible and easy, and their rhythm resilient.' *Bedfordshire Times and Independent,* 30 March 1928, p. 9.

84 'Two passages might have been improved: the opening by the ladies in unison, which was slow and a little dull, and the page or two near the end following the altos' entry 'stick of incense'. That heavy entry momentarily spoilt the atmosphere created by the soloists, and the succeeding unaccompanied passages should have been sung with a whispered *pianissimo*.' Ibid.

85 At the end of the review of the December 1927 concert, a note had stated that the soloist in March would be Ethel Furmidge.

86 *Bedfordshire Times and Independent*, 30 March 1928, p. 9.

87 Ibid.

usual impossibility of going through the work with the full orchestra, and the actual difficulty of the scoring, the chorus came through with credit to themselves and to the conductor. It was something to have attempted so formidable a work at all.'[88] The limited rehearsal time, especially of the local orchestral players with the professionals from London, does seem to have been a real problem. This concert coincided with the Schubert centenary week, so the second half was devoted to shorter orchestral and choral works by that composer.

The last work of the season, performed in March 1929, was Brahms's *German Requiem*. The reviewer referred to this in his review of *The Music Makers*. He hoped that special attention would be given to the more delicate – and difficult – part of good choral singing, the lighter shade of tone and the subtleties of rhythm. In the event, he was happy with the result, as far as the chorus was concerned.[89] However, the reviewer takes the orchestra to task for overwhelming one of the two soloists, the soprano Hilda Howe, who was a local singer.[90] Keith Falkner, who sang twice for the Choral Society, notably in Haydn's *Creation* in 1928, was the baritone soloist and made a very good impression.[91] This performance was given in the Corn Exchange, and the reviewer notes with regret that there were many empty seats.

Brahms's *German Requiem* was repeated in November, in St Paul's church, the day after the eleventh anniversary of the signing of the Armistice. This time there was a full to overflowing audience. Hilda Howe was again the soprano soloist, but the baritone soloist for this performance was George Parker. The report is lyrical about the setting and, on the whole, favourable about the performance: 'Requiem … rest. That was truly the gift that the noble music of Brahms brought as it rose, sombre and yet exultant, among the pillars and arches of the old church.'[92] There is not much room in St Paul's church for a full chorus and orchestra and it is not clear how all the performers fitted in.

As Bedford is the home town of John Bunyan, it is perhaps not surprising that the Musical Society should have performed Bantock's *The Pilgrim's Progress*, commis-

88 *Bedfordshire Times and Independent*, 23 November 1928, p. 10.

89 'The long and sometimes intricately-scored choruses were sung with confidence and feeling, and the rich smooth tone of the sopranos was especially praiseworthy. In such choruses as "All flesh doth perish" and "Blessed are the Dead", where reverent treatment was called for, a little more true *piano* singing would, perhaps, have been an improvement … But no fair criticism can hide the fact that a lot of hard work had gone into the preparation of the work.' *Bedfordshire Times and Independent*, 29 March 1929, p. 9.

90 'One's only criticism of the orchestral playing is concerned with their accompaniment of the soloists: Miss Howe in particular would have been given a much better chance had some of the instrumentalists not obtruded themselves.' Ibid.

91 'Mr. Falkner's resonant and finely controlled voice was admirably suited to the music and he realised in his singing the full austerity of the Psalmist's "Lord, make me to know what the measure of my days may be".' Ibid. Keith Falkner was subsequently director of the Royal College of Music 1960–74, immediately preceding Sir David Willcocks.

92 The reviewer continues: 'Both chorus and orchestra reached a high standard of technical accomplishment and it was evident all through that they knew their work thoroughly. If there was one exception to this it was in the latter part of the chorus "Lord make me to know" where there seemed a little uncertainty among the sopranos and the consequent preponderance of male voices marred what as otherwise a good balance of the parts … The chorus 'How lovely are Thy dwellings' (the memory of which lingered pleasantly in the mind from the first performance of the 'Requiem') was again beautifully done.' *Bedfordshire Times and Independent*, 15 November 1929, p. 10.

sioned by the BBC for the tercentenary of Bunyan's birth.[93] The first performance, which was broadcast from the Queen's Hall, London, was given in November 1928. The Bedford performance was given on 25 February 1930. The *Bedfordshire Times and Independent* had a very long preview (a full column and a bit of the broadsheet paper) in the previous week's paper. There is an interesting comparison to Elgar's *The Dream of Gerontius*.[94] Granville Bantock had hoped to attend the performance, but telegraphed to say that he was unable to come.

The Queen's Hall performance had a choir of three hundred and an orchestra of eighty. Despite being on a much smaller scale, Mr W. A. Attenborough, the former MP for Bedford, reckoned that the Bedford performance was 'marvellous'. There are two main choruses, a chorale 'The Pilgrim now hath Found His Lord' and what the reviewer describes as 'the great closing chorus', 'In Praise of Famous Men'. Six soloists are required, and the ladies' parts were all sung by local singers. Keith Falkner was again the baritone soloist, taking the part of Bunyan the Dreamer. The second half of the concert: 'with the best will in the world, must be called a-rough-and-ready performance of Mendelssohn's "Hymn of Praise".'[95]

At the annual general meeting held in July 1930, Herbert Colson said that he would very much like to perform Bach's Mass in B Minor but felt that the Musical Society was not strong enough – so he suggested Mendelssohn's *St Paul*. He also suggested a second concert with a miscellaneous programme, including Dr Cyril Rootham's *For the Fallen*; he thought it might be possible to get Dr Rootham to come from Cambridge to conduct.'[96] In fact, *For the Fallen* was not performed. *Hiawatha* was chosen instead.

St Paul was performed in St Paul's church towards the end of November. It is clear from the review that something was wrong with the Musical Society: 'Those – the unfortunate critic among them – who could neither fail to remember that this was the opening of the Musical Society's concert season nor escape concentration on the more technical aspect of the performance must have gone away in varying degrees of disappointment and depression ... any true and impartial record of the performance must contain the admission that Bedford Musical Society could and should have produced a better rendering than it did of this familiar and comparatively easy oratorio.'[97] The critic thought that Herbert Colson worked hard but: 'Clearly given leads were missed, especially by the sopranos who were unusually

93 Granville Bantock's knighthood was announced in the New Year's Honour's list 1 January 1930. The preview, 21 February, refers to him as Professor Bantock and Dr Bantock. The review, 28 February, gives him his new title (Sir) in the opening paragraph but reverts to Dr Bantock in the second paragraph.

94 'In general style the work bears some similarity to Elgar's *The Dream of Gerontius*, that is to say, there are angels, devils, lost souls and an earthly choir, together with the voices of Christian, Apollyon, and Bunyan himself. In places the reminiscence is even stronger – not that Bantock's music is actually like Elgar's but the effect on the listener is similar as might be expected seeing that in both works the theme is that of a journey through spiritual realms to the Celestial City.' *Bedfordshire Times and Independent*, 21 February 1930, p. 10.

95 *Bedfordshire Times and Independent*, 28 February 1930, p. 11.

96 Elgar had also planned to use Laurence Binyon's poem for his own *For the Fallen*, but initially did not because Rootham was already working it. Elgar eventually returned to the theme, after much persuasion, calling his work *The Spirit of England*. This upset Rootham. See Northrop Moore, *Edward Elgar*, p. 700. Freddie E. Stevens (chorus master for the Musical Society 1952–65) knew Cyril Rootham at Cambridge in the early 1930s.

97 *Bedfordshire Times and Independent*, 28 November 1930, p. 10.

weak throughout: and even the steadfast basses floundered for a couple of pages in the chorus "O great is the depth".'[98] The orchestra fared a little better, though some of the wind parts were filled in by the organ. All the soloists were local – reducing expenses – and two of them were badly out of tune. The two are not identified. The review ends with the hope for a really splendid performance of *Hiawatha* in the spring.

Hiawatha was performed in March 1931. The Musical Society was joined by Kempston Musical Society, and the Corn Exchange was almost full. The reviewer notes: 'The choir was augmented by members of the Kempston Musical Society (by the courtesy of Mr. G. Ramsey) and as a result the balance between the voices and orchestra was nearer the ideal than could otherwise have been possible. Even so, a still stronger chorus, especially in the male voice parts, would have been an advantage.'[99] Bedford and Kempston combined could apparently muster only eleven tenors, and, though these did remarkably well, there were times when the volume necessarily fell short of the requirements: 'The performance ... was a distinct success, and a considerable part of the credit for this – as Mr. Colson would admit – is due to Mr. Cyril Gell, who in the absence from the town of the Hon. Conductor, undertook the training of the chorus at all but the last two or three practices.'[100] Despite the problems, the review concluded on a positive note: 'In general, it can be said that the whole performance, despite the incidental imperfections that have been referred to, was thoroughly enjoyable and provided one of the best choral concerts the Musical Society has given for some time.'[101] This was, unwittingly, a valedictory compliment.[102]

Bedford Choral Society concerts, 1925–33

The Bedford Choral Society, with its new name, its formal connection to the Free Church Council severed and new conductor, made a significant contribution to the musical life in Bedford over the next few years, although the number of singers was small compared to the numbers that had initially sung with the Free Church Choral Union.

Arthur Parris was a conservative musician who was well suited to the Choral Society's aims. The first concert was *Acis and Galatea*. The concert was given on 16 April 1925, much later than originally planned in October 1924, when Percy Burke was still conductor.[103] Quite a number of members of the original Choral Union were reported to have left when the Choral Society became independent: 'The chorus was only seventy strong but it was obvious that the best material remains out of the old Free Church Choral Union chorus and that the present chorus is capable of much

98 Ibid.
99 *Bedfordshire Times and Independent*, 20 March 1931, p. 9.
100 Ibid.
101 Ibid.
102 Rather poignantly, in view of subsequent events, immediately under the review of *Hiawatha* in the *Bedfordshire Times and Independent* is a report about Harry Harding's will, stating the gross value of his estate.
103 The delay in holding a concert at this time may have been because the Bedford Festival was held in the first part of March. The Musical Society seems also to have been similarly affected.

better work than it gave on this occasion.[104] … Mr. Parris has already obtained good balance and flexibility.'[105] The only accompaniment was that of pianoforte (Madeleine Lovell) and organ (Marshall Palmer). The comments of a correspondent to the *Bedfordshire Times and Independent*, highlighting the lack of an orchestra, followed the review: 'I enjoyed the concert as a reminder of the delightful work which I have heard many a time, but I was disappointed in its production on this occasion. The chorus was very good. The recitatives, as accompanied by with organ, were excellently given … The pianist supported the Chorus firmly and accurately, but Handel requires a volume of support – strength and power. The attempt to interpret Handel with a piano simply was a distinct failure. The absence of strings, really a full orchestral accompaniment, makes one say it should never again be attempted.'[106] There was only a moderate attendance. The reviewer felt that they deserved better support from the public. After this concert, the Choral Society used a string orchestra, augmented by organ and sometimes piano.

Arthur Parris conducted all the Choral Society's concerts. Marshall Palmer recalled working as organ accompanist with him:

> I came to know Mr. Parris well at that time. He would invite me to his house and we would go through the score together, marking in the parts he needed me to play. He sat with cigarette in holder; I sat by his side, armed with coloured pencils … The Corn Exchange organ was a semi-tone higher than piano or strings, so everything had to be transposed down a semi-tone. Sometimes I would just mark my score 'In A flat' but more complicated scores would have scraps of manuscript pasted over them. It could be quite nerve-racking.[107]

The Choral Society was on a smaller scale than the Musical Society and its choice of music more conservative, although there was some overlap. Arthur Parris thought that it was best to stick to oratorios, mostly by Handel, and this is what the Choral Society generally did.[108] This no doubt accounts for some of the Choral Society's success, filling a void, as it were, because the Musical Society did not perform any of Handel's oratorios under Herbert Colson.

At the July 1925 annual general meeting, Arthur Parris said that the next concert was to be a performance of Mendelssohn's *St Paul* on 26 November. The next concert was actually a performance of *Messiah,* and was performed in December 1925: 'the first of an intended series of annual Christmastide performances of Handel's "Messiah".'[109]

Mendelssohn's *St Paul* was not performed until February 1926. The reviewer congratulates Arthur Parris for securing, despite some difficulties, an enjoyable performance: 'There were gaps in the ranks of the chorus [presumably because of

104 There is a further reference to the drop-out in the review of *St Paul*, in February 1926: 'The original chorus of the Free Church Choral Union has dwindled to comparatively small but by no means insignificant numbers and its best quality survives in the Choral Society.' *Bedfordshire Times and Independent*, 12 February 1926, p. 9.
105 Ibid.
106 Ibid.
107 H. Marshall Palmer, *Memoirs*.
108 See the report of the Choral Society's annual general meeting in the *Bedfordshire Times and Independent*, 17 June 1927, p. 9.
109 *Bedfordshire Times and Independent*, 25 December 1925, p. 12.

the flu epidemic].[110] The absence of the organ naturally was felt by a chorus that is used to its support, but it would have been felt less if the singers had known their parts better … It was particularly unfortunate that it had been decided to dispense with the woodwind and brass [a reasonable decision if only for reasons of economy] and rely on strings and organ … If the chorus had been as good all through the performance as they were at the end, the performance might have been described as an unqualified success.'[111] The Corn Exchange was only half-filled for this concert. The reviewer felt that there were great possibilities in this chorus, and that the audience's obvious enjoyment of their singing should encourage them to go ahead and give increasing attention to the finer points of their art – ensemble, rhythm, phrasing, accentuation, gradation and variety of tone.

The Choral Society's next concert was held in May, less than two weeks after the end of the General Strike: 'The Corn Exchange was well filled for the last concert of the season … The programme was miscellaneous, no big work being performed. An interesting feature of the concert was that most of the music was fresh to Bedford listeners.'[112]

The chorus's biggest task was a performance of Brewer's *Summer Sports*, which was completed in 1911. This consists of five songs, originally from the Elizabethan period, together with an orchestra. The title comes from a song by Thomas Dekker, 'Summer Sports'. The work also includes his 'Golden Slumbers'. There was a string orchestra, and the pianist was Madeleine Lovell. Carrie Tubb was the soloist in a number of the shorter songs, though not in *Summer Sports*. The reviewer was slightly critical of her singing on this occasion.[113]

The Choral Society performed *Messiah* once again in December 1926. This had now become an annual event.[114] 'It was a pleasure not only to see increased numbers in the choir, but more especially to hear a real improvement in the choral work which, on the whole, was sound and gave much enjoyment.'[115] There is a detailed description of how the various parts of the choir performed.[116] Arthur Parris was complimented for his work at rehearsals. Keith Falkner was also complimented:

110 Marshall Palmer, the organist, was one of those affected, succumbing at the eleventh hour.

111 *Bedfordshire Times and Independent*, 12 February 1926, p. 9.

112 *Bedfordshire Times and Independent*, 28 May 1926, p. 8.

113 'Her voice was as beautifully clear and "open" as ever and her technique is as good as in the past. In the face of such finished singing it seems a pity to find any fault but Miss Tubb's intonation on Thursday just spoilt her singing occasionally: she was never singing really flat but she was frequently just going to be. That was principally in her slow sustained songs.' Ibid.

114 'A fairly large audience gathered in the Corn Exchange on Thursday evening to hear what has now become the Bedford Choral Society's annual performance of Handel's Messiah.' *Bedfordshire Times and Independent*, 24 December 1926, p. 9.

115 Ibid.

116 'The choir is well-balanced and keen. The sopranos sang with bright, fresh tone, and except for a few weak entries (apparently due to nervousness, for which there was no need) their attack was good. Their intonation was true, and the enunciation has improved in a marked degree. The contraltos were a little less successful; although they sang with good, broad quality of tone, the effect was a little lacking in variety and inspiration. Their singing, however, was useful because of its reliability. It is a pity the basses are small in numbers, for more were certainly needed to make a really good balance, particularly as the tenors were very strong and might really have been toned down at times. All the men, however, showed excellent team work. The choral balance might be improved on another occasion by better seating arrangements; it was unfortunate that some of the sopranos were placed below the tenors.' Ibid.

'Mr. Keith Falkner (bass) used his fine voice in the musicianly way that Bedford audiences have learned to expect from him.'[117]

A performance of *Hiawatha* followed in February 1927.[118] The review describes the usual accompaniment.[119] Marshall Palmer recalled a particular mishap during this performance:

> I only ever remember making one awful boob. This was at the end of 'Hiawatha'. The choir sang all three parts of Coleridge-Taylor's tuneful work. In Part III, 'The Departure', as Hiawatha is sailing across to his hereafter, I had to hold on a low pedal note for several pages as the chorus mounted to a climax. The sopranos reach a high B natural, the whole choir singing *fortissimo* 'to the hereafter' and on the 'aft …', the orchestra comes in *fff* – all should be thrilling and majestic. I would prepare full organ to go into action but when the exciting moment came, I crashed out the chords in the original key. When I heard the sound that I was making, I quickly reverted to the correct key but it did not make for good listening. I slipped out that night having turned off the water-engine, got on my bicycle and rode home with burning cheeks.[120]

The reviewer does not seem to have noticed and the only comment is generous: 'Miss Lovell (piano) and Mr. Palmer did a great deal of the difficult work with unobtrusive reliability.'[121] Doris Vane was one of the soloists: 'Doris Vane needs no introduction to Bedford audiences, nor indeed to any who have a wireless set. She sang Hiawatha with the earnestness, the sincerity and the rich beauty of tone that one always expects from her, and not in vain.'[122]

According to the review, the Corn Exchange was full for the performance of *Hiawatha*. However, at the following annual general meeting, it was stated that there would have been an even better audience had not a Clara Butt concert followed soon afterwards.

The main concert in the following season was a performance of Haydn's *Creation* in February 1928. The review opens by referring to Haydn's humour:

> One always suspects 'Papa' Haydn of having had his tongue in his cheek when he wrote parts of 'The Creation'. The man who could introduce sudden *sforzandi* into his music with the avowed intention of "making old ladies jump' could scarcely be expected to resist the obvious temptations of the Creation story, as compiled for the oratorio from Genesis and Paradise Lost.[123] Such phrases as 'cheerful stands the tawny lion', 'with sudden leap the flexible tiger appears', and 'in long dimension creeps, with sinuous trace, the worm', simply

117 Ibid.

118 There is a comment about Coleridge-Taylor in the *Oxford Companion of Music* that seems particularly apposite for the Choral Society at this period: 'Nevertheless, he provided British (and to some extent American) choral societies with material of distinction – and a new 'flavour' that came as a welcome relief from existing conventions.' Scholes, *Oxford Companion of Music*, pp. 180–1.

119 'As on previous occasions, the full orchestration, on which depends much of the picturesqueness of the setting, was dispensed with, but the substitute was excellent, consisting of a small but efficient string orchestra (skilfully led by Mrs. H. W. Robinson), harp (Miss Gwen Melhuish) – they usually used harp – pianoforte (Miss Madeleine Lovell) and organ (Mr. H. M. Palmer).' *Bedfordshire Times and Independent*, 25 February 1927, p. 12.

120 H. Marshall Palmer, *Memoirs*.

121 *Bedfordshire Times and Independent*, 25 February 1927, p. 12

122 Ibid. Doris Vane sang regularly at the Promenade Concerts 1915–31.

123 Early in *The Creation* the chorus sings 'Let there be Light'. 'Light' is suddenly and unexpectedly sung very loudly – *forzando* (*sf*).

> had to be translated literally by such a picture-painter as Haydn, ... and the translation is vastly tickling to the modern ear. Nor can the audience now resist a smile at the quaintly idyllic picture of Adam and Eve in their Eden bliss. And why should we?[124]

The performance seems to have been a success and, except for an unlucky accident for the chorus at the beginning, it was a good sound performance. The 'accident' was unspecified.

The bass soloist was, once more, Keith Falkner. The review ends with a note about his dress clothes having been stolen as he travelled to the concert. Marshall Palmer gives an entertaining account of the occasion in his memoirs:

> In February 1928, Bedford Choral Society was rehearsing Haydn's 'Creation' and I was to play the Corn Exchange organ for the performance. At the dress rehearsal that afternoon, Mr. Parris, the conductor, summoned me down from the organ and told me that Mr. Keith Falkner, who was a bass in St. Paul's Cathedral choir, had had his suitcases stolen on his way from St. Pancras to Bedford. He was to go on a longish tour and both his evening dress suits were in one of the suitcases. He had arrived at the rehearsal in a splendid golden brown suit of 'Plus Fours' which I had admired from the organ console. I was asked if I could lend him a suit for the evening. We looked at each other – he was not so tall as my six foot, five inches and certainly much fuller and bigger built. In the end, he decided not to borrow from me but turned up in his 'Plus Fours' to take his place by the soprano and tenor, both resplendent in evening dress. I am sure that Mr. Parris must have explained the situation to the audience who were naturally sympathetic. His glorious voice made apologies unnecessary, but the headline in the Daily Express the next day was 'ADAM IN PLUS-FOURS AT BEDFORD'.[125] Keith told me when he came to sing at Letchworth Free Church some years later that he had never felt such a fool as at that concert and that the thief had been caught. The only damage was that all the names had been neatly removed from every article of clothing and every musical score.[126]

The major concert in February 1929 was Handel's *Belshazzar*. The review opens with the rather extraordinary (and probably incorrect) statement that *Belshazzar*, composed in 1744, had only twice been performed in this country. The Choral Society used the recently published and simplified edition without the double choruses. The reviewer commended the Society for its policy of breaking new ground, although this made very heavy demands on the chorus and orchestra. *Belshazzar* was the only rarely performed (i.e. not popular) large-scale work that was sung by the Society. The Choral Society, and particularly Arthur Parris, was complimented in the review on the success of the performance.[127] Mrs Coltman, the contralto soloist, was a local singer. Frank Phillips, the bass soloist who took the

124 *Bedford Record*, 28 February 1928, p. 2.

125 This is a lovely story but the author was unable to find this headline in *The Daily Express*.

126 H. Marshall Palmer, *Memoirs*.

127 'The choruses were managed admirably by a choir that was somewhat depleted in numbers. More male voices would have improved the balance, and the lack of tenors occasionally resulted in an unfortunate effect upon the tone of the few valiant gentlemen … It speaks well, therefore, for both the enthusiasm and the ability of Mr. Parris and his forces that their venture was justified by the results … The otherwise excellent playing of the orchestra, of which Mrs. H. W. Robinson was leader, was marred in places by uneven entries, a tendency especially noticeable in the accompaniment of the soloists.' *Bedfordshire Times and Independent*, 22 February 1929, p. 12.

part of Daniel, taught singing classes in Bedford. Before the performance, the whole gathering sang the hymn 'Now Thank we all our God' in gratitude for the King's progress towards good health.[128]

The Choral Society performed *Elijah* in February 1930. For this performance, they were augmented by members of the Rushden Park Road Baptist Church Choir, as they were in several other concerts at this time. As a result of the choir being augmented, there were too many sopranos, while there was the usual shortage of tenors. The reviewer thought a smaller and more balanced choir would have been preferable and considered the performance only 'adequate'. He also thought that Arthur Parris should have undertaken more 'drilling' but was complimentary about the four soloists, referring to them as, 'all accomplished and experienced singers'.[129] He does not give any details about their backgrounds, however.

Marshall Palmer recounts in his *Memoirs* a performance given by the Choral Society in Bedford Prison late in 1930 or early in 1931:

> The Choral Society was asked to sing 'Messiah' in the main building of Bedford Prison. My mother's choir had been visiting the prison for several years singing carols in the Chapel. It was quite a moving experience for singers & prisoners, one of whom was Rouse, the murderer, who was later hanged at the prison.[130] However, a large choir assembled in the lofty, forbidding building which reminded me slightly of the old Crystal Palace, in that it was a cruciform shape. The walls were iron stairways with levels of little galleries leading to the cells. The prisoners were in the main body of the hall, opposite the choir and also in the two side aisles. I was given a large, elderly grand piano on which to play but it was too far away from Mr. Parris and I could not see him well. I asked the Governor if the piano could be moved. He agreed and signalled to a couple of men who moved it under my direction. I could see that they looked at the piano rather knowingly and one glanced at the 'fall' to see the make of the instrument. After the performance, the Governor, Mr. Pickering, told me that both men were musicians, one was a F.R.C.O. and neither was 'in' for violent crime, rather embezzlement or such. I remember the acoustics in the lofty building were very good and the choir sang well.[131]

The main concerts in February 1931 and 1932 were, respectively, Handel's *Samson* and *Judas Maccabaeus*. Both performances were again augmented by

128 Ibid. The author has Mary Whitchurch's score of *Belshazzar* (the abridged edition) with her note showing the date of the concert. The names of the soloists are written in the front of the copy.

129 H. Marshall Palmer, *Memoirs*.

130 Marshall Palmer does not give the date of the prison concert, but it is possible to date it from this reference to Alfred Arthur Rouse, the murderer. Rouse was hanged on 10 March 1931 for a crime committed on 5 November 1930. Rouse was found guilty of the murder of a hitch-hiker in his (Rouse's) car. It is possible he was attempting to fake his own death because of domestic problems – as well as being married he had several girlfriends, at least two of whom became pregnant from knowing him. He therefore needed to disappear in order to avoid inevitable trouble. Rouse claimed that the car exploded when the hitch-hiker lit a cigarette after he himself got out of the car. Rouse was identified through the car's number plate, arrested, tried for murder and hanged in Bedford gaol. The victim was never identified, making it a very unusual case. According to the Wikipedia article, Rouse studied music at evening classes and had considerable musical talent and a good baritone voice. Rouse also learnt to play the piano, the violin and the mandolin. Wikipedia, http://en.wikipedia.org/wiki/Alfred_Rouse, accessed 8 April 2015.

131 H. Marshall Palmer, *Memoirs*.

Rushden Park Road Baptist Church Choir.[132] It is pretty clear from the reviews that neither performance was of a very high standard. Also, neither performance was well supported, with a 'painfully large proportion of empty seats' for *Samson*.[133] In both the 1931/32 and 1932/33 seasons, there were also concerts in November. In both of these the main works were by Coleridge-Taylor, in November 1931 a performance of *Kubla Khan*, and in November 1932 *A Tale of Old Japan*. The latter was once again spoiled, the reviewer thought, because of the imbalance in the choir, with a shortage of basses and especially tenors. There was some good singing but: 'in the softer passages the delicate singing that is so essential to a performance of this work was largely missing. Nor were the attacks and precision always very good.'[134] The baritone soloist was the twenty-seven year-old Boyd Neel. Born in 1905, he qualified as a naval officer and doctor of medicine, but then turned to music. Two years after singing with the Choral Society he founded the well-known Boyd Neel Orchestra. He was the only one of the four soloists whom the reviewer felt was confident in the cantata.

The Choral Society's final concert, performed in February 1933, was another performance of Haydn's *Creation*. There was a larger than usual audience for this popular work. The choir, augmented once more by Rushden Park Road Baptist Church Choir, seems to have sung as well as they ever had done, with only the alto section appearing to 'lack vitality', possibly because there were fewer of them than usual. The orchestra rather spoiled the performance, however.[135] Mrs H. W. Robinson, who had led the Choral Society's orchestra for most of their concerts, let it be known that she would stand down after this performance.

Organisation of Bedford Musical Society

The annual general meeting reports in the *Bedfordshire Times and Independent* are comprehensive and give many details about the running of the Musical Society, they include: information about the election of officers – the key players – and committee members; summaries of the secretary's and treasurer's reports; and plans for forthcoming seasons. In the early years, meetings were held at the Working Men's Institute, but from 1926 they were held at the General Library (now the Harpur Suite).

132 See *These Years Have Told: The Story of Park Road Baptist Church, Rushden*, by George E. Bayes, (Rushden, 1951). On page 89 there is a little about the choirmaster at the time that the choir from this church sang in Bedford: 'Mention must be made of the retirement, after twenty-one years' service of the choirmaster, Bernard Tompkins, a son of the Rushden manse. During his term of office, great strides were made in the musical side of the worship … Largely through Mr. Tomkins's professional connections, annual choir festivals became the occasion for visits of eminent artistes of national reputation. Crowded congregations supported these musical services and Park Road Baptist Church became noted for its good music. The successful presentation of oratorios was another regular feature developed by this talented choirmaster.' Bernard Tomkins advertised regularly that he taught singing at Rose's Music Store in Bedford on Fridays and Saturdays, e.g., *Bedfordshire Times and Independent*, 17 July 1931, p. 8.

133 *Bedford Record*, 17 March 1931, p. 1.

134 *Bedfordshire Times and Independent*, 25 November 1932, p. 12

135 The reviewer blamed this on insufficient practice and suggested that a simpler accompaniment might have been better. 'The opening was promising and in the earlier parts of the work the accompaniments of the choruses were full and effective. But later there came disintegration and even actual breakdown. How the soloists managed to finish the duet "Grateful consort" still remains a mystery: if it had not been for the intervention of the organ they would probably have gone practically unaccompanied to the end. *Bedfordshire Times and Independent*, 17 February 1933, p. 7.

At the annual general meeting in June 1924, Richard Allen resigned as president. Harry Harding was nominated, but did not accept the appointment and Lady Lawson-Johnson was subsequently elected. Mr W. A. Attenborough was elected to replace her in 1928. Mrs Whitchurch replaced him between the 1930–31 annual general meetings, presiding at the annual general meeting in 1932, and at a crucial one in 1933.

There were six vice-presidents in 1924, including two Harpur Trust head teachers, Mr H. W. Liddle and Miss Westaway. Miss Walmsley and Miss Stansfield were also vice-presidents. By 1929 there were nine vice-presidents, including all the Harpur Trust head teachers. Mr Grose-Hodge of Bedford School was one of them. Other vice-presidents included J. Arnold Whitchurch and Richard Allen, and the mayor for that year, Mr G. H. Barford, who was also president of the Choral Society.

Dr Harvey Goldsmith remained honorary secretary throughout this period, having originally been appointed in 1904, though from 1928 Mr W. G. Walker was joint honorary secretary. Mr W. T. (Tom) Baker was the librarian, as his father had been before him. He was also elected honorary treasurer at the annual general meeting of 2 June 1927 on the resignation of Captain Ray. Mr Baker asked to be allowed to continue as librarian 'as a labour of love'.

Several people were involved with both the Musical Society and with the Choral Society, notably Mr and Mrs J. A. Whitchurch and Mr G. H. Barford. And while Mr A. E. Storr was chorus secretary of the Musical Society, Mr E. Storr (his father) was treasurer of the Choral Society.

The financial position of the Musical Society looms very large in annual general meeting reports. Under the headline 'Bedford Musical Society' there was usually a sub-heading about the financial position, which varied from year to year, as the following examples show: 1925, 'A Deficit to Reduce'; 1926, 'Improved Financial Position'; 1927, 'Difficult Financial Position'; 1929, 'An Unsatisfactory financial position'; 1930 (surprisingly!) 'Another Good Year'. The statement of accounts reported at the 1927 annual general meeting is the fullest report of any annual general meeting during these years.[136]

The chairman, Mrs Whitchurch, said at the 1927 meeting that the Society ought not to have an overdraft, and that she hoped every member would make an effort to get rid of the debt. She thought that the concerts in Bedford were very cheap and that the prices of seats could be raised. Drawing room concerts by the members would also be a dignified way of raising extra money for the big concerts.[137]

The 'improvement' in 1930 was short lived. The bank overdraft was down to £5 8s 1d from the £74 14s 3d reported at the 1929 annual general meeting. In 1931,

136 'The statement of accounts for the season 1926–27 showed receipts amounting to £397 / 16 / - , which included £135 / 14 / - in subscriptions; £167 / 7 / - in concert tickets; patrons' donations, £50 ; music, £41 ; and sundries, £3 / 5 / - . The payments included £123 to artistes for the three concerts, hire of halls £42 / 14 / - ; cost of platform and chairs, £51 / 9 / - ; printing and advertising, £60 / 17 / - ; tax stamps, £38 / 15 / - ; music, £52 ; hire of piano £9 /10/ 6 ; and other small items; total £483 / 15 / - , or £65 / 18 / - in excess of the receipts. The balance sheet as at 5th May. 1927, showed bank overdraft £130 / 16 / - , and outstanding cheques £10 / 18 / - . The assets amounted to £112 / 3 / - . and £7 / 10 / - was deposited in advance booking of the hall for the season 1927–28. The accounts were audited by Mr. W. Shepherd'. *Bedfordshire Times and Independent*, 10 June 1927, p. 12.

137 Ibid.

however, there was a £200 deficit. It is, perhaps, not surprising that there were financial problems, in view of the country's bleak economic position at the time.

Organisation of Bedford Choral Society

No minute books for the Bedford Choral Society have survived. The information there is about the running of the Society – and it is good information – comes from reports in the *Bedfordshire Times and Independent*, especially regarding the appointment of Arthur Parris, and details of subsequent annual general meetings.

In his treasurer's report to the 1924 annual general meeting at the end of May, Mr E. Storr stated that: 'the Union had paid all debts (applause). It had paid off £42 from last year. A small amount stood against them at the bank, but subscriptions due from members would clear it off. So that the Union had had a very satisfactory year.'[138]

At the adjourned annual general meeting on 4 October 1924, Mr E. Storr reported that the Choral Union had an overdraft of £1 5s 5d, and that bills sent in since the audit brought the deficit up to nearly £2.

The report of the 1927 annual general meeting, with the sub-heading 'ENCOURAGING REPORTS', opens with: 'The Mayor (Ald. G. H. Barford), President of the Bedford Choral Society, was in the chair at the annual meeting on Monday in St. Paul's Wesleyan School, and was supported by Mr. A. F. Parris, Hon. Conductor, Mr. G. Pleasant, and Mr. H. C. Piper, Hon. Secretary.'[139] There then follows detailed information about the accounts and the election of officers and committee members. Mr Pleasant and Mr Piper were elected as joint secretaries. Mr E. Storr, who was organist and choirmaster at Kempston East Methodist church, continued as treasurer (he finally retired in 1931 because of his age; he was seventy-nine). Mr S. French was named as assistant conductor and Marshall Palmer as organist. Seven of the fifteen members of the committee were women. 1927 was probably the Choral Society's most successful year and this is reflected in the report.

Closure of the Bedford Musical Society

The Musical Society did not put on any choral concerts after the 1931 annual general meeting, though it did not disband for another couple of years. It closed down rather suddenly in the autumn of 1933. The main reason was identified by Mr Pinnock at a crucial 1932 annual general meeting where he said that the real question was that of membership: 'Rightly or wrongly, I have come to the conclusion that in a town like Bedford there is not room for two societies ... I hope that from this meeting an effort will be made to see if it is not possible to have one good musical society in the town rather than two who, if they are not on the rocks are very near to it.'[140]

Bedford did not have a large enough population to sustain two societies. So both the Musical Society and the Choral Society suffered from a shortage of singers, especially men, and from poor audiences at concerts as a result. The logical thing would have been to combine. But while the Musical Society was closer to the Established Church, the Choral Society was rooted in nonconformity having started out

[138] *Bedfordshire Times and Independent,* 6 June 1924, p. 13.
[139] *Bedfordshire Times and Independent*, 17 June 1927, p. 9.
[140] *Bedfordshire Times and Independent*, 1 July 1932, p. 10.

as a coalition of nonconformist choirs. There was some programming overlap with both societies including works by Mendelssohn and Coleridge-Taylor. However, the Musical Society did not perform any works by Handel, while the majority of the works performed by the Choral Society were Handel's oratorios.

According to Herbert Colson, in an interview soon after the Musical Society's closure: 'the loss of enthusiasm by members of the two Societies themselves might be attributed to a falling off of the interest taken by the General Public in their performances. This, in its turn, might be due to broadcast music. No amateur production could compete with the wireless.'[141] However, Herbert Colson was incorrect when he said: 'There was a decline in the Victorian period and we are now emerging from that decline.'[142] Far from declining during the Victorian period, choral music grew hugely from quite small beginnings in the 1850s and 1860s, and in Bedford was very strong while Philip Diemer was conductor. Harry Harding then continued and strengthened choral music in the town. Herbert Colson seems to have lacked the personal and organisational skills of his predecessors, and he failed to maintain and develop the Musical Society and to attract sufficiently large audiences. Something must have spurred Arthur Parris to move to the Choral Society, and whatever it was, the existence of the Choral Society no doubt exacerbated the problems that faced the Musical Society, as Mr Pinnock observed. Another factor in the failure of both societies was, almost certainly, the shortage of men, probably because so many men had been killed in the First World War. This shortage was regularly referred to in reviews.

At the annual general meeting of the Musical Society held on 1 July 1930, it was reported that there was: 'a better financial position than at any time during the past five years.'[143] However, as already mentioned, Mendelssohn's *St Paul*, performed in November 1930, was a poor concert. *Hiawatha*, performed with assistance of the Kempston Musical Society in March 1931, was more successful, but not enough to save the Society.

The 1931 annual general meeting should have been held towards the end of June or early in July, but it was postponed to September. Towards the end of August, the following report appeared in the *Bedfordshire Times and Independent*:

> A CRITICAL POSITION: MANY MORE MEMBERS – AN URGENT APPEAL, Having completed its 64th season, Bedford Musical Society finds itself in serious financial straits. At the moment there is a deficit of nearly £200, attributed to insufficient support and poor attendance at concerts, and unless many more members and supporters come forth, the Society may have to discontinue its activities … In these circumstances, the officers of the Society have issued an appeal, in which they state: 'The society has a nucleus of the best singers in the district numbering about 100. Unless another 100 performing members are secured it is practically impossible to carry on. The Society has 50 instrumentalists of a high calibre and needs many more. The Society has non-performing members who pay an annual subscription and needs 100 more.' [The

[141] *Bedfordshire Times and Independent*, 17 November 1933, p. 10.
[142] Ibid.
[143] *Bedfordshire Times and Independent*, 4 July 1930, p. 10.

> following] … personal letter, addressed 'To all lovers of music' has been issued by Mrs. Whitchurch as President.[144]

Although the Corn Exchange had been nearly full, receipts from *Hiawatha* were insufficient to meet all the Musical Society's expenses. Normally the deficit would have been made up by members' subscriptions, but a shortfall of members resulted in the deficit of nearly £200 not being made up. There is no report in the *Bedfordshire Times and Independent* of the September annual general meeting, postponed from July.

The Musical Society did not hold any concerts during the 1931/32 season, but rehearsals were maintained. However, only the more enthusiastic members attended. The 1932 annual general meeting was held on 28 June and was a critical one. The very full *Bedfordshire Times and Independent* report is headed, 'LONG DISCUSSION AT ANNUAL MEETING.' The sub-heading is, 'CHORAL ACTIVITIES SUSPENDED FOR A YEAR.' The annual report was read by the joint-secretary, Mr W. G. Walker, because Harvey Goldsmith, who usually introduced the secretary's report, was not present. There had been no concerts during the season because there were too few singing members for the conductor to prepare a work for public performance. There were only about sixty members of the chorus and thirty-five in the orchestra. Mr Beagley, who had sung with the Musical Society for nearly fifty years, said it was impossible to go on when only three or four tenors and basses attended the practices: 'If you would only give me one more year to make it my fiftieth, how happy should I be; but how are you going to get your members if you do go on?'[145]

The committee had not felt justified in incurring any more debts – having lost heavily on concerts in the previous season. A proposal to close the Musical Society was put to the meeting but not finally agreed upon.[146] It was, however, agreed that the orchestral section should continue to function, the debts be paid, and the choral section be left in abeyance for twelve months. Mr Pinnock said he thought that there was a lack of enthusiasm to sing choral music. He nevertheless proposed an amendment to the motion: that efforts should be made to meet with representatives of other musical societies in the town with a view to amalgamation and to forming one society. This amendment was lost by a large majority.[147]

In a letter to the *Bedfordshire Times and Independent* following the meeting, Mary Palmer gave three reasons for the Musical Society's failure, she stated that: musically, there was a lack of enthusiasm and real hard work at rehearsals, so concerts were not first rate; there was a lack of cordiality and friendliness among members; and that the 5s subscription, and the cost of music was rather a lot

144 *Bedfordshire Times and Independent,* 21 August 1931, p. 7.

145 *Bedfordshire Times and Independent,* 1 July 1932, p. 10.

146 Ibid. The proposer was Mrs Wells. The dissolution of the Musical Society was agreed in principle.

147 Ibid. The Musical Society's income was just over £50, despite there having been no concerts and expenditure was approximately £22. However, the liabilities were approximately £50–£82 for a bank overdraft and £32 owed to sundry creditors. The Musical Society had certain assets of nearly £100, so was actually solvent, but they could not – or did not wish to – realise these because of the bank overdraft and the perceived need to keep a little 'nest-egg'.

for some people.[148] Lastly, she suggested that her forty-strong mixed choir should disband so they could throw their lot in with the Musical Society.[149]

At the 1933 annual general meeting, it was agreed to wind up the Society. Mrs Whitchurch, whom the *Bedfordshire Times and Independent* refers to as Miss Whitchurch, said in her opening remarks that it would be a terrible thing to dissolve the Society and she could not believe that it should be allowed to happen or that it was not possible to get more members.[150] The only person to speak against disbanding the Society was Mr W. T. Baker, the honorary treasurer. He still believed, 'from the bottom of his heart', that the Musical Society could be resuscitated. Herbert Colson formally resigned, expressing 'great grief' at having to do so.

Only about thirty members attended the meeting, but as a two-thirds majority was required to wind it up, a postal ballot had to be held. Once it was agreed by the meeting that this should be arranged, the meeting was adjourned until replies were received. And so, after sixty-six years, the Bedford Musical Society ceased to exist.

Closure of Bedford Choral Society

The closing down of the Choral Society was rather sad. It was more sudden and unexpected than the closure of the Musical Society. The 1933 annual general meeting was held on 26 July, and the secretary's report was moderately optimistic in tone: 'the Secretary commented upon the harmonious working of the society and said its success was the more remarkable in view of the difficulties that were being experienced by older and better known societies throughout the country. He was certain that there were a number of people who had never been to their concerts and who, if they could be persuaded to tear themselves away from their wireless sets for once and to hear the real thing, would thereafter, be regular members of the Society's audiences.'[151] The secretary, George Clark, thanked Mrs. Makings in particular for arranging whist drives which had augmented the Choral Society's funds.[152] The treasurer's report showed that the Choral Society was nearly £15 in credit. Arthur Parris's suggestions for works to be performed during the forthcoming season, Brewer's *Summer Sports* in November, and *Hiawatha* in February were approved. The secretary referred to the need for more members and more patrons. Apart from this, the Choral Society appears to be 'ticking along nicely' if not thriving.

Financial concerns in 1933 were not the most pressing problem facing the Choral Society, or the cause of its demise. It was announced in the press that rehearsals for *Summer Sports* would begin in September at the Girl's Modern School.[153] The Choral Society had previously performed this work in May 1926. The next report is from the *Bedfordshire Times and Independent* of 3 November 1933, and is given here in full:

148 *Bedfordshire Times and Independent*, 15 July 1932, p. 9.

149 A week earlier there was also a letter from Mr S. W. Churchill, organist of St Peter de Merton church, Bedford, saying that the closing down of the Musical Society, with its long and honourable record of work was a musical calamity. He goes on to speak of the lovely voices in Mrs Palmer's Choir and the number of men singing in the Polychordia at the Competitive Musical Festival. There is a memorial to Mr Churchill in St. Peter's church. *Bedfordshire Times and Independent*, 8 July 1932, p. 9.

150 *Bedfordshire Times and Independent*, 30 June 1933, p. 12.

151 *Bedfordshire Times and Independent*, 28 July 1933, p. 8.

152 George Clark's daughter, Barbara, was secretary of the Bedford Messiah Choir in the 1990s.

153 *Bedfordshire Times and Independent*, 22 September 1933, p. 9.

BEDFORD CHORAL SOCIETY TO CLOSE DOWN THROUGH LACK OF ENTHUSIASM

At a special general meeting of members of the Bedford Choral Society on Tuesday evening, it was unanimously decided to close down. A small sub-committee was appointed to wind up the affairs of the Society, which is financially sound. The balance is to be given to the Bedford County Hospital.

It is understood that a general lack of support and enthusiasm among the members of the Society was the reason for the decision. The Society were to have performed 'Summer Sports' by A. Herbert Brewer, at the end of this month, but this work, which was given a few years ago, proved to be unpopular amongst the choral members and the attendances at practices were so poor that the possibility of the work being performed was very remote. The position became such that it was imperative to call a special general meeting, and at this meeting, the decision to close down was taken. The Society was begun immediately after the war as the Bedford Free Church Choral Union. It was then composed mainly of members of Free Church choirs, with Mr. Percy Burke as conductor. When Mr. Burke left Bedford for London, an appeal for support was made to the town, with satisfactory results, the title was changed, and Mr. Parris was elected conductor.

The present officials are: Mr. J. Arnold Whitchurch, President; Mrs. E Murray and Mr. G. H. Ratcliffe, Vice-Presidents; Mr. A. F. Parris, Hon. Conductor; Mrs. Makings, Hon. Treasurer; and Mr. G. Clark, Hon. Secretary.[154]

The Choral Society had always struggled both to retain members (following its severance of close links with the Free Churches Council) and to attract audiences. Its concerts had always been on a smaller scale than those of the Musical Society and it had humbler aspirations, but it had fulfilled a need in Bedford for traditional choral works. Its demise apparently occurred without a murmur of dissent. But some of the individuals who were involved with the Choral Society would have a further role in Bedford's musical history.

[154] *Bedfordshire Times and Independent*, 3 November 1933, p. 26.

Chapter Six

Entr'acte, 1933–41

> That this Society, with its long and honourable record of splendid work, should cease its activities or any part of its work is a musical calamity.[1]

With the demise of both the Musical Society and the Choral Society in 1933, there followed a period where there was no choir able to perform large scale choral works with some form of orchestral accompaniment. However, there were a number of choirs in the town, and a considerable amount of live choral music was performed during the period 1933–40. There were also regular orchestral and chamber music concerts. This chapter will look at the variety of musical activity that continued during these years.

The Mary Palmer Choir

Mary Palmer (1868–41), *née* Cowley, was the wife of the prominent editor of the *Bedfordshire Times and Independent* newspaper.[2] She originated from Brighton and gained scholarships at the Brighton School of Music (then an unofficial branch of the Royal Academy of Music in London): 'As a singer and pianist, her services were of great demand at Brighton concerts, her soprano voice being notable for its purity and range … She was handicapped by ill-health and was virtually an invalid over a period of years … But in the last twenty years of her life her health showed some signs of improvement.'[3]

Mary Palmer was an early and enthusiastic supporter of the Bedford Festival. Initially, she trained children's choirs to compete. She formed a ladies' choir in the autumn of 1924, and they sang in the Bedford Festival in the following March. She formed a mixed choir in 1925. The ladies' choir comprised about thirty members and they were joined by about twenty men to form the mixed choir. The choir was well regarded and even sang for the radio, as her obituary says:

> The Mary Palmer Choir gained an enviable reputation wherever they sang. Although there were the ladies' and mixed voice choirs performing separately there was actually one choir, a friendly body of people whom Mrs. Palmer inspired with her own love of singing. They sang together as her friends; they appreciated the value of preparing for and competing at music festivals and their numerous successes were a testimony to Mrs. Palmer's ability as a choir-trainer. Always Mrs. Palmer expected the best of which they were capable and she

1 R. W. Churchill, organist of St Peter's church, Bedford. Extract from a letter to the *Bedfordshire Times and Independent*, 8 July 1932, p. 9. There is a memorial to him in St Peter's church, Bedford.

2 William Palmer was editor from 1895 until his death in 1922.

3 From Mary Palmer's obituary (headed 'MRS WILLIAM PALMER') in the *Bedfordshire Times and Independent*, 17 January 1941, p. 7.

> achieved remarkable success in this endeavour. The Mary Palmer Choirs were familiar competitors at the annual festivals in Bedford, Northampton, Leamington, Bourneville (Birmingham), Kettering, Peterborough, Leicester, Hastings and Nottingham. In May 1927, the choir had the distinction of broadcasting from Savoy Hill (2LO); ten years later, Mrs. Palmer again conducted her singers before the microphone - at Broadcasting House – and in August 1938 another programme was given by the choir 'on air'. On each occasion, half an hour's programme of part-songs was given on a National and Regional wavelengths.[4]

Marshall Palmer wrote an account of the 1937 broadcast at Broadcasting House for the *Bedfordshire Times and Independent*:

> It may be of interest to record the experiences of this Bedford choir (some fifty strong) … Having assembled outside the building shortly before 3 p.m., we were admitted to the entrance hall one by one (and counted – which was reminiscent of the preliminaries to a prison concert!) … we were shepherded to respective cloak-rooms where all but necessary clothing was politely taken from us: it is said that engineers are likely to become hysterical if anything resembling an overcoat or an umbrella enters a studio, for such things actually affect perfect broadcasting adversely. We were then herded into a very small studio … It had apparently (by some error) not been realized that the choir was so large … arrangements were made for us to move to a larger studio – 'BB' – that was used for some Variety broadcasts … Here a platform accommodated two new 'Bosendorfer' grand pianofortes, the whole choir, and the announcer's desk … Mr. Bradley (the Balance and Control official eventually responsible for putting us 'on the air') and two overalled assistants first put us at our ease, and then – to our Balance Test … Mr. Bradley listened in the adjoining room, returned and moved the 'mike' and piano, and so on – until 3.45. when we were free to sit and talk. At 3.50 there was a general murmur, 'Look, there is Mr. Stuart Hibberd!' and through the glass windows of the listening-room – the Chief Announcer braved the interested gaze of many female eyes! … By 4 o'clock we were on the platform and dead quiet; a moment later red lights flickered and then stayed on; Mr. Hibberd spoke naturally … and then we were singing. Were we broadcasting? – yes, but really it seemed hard to realize this … we sang for the sheer joy of making music – which is not always easy to do, but which is the proper way to do such a thing.'[5]

The programme, conducted by Mary Palmer, with accompanist, Marshall Palmer, mainly consisted of short English choral works from the twentieth century and included one work by Marshall Palmer himself.[6]

Mary Palmer was an active member of the Bunyan Meeting church until her move to Woburn Sands. According to her obituary: 'In 1937, 1938 and 1939 the choir formed the foundation of a larger choirs summer Festival Service of Music in

4 Ibid.

5 *Bedfordshire Times and Independent*, 30 April 1937, p. 13. The choir's visit took place on 18 April 1937.

6 The first part of the programme for mixed voices was: 'Full Fathom Five' (Charles Wood); 'Alleluia' (H. Marshall Palmer); and 'When Mary thro' the Garden Went' (Charles Stanford). This was followed by a section for women's voices: 'The Lord is my Shepherd' (Schubert); 'Orpheus with his Lute' (Edward German); and ''Tis time, I think, by Wenlock Town' (Thomas Armstrong). The concert concluded with two more songs for mixed voices: 'O Can Ye Sew Cushions? ' (arr. Bantock); and 'My Soul, there is a Country' (Parry). Detail of the music performed comes from *The Radio Times*, 16 April 1937, p. 20

Woburn Church, an event which was instituted by Mrs. Palmer's youngest son, Mr. H. Marshall Palmer, A.R.C.O.'[7]

Mollie Winter, who sang with the Musical Society from the 1950s until 1997 (by which time it had become the Bedford Choral Society), recalls singing in Mary Palmer's choir:

> I came to Bedford from Nottingham in 1936 and joined Mrs. Palmer's choir straight away. I had been married for two years. Tom (my husband) was in Lloyd's Bank. Marshall Palmer was organist of Woburn Parish Church. Mary's daughter, May used to come to the choir. They lived in Woburn from 1935 onwards and used to go to competitive music festivals all over the country. Mary Palmer was quite elderly and not very strong and rather thin. Marshall, her youngest son, sometimes took rehearsals and sometimes conducted. His mother worried about him as he had not got a proper job and yet he was so musical. He taught piano privately. He lived in Glebe Road. I went for piano lessons but singing came more easily so I did not carry on long with the piano. I enjoyed being in Mary Palmer's choir. We used to go to Hastings. I remember winning £20–00. There were about thirty of us in the choir. You were not all allowed to enter for competitions. Mary used to pick and choose, rather. Mostly we sang three part pieces, but sometimes four part songs. Some of the adjudicators at competitions were well known composers. We used to meet Armstrong Gibbs, Thomas Armstrong, Herbert Howells and Helen Henshaw. My first baby was born in 1940, so I was not singing at the time that Mary Palmer died.[8]

Mary Palmer made her last appearance with the choir in 1940. She died in January 1941 at the age of seventy-three, leaving three sons and one daughter. Mollie Winter adds: 'After Mary's death, several of those who had been in the Mary Palmer Choir joined a choir run by Mrs Ethel Budd, organist of St Paul's Methodist church in Harpur Street [where Bedford Central Library now is]. Mrs Budd's choir maintained the tradition of involvement in music competitions in the late 1940s and early 1950s.'[9]

The Polychordia

This male-voice choir was formed by Herbert Colson a year after the last performance by the Musical Society in March 1931. *Bedford Music – A Year Book,* published in 1947 and 1948 to give information about a wide range of musical activities in the Bedford area, says of the Polychordia: 'The Polychordia Male Voice Choir was formed in 1932 with 50 members. Competitions have been entered in many parts of England, and Concerts have regularly been given for charitable purposes.'[10] It seems that many of the singers in the Polychordia were staff at Bedford Modern School.[11] Asked towards the end of his life about his conductorship of the Polychordia: 'Mr. Colson's eyes lit up. This had been one of his "hobbies", and he loved it. "One of the finest things that anyone can do is to run a male voice choir like that", he said "They

7 *Bedfordshire Times and Independent*, 17 January 1941, p. 7.
8 Personal interview with Mollie Winter by the author.
9 Ibid.
10 *Bedford Music - A Year Book 1947*, p. 20.
11 Personal interview with Joe Pinnock by the author. George Thompson, a member of the Bedford Orpheus Choir and Bedford Choral Society, confirmed this.

were all jolly good fellows, and theirs was the pleasantest company imaginable. They have sung in competitions all over the Midlands, including Birmingham, Nottingham and Leicester. They have had some grand times, and raised a fair bit of money for charity, too."'[12]

The Polychordia first performed at the Bedford Festival in the spring of 1932. On 28 February 1933, they took part in a concert that also included the Musical Society orchestra. The orchestral works were Beethoven's Symphony No. 5, Wagner's *Siegfried Idyll* and Grieg's *Peer Gynt Suite*. They were conducted by Mr de Choisy. Herbert Colson conducted the Polychordia in interludes between the orchestral works. In November 1933, the Polychordia gave a further concert in the Town Hall. This time, the bulk of the concert was choral music, with interludes played on the violin by Alfred de Reyghere with Miss A. de Reyghere as piano accompanist. The Polychordia's songs included Elgar's 'Reveille', Coleridge-Taylor's 'Lee Shore' and 'Old King Cole'. Evelyn Bryan, of the BBC and Provincial Concerts, was the soprano soloist.[13]

Herbert Colson was conductor of the Polychordia until the beginning of 1947, but owing to ill-health he handed over to Mr E. G. Tebbutt.

The Bedford Orpheus Choir

Captain Percy Burke, one-time conductor of the Free Church Choral Union before it became the Bedford Choral Society, re-appeared in the mid-1930s to form the Bedford Orpheus Choir. In August 1935, Percy Burke wrote to the *Bedfordshire Times and Independent* setting out his proposals. First there is an editorial introduction: 'Elsewhere in this issue, Capt. Percy Burke, once conductor of the Choral Union, announces his intention to form a choir and, with the help of his London Orchestra, to give a performance of "Hiawatha" in February.'[14] In the following letter, Percy Burke explains the circumstances that have led to his decision:

> Sir, – Many times during the past three years members of my old choirs have asked me when I was going to give them an opportunity of a real good sing … I thought it would be difficult to find twenty vocal enthusiasts in the once very chorally-minded Bedford … One particular keen member has greatly surprised me by presenting me with a list of over twenty names of those who would like to sing again under my conductorship … I feel I must at least endeavour to keep faith with those good folk … I have decided that if any work would quicken the pulse of the invalid art of choral singing, it is the inspiring and ever pleasing 'Hiawatha' by Coleridge-Taylor … I hope to enlist the help of my London Orchestra, and this, coupled with the fact that the renovated Corn Exchange organ would be anxious to show its paces... and with the engagement of first class artists, should give us the ingredients necessary for a very successful evening next February … Owing to the fact that I am only at home at weekends, the rehearsals must be held on Saturday evenings, but what Saturday evenings we used to have … Percy Burke Musical Director Wandsworth Technical Institute 39 Castle Road Bedford.[15]

12 Report of Herbert Colson's retirement from Bedford Modern School. *The Bedfordshire Times and Bedfordshire Standard*, 5 August 1949, p. 6.
13 *Bedfordshire Times and Independent*, 10 November 1933, p. 10.
14 *Bedfordshire Times and Independent*, 30 August 1935, p. 10.
15 Ibid.

In an editorial footnote the question is raised as to whether the Corn Exchange organ would be ready, as work on the organ was not expected to start until next spring, but concludes that the organ is not essential for *Hiawatha*.

The reality, however, was rather different from Percy Burke's original – rather grandiose – ideas. The Orpheus Choir was formed with approximately fifty members. George Thompson, who subsequently sang with the Bedford Choral Society (as Bedford Musical Society had by then become) until the year 2000, recalls:

> There's a photograph of the old Bedford Orpheus Choir. I took it at a social evening. When I joined the Orpheus Choir, Captain Percy Burke was the conductor and we only did two works, *Hiawatha* and the *Messiah*. We used to do the whole of *Hiawatha*, the three parts, and we went all over the place, singing that. On Good Friday we would, perhaps, do the *Messiah*. I remember going to Potton, going to Shefford and going to Ampthill Methodists and I think we went to Bletsoe church. In those days, there was a Mr Davies, of Cranley Outfitters. He was a Moravian, I think, and a local preacher, and he used to sing in the choir and he was a very keen walker. After these Good Friday concerts, he used to say to me: "We're not going back in the coach, George, are we? We may as well walk." I remember walking back from Potton and from Ampthill with him – just the two of us.[16]

The Bedford Messiah Choir

The Bedford Messiah Choir, which is still extant, was founded by W. G. Poole in 1937. W. G. Poole was a personnel manager, later general manager, at W. H. Allen and Sons Ltd, the Bedford engineering company. He started annual performances in the Bromham Road Methodist church (still visible behind a modern shop front, almost opposite Holy Trinity church) as the first major event of the Christmas season. To him it was an act of worship rather than a musical performance. As a result, the quality of the performance and the ability of the singers took second place.[17] George Thompson remembers singing in one or two of the earliest performances, but found himself sitting next to people who were, as he put it, 'all over the place', so he did not continue to sing with them.[18] W. G. Poole conducted the choir until the late 1950s.

Orchestra and instrumental music

A surprising amount of orchestral and instrumental music was performed in Bedford at this time. With the looming demise of the Musical Society, the orchestra was renamed The Bedford Orchestral Society and carried on. A preview from the period states that: 'They will shortly renew their activities on the same lines as last year under the conductorship of Mr. Jean de Choisy. There are still a few vacancies for members.'[19] The Orchestral Society seems to have flourished during the 1930s as a review from early 1938 states: 'By no means that least important service that Mr. Jean de Choisy, conductor of the Bedford Orchestral Society, has in recent years

16 Personal interview with George Thompson by the author. George Thompson was examined by Granville Bantock for his Trinity College piano examination and, as top student, was awarded a prize.
17 Personal interview with Brian Caves by the author. Brian Caves was the organist of the Bunyan Meeting in the 1970s and 1980s, and conducted the Messiah Choir in the 1970s and 1980s.
18 Personal interview with George Thompson by the author.
19 *Bedfordshire Times and Independent*, 22 September 1933, p. 9.

rendered to the music of Bedford is the really remarkable tradition, now firmly established, that he has built up with regard to audiences at the Society's annual concerts.'[20] A review of a February 1939 concert was similarly enthusiastic. This concert included Bruch's 'most familiar' violin concerto.[21]

The Bedford Music Clubs

A report in the *Bedfordshire Times and Independent* of 22 September 1933 refers to two series of chamber music concerts.[22] There were two organisations, each claiming the title of Bedford Music Club, each with a concert programme list and dates.

The locally-based Music Club, founded in 1924, flourished throughout the 1930s and promoted chamber concerts. They met at Bedford High School, and Miss H. B. Norman was the honorary secretary and treasurer. The programme for the 1933/34 season included the Brosa Quartet, the Trio Players (Gerald Moore, Edna Kersey and Cedric Sharpe), Harriet Cohen and Lionel Turtis. Over the next few years the musicians who came to Bedford included the accompanist Gerald Moore, Isobel Baillie, Leon Goossens and Peter Pears (as a member of the New English Singers in January 1937). Many of the reports of these concerts were written by Marshall Palmer.

The London-based Music Club, which claimed to be, 'the original Bedford Music Club', was under the direction of the Imperial Concert Agency, 175 Piccadilly, W1, from where season tickets could be obtained. It is not clear how long this music club survived.

The outbreak of the Second World War

By 1939 the Bedford Competitive Music Festival or 'Eisteddfod', formed in 1921, had become one of the biggest music festivals in the country.[23] Most of the town's leading musicians were involved with it in some way and Harry Harding had been especially so, until his death in 1930. With the outbreak of war in September 1939, it was no longer possible to continue with all the musical activities in the town. Many men were called up for active service or were involved in the Home Guard or other duties locally. The Music Festival was put under wraps for the duration of the war and the Bedford Music Club did not put on any concerts either.[24] There were, however, a number of orchestral concerts held in the Corn Exchange, with some nationally-prominent musicians taking part. Among them were Sir Henry Wood with the London Symphony Orchestra (at the beginning of August 1940) and Basil Cameron, who conducted the London Philharmonic Orchestra in December 1940 and the London Symphony Orchestra in May 1941. Also, Myra Hess gave a piano recital early in 1941. As Marshall Palmer put it in one of his reviews, Bedford was

20 *Bedfordshire Times and Independent,* 25 February 1938, p. 11.

21 Violin Concerto No. 1 in G Minor.

22 *Bedfordshire Times and Independent*, 22 September 1933, p. 16. This report includes details of the two Bedford Music Clubs, a report about the Bedford Orchestral Society rising from the ashes of the Bedford Musical Society and details of rehearsals for the Choral Society's November concert, which was to have included Herbert Brewer's *Summer Sports* – the concert which never took place, as described at the end of chapter five.

23 *Bedford Music – A Year Book 1947*, pp. 9 and 19.

24 Ibid.

really on the musical map.[25] It is possible that the Corn Exchange was being tested as a suitable future venue for the BBC Symphony Orchestra with these concerts.

There was one notable concert, mostly of local musicians, which could be described as a *finale* to the period 1933–40. This concert, a performance of *Elijah* in 1940, was promoted by the Music Festival. The foreword to the programme states: 'Owing to the war it was found impossible to hold the Competitive Music Festival this year and in order to keep together, the many Choirs in our County which for years competed at the Festival, it was decided that a Choir and Orchestra should assemble together, under the conductorship of Mr. H. J. Colson and present Mendelssohn's great work, "Elijah" as a special effort.'[26]

The concert was scheduled for 16 May - this date is shown in the programme – but the performance had to be postponed, owing to the critical situation brought about by the war. Neville Chamberlain resigned as prime minister after a vote of no confidence in the House of Commons on 10 May, and Winston Churchill formed the National Government and War Cabinet over the next few days, 11–15 May. Germany invaded Holland at the same time and then invaded France, which fell before the end of the month. The deliverance from Dunkirk occurred between 26 May and 4 June. The *Elijah* concert was finally held on 26 September, during the blitz (7 September – 3 November).

The chorus was 250 strong with members of many local choirs taking part including the Bedford Polychordia Choir, Bedford Orpheus Choir, Biggleswade Ross-Boughton Choir, Bunyan Women's Guild Choir, Fenlake Fellowship Choir, Mary Palmer's Choir, Podington, Hinwick and Farndish Choirs, Queen's Works Musical Society, Shefford Choral Society, St Cuthbert's Mothers' Union Choir, and the Wesley Hall Mothers' Union Choir.

The orchestra comprised only twenty-two players with organ accompaniment. The singers are listed and include George Thompson who was at home in Bedford on leave at the time. The *Bedfordshire Times and Independent* reported on the performance: 'The Committee of the Bedfordshire Competitive Music Festival are to be congratulated on their courage and determination in carrying through the performance of the Elijah on Thursday evening at the Bedford Corn Exchange, despite the very trying present conditions. They were rewarded by a large audience of music-loving and Festival supporters who, I think, in their turn deserve to be praised for sportingly turning up and defying the sirens.'[27]

The article includes of a long account of why the concert was being held, who was taking part, a lengthy passage entitled 'Mendelssohn's Masterpiece' and details of the soloists:

> The performance, under the direction of the Festival's chairman, Mr. H. J. Colson, F.R.C.O. reached a very high standard. The four soloists were all artists of repute and well known to Bedford audiences. Miss Stiles Allen has adjudicated at our Festival on several occasions and she is, of course, one of the best-known singers on the concert platform to-day. Her performance on Thursday evening showed, I thought, slight signs of tiredness, but her voice

25 *The Bedfordshire Times and Bedfordshire Standard*, 30 May 1941, p. 5.
26 Bedford Competitive Music Festival, *Elijah Programme*, (Bedford, 1940). Author's collection.
27 *The Bedford Record*, 1 October 1940, p. 4.

> was as lovely as ever. Miss Margaret Balfour, who sang the contralto part, was exemplary in enunciation and interpretation. Mr. Edward Reach, the tenor, was in splendid form and sang with dramatic intensity. Bedfordians who had been looking forward to the appearance of their own Mr. Frank Phillips were disappointed that his important duties at the B.B.C prevented him from taking part. His place was admirably taken by Mr. Arthur Fear, who sang the part of Elijah magnificently. The choruses were all very brilliantly sung with precision and vigour, and Mr. Colson secured results which would have done credit to any choral body – amateur or professional. The orchestra was efficiently led by Mr. A. de Reyghere, A.R.A.M., and Dr. Probert Jones did valuable work at the organ, though we missed the wood-wind which is always such an outstanding feature of Mendelssohn's scoring. I class this performance as worthy of ranking with the best of any choral efforts given in Bedford in recent years, and I offer sincere congratulations to Mr. H. J. Colson and to all those who took part in such an outstanding performance. PC[28]

This concert was something of a swan-song for a number of the choirs and looked back to the period before the demise of the Musical and Choral Societies in 1933. But it also looked forward to when there would, once more, be performances of large scale choral works in the town.

Mary Palmer died on 13 January 1941, four months after the *Elijah* concert was held. Her choir did not survive, but as Mollie Winter has noted, several members joined Mrs Budd's choir. Herbert Colson remained in charge of music at Bedford Modern School and organist of St Paul's church until the late 1940s although he was not involved with the upsurge in choral singing that was about to unfold. Percy Burke lived in Bedford until the late 1960s but, like Herbert Colson, did not continue to take an active part in music in the town or continue to be conductor of the Orpheus Choir, though it survived into 1950s.

[28] PC is probably Peter Churchill of 67 Foster Hill Road, Bedford, a piano teacher. He advertised in the *Bedfordshire Times and Independent*, for example on 16 July 1937, p. 7.

Chapter Seven

Reformation, 1941–43

> Several members of my mother's choir had been suggesting that the Bedford Musical Society should be revived. As I had often had to conduct the Mary Palmer Choir when she was ill, and had formed and conducted the Clarendon Male Voice Choir in the thirties, it was to me they turned to set things in motion.[1]
>
> Actually the meeting to re-form the Bedford Musical Society took place the week after we were married in September 1941 and Marshall was in bed with a high temperature and an ear infection, so I represented him at that meeting and cycled home the thirteen miles to Woburn Sands afterwards! Devotion?! [2]

Until the beginning of 1941, Marshall Palmer had been the paid organist of Woburn parish church, but his contract was terminated by the twelfth Duke of Bedford. The Duke, who inherited the title in 1940, was opposed to the war against Hitler. Before succeeding to the title the Duke was well-known as a pacifist, and was prepared to give Hitler the benefit of the doubt. He founded the right wing British People's Party in the summer of 1939 with two others, one of whom had been a member of Sir Oswald Mosley's British Union of Fascists. The new party was suspiciously pro-German. In his autobiography *A Silver-plated Spoon*, the Duke's son John, later the thirteenth Duke of Bedford, describes his father's treatment of the vicar:

> At the beginning of 1941, he [the 12th Duke] was off on another tack. One of our oldest family obligations had been to pay the vicar's stipend at Woburn Parish Church. My father had made up his mind that the Church of England was supporting the war and decided to stop these payments and join the Plymouth Brethren ... Things got so bad that I felt I had to make some gesture to retrieve the family honour, so my wife and I went down to pay a courtesy visit on Archdeacon Martindale the day before he left the vicarage.[3]

Just weeks after his mother's death, Marshall Palmer received similar treatment from the Duke. There is a report in the *Woburn Reporter* of 11 February 1941:

> Mr. H. Marshall Palmer, organist at St Mary's Church, Woburn, for ten years, is refusing to give up this appointment even though he has received a month's notice from the Duke of Bedford to terminate his employment ... To a reporter of this journal he said: 'The Duke has "sacked" me, but I am simply not going. The Duke can't turn me out – St. Mary's is not a private place of worship and I intend to carry on. To lose the £125 a year of my income is a big blow, but if

1 H. Marshall Palmer, *Memoirs*.
2 Personal communication to the author from Sylvia Palmer.
3 James John Russell Bedford, Duke of, *A Silver-plated Spoon; The Story of the Dukes of Bedford, including the Author's own Life* (London, 1959), pp. 147–8.

> the congregation can't afford to pay me, I shall play for nothing. I am not going to let them down.'[4]

So he stayed on as organist but lost his £125 p.a. stipend.[5] The Duke's action may have led him to turn his energies to reforming the Bedford Musical Society.

Marshall Palmer had had a somewhat chequered career combining journalism – members of his family edited *The Bedfordshire Times* newspaper series over a number of years – with being an organist and music teacher.[6] By 1941 he was a teacher at Bedford Modern School. He had also been teaching at Owen's School after its evacuation from Islington to Bedford in 1940, after which time the school shared Bedford Modern School's premises for the duration of the war.[7]

Marshall Palmer's decision to reform the Musical Society was no doubt also influenced by the BBC Symphony Orchestra's arrival in Bedford. Altogether, about two hundred players and people associated with the administration of the orchestra came to the town. They left Bristol because there had been heavy bombing there. Nicholas Kenyon refers to the move in his history of the BBC Symphony Orchestra:

> W. W. Thompson's assistant, Dorothy Wood, was sent to Bedford for a week in July and had reported favourably on the facilities at the Corn Exchange, Bedford School and the churches and chapels which were to be made available for the Orchestra's use … The Symphony Orchestra was due in Bedford on 30 July 1941. Most of the Orchestra travelled there by special train … which went by a complicated cross-country route to avoid London. Boult characteristically decided to make the journey on his push-bike.[8]
>
> Concert-giving began in Bedford on 17 September 1941, at 7 p.m. All major concerts were to be given in the Corn Exchange, a hall which proved to have good acoustics. 'A reasonably good studio, but a rather over-powering concert-hall', said Boult.[9]

Marshall Palmer wrote to *The Bedfordshire Times and Bedfordshire Standard* (for which he had been a music critic for several years) proposing the formation of a new choral society. The letter was printed on 8 August, a few days after the arrival of the BBC Symphony Orchestra in Bedford.[10] The letter is several paragraphs long, and includes references to his mother, the late Mary Palmer, and to her choral work. The main points he made were: that there had not been a permanent large choir in Bedford for some years; the formation of a new choral society would be supported

4 This report was amongst Marshall Palmer's papers loaned to the author by Sylvia Palmer.

5 In the report of his leaving Bedford at the beginning of March 1943, *The Bedfordshire Times and Bedfordshire Standard* states that he had been organist of Woburn for eleven and a half years.

6 Marshall Palmer advertised regularly in *The Bedfordshire Times and Bedfordshire Standard*, for example on 8 August 1941, p. 6. The advertisements state that he receives pupils for pianoforte, singing, theory and organ at Fraser's Studios in Harpur Street, Bedford, and in Woburn Sands, and at pupils' homes.

7 There is a commemorative plaque given by Owen's School at the eastern entrance to the Harpur Centre (the site of Bedford Modern School during the Second World War). There is also a reference to Marshall Palmer in Martin Mitchell and David Bernstein, eds, *Well Remembered Fields: The Story of One School's Evacuation 1939–1945* (unknown, 2003), p. 188.

8 Nicholas Kenyon, *The BBC Symphony Orchestra: The First Fifty Years 1930–1980* (London, 1981), p. 170.

9 Ibid., p. 176.

10 *The Bedfordshire Times and Bedfordshire Standard*, 8 August 1941, p. 6.

by the public; and the choir would, he hoped, be accompanied by a famous orchestra and probably be under the direction of a well-known conductor in at least one concert a year. He asked supporters of the idea to contact him as tangible evidence of assistance before making any public announcements.

Marshall Palmer's letter generated a mixed response in *The Bedfordshire Times and Bedfordshire Standard.* There was adverse reaction from Mr H. J. Billingham, secretary of the Bedford Orpheus Choir, who suggested that instead of contacting Marshall Palmer about his: 'nebulous choir, readers of the paper who are interested should contact him, Mr. Billingham, about joining a "real live choir".'[11] In his reply, Marshall Palmer resolved that if the venture succeeded, it would do so because friends of his (old and new) had got together to sing, loved music, and would give pleasure to many others, and for no other reason. In a further letter, published on 12 September, he added that he: 'lives fourteen miles from Bedford, in the wilds of Buckinghamshire [Woburn Sands!]'.[12]

Meanwhile, the day following Marshall Palmer's second letter (13 September), he was married at St Mary's church, Woburn, to Sylvia Buxton. Sylvia had been head girl at the Bedford Girls Modern School for the academic year 1938/39. Sylvia and Marshall Palmer had only met in April. The report of the wedding says of Sylvia that, 'she was an amateur actress of more than average ability'.[13]

Almost immediately after his wedding, Marshall Palmer recalls in his memoirs: 'I was asked to put an advertisement in The Bedfordshire Times inviting any who might be interested to a meeting at the Dujon Cafe on 22 September. Unfortunately, I was ill that day with an ear infection, so, bravely, Sylvia stepped into the breach and, helped by my good friend Mr. Harry Page, put my ideas to a keen nucleus of choristers.'[14]

Sixty people attended the initial meeting at the cafe, above the Dudeney & Johnson grocery store (the building now used by Lloyd's Bank). The former secretary of the Mary Palmer Choir, Leslie Martin, acted as chairman. There was some debate about whether the choir would perform oratorial or operatic works; no conclusion was reached.[15] The name 'Bedford Choral Society' was suggested. Sylvia Palmer said that she would ask the permission of the conductor of the old Bedford Choral Society (Arthur Parris) to use that title. Marshall Palmer's recalls that: 'A small committee was formed and Sylvia asked to be Secretary.'[16]

A second meeting was held on 30 September, and it was agreed that the name used for the Society should be the Bedford Musical Society, on the strong recommendation of Arthur Parris, who said that he: 'regarded the decease of that Society

11 *The Bedfordshire Times and Bedfordshire Standard*, 15 August 1941, p. 5.

12 *The Bedfordshire Times and Bedfordshire Standard*, 12 September 1941, p. 7.

13 *The Bedford Record and Circular*, 16 September 1941, p. 4. See also *The Bedfordshire Times and Bedfordshire Standard*, 19 September 1941, p. 4.

14 H. Marshall Palmer, *Memoirs*. The author was unable to find the advertisement referred to here.

15 At the next meeting, Marshall Palmer stated his wish that the society should sing either oratorios or miscellaneous short choral works, and not consider the performance of operas in concert version.

16 H. Marshall Palmer, *Memoirs*. He continues: 'The last train home to Woburn Sands left St. John's station at 7.15p.m. so the only option in those days was to cycle the fourteen miles home. Sylvia and I did this on many occasions after rehearsals, but that night she cycled home on her own sometimes in foggy conditions. We were both relieved when she reached home at 11p.m. to a warm supper provided by my sister May.'

some years ago as one of the saddest things that had happened to Bedford's music ... [and] strongly urged that they should call themselves the "Bedford Musical Society" to revive old memories and not allow old associations to die away.'[17] As Marshall Palmer put it in his *Memoirs*: 'They decided that they would like the Society, run by my dear master and mentor, Dr. H. A. Harding, revived.'[18] Sylvia Palmer affirms that the Society saw itself as being reformed.[19] This is borne out by the title inside the front cover of the first *Minute Book*, 'Bedford Musical Society Reformed October 1941'.[20] The programme for the first concert puts it like this:

> This is the first concert given by the newly constituted Bedford Musical Society, who wish to continue the fine work done for so many years by the former Society of the same name and by the late Bedford Choral Society. The new Society seems to represent choralism in the town and district and to have as members all singers and instrumentalists who wish to perform the major works of the choral repertoire. It is hoped that this will be the first of many concerts.[21]

This hope has been more than adequately realised.

It was agreed at the 30 September meeting that Handel's *Judas Maccabaeus* should be performed as the first concert, and that the performance should be on 26 March (ten days before Easter) in Bedford Modern School. The first rehearsal was arranged for Monday 6 October at 7.30p.m. at the Dujon Cafe. From then on, weekly rehearsals were held on Mondays, as they have been ever since. *Judas Maccabaeus* was chosen as being topical for wartime as explained in the review in *The Bedford Record and Circular*: 'Handel in his famous oratorio "Judas Maccabaeus" celebrated the successful struggle of the Jewish people against the Syrians under Gorgias ... And "Judas" – an oratorio of freedom – has the authentic consolatory ring for our war-assaulted ears and minds.'[22] It was composed in 1746, having been commissioned by Frederick Prince of Wales, to celebrate the English victory over the Young Pretender at Culloden and the return of the victorious general, the Duke of Cumberland, to London. It was not a glorious victory. Cumberland treated the defeated Scots very cruelly, earning the title 'Butcher Cumberland'. Handel probably did not know of Cumberland's reputation at the time.

The performance of *Judas Maccabaeus* was the first of only four of the Musical Society's concerts that Marshall Palmer conducted. The chorus and orchestra consisted of a hundred performers, Marshall Palmer 'exchanging', as the reviewer

[17] *The Bedfordshire Times and Bedfordshire Standard*, 3 October 1941, p. 10. At the meeting, Marshall Palmer said that as far back as 1933 he had made efforts to form such a choir (as the Bedford Musical Society) and many present would recall the brief life of the 'Bedford Philharmonic Society'. This is the only reference that the author has come across to the 'Bedford Philharmonic Society'.

[18] H. Marshall Palmer, *Memoirs*.

[19] Sylvia Palmer explained, in a personal letter to the author, how Marshall Palmer saw that Bedford Musical Society as being reformed: 'Dr. Harding had been in charge. He was Marshall's revered teacher and mentor for many years. The thought that he, Marshall, should put on his (Dr. Harding's) mantle was humbling but attractive ... it was a re-forming of the choral side of the old Bedford Musical Society. At that time there was a Symphony orchestra, under bandmaster Thorpe, giving regular concerts.'

[20] *Minute Book 1941–43*, BLARS X817/1/6. This *Minute Book* includes a list of committee members and names and addresses of sopranos, altos, tenors and basses as of October 1941 and May 1943. The minutes commence in 1942.

[21] Bedford Musical Society, *Programme for Handel's 'Judas Maccabaeus'*, 26 March 1942, p. 4.

[22] *The Bedford Record and Circular*, 31 March 1942, p. 2.

put it, 'the critic's seat for the conductor's rostrum'.[23] Marshall Palmer wrote of the soloists in his *Memoirs*: 'Because the BBC Singers were in Bedford, I was able to have three of their group as soloists – Margaret Rees, soprano, Margaret Rolfe, contralto, and Stanley Riley, bass.[24] My old friend, Eric Barnes of St. Paul's Cathedral choir, was unable to come himself but another member of that illustrious choir, Tom Purvis, came to sing – especially the famous air "Sound an Alarm".'[25] The programme acknowledged the Musical Society's indebtedness to the BBC and the Bedford Symphony Orchestra, for what is termed 'friendly co-operation'.

The reviewer for *The Bedford Record and Circular* was very favourable towards the performance, although there were some minor blemishes.[26] The reviewer hoped that this would be the first of many concerts and considered that: 'the new Society has launched itself with such enterprise and genuine musical achievement that it deserves and will surely attain a proud and progressive history in the choral art of Bedford.'[27] The review states that there was a large and enthusiastic audience and that the profits were to go to the Bedfordshire Rural Music School.

There is no record of the minutes of committee meetings before 7 June 1942. The first *Minute Book*, already referred to, has the first segment torn out and begins with the names of the sopranos listed alphabetically, starting from 'A'.[28] There are fifty-five names, written in ink (by Sylvia Palmer) and a number of additions, deletions and amendments to the list made in pencil. It is not clear if these are the names of the singers in *Judas Maccabaeus*.

The second concert of this new period was given by the Musical Society in mid-July 1942. The main work was Vaughan Williams's *Dona Nobis Pacem*. The review in *The Bedford Record and Circular* gives the background to the work: 'written in 1936, [it is] a kind of musical tract for the times, composed when the fear of war dominated the nation. To hear it now when that fear has been translated into grim and horrific reality is to be moved, exhilarated and even tormented by the contrast between human hope and experience.'[29]

The concert included a number of shorter works including Bach's 'Peasant' cantata; songs by Purcell, Holst, Delius, Stanford and Bairstow; and 'The Conductor's Song' – Marshall Palmer's own setting of 'These Things Shall Be', four verses from the poem by J. Addington Symonds. Members of BBC Theatre Orchestra took part. The soloists were Elsie Suddaby and Roy Henderson, both of whom had

23 Ibid.

24 According to the programme and to the review, Joseph Farrington, not Stanley Riley, was the bass soloist. Stanley Riley sang a year later at the Musical Society's performance of *Messiah*.

25 H. Marshall Palmer, *Memoirs*.

26 He wrote that: 'the chorus and orchestra gave a vigorous and finely-shaded interpretation of this masterpiece. The chorus produces a rich tone, has a bright and confident attack and is flexible and alert, not least in the *pianissimo* passages … The orchestra … would have been advantaged by a larger personnel, but it played with excellent spirit and rhythmic feeling; its co-operation with the choir was vital and happy.' *The Bedford Record and Circular*, 31 March 1942, p. 2.

27 Ibid.

28 'Sopranos (Cont.)' is what is actually written, suggesting this follows on from another page. A much longer list of names, dated May 1943, also precedes the minutes. The title page also contains the names of the officers and committee. Mr Bilham's name is incorrectly spelt as 'Billingham'. Mr Billingham was the conductor of the Orpheus Choir.

29 *The Bedford Record and Circular*, 14 July 1942, p. 4.

sung with Musical Society previously. Of this concert Marshall Palmer wrote in his *Memoirs*:

> My suggestion was to tackle Vaughan Williams's 'Dona Nobis Pacem'. This work proved to be a real challenge but a very rewarding one. It required a very full orchestra and two very good soloists. I had become friendly, through my reporting of BBC concerts, with C. B. Rees, the BBC's press officer. He put me in touch with the players in the BBC Theatre Orchestra who were glad to have the opportunity to play in different kinds of music. The brass section, particularly, provided a valuable addition to Bedford's local players. The latter provided the main string section and a fair proportion of wood-wind. The Committee supported the need for first-class soloists. We were indeed fortunate that Elsie Suddaby and Roy Henderson were able to sing for us. The Corn Exchange was full for this, our second concert. The audience responded well to this disturbing Vaughan Williams' masterpiece.[30]

The reviewer, from *The Bedford Record and Circular*, thought that the concert had: 'too generous an allowance of music, especially in days when adequate is not too easy and war needs have taken so many men away … but the music had obviously been studied with imagination as well as diligence, and Bedford music-lovers are indebted to Mr. Palmer for the opportunity to hear this magnificent music.'[31] Of the two soloists, he wrote of their performance in the 'Peasant' cantata: 'Miss Suddaby and Mr. Henderson evidently enjoy their Bach – and communicated to all their own relish.'[32]

Following the Society's performance of *Dona Nobis Pacem,* Marshall Palmer recalled that: 'Several members of the choir came up with Sylvia & me to the Royal Albert Hall to hear the work, and Vaughan Williams's "Sea Symphony" on the occasion of the composer's 70th birthday. We found both works so compelling that I wanted to try the "Sea Symphony" at our next venture, but the Committee, I think perhaps wisely, decided to consolidate the Society's position and begin rehearsing carols for a Christmas concert in Holy Trinity church and *Messiah* at Easter.'[33]

The Musical Society approached the Granada Cinema as a possible venue for the carol concert because the Corn Exchange was already booked up, but the cost would have been twenty-five guineas, which was too much. Miss Westaway, headmistress of the High School, was also approached but the High School was not 'blacked-out', so arrangements were made to hold the concert in Holy Trinity church. The concert was held on 21 December and the church was packed. *The Bedfordshire Times and Bedfordshire Standard* report notes: 'between such well-tried favourites as "God rest you merry, Gentlemen" and "The First Nowell" we heard three groups of modern carols by the choir, including Marshall Palmer's own delightful setting of a sixteenth century German carol.'[34] A silver collection was taken in aid of the Bombed Churches Fund.[35]

30 H. Marshall Palmer, *Memoirs*.
31 *The Bedford Record and Circular*, 14 July 1942, p. 4.
32 Ibid.
33 H. Marshall Palmer, *Memoirs*.
34 *The Bedfordshire Times and Bedfordshire Standard*, 25 December 1942, p. 7.
35 'Silver collections' were common before the introduction of decimal coinage in 1971. The idea was to encourage donors to give higher value (i.e. silver) coins rather than 'copper' coins.

The news that Marshall Palmer would be leaving Bedford became public at the beginning of March 1943 and was reported in the local press.[36] He was leaving to take up the appointment of assistant musical director at Cheltenham College. After wishing him well, the report continues: 'Many readers, too, will miss the spirited and well-balanced critiques of musical performances which have appeared in this newspaper under the initials "H.M.P." for the past seven years.'[37]

Holy Trinity church was the venue for Marshall Palmer's last concert with the Musical Society, *Messiah*, on 15 April 1943. *The Bedfordshire Times and Bedfordshire Standard* made one of its rare errors when it reported that the performance was on 15 March. The review goes on: 'The occasion was one of special interest since it marked the last public appearance before his departure from the town of Marshall Palmer who had been the Society's conductor since its inception: and there could have been no more fitting conclusion to the great work he has done for music in Bedford than this highly successful performance.'[38] Marshall Palmer writes: 'Margaret Rees, Gladys Ripley, Tom Purvis and Stanley Riley were the soloists at that performance … with Jack Mackintosh from the BBC orchestra playing the solo trumpet. Norman Frost, now music master at BMS [Bedford Modern School], played the organ and was to take over conducting the choir.'[39]

At the annual general meeting of the Musical Society on the 19 April, a presentation was made to Marshall and Sylvia Palmer. Marshall Palmer recalled: 'Our final meeting with our loyal musical friends in Bedford was a moving affair. Sylvia and I were given a beautiful silver cake dish and an Entree dish, both of which are still treasured possessions of a happy association with Bedford Musical Society.'[40] The Society then had to appoint, at that same meeting, not only a new honorary conductor, but also a new honorary secretary.

The Musical Society today owes Marshall Palmer an enormous debt of gratitude. He seems to have come along at just the right moment and to have had just the right ingredients for the Society's reformation – musical and conducting skills, vision, the ability to communicate and inspire, and organisational skills. The reason for the Musical Society's immediate and long-term success can probably be summed-up in the conclusion to the newspaper report of March 1943, about his leaving Bedford: 'In September 1941 [he] formed the new Bedford Musical Society, a project which was very near to his heart and which has already laid the foundation for a bright and healthy future.'[41]

[36] *The Bedfordshire Times and Bedfordshire Standard*, 5 March 1943, p. 11.
[37] Ibid.
[38] *The Bedfordshire Times and Bedfordshire Standard*, 23 April 1943, p. 8.
[39] H. Marshall Palmer, *Memoirs*.
[40] Ibid.
[41] *The Bedfordshire Times and Bedfordshire Standard*, 5 March 1943, p. 11.

Chapter Eight
Great Expectations, 1943–47

> Mr Frost ... has found a field for his undoubted talent as a conductor in the town and he has made a name for himself … he is a competent musician and very enthusiastic … He is, like most music masters I have known, somewhat temperamental but not unduly difficult.[1]

> About five hundred members of the B.B.C. Staff came to Bedford ... The movement back to London begins on 18th July 1945, when the Symphony Orchestra returns. In the past four years about 8,000 broadcasts have been made from Bedford. The Theatre Orchestra and the Singers are to remain here a little longer.[2]

Norman Frost (1903–90)

Norman Frost was appointed honorary conductor at the special general meeting on 19 April 1943, the same meeting at which a presentation was made to Marshall Palmer. The appointment was initially for the remainder of the season only, but he was re-elected at the annual general meeting held at the end of July 1943. At that meeting, another profoundly significant appointment was made, that of Margaret Robertson, who was elected as secretary.

Norman Frost's main academic qualification was in music. However, he had been appointed at Bedford Modern School in 1941 as a teacher of English.[3] Norman Frost was born and grew up in Hampshire, and was articled as a pupil to the organist of Winchester Cathedral, Dr William Prendergast, 1920–23. He then studied organ and piano under Arnold Goldsborough at the Royal College of Music 1924–25. In 1926 he was appointed senior music master at Barnard Castle School, an appointment that he held for nine years. In 1935 he was appointed, again as music master, at Firth Park School, Sheffield. This school's choir was broadcast by the BBC on the eve of the coronation of George VI in May 1937, as a tribute from the schools of England. During Norman Frost's time at Firth Park School he conducted a variety of well-known choral works.[4]

Norman Frost was then appointed as an inspector for the Board of Education, and although his appointment was as a music specialist, his duties were in the main for general work, for which it was eventually decided he was not suitable.

1 Letter of H. W. Liddle, headmaster of Bedford Modern School, 7 December 1944, Bedford Modern School Archive.

2 'Farewell B.B.C.', an article in *The Bedfordshire Times and Bedfordshire Standard*, 13 July 1945, p. 10.

3 The author is grateful to Richard Wildman, archivist at Bedford Modern School, for information about Norman Frost's background.

4 These included parts one and two of *Messiah*, Purcell's *King Arthur*, Stanford's *Songs of the Fleet*, Elgar's *Banner of St George*, and Bach's *Christmas Oratorio* (in Sheffield City Hall).

He resigned and looked for a non-musical post, as vacancies for music teachers were scarce.[5] He was appointed as English master at Bedford Modern School and started in January 1941 on a temporary basis. He was offered a permanent post a year later.[6] He remained at the school for the rest of his working life, mainly teaching the lower classes of the school. The head of music at the school was, at the time of his appointment, Herbert Colson, with whom Norman Frost reputedly did not get on. When Herbert Colson retired in 1949, Norman Frost applied for his job, but was not appointed, partly because he had proved himself to be an effective and challenging English teacher, and partly because the then headmaster, J. E. Taylor, thought that he was unsuitable for the post.[7] Frederick (Fred) D. S. Rawlins was later appointed. Norman Frost did, however, teach music at Owen's School following Marshall Palmer's move away from Bedford. Norman Frost was also, for a time in the 1940s, organist and choirmaster at Holy Trinity church, and was one of Philip Diemer's successors.

The president of the Musical Society at this time was J. Arnold Whitchurch, formerly president of the old Choral Society. He acted as chairman throughout Norman Frost's tenure. Arnold Whitchurch was a very prominent figure in Bedford. Most notably, he was chairman of the County Hospital Board. He was also a county councillor. The secretary was Margaret Robertson, who was appointed when Sylvia Palmer resigned. She remained in post until the mid-1950s and was very active on the committee. She continued to be influential in the Society until her untimely death in the late 1970s.

The first concert that Norman Frost conducted was held on 14 October 1943 in Bedford Modern School hall. There were two works in this concert, Purcell's *King Arthur* and Borodin's *Polovtsian Dances*. The factual review is by J.H.M.S. (John Henry Miller Sykes) who was to be the music correspondent for *The Bedfordshire Times and Bedfordshire Standard* until the mid-1960s.[8] The soloists in *King Arthur* were Margaret Rees (soprano), Bradbridge White (tenor) and Stanley Riley (bass). A string orchestra, led by Ivan Goulding, accompanied the chorus. In addition, for the *Polovtsian Dances* the orchestra was joined by woodwind and brass reinforcements: 'Mr. Frost was able to call on the same players – save perhaps the competent Master David Goslin as second clarinet – that served Sir Thomas Beecham and the gilded assemblage at pre-war Covent Garden when they, too heard the Polovtsians dance

5 According to Fred Rawlins, the reason for his resignation was that he fell out, as he was prone to do, with Geoffrey Shaw, the chief inspector of music.

6 The headmaster at the time of Norman Frost's appointment was H. W. Liddle.

7 In a letter of reference for the post, the Rev. H. Spence stated that Norman Frost was a very good musician, had a wide knowledge and was an extremely competent choir trainer who could hold the attention of a choir and get the results he wanted. Letter of Rev. H. Spence, undated, in response to a letter dated 25 February 1949, Bedford Modern School Archive.

8 J.H.M.S. was a prolific writer for the newspaper. He died on 20 November 1966 in Bedford Hospital, aged 60, after a short illness. At the time of his death he lived at 71 Chaucer Road, Bedford, and was married with one daughter. His *Bedfordshire Times* obituary includes information by R. B. Payne, also a *Bedfordshire Times* music correspondent: 'Mr. Sykes had a good sense of judgement in musical matters and a wealth of musical experience, having in his youth come under the influence of the late Arthur Somervell, for many years chief musical inspector for the Board of Education, He became friends with Frederick Thurston, the clarinettist, and Yehudi Menuhin, during the war when they were based in Bedford.' *Bedfordshire Times*, 25 November 1966, p. 23.

their hectic measures.'[9] J.H.M.S. notes that they were all fresh from their triumph in the broadcast of the Beethoven Mass the previous evening. He is complimentary about the choir and notes Norman Frost's exuberant enthusiasm: 'we have seldom seen any conductor with such energy.'[10] He also approved of Norman Frost's: 'Beecham-like manner with latecomers to the audience [which] was delicious.'[11] It was perhaps a bit hard not to allow for a few latecomers in war-time conditions.

The Christmas carol concert followed on Thursday 23 December, in Holy Trinity church. The music performed included part of Bach's *Christmas Oratorio* as well as traditional Christmas carols. The small string orchestra, assembled for the occasion, did not play very well according to the reviewer: 'It seldom played, and there were painful moments when it was both out of tune and out of time.'[12] Interestingly, in view of his apparently cool relationship with Norman Frost, Herbert Colson played the organ.

The main work in the concert held at the end of April 1944 was another performance of that old favourite, *Hiawatha's Wedding Feast*. The concert also included Brahms's *Song of Destiny* and Parry's *Blest Pair of Sirens*, and was given, once more, in Bedford Modern School hall. The 'large' chorus – the number of singers is not specified – was supported by an orchestra of about thirty-seven. At the start of the concert, Norman Frost thanked the professional musicians taking part for their assistance, especially the leader of the orchestra and: 'that distinguished musician, Ernest Hall, the principal trumpet of the B.B.C. Symphony Orchestra, who had appeared on this occasion as a modest amateur violinist.'[13] The reviewer, J.H.M.S., thought that the soloist Jan van der Guch's voice was delicate, graceful and subtle, but not strong enough to be heard over the orchestra: 'we have often enjoyed [his voice] over the radio, where amplification of the solo to override a full orchestra is merely a matter of mechanical control; but for "Onaway, Awake!" we needed a heroic tenor whose clarion voice would of itself dominate the triumphant supporting orchestration, and this we were not able to hear in Thursday's performance.'[14]

The choir's contribution at the next concert, early in July, was to sing four madrigals and a few more recent songs. Louis Kentner was soloist in Bach's Piano Concerto in D Minor with the Bedford String Orchestra.[15] Louis Kentner also played works by Chopin and Liszt, of which he was a noted performer. There were 600 people in the audience, so it was fortunate that the setting was the Corn Exchange, rather than a smaller venue.

The 1944 annual general meeting was held in July, and Norman Frost spoke at length to the Society's members.[16] The thrust of his argument was that the Society

9 *Bedfordshire Times and Bedfordshire Standard*, 22 October 1943, p. 5.

10 He continues: 'The choral work was remarkably efficient at all times. In the days of difficult transport arrangements and innumerable calls on leisure time, very great credit is due to the Society, under Mr. Frost's guidance, which they had obviously put in at rehearsal.' He also notes that the chorus kept up in the *Polovtsian Dances* while retaining clear enunciation. Ibid.

11 Ibid.

12 *The Bedford Record and Circular*, 28 December 1943, p. 4.

13 *The Bedfordshire Times and Bedfordshire Standard*, 5 May 1944, p. 7.

14 Ibid.

15 Louis Kentner was born in Karvinna, then in Hungary, but now in the Slovak Republic. He settled in England in 1935. He gave the first performance of Bartok's Piano Concerto No. 2.

16 *The Bedfordshire Times and Bedfordshire Standard*, 21 July 1944, p. 10.

should be broad-based, with relatively more orchestral music and less choral music. He believed that larger audiences could be gained for the former and that interest in choral music was waning. He also anticipated that the BBC Symphony Orchestra would return to London during the following year.

The reviewer of the final concert given in 1944 (not identified, though probably J.H.M.S) thought that it was excellent. But he did not approve of the choice of programme, especially the main work, Elgar's *Music Makers*. He complained that: 'the composer has assembled quotations from all the more sober and sanctimonious of his works.'[17] He blamed the programme for the Corn Exchange being only three-quarters full. A full-scale orchestra had been engaged, 'from among the finest players in the country'. This was led by Paul Beard, leader of the BBC Symphony Orchestra 1936–62. The reviewer also thought that the orchestra drowned out Janet Howe, soloist in Elgar's *Sea Pictures*, just as they had drowned out Jan van der Guch in April: 'our enjoyment was marred in that we were seldom able to hear the singer. In this matter of accompaniment, one may express some surprise that the orchestra themselves did not realize that there was no soloist's microphone with which the knob-twisters would correct the balance.'[18]

The first concert of 1945 was held in March, in the last days of the war in Europe. The programme was modest. The choir sang 'Madrigals and Modern Pieces', as one of the sub-headings in the review puts it.[19] The modern pieces were four *Songs of Springtime* by E. J. Moeran, who was much approved of by J.H.M.S. As in the July 1944 concert, there was a prominent piano soloist. This time it was Benno Moiseiwitsch. The main work played by him was Mussorgsky's *Pictures at an Exhibition*, as originally written, for solo piano.[20] No orchestra was engaged for this concert.

Ida Haendel was the soloist at the next concert, early in July. She played Bach's Violin Concerto in E Minor, accompanied by the Bedford String Orchestra. The choir's contribution was a set of madrigals by Orlando di Lasso and some English folk songs arranged by Vaughan Williams. This was the format preferred by Norman Frost, according to minutes of the committee meeting held just a few days later.[21]

17 *The Bedfordshire Times and Bedfordshire Standard*, 24 November 1944, p. 7.

18 Ibid.

19 *The Bedfordshire Times and Bedfordshire Standard*, 23 March 1945, p. 6.

20 Freddie E. Stevens (chorus master for the Musical Society 1952–65) was stationed in Oxford during the war as was Moiseiwitsch's nephew, Alec Kennard. When Moiseiwitsch came to perform there, his nephew introduced Freddie Stevens to him. The final work that Moiseiwitsch played at the concert was Beethoven's *Appassionata Sonata*. Moiseiwitsch and Freddie Stevens travelled together by train to London the next day and Moiseiwitsch persisted in asking Freddie's opinion of the performance. Eventually, Freddie said that he thought that he had played the last movement much too fast and that it sounded like an underground train. Moiseiwitsch, expecting to be complimented, was most put out and there was no further conversation between them on the journey. When Moiseiwitsch was next in touch with his nephew, he asked after his nephew's 'sardonic friend'. Personal interview with Freddie Stevens by the the author.

21 At the committee meeting Norman Frost is reported as saying that: 'he was not prepared to continue if the members wished to do big works, as he was not prepared to accept responsibilities outside the actual conductorship and preparation of works with the choir and orchestra. Others must relieve him of all outside responsibilities. He had discussed the problem with Sir Adrian Boult and Mr. Raybould who had suggested either unaccompanied works, or large works with a loss of £60 – £70 on each concert.' Norman Frost also found the responsibility of organising larger scale concert quite challenging. This outburst may have generated more support, as the first concert of 1946 was *Elijah*. *Minute Book 1944–48*, 9 July 1945, BLARS X817/1/7.

Soon after this concert, the BBC Symphony Orchestra returned to London, to be followed a little later by the BBC Theatre Orchestra and the BBC Singers. This was a huge loss to Bedford. *The Bedfordshire Times and Bedfordshire Standard* of 13 July had a lavish article, under the heading 'Farewell, B.B.C.! by J.H.M.S.'[22] The article included a 'Thank You' letter from Sir Adrian Boult and interesting facts about the BBC's stay in Bedford. There are details of the studios used; the number of public concerts given, mostly by the BBC Symphony Orchestra (there were about sixty); and photographs of some of the leading conductors and soloists. There are also lists of the famous soloists and composers who came to Bedford, and details of first UK performances of new works given in the town. A few 'Outstanding Occasions' are referred to, one of which was a concert conducted by Sir Henry Wood in December 1941 in honour of Stalin's birthday!

On Friday 10 August, the Musical Society was broadcast on the BBC Home Service (now Radio 4) for twenty minutes in the morning. The programme had been recorded earlier in the month. *The Bedfordshire Times and Bedfordshire Standard* report commented approvingly on the high standard of the choir conducted by Norman Frost and stated that this was the first time a radio audience had heard Bedford's music, with the exception of the broadcast of carols on Christmas morning in 1944 when the choir joined the BBC Chorus. Generally speaking, the report is complimentary: 'The programme was typical of the catholicity of the Society's work, ranging from madrigals by Bennet and Orlando di Lasso, of the sixteenth Century, to Vaughan Williams and Moeran.'[23] Parry's famous motet 'My Soul, there is a Country' was also included in the programme.

The main work in the December 1945 concert was a performance of Bach's motet 'Jesus, Priceless Treasure'. The reviewer thought that this was really unsuitable for the choir, primarily because it was too difficult for amateurs and would have stretched even the BBC Singers. Some movements from *Messiah* were also included, accompanied by the Corn Exchange organ. The piano soloist was Irene Scharrer who played Bach, Chopin and Schubert. The Bach motet may have been 'unsuitable', but there was nevertheless a large audience.

The Musical Society was once more on familiar territory with Mendelssohn's *Elijah* at the end of March 1946. The reviewer notes the significance of this performance: 'Taken all in all, this was the most important musical occasion which has happened in Bedford since the B.B.C. left ... the Musical Society deserves the highest commendation ... No musical body, including the powerful London choral societies, could have put it on in a better manner.'[24] This is high praise indeed, even if it is from a provincial reviewer.[25] Norman Frost's: 'tireless energy compelled a response which was worthy of an oratorio whose musical invention was the most powerful and more equal to the greatness of the story it had to tell than was the always genteel and frequently insipid music of Mendelssohn.'[26]

22 *The Bedfordshire Times and Bedfordshire Standard*, 13 July 1945, p. 10.
23 *The Bedfordshire Times and Bedfordshire Standard*, 17 August 1945, p. 6. In the review of the Musical Society's next concert (*The Bedfordshire Times and Bedfordshire Standard*, 14 December 1945, p. 5) there is a reference to the Society having taken part in several broadcasts.
24 *The Bedfordshire Times and Bedfordshire Standard*, 29 March 1946, p. 5.
25 The reviewer was probably J.H.M.S., although the review is unattributed.
26 *The Bedfordshire Times and Bedfordshire Standard*, 29 March 1946, p. 5.

There was a formidable line-up of professional soloists, Isobel Baillie, Muriel Brunskill, Roy Henderson and Walter Widdop. The reviewer is somewhat critical of three of the soloists. Although he commends Isobel Baillie for her: 'impeccable soprano, faultless in intention, phrasing and clarity of enunciation, as always', he thought she occasionally had an edgy quality.[27] Muriel Brunskill is said to have been: 'out of sympathy with the gracious spirit of the work' when she sang the tender 'O Rest in the Lord'. And Walter Widdop, although complimented for his Italian-like rich smoothness: 'suffered as times from a slight hardness in the upper register'.[28] Fulsome praise is reserved for Roy Henderson, the bass soloist who took the part of Elijah, who: 'brought a sincere conviction to a voice whose full round tone gave us unalloyed pleasure'.[29]

The reviewer's comments about the huge choir were highly favourable. The choral work, he thought, was alert, sound and vigorous, but the eighteen string players of the Riddick String Orchestra were not really adequate for the choir, even though there was organ accompaniment as well. He did recognise, however, that Norman Frost seemed to have got the best out of the players.[30] This performance of *Elijah* was the last concert of the season.

George Thompson and Kate Freyhan both sang for the first time with the Musical Society in this performance of *Elijah*. George Thompson, who had sung with the Orpheus Choir in the 1930s, was to sing first bass with the choir until the late 1990s, although not continuously. Kate Freyhan, a contralto, also sang with the choir for over thirty years, and went on to become assistant chorus master, a post she held for many years. Kate Freyhan was married to Hans Freyhan, a colleague of Norman Frost's at Bedford Modern School. From 1942–46, Hans Freyhan taught German, but like Norman Frost he had trained as a music teacher.

The Musical Society did not hold the usual summer concert in 1946. Norman Frost had said at the February committee meeting that he would be unable to undertake the concert for reasons of health, and the committee agreed.[31]

During the summer and autumn of 1946 the Musical Society's *Minute Books* include various references to the possible formation of a full-time professional orchestra in the area, with Arts Council backing. The plan was to have this in place by September 1947. The Musical Society hoped to be directly involved with the establishment of the orchestra and, of course, to benefit from it. During the 1946/47 season the Society promoted several orchestral concerts played by professional orchestras. Norman Frost conducted two of them. The Musical Society's use of professional orchestras may have been in anticipation of involvement with the proposed new orchestra, or in order to take advantage of the Arts Council funding

27 Ibid.

28 Ibid.

29 Ibid. Roy Henderson was one of the few people born in the nineteenth century who lived until the twenty-first century. He was one of the original soloists in Vaughan Williams's *Serenade to Music*, first performed in 1938.

30 *The Bedfordshire Times and Bedfordshire Standard*, 29 March 1946, p. 5. The programme lists the 136 singers and eighteen members of the Riddick String Orchestra. Hans Freyhan overestimated a little when, following the death of Norman Frost in March 1990, he wrote to *The Bedfordshire Times and Bedfordshire Standard* saying that that there were 150 members of the choir.

31 *Minute Book 1944–48*, 11 February 1946, BLARS X817/1/7.

that was then available. The Musical Society certainly seems to have had big ideas, as did Norman Frost.

Norman Frost had first suggested his being elected in a professional capacity at the committee meeting that preceded the annual general meeting in July 1945. He raised the same question again at the meeting that followed the 1946 annual general meeting. He seems to have hoped that he would have a part to play in the Society's involvement with the new orchestra. The minutes include a number of references to him: 'resenting criticism and lack of respect for his position', and 'his hopes of being paid as a professional'.[32]

The first of the three orchestral concerts sponsored by the Musical Society during the 1946/47 season was that given by the London Symphony Orchestra on 7 October 1946. The programme included Rachmaninoff's Piano Concerto in C Minor and Schubert's 'Unfinished' Symphony. This was the first time that programme notes appeared in the printed programme to accompany the concert.[33] The notes were written by J.H.M.S and included information about the London Symphony Orchestra and its history. The number of instrumentalists is not stated. It is likely that there were between forty and fifty. Before the concert, the vicar of St Paul's church had been asked to ensure that the bell-ringers did not practise on Mondays when there were concerts, and a donation was made to thank them for making alternative arrangements.[34]

The second orchestral concert was given a month later. Norman Frost conducted again, and this time the Jacques Orchestra played in Bedford School hall, a setting which impressed the reviewer, J.H.M.S.[35] The programme included two works by Vaughan Williams, his Oboe Concerto – the soloist was Leon Goossens – and his *Pastoral Symphony*. On the morning of the concert, the music critic of *The Times* had written that the duties of a conductor were to keep time and to find the melody and bring it out. *The Bedfordshire Times and Bedfordshire Standard* reviewer quotes this and then comments: 'We have never heard Mr. Frost do both these things better than he did on Friday last.'[36]

Between the second and third orchestral concerts, Norman Frost conducted the Musical Society's performance of *Messiah*, on 2 December 1946. With the line-up of soloists, this was, perhaps, one of the most memorable performances that the Society has ever given. The reviewer, J.H.M.S., wrote: 'The soloists were the quartet of singers who are recognised as the greatest this country has to offer for oratorio, and the Musical Society is to be congratulated on arranging their presence.'[37] They

32 *Minute Book 1944–48*, 25 July 1946, BLARS X817/1/7. It is not clear if Norman Frost received any payment for taking rehearsals and conducting. If he did not, it is possible that what he was really asking for was a fee for this work. However, in view of the discussions that were taking place at the time about the formation of a local professional orchestra he may have had bigger ideas.

33 Before 1946, programmes had included the names of the Musical Society's patrons and performing members and the names of the soloists and orchestral players. But there were no biographical notes about the soloists, or notes about the music. Some programmes did not have programme notes 1946–50, but after 1950 they nearly always did. Notes about the soloists were not included until the 1980s.

34 The Bedford Symphony Orchestra also gave the ringers a donation for not ringing when their concerts were held on Monday nights.

35 In his autobiography *My Own Trumpet* (London, 1973), p. 120, Sir Adrian Boult refers to Bedford School hall: 'This place with its wooden galleries made a fine soundbox.'

36 *The Bedfordshire Times and Bedfordshire Standard,* 15 November 1946, p. 5.

37 *The Bedfordshire Times and Bedfordshire Standard*, 6 December 1946, p. 7.

were Isobel Baillie (soprano), Kathleen Ferrier (contralto), Heddle Nash (tenor) and William Parsons (bass) - and they were a great quartet indeed. Kathleen Ferrier had only started to sing professionally during the war years, so this concert was quite early in her tragically short career. The reviewer wrote: 'The contralto who is rapidly rising to international fame … showed us – specially in "He was despised" – why she is so unanimously appreciated.'[38] Kate Freyhan recalled: 'I was so impressed with her voice. It was so wonderful. I did what I should not have done during the rehearsal. I got up out of my seat and went down into the hall so I could watch her.'[39] The orchestra was the Boyd Neel Orchestra. Paul Steinitz played the organ. By this time he had founded the London Bach Society and was a senior lecturer at Goldsmith's College in South London and a professor at the Royal Academy of Music. He was also conductor of the Bedford Symphony Orchestra.

The review opened with a comparison of the Bedford performance of *Messiah* with a performance by the Oxford Bach Choir of Handel's *Ode for St Cecilia's Day* to which the reviewer had been the previous evening. The Musical Society: 'had nothing to fear from the august Oxford choir.'[40] He also thought that the playing of the amateur orchestra at the Oxford concert was deplorable. *Messiah*, he wrote, is a great dramatic – almost operatic – work, and he did not think in the light of this that the Bedford choir was quite as good as it should or could have been.[41] The review ends with the comment that: 'The hall was more than full: it was packed.'[42]

The third orchestral concert of the season was a Beethoven programme, held on 7 February 1947. The orchestra was the New London Orchestra, and the conductor was Alec Sherman. This concert took place quite early in the very cold winter of 1947. The coldest spell began in Kent and East Anglia on 22 January. By 25 January, there was snow in Bedford and the surrounding area, and by 30 January the whole country was covered. February was one of the coldest months ever recorded in the United Kingdom. At Woburn on 25 February, a temperature of minus twenty-one degrees centigrade was recorded. There were food and power shortages and transport was severely disrupted by drifting snow. It is to the Musical Society's credit, and to the credit of the visiting orchestra, the soloist and the conductor, that the concert went ahead as planned. The only reference to the cold in the review was a note at the end: 'Bad weather was responsible for a few vacant seats, but the response to all three works was enthusiastic.'[43]

The cold weather lasted until mid-March. The last of the Musical Society's concerts that Norman Frost conducted was Brahms's *German Requiem* and Symphony No. 2. This concert was scheduled for 21 March, but due to the sudden thaw there was widespread flooding.[44] The soloists and members of the orchestra

38 Ibid.

39 Personal interview with Kate and Hans Freyhan by the author.

40 *The Bedfordshire Times and Bedfordshire Standard*, 6 December 1946, p. 7.

41 'The Society's conductor, Mr. Norman Frost, did not spare himself, and his clear beat and magnetic gesture should have sufficed to draw out from the chorus the last accentuation which somehow failed ever to send the cold shiver down the spine.' Ibid.

42 Ibid.

43 *The Bedfordshire Times and Bedfordshire Standard*, 14 February 1947, p. 5.

44 Personal interview with Bill Knight by the author. Heavy rain and melting snow caused the flooding. Because the ground was still frozen, the ground could not absorb the large amount of water. At Dame Alice Harpur School, the school hall started to flood during the school assembly. The headmistress took

– The New London Orchestra – could not travel to Bedford, so the concert was held just over a month later, on 28 April. The soloists were Roy Henderson and Ena Mitchell. For the first time, Hans Freyhan wrote the programme notes, as he subsequently did for most of the Musical Society's concerts for just under fifty years until his death in 1996. His notes were always erudite, informative and succinct, and his style is quite distinctive.

The reviewer, once more J.H.M.S., considered the Brahms's Requiem one of the most difficult works to perform, and consequently wrote that: 'for a work which would extend even professional singers, Mr. Frost could not draw from his large chorus anything like the required standard ... If the choir did not score three marks for a perfect answer, they deserve a full two for a brave try – a brave try indeed!'[45]

J.H.M.S. thought that the playing of the Brahms's symphony was ragged, but his main criticism reminds us of a recurrent problem in the 1920s – soloists and instrumentalists having to leave concerts early to catch their trains back to London: 'Mr Frost mistakenly attempted to permit the players to catch their train back to London by playing the last Movement (of the Symphony) at almost twice the normal speed.'[46]

This was the last time that Norman Frost conducted the Musical Society during his short but influential tenure. When arrangements for concerts for the 1947/48 season were being made, the London Symphony Orchestra would only agree to play with a conductor of national reputation. Similarly, the Jacques Orchestra would only play with their conductor, Dr Jacques. Early in June, according to the minutes:

> The Secretary [Margaret Robertson], reported that, acting on the instructions of the sub-committee, she had tried to engage orchestras for next season. Miss Bass of Ibbs & Tillett explained that the orchestras were not prepared to accept engagements under the Society's Hon. Conductor. The Hon. Conductor, realising the difficulties facing the committee had immediately offered his resignation. After expressions of deep regret, the Hon. Conductor's resignation was unanimously accepted.[47]

At the annual general meeting in July, Norman Frost said he considered it an honour to be standing down and to be replaced by Clarence Raybould. Whatever his personal feelings, he behaved with very good grace. The minutes of the meeting record that: 'A vote of thanks was moved by the President, Mr. J. Arnold Whitchurch, in the warmest terms, for his excellent work over many years.'[48]

The Musical Society certainly expanded and prospered while Norman Frost was conductor. When he was appointed, the Society was quite small with some sixty

control and told the girls leave in an orderly fashion and not to panic. Hans Freyhan, who was playing for that assembly, started to play Handel's *Water Music*. See also Richard Wildman, 'The Bedford Flood, 1947', *The Bedfordshire Magazine*, vol. 26, no. 201 (Summer 1997), pp. 11–15.

45 *The Bedfordshire Times and Bedfordshire Standard*, 2 May 1947, p. 5.

46 Ibid.

47 *Minute Book 1944–48*, 2 June 1947 and 16 July 1947, BLARS X817/1/7.

48 The minutes of the committee meeting of 6 August 1947 record a request for a fuller statement under Any Other Business. The reply was: 'a more intimate explanation might not be to the Society's best interests, or to Mr. Frost's.' *Minute Book 1944–48*, 6 August 1947, BLARS X817/1/7.

members and a deficit of £15. When he resigned as conductor, it had increased to over 600 members and the bank balance stood at over £350.[49]

There was some ill-feeling at the way Norman Frost was edged out for the appointment of Clarence Raybould. Hans Freyhan, a colleague of Norman Frost's at Bedford Modern School at the time, expressed this view to the author many years later, and felt that the situation had been engineered. Norman Frost had no further involvement with the Musical Society. He continued to teach at Bedford Modern School, channelling his energies into teaching drama. He taught there until 1967. After he retired he continued to live in Bedford. He died in 1990. He is fondly remembered by many former pupils of the school, although his hypercritical teaching methods caused lasting resentment in others.

During the period when Norman Frost was conductor, several very influential members came to the fore, members who would have a profound influence on the Musical Society for many years to come.

Margaret Robertson (1905–78)

Margaret Robertson, who was born in Suffolk, joined the Musical Society at its reformation in 1941. She was then a teacher at the Harpur Secondary School in Horne Lane and was a colleague of Fred Rawlins, 1946–48. Subsequently, she moved to Oakley Junior School, where she was head teacher for many years. She was elected honorary general secretary in 1943 in succession to Sylvia Palmer, when Sylvia and her husband Marshall moved to Cheltenham. Margaret remained as general secretary for twelve years, resigning in 1955. She was subsequently elected chairman and remained a driving force within the Society. Deirdre Knight, a member of the choir, recalled:

> In a sense, she *was* the Musical Society – for thirty years. I don't know what it was. She was General Secretary, then she moved up to be Chairman. She was wonderful, really. There has never been anyone like her before or since. Absolutely enthusiastic; all the way, wasn't she? She used to go out of her way to meet people, to resolve problems, to help, and to advise. She was a leading member of the National Federation of Musical Societies for a number of years, and instrumental in bringing good music to Bedford. Oakley Junior School was a kind of show-place. She retired in 1972 and only had a few years of retirement.[50]

The *Minute Books* are in her strong, firm hand and the minutes are clear, concise and informative.[51] She was very influential in much that occurred in the period 1947–58 within the Musical Society – more so than in her first few years as general secretary, when Norman Frost was the conductor, and the dominating force.

49 The numbers (60 and 600) quoted here are from Norman Frost's (unsuccessful) application for the post of musical director at Bedford Modern School in 1949, following the retirement of Herbert Colson. According to the programme for the April 1947 Brahms concert there were 20 patrons, 339 subscribing members, and 138 chorus members, a total of 497. Application for post of musical director, Norman Frost, 12 February 1949, Bedford Modern School Archive.

50 Personal interview with Bill and Deirdre Knight by the author.

51 BLARS X/817/1/7, X/817/1/8 and much of X/817/1/9.

Kate (1909–98) and Hans Freyhan (1909–96)

Kate and Hans Freyhan were hugely influential within the Musical Society between the late 1940s and 1990s.[52] Hans Freyhan was born in Berlin. His father, Max, was a lawyer but his real interests were literature, the theatre – he wrote theatre criticisms professionally – and music. He was also a good pianist. Hans Freyhan's mother had trained as a singer, and he himself started to learn the piano at the age of nine, later taking up the cello and the organ. He studied musicology, German language and literature and philosophy at Freiberg University, and subsequently studied to become a teacher at Berlin University. After qualifying, Hans Freyhan started teaching music in a grammar school, but quite soon, at the age of twenty-three, he was 'forcibly retired' (his words) because, following the Nazi rise to power in 1933, Jewish people were forbidden to teach in state schools. From then on, he had to earn a living teaching at independent schools and taking private pupils.

Kate Freyhan (*née* Lévy) was born and grew up in Hamburg where her father was a solicitor. She studied a range of subjects, also at Freiberg University, which is where she and Hans Freyhan met. Her father was successful in a number of actions brought by Jewish people, and in 1936 the police came to arrest him. His family said, 'You cannot take him from where he is now', which annoyed the police very much; he had died a week or two earlier in hospital from peritonitis. If he had not died, he would probably have perished in a concentration camp, as Kate Freyhan's mother did later, in Auschwitz.

Hans Freyhan was given a year's visa for a post at a school in Brighton in 1938. The school offered temporary posts as a way of helping Jewish people who were suffering persecution in Germany. A colleague of Hans Freyhan - a fellow teacher - had seen the advertisement and had intended to apply, but told Hans to submit an application for the post because he had a wife and a young child. The teacher and his elderly mother subsequently perished. Hans Freyhan left Germany first and Kate followed soon afterwards with their son, Peter, then less than a year old. The war began within a few months. Because aliens were not allowed to live on the south coast in case they were spies, Hans Freyhan had to leave the post in Brighton. Despite the persecution of Jewish people in Germany, the British authorities feared that there could be spies amongst them. He was taken into custody and sent to the Isle of Man where he, along with many other Jewish people, was interned. Among other internees were three members of the Amadeus Quartet – they formed the quartet in 1947.[53] Hans Freyhan spoke quite highly of the British authorities on the

52 It was to Hans and Kate Freyhan that the author first turned when he started researching the history of the Society. He will never forget that first afternoon spent with them when they showed him some of the early concert programmes and described, very movingly, how they had had to leave Germany and how they had come to settle in Bedford. The author wrote in his *Diary*: ' I had a wonderful, absorbing time – it meant so much to talk to these very kind, warm people who have done and given so much to local music. They talked, too, of their leaving Germany and of their early days in England. I expected to stay with them for over two hours, but stayed for four hours … Hans is rather frail but mentally so alert. Kate, too, is mentally very alert – incredibly so, but has a spinal injury so walks with great difficulty.' Michael Benson, *Diary*, 24 March 1991. There is a full page about Kate and Hans Freyhan in *The Bedfordshire Times*, 21 June 1991, p. 8, that includes background information about the couple.

53 In Mary Wesley's novel *The Camomile Lawn* (London, 1984), a Jewish musician who had escaped from Germany is interned in the Isle of Man for the same reason.

Isle of Man. They organised football matches between the camps and he was able to take part in concerts and give lectures on music.

Meanwhile, Kate Freyhan was struggling with two very small children on eleven shillings a week in a house in Hemel Hempstead with outside toilets. The vicar of Ramsey, in the Isle of Man, whom Hans had met there, had a sister in Hemel who helped Kate find improved accommodation. After Hans Freyhan's release from internment, the family left Hemel Hempstead because of an outbreak of measles and were offered relocation in Bedford or Rickmansworth. They chose Bedford because they had heard of the schools. For their first few weeks in the town, along with many others, they slept in a church hall while the authorities sought billet accommodation for them. Eventually accommodation was found in a house in Pemberley Lane with Miss Parker-Ford, the wealthy but unmarried daughter of a former vicar of St John's church, Bedford. At first she refused to have them, but changed her mind when she heard that Hans Freyhan was a musician. When the Freyhan's first moved in she was rather cold and reserved and expected the children to be quiet, but she soon warmed to the family and they became good friends. Miss Parker-Ford helped Hans Freyhan to find his first job in Bedford, teaching German and French at Bedford Modern School. Earlier, Hans Freyhan had written to Herbert Colson about teaching music there. Herbert Colson had written a post card back saying that he believed that there was 'no chance' of a post teaching music in Bedford.

As early as October 1941, there are newspaper reports of Hans Freyhan giving talks about Schubert and Brahms under the auspices of the Bedfordshire Rural Music School, and playing the piano in a performance of one of Brahms's Cello Sonatas.[54] Kate Freyhan began teaching recorder in the town and was soon asked to join a Bedford Modern School orchestra playing oboe parts as there were no oboists.[55]

In November 1946, Norman Frost spoke to Hans Freyhan about the possibility of his becoming the Musical Society's accompanist. According to the minutes: 'He was willing to act as honorary accompanist, provided he did not lose any professional engagement; if he accepted the position in a professional capacity he would require £1.1s. [one guinea] per rehearsal.'[56] He was taken on for a limited period. This was probably on a voluntary basis because in March 1947 it was agreed that he should be paid. The question was raised as to whether, as a member of the Society, he should be receiving remuneration. However, he did not remain accompanist for very long because he started work a few months later in Yorkshire and then took on a teaching post at St Neots.

Hans and Kate Freyhan's strong links with the Musical Society had begun, and their story, and that of Margaret Robertson, continues in the following chapters.

[54] *The Bedfordshire Times and Bedfordshire Standard,* 3, 10 and 17 October 1941, pp. 10, 10 and 8 respectively. The 17 October 1941 report refers to him as 'H. W. Treyhan'.

[55] Kate Freyhan recalled leaving her younger son, Michael, in the hall during rehearsal, and by the end of the rehearsal, he was humming the second movement from Schubert's Symphony in C, though at that stage, he was too young to be able to speak.

[56] *Minute Book 1944–48,* 14 November 1946, BLARS X817/1/7.

Chapter Nine

Bach comes to Town, 1947–59

> It is with the greatest possible pride that the committee of the Bedfordshire Musical Society announces that Mr. Clarence Raybould has consented to become the Society's conductor. By doing so, Mr. Raybould does honour not only to the Society but to the town at large which first became acquainted with him when the B. B. C. Symphony Orchestra lived and played amongst us during the war. We then began to know him not merely as a name in the "Radio Times" but as a delightful personality as well.[1]

Clarence Robert Raybould (1886–1972)

Clarence Raybould, the Musical Society's new conductor, was born in Birmingham. He was, in 1912, the first person to receive a music degree at Birmingham University. He joined the Midland Institute of Music that same year as a teacher of harmony and counterpoint. He subsequently worked with Rutland Boughton as accompanist, coach and conductor of the Glastonbury Festival and, after that, performed the same role for the first Beecham Opera Company.[2] He then moved to the British National Opera Company, having already established a modest reputation as a conductor and composer before the outbreak of the First World War. His opera, *The Sumida River,* was performed in 1916 in Birmingham. After the war, he worked as a pianist and accompanist, travelling widely. He worked for the Columbia Gramophone Company 1927–31, and later in films, as a composer, arranger and conductor of film music.

Before his appointment to the BBC, Clarence Raybould had conducted the BBC Symphony Orchestra several times. The first time was in January 1935, in the first United Kingdom performances of Roger Sessions's *The Black Maskers*, George Gershwin's *Second Rhapsody* and Aaron Copland's *Dance Symphony*. In the same year, he also conducted the first performance and world premiere of Mozart's Rondo in A. He was appointed chief assistant conductor of the BBC Symphony Orchestra in 1938 by which time he had conducted new works at fourteen of the orchestra's concerts. He was then nearly fifty-two years old. He moved with the orchestra from London to Bristol, and then from Bristol to Bedford in 1941, and remained chief assistant conductor for the duration of the Second World War – all the time that the orchestra was resident in Bedford. He and his wife lived at 9 Everard Road,

[1] Margaret Robertson, in a letter to *The Bedfordshire Times and Bedfordshire Standard,* 25 July 1947, p. 5.

[2] Rutland Boughton was an English composer. Michael Kennedy in the *Oxford Dictionary of Music* (Oxford, 1985), p. 93, writes: 'Inspired by Wagner's theory of music drama, [he] conceived the idea of an Eng. Beyreuth at Glastonbury for perf. of series of mus. dramas, based on the Arthurian legends, by himself, with Reginald Buckley as librettist. First fest, held in 1914 when his "The Immortal Hour" (1912–13) was perf.' See also Michael Hurd, *Rutland Boughton and the Glastonbury Festivals* (Oxford, 1993).

Bedford, until 1950. As a conductor at the BBC he was a great success. Nicholas Kenyon writes: 'Over the following nine years, Raybould did an enormous amount of work with the orchestra.'[3] Sir Adrian Boult, in his autobiography, *My Own Trumpet*, writes: 'During this time, the assistant conductor of the Orchestra was Mr. Clarence Raybould, a very distinguished musician, who had great experience also as a chamber music pianist and accompanist. He was with us for a large number of years and did yeoman service as he was very popular with the orchestra.'[4]

Clarence Raybould retired shortly after the orchestra returned to London, six months before reaching the BBC's staff retirement age of sixty.[5] Following his retirement he became involved in working with young musicians. He taught at the Royal Academy of Music where he conducted the senior orchestra and he was also the first conductor of the National Youth Orchestra of Wales, which he helped to found in 1945. He remained its conductor until 1966.[6] He was appointed conductor of Bedford Musical Society at the July 1947 annual general meeting. In the letter to *The Bedfordshire Times and Bedfordshire Standard* quoted at the start of this chapter, Margaret Robertson also wrote: 'Further acquaintance has served to increase our regard for him both as a man and as a musician: and we are happy to think that Mr. Raybould now declares himself a Bedfordian by thus honouring the town of his adoption … There can be very few amateur societies which have ever been fortunate enough to enjoy the services of so distinguished a musician as Mr. Raybould.'[7]

The roles of chorus master and accompanist were obviously very important as Clarence Raybould was regularly away, and the Musical Society took some trouble in making these appointments. Paul Steinitz, conductor of the Bedford Symphony Orchestra and Mr Frederick (Freddie) E. Stevens, the newly appointed county adviser for music and drama, were proposed for the post of chorus master: 'whichever proved to be the most willing or acceptable on the best possible terms.'[8] In the event, neither man was appointed, and Daphne Braggins was elected chorus master on 5 September 1947, at the end of that very hot summer, having originally been suggested for the post of accompanist. She remained in post for three years – until shortly after her father stood down as chairman, in 1950. Her father was Alderman Archibald Braggins, a former mayor of Bedford, who owned a large store on the corner of Harpur Street and Silver Street. The store was taken over by Beales in the 1980s.

Daphne Braggins was a student at Bedford High School, which she left in 1933 to go to the Royal College of Music. In 1936 she won the Royal College of Organists Lafontaine Prize and this was followed by the Turle Scholarship for Music at Girton College, Cambridge, in 1937. She graduated from Girton College with a

3 Kenyon, *The BBC Symphony Orchestra*, p. 133. Nicholas Kenyon probably includes Raybould's two years working for the BBC before he was formally appointed as chief assistant conductor.

4 Boult, *My Own Trumpet*, p. 97.

5 See Kenyon, *The BBC Symphony Orchestra*, p. 220, with reference to Sir Adrian reaching this age on 8 April 1949.

6 Obituary of Clarence Raybould, *The Times*, 29 March 1972, p. 16.

7 *The Bedfordshire Times and Bedfordshire Standard*, 25 July 1947, p. 5.

8 The minutes for the 6 August committee meeting suggest either Dr Steinetz, at a fee of 3gns per rehearsal plus expenses, or Dr Willcocks of Kings College, Cambridge, for chorus master. It was pointed out that Dr Willcocks had just been appointed to Salisbury Cathedral. See William Owen, ed., *A Life in Music: Conversations with Sir David Willcocks and Friends*, (Oxford, 2008), pp. 77–8

Bachelor of Music degree in 1940. From Cambridge she went to Dublin for post-graduate study and became a Doctor of Music in 1951. Academic life obviously suited her because she took an English and Music BA degree at Cambridge in 1955.[9] She inherited a large house in Rothsay Road (now Lillibet Lodge) from her father.[10] Although she was a gifted musician, her appointment may have owed something to the fact that her father was chairman of the Musical Society at the time.

Concerts, 1947–52

Although one of the original aims of the Musical Society was the encouragement of instrumental as well as choral music, apart from the orchestral concerts in the latter part of the 1920s under Herbert Colson, the Society had mainly concentrated on choral works. The 1947/48 membership card includes the constitution. One of the two objects of the Society is: 'To provide a regular series of first-class orchestral and choral concerts, to maintain Chorus as part of its organisation, and engage orchestras and solo artistes of high repute.'[11]

During the period that Clarence Raybould was conductor, there were nearly as many orchestral concerts as choral concerts. The Society was ambitious, and because generous grants were available it saw itself as going from strength to strength. Professional orchestras played at all concerts during Clarence Raybould's first few years as conductor. There were significant changes in 1952, but the overall pattern of concerts did not change. Clarence Raybould included a number of recently-composed choral works in his concerts, for example, Vaughan Williams's *Dona Nobis Pacem*, Ireland's *These Things Shall Be*, Bliss's *Pastoral: Lie Strewn the White Flocks* and Kodály's *Psalmus Hungaricus* and *Missa Brevis*. He also conducted the first performance in Bedford of Fauré's Requiem. Otherwise, the programmes of choral concerts that he conducted over the years were surprisingly conventional and included Handel's *Messiah* (twice) and *Acis and Galatea*, Mendelssohn's *Elijah*, Haydn's *Creation* and Coleridge-Taylor's *Hiawatha's Wedding Feast.* The orchestral concerts conducted by Clarence Raybould were more adventurous, with two symphonies by Sibelius, and Vaughan Williams's Symphony No. 6. Several concerts included a number of shorter, mostly modern works.

The first concert that Clarence Raybould conducted was an orchestral concert near the end of September 1947, and the first choral concert was *Acis and Galatea*, early in November 1947. The latter concert also included Mozart's Symphony No. 38 (known as the 'Prague Symphony'). The reviewer, J.H.M.S., was usually deferential to Clarence Raybould, but on this occasion he was somewhat critical, not so much of Clarence Raybould himself, but of the programme content – full-length performance of Handel does not appear to have been to his taste.[12] The review states that the work lasted from 7.45p.m.–9.14p.m. and there was no interval.

9 Stephen J. Weston, *The Organ and Organists of Bedford High School 1898–1998* (Bedford, 1998), p. 9.

10 The author remembers delivering a letter, wrongly delivered to his address in Waterloo Road, Bedford, to Daphne Braggins at her house nearby in Rothsay Road. He noticed several pianos in one of the downstairs front rooms. It was obvious that the house was occupied by a musician.

11 1948/49 *Membership Card*, given to the author by George Thompson.

12 He opens the review with the following tale: 'Sooner or later, when professional musicians discuss Handel, someone will tell the story of the double-bass player who dreamt he was playing "Messiah" and

Today, this would be regarded as an unconventional view of Handel. J.H.M.S. writes that the repetition in Handel's works helps to explain why there was a small audience.[13] 'The hall was only half-full, and one scarcely wondered why no more music-lovers had bothered to attend ... They should choose better programmes.'[14] J.H.M.S. is, however, very complimentary about the performers, the soloists, the chorus and the augmented Boyd Neel Orchestra: 'True gems were there, glowing and alive, and they were magnificently sung by chorus and soloists alike.'[15]

Just over a month later, the Boyd Neel Orchestra joined the Musical Society's chorus again, in a performance of *Messiah*. The review (the author is not identified this time) is positive and complimentary: 'Mr. Raybould electrified his choir and Dr. Boyd Neel's Orchestra into the ineffable verve Handel so insatiably demanded.'[16] The review ends on a positive note, too: 'At the right moments Mr. Raybould was assisted in his brilliant work by Miss Daphne Braggins at the organ and Mr. Eskdale with his solo trumpet. The hall was solidly filled and many had to stand.'[17]

The orchestral concert that followed in February 1948, for which the Riddick Strings played, was poorly attended. So much so, that: 'Mr. Raybould addressed them [the audience], and while congratulating the few on being present, said he was disgusted with the many who were absent.'[18] The programming *may* have been partly to blame on this occasion.[19]

For the last concert of the season, held in March, a large contingent of the London Symphony Orchestra joined the Musical Society's chorus in Kodály's *Psalmus Hungaricus* and Vaughan Williams's *Dona Nobis Pacem*, and also performed orchestral works by Beethoven and Mendelssohn. J.H.M.S. writes: 'It was pleasant to hear the choir demonstrate that music more modern than that of Handel found

when he woke up he found that he was.' The implication of this anecdote is that uncut Handel means: 'endless contrapuntal repetitions in arias, and the length of *Acis and Galatea*.' *The Bedfordshire Times and Bedfordshire Standard*, 7 November 1947, p. 5.

13 When Clarence Raybould was asked about a critical review, written by J.H.M.S. (John Sykes), of a concert that he had conducted at a subsequent rehearsal, he said 'Mr. Sykes is an electrician: I am a musician'. This anecdote was related to the author by George Thompson, a member of the choir. This comment was made at a rehearsal following the performance of Verdi's Requiem in March 1949. Mr Sykes was, however, no ordinary electrician. In his *Bedfordshire Times* obituary his prowess is praised: 'A brilliant electrical engineer he combined with this skill great journalistic and broadcasting ability … He was founder and editor of "Direct Current", European technical editor of "Electrical World" of New York, editorial assistant to "Water Power" and consultant on high voltage engineering to a division of Enfield Rolling Mills Ltd. Articles under his signature appeared in almost every electrical journal in the world, and his advocacy played a great part in the recent extension of the use of direct current for the transmission of high voltage power. He made over 1,000 broadcasts on electrical and scientific subjects on BBC sound and television services … He was author of a number of books on electrical practice: "The Guide Book to Electricity", "Beginner's Guide to Electrical Wiring", "Beginner's Guide to Automobile Electrical Equipment" … For 17 years he was engineer-in-charge of the first section of the British high voltage grid and it was on this account that he came to live in Bedford.' *Bedfordshire Times*, 25 November 1966, p. 23.

14 *The Bedfordshire Times and Bedfordshire Standard*, 7 November 1947, p. 5.

15 Ibid. The Boyd Neel Orchestra and the Riddick Strings would normally have comprised between twenty and thirty players. *Minute Book 1951–53*, 16 April 1953, BLARS X817/1/9.

16 *Bedford Record & Circular*, 16 December 1947, p. 2.

17 Ibid.

18 *Bedford Record & Circular*, 24 February 1948, p. 8. This review ends with the comment: 'A fuller notice will appear in Friday's *Bedfordshire Times*.'

19 The concert included works by Bach, Piano Concerto in F Minor; Elgar, *Introduction and Allegro for Strings*; Turina, *Rapsodia Sinfonica*; Bloch, Concerto Grosso; and Wiren, *Serenade for Strings*.

them unafraid … Mr Raybould, the Society's famous conductor, made the choir sing as they have seldom sung before, and it was a refreshing and encouraging sound.'[20] Despite the inclusion of two modern works, there was a packed audience.

The opening concert of the new season was orchestral, and included Sibelius's Symphony No. 2. J.H.M.S. is a little critical of the programming – three works from the late nineteenth and early twentieth centuries, but he then writes: 'the opportunity of hearing Mr. Raybould interpret the music of his friend Mr. Sibelius was more than ample compensation.'[21]

The next concert – the first of the season with the chorus – was in mid-November and included Brahms's *Liebeslieder* waltzes. For these, there was piano accompaniment (for four hands) for the choir, rather than orchestral accompaniment. Brahms's Four Trios for Female Voices, Harp and Two Horns was also performed. J.H.M.S. paid tribute, as he regularly did, to Daphne Braggins for her work in training the choir. One of the horn players was Charles Farncombe, who was soon to be appointed chorus master for the Musical Society.

There was an odd reference to the November concert at the following annual general meeting in July: 'Miss D. Robertson ... recalled that the second concert in last season's programme had "lost the confidence of the members and the opportunities of a broadcast".'[22] It is not known what the broadcast was or why the members had lost confidence.

An orchestral concert given by the Riddick String Orchestra in mid-February 1949 included what J.H.M.S. referred to as 'a robust and purposeful' performance of Bach's Brandenburg Concerto No. 3 and a 'delightful' performance of a work by the Italian composer Mario Pilati, his miniature *Suite for Pianoforte and Strings*.[23]

At the end of March 1949, Clarence Raybould conducted his most significant performance as conductor of the Musical Society. This was Verdi's Requiem, with the London Symphony Orchestra. It was certainly the grandest concert in scale, and was sung in Latin, which was probably a first for the Musical Society.[24] This fact is not stated in the review. The programme contains the Latin text, the English translation and the names of the performers; there are no programme notes. The concert included Kodály's *Missa Brevis*, which was also probably sung in Latin, as the Latin text together with the English translation is included in the programme. The reviewer, E.L.N., gives little description of the performance, but does praise the chorus and orchestra.[25] He was very complimentary about the soloists, one of whom was Richard Lewis (tenor), and he wrote that the success of the performance

20 *The Bedfordshire Times and Bedfordshire Standard*, 26 March 1948, p. 5.

21 *The Bedfordshire Times and Bedfordshire Standard*, 8 October 1948, p. 6.

22 *The Bedfordshire Times and Bedfordshire Standard*, 27 July 1949, p. 5.

23 *The Bedfordshire Times and Bedfordshire Standard*, 25 February 1949, p. 5.

24 George Thompson, who took part in the concert confirmed the fact that the concert was sung in Latin in a personal interview with the author. Margaret Robertson also referred to it as, 'Verdi's Latin Requiem' at the following year's annual general meeting.

25 He wrote: 'chorus and orchestra ... achieved a magnificent volume of sound in the tremendous climaxes, and beautiful quality of tone in the pianissimo passages. There may have been a hint of uncertainty on the part of the chorus once or twice, and they were sometimes put to it to compete with Verdi's heavy orchestration, but there were few ragged entries, and the high standard of performance bore evidence of excellent work on the part of the chorus master, Miss Braggins.' *The Bedfordshire Times and Bedfordshire Standard*, 8 April 1949, p. 7.

was a tribute to the personality and great skill of Clarence Raybould. Otherwise, he seems almost out of his depth and makes no detailed comments on the performance of either work and no comment on the size of the audience.[26]

At the July 1949 annual general meeting, it was announced that the next season's concerts had been planned deliberately for their popular appeal. The president, Ald. J. Arnold Whitchurch, welcomed this decision, 'This is like old times', he is quoted as saying.[27] Reading between the lines he is implying that the previous season, with a number of unfamiliar works, had not been a success.

Hans Freyhan was appointed accompanist at the start of the year, but had to resign six months later because he was due to work away from Bedford (in Yorkshire) after the summer holidays. Early in the season, Daphne Braggins was absent from one of the rehearsals without arranging for someone else to take it. Someone suggested that Kate Freyhan, who conducted a number of smaller choirs, should take that rehearsal. Kate Freyhan agreed and was subsequently appointed assistant chorus master. She held this post 1948–74.[28]

The new season opened with the London Philharmonic playing an orchestral concert at the end of September. *Elijah* followed at the end of November. The Musical Society was assisted by the augmented Riddick String Orchestra. The reviewer, E.L.N., was very complimentary about the performance.[29] There was a fine line-up of soloists, Jennifer Vyvyan (soprano), Anne Wood (contralto), Heddle Nash (tenor) and Roy Henderson (bass). Of Roy Henderson, who sang the part of Elijah, the reviewer wrote: 'To hear his singing of the beautiful aria "It is enough", was a most moving experience.'[30] The twenty-four year old Jennifer Vyvyan had studied at the Royal Academy of Music with Roy Henderson and joined the cast of Glyndbourne in 1948. In 1950 she went on to study in Switzerland and subsequently had a very successful, though tragically short, career as an opera singer and concert performer.[31] Daphne Braggins was not available to play the organ, so Frederick (Fred) R. S. Rawlins played instead, at short notice.

At the end of January 1950, the then Labour MP for Bedford, Mr Skeffington-Lodge, contacted the secretary of the Musical Society to ask if the Society would give up the concert due to be held in the Corn Exchange on the 16 February. This was so that Clement Attlee, the prime minister, could speak there in the run up to the general election. Following a lengthy discussion at a special committee meeting, it was unanimously agreed to decline the request because heavy losses would be incurred. The secretary wrote to Mr Skeffington-Lodge accordingly:

[26] It is not known who the reviewer E. L. N. was.

[27] *The Bedfordshire Times and Bedfordshire Standard*, 28 July 1950, p. 7.

[28] Personal interview with Kate and Hans Freyhan by the author.

[29] Of the choir he wrote: 'The choir sang well and were usually quick to respond to the demands of the conductor's baton. The balance was good on the whole in spite of the comparatively small number of tenors and basses.' *The Bedfordshire Times and Bedfordshire Standard*, 8 December 1949, p. 6.

[30] Ibid.

[31] Jennifer Vyvyan died in April 1974, soon after her forty-ninth birthday as a result of complications from a bronchial and asthmatic condition that she had been struggling to control over a number of years. See the Bach Cantatas website, http://www.bach-cantatas.com/Bio/Vyvyan-Jennifer.htm, accessed 29 November 2014.

> I am instructed by my Committee to inform you that they have carefully considered your request … and have decided, with regret, that it is impossible for the Musical Society's concert arranged for 16th February in the Bedford Corn Exchange to be cancelled … Our contract with the Philharmonia Orchestra dates back to May 1949 and our commitments amount to almost £400.[32] Our chorus has been rehearsing for months and we have sold many tickets … These facts make it quite impossible for us to let you have the Corn Exchange on 16th February, because it is impossible for us to renounce our liabilities … I remain.[33]

The Musical Society may have done the prime minister a favour, as he held an open air meeting, as reported in *The Bedfordshire Times and Bedfordshire Standard* of 17 February:

> PREMIER DRAWS CROWD OF 10,000 AT BEDFORD, 'Labour Puts First Things First'. The visit of the Prime Minister, the Right Hon. C. R. Attlee, to Bedford yesterday (Thursday) evening was marked by the biggest political meeting the town has ever known. Police estimated that nearly 10,000 people were crowded in and around the Market Square long before the Premier spoke. Traffic was diverted as people surged from the pavements and thronged the High Street. Even after Mr. Attlee had begun to speak people were seen joining the rear of the crowd.[34]

Despite the crowds, Clement Attlee's visit did not have the desired effect. Mr Skeffington-Lodge lost the seat to the twenty-nine year-old Christopher Soames, Winston Churchill's son-in-law, in the election on 23 February. The Labour Party won the election nationally, but with a much reduced majority. Clarence Raybould subsequently wrote personally to Clement Attlee.[35]

The concert that Mr Skeffington-Lodge had hoped the Society would cancel was, according to J.H.M.S., a triumph. He very much approved of the chorus's singing of Parry's *Blest Pair of Sirens* and Borodin's *Polovtsian Dances*. The orchestral works included Sibelius's Symphony No. 5: 'where once again we rejoiced in wonderful orchestral ensemble. When it was realised that the country's supreme horn player, Mr. Dennis Brain, and many other distinguished solo executants were to be found in the orchestral ranks, this was not surprising.'[36] There is no comment about the size of the audience in the review, which suggests that it was good without being a sell-out.

Five weeks later, in their fourth and final concert of the season, the Musical Society performed Haydn's *Creation* with the Riddick Strings. Among the soloists was the well-known soprano, Isobel Baillie, about whom J.H.M.S. is very complimentary: 'Her very wonderful soprano voice – true, clear, and rich in every part of its compass – can seldom have been heard to better advantage than in the air

32 The normal size of the larger London orchestras on their Bedford visits seems to have been between fifty and sixty players, according to the minutes of 19 January 1950, although for the concert in March 1948, which included Vaughan Williams's *Dona Nobis Pacem* and Kodály's *Psalmus Hungaricus*, additional players were required.

33 *Minute Book 1948–51*, 28 January 1950, BLARS X/ 817/1/8.

34 *The Bedfordshire Times and Bedfordshire Standard*, 17 February 1950, p. 7.

35 *Minute Book 1948–51*, 16 March 1950, BLARS X817/1/8.

36 *The Bedfordshire Times and Bedfordshire Standard*, 24 February 1950, p. 7. Dennis Brain was killed in a road accident in the late summer of 1957 when returning to London. He was driving a Triumph sports car.

"With verdure clad".'[37] However, he also states, questionably, that the work does not provide many opportunities to extend the chorus. At the end of the performance, Clarence Raybould thanked the large audience for coming and asked for their support for the next season: 'We shall be here again next year, so don't forget to come and see us.'[38] This is something of a contrast to his speech after the concert two years earlier, in February 1948.

There is one very significant item in the minutes of the committee meeting in June 1950. This reads: 'Mr. Raybould raised the question of Chorus rehearsals, now that he had left the town. The Committee thought a professional Chorus Master ought to be appointed and the Secretary would ask Mr. Raybould if he could nominate anyone.'[39] Clarence Raybould had moved from Bedford to London in the first half of 1950, and Archibald Braggins had indicated that he would be standing down as chairman due to ill-health. Both of these facts could have had some bearing on the decision to replace Daphne Braggins.[40] At the next committee meeting, shortly before the July annual general meeting: 'It was agreed to write to the Chorus Master giving Mr. Raybould's and the Committee's views on a change of Chorus Master.'[41] The committee met again in the September when the following was recorded: 'A formal note was read from Miss Braggins resigning from the Chorus Mastership of the Society "for private reasons".'[42] The minutes state, somewhat hypocritically, that the resignation was accepted with regret and that tributes were paid to Miss Braggins's work for the Society.

Charles Farncombe was nominated to replace her, and at a committee meeting immediately after the annual general meeting of 25 July 1950 a sub-committee was appointed to interview him, to appoint if they thought him suitable, and to agree a fee. At the September committee meeting, members of the sub-committee confirmed Charles Farncombe had been appointed and terms agreed.

Charles Farncombe, who was born in 1919, was a chorister at Canterbury Cathedral before going on to Dulwich College. When he left school, he studied civil engineering and later worked for the construction company, John Mowlem. He served in the Second World War in France where he was injured. While recovering, he decided to make a career in music and took up the French horn. After studying at the Royal School of Church Music, he studied at the Royal Academy of Music 1948–51. So it was at the start of his last year at the Royal Academy that he took on the role of accompanist for the Musical Society. He was encouraged by Vaughan Williams, who got to know him at the Royal Academy, to start conducting, and in 1955 he founded the Handel Opera Society. This did much to help revive the popu-

[37] *The Bedfordshire Times and Bedfordshire Standard,* 7 April 1950, p. 10.

[38] Ibid. In the concert review, there was a reference to a recent *Sunday Times* article about Haydn's *Creation*: 'its naive pastoralities where the tawny lion well-behavedly roars in the orchestra, and the "Fleecy, meek, and bleating flocks" have their counterparts in the woodwind, provide an evening of what the Rev. Bernard Croft called, in the Sunday Times of the week-end after the concert, "holy fun".'

[39] *Minute Book 1948–51*, 21 June 1950, BLARS X817/1/8.

[40] Ibid. He was offered the vice-chairmanship before the annual general meeting, but declined it. He lived until 1972.

[41] Freddie Stevens, who was a committee member by this stage, told the author that Daphne Braggins upset some people and that the secretary, Margaret Robertson, had in effect sacked her, although Daphne Braggins was a very good musician.

[42] *Minute Book 1948–51*, 11 September 1950, BLARS X817/1/8.

larity of the composer's operas and oratorios, though sadly the organisation only survived until 1985. But the aims had been achieved, for Handel's operas are now regularly performed.[43]

Despite more popular programmes during the 1949/50 season, the Musical Society lost nearly £800 on its four concerts. A number of generous grants from the Arts Council, from Bedford Corporation and Bedfordshire County Council enabled the Musical Society to continue to promote high class concerts.

The first concert of the new season, an orchestral concert, was held early in October 1950. The main work was Vaughan Williams's Symphony No. 6, which J.H.M.S. suggests is: 'one of the greatest, if not the greatest written in our time'.[44] He was obviously impressed by the performance, given by the London Symphony Orchestra. Other works in the concert were by Brahms, Debussy and Dohnányi. However, the Corn Exchange was only two thirds full, resulting in the headline, 'Poor Support for Musical Society.' There is a reference in the review to Clarence Raybould being, 'fresh from his triumphs in Washington'. It is not clear what his triumphs actually were.[45]

A performance of *Messiah* followed in December, with the Riddick String Orchestra. The reviewer suggests that the solo singing was disappointing because of the immaturity of the singers. The Musical Society had decided to engage younger soloists, no doubt to save costs. At the committee meeting that followed a few days after the performance, Mrs Olive Parris, wife of Arthur Parris, thought the experiment with young soloists should not be repeated because of the audience reaction and because some members of the choir thought that the performance had been 'dull'.[46]

The orchestral concert given in February 1951 was more like some of the concerts that Clarence Raybould conducted soon after his first appointment, with several shorter pieces, a number of them modern. The reviewer, E.L.N., writes: 'If we sometimes merit the accusation of being musically conservative and loth to give contemporary music a hearing, our lugubrious critics would have had little cause for complaint at the enthusiasm of the audience in the Corn Exchange.'[47]

The main work at the choral concert given in April was Fauré's Requiem. The choir was accompanied by the London Philharmonic Orchestra. This concert rounded off the season. Although Fauré composed the Requiem 1877–90 – originally with just organ accompaniment – it did not achieve general popularity until after the Second World War.[48] The concert opened with the prelude from Elgar's *The Dream of Gerontius*. The reviewer, J.H.M.S., points out an imbalance in the chorus with far more sopranos and contraltos than tenors and basses, but he compliments Charles Farncombe and Clarence Raybould for managing to conceal this lack of symmetry and produce a full and rich sound. The soprano soloist, Margaret Ritchie, was very well-known at the time. Also included was Ireland's *These Things Shall*

43 Charles Farncombe, obituary, *The Times*, 2 August 2006, p. 49.
44 *The Bedfordshire Times and Bedfordshire Standard*, 13 October 1950, p. 5.
45 Ibid.
46 *Minute Book 1948–51*, 20 December 1950, BLARS X817/1/8.
47 *The Bedfordshire Times and Bedfordshire Standard*, 13 April 1951, p. 7.
48 Kennedy, *Oxford Dictionary of Music*, p. 242.

Be, something of a contrast to the Fauré, and Holst's *King Estmere*, which J.H.M.S. liked, referring to it as a 'happy piece'.[49]

At the annual general meeting in July, a financial loss of nearly £770 on takings at concerts was announced. This was nearly as large as that of the previous season, though after deficit grants, donations and subscriptions were taken into account, there was only a shortfall of just over £25. The situation was still serious. Margaret Robertson announced that the Arts Council would be cutting the budget for the forthcoming year by a third – to £200 – and that it would be necessary to operate on a much smaller scale. She said that she felt like the prophet of doom. A motion was carried saying that too much money was being spent on orchestras.[50]

At the end of September 1950, the Town Council announced that the Corn Exchange organ was to be disposed of.[51] Following this statement, *The Bedfordshire Times and Bedfordshire Standard* published three letters.[52] One of the writers (who does not give his name) quotes Ald. A. J. Canvin, who had stated that, since 1936, a total of £1,668 8s 7d had been spent on the organ, but the income from its use had only been £32 2s 6d. This writer makes the point that the organ was in constant use when the BBC were in Bedford and asks what the BBC paid towards its maintenance. His question appears to have gone unanswered. A year later, it was reported that the Corn Exchange organ was to be sold to Messrs. J. W. Walker for £400.[53] This report also stated that the Harpur Trust had been approached to see whether the organ could be acquired for Bedford Modern School, but that it had not been possible to arrange this.[54]

The main work in the December concert was *Hiawatha's Wedding Feast*. The tenor soloist, who sang the famous 'Onaway, Awake!', was Frank Titterton and there was a 'scratch' orchestra led by Ronald Good. The audience was disappointing despite this being a popular programme, because, according to J.H.M.S., there was an outbreak of fog and frost so severe that it had even hampered the conductor, who was late for the rehearsal. The last paragraph of the review is 'second hand' because the reviewer had another engagement. He did not notice, apparently, what one member referred to at the subsequent committee meeting: 'a lack of organisation that was criminal, no stands, Mr. Raybould's music appeared to be mixed up, the Chorus Master not present.'[55]

The Boyd Neel Orchestra played at an orchestral concert in February 1952, less than a week after the funeral of King George VI.[56] This concert had an eight-

49 *The Bedfordshire Times and Bedfordshire Standard*, 13 April 1951, p. 7.

50 *The Bedfordshire Times and Bedfordshire Standard*, 27 July 1951, p. 8.

51 *The Bedfordshire Times and Bedfordshire Standard*, 29 September 1950, p. 7.

52 *The Bedfordshire Times and Bedfordshire Standard*, 6 October 1950, p. 5 (two letters) and 13 October 1950, p. 5 (one letter).

53 Report of the Town Council meeting, *The Bedfordshire Times and Bedfordshire Standard*, 26 October 1951, p. 7. See also BLARS BP43/44 and BP43/6.

54 In a letter to the author of 31 January 1996, J. W. Walker & Sons Ltd confirmed that the organ was purchased in November 1951. By that stage the organ bore the label Peter Conacher & Co of Huddersfield, who had presumably undertaken the renovation work in 1936. The letter states that the company has no record that the organ went whole to any one destination, and that the parts were probably used in various contracts. The general shortage of funds and materials at that time obliged organ builders to use good quality second-hand material in lieu of new material for most repair and renewal work.

55 *Bedford Record & Circular*, 18 December 1951, p. 2.

56 On 15 February 1952.

eenth century flavour, though only three of the seven works performed were actually composed before the year 1800. There was a good audience, suggesting to the reviewer the popularity of what he referred to as chamber music.[57]

The final concert of the season, held at the beginning of April, was another choral and orchestral concert, again with a 'scratch' orchestra. The main work was Handel's 'Dettingen' Te Deum, but the concert also included Bach's Brandenburg Concerto No. 3 and Bliss's *Pastoral: Lie Strewn the White Flocks*. The audience for the concert was very small, and the president, J. Arnold Whitchurch, commented at the annual general meeting in July that: 'He was bitterly ashamed of the small audience for the Society's final concert this year.'[58] The treasurer, Mr D. J. Clark, reported that sales of tickets for this concert were the lowest on record.[59] Even without changes to funding arrangements, the Musical Society would have had to do something to remedy the situation, but external factors were about to force their hands.

The general election of October 1951 was won by the Conservatives, with a small but decisive majority. This had a profound significance on funding for the arts and on the Musical Society. Generous public funding for the arts had been available under Article 132 of the Local Government Act 1948. Following changes to the provision of subsidies, Arts Council grants were cut, and support for the Musical Society from both Bedford Corporation and Bedfordshire County Council was substantially reduced.

As a result the Society was forced to review its policies and future programmes. The outcome of the review was that Freddie Stevens was asked if he would take on the job of chorus master at no cost, and Fred Rawlins was asked if he would continue as accompanist in an honorary capacity.[60] Freddie Stevens was at the meeting where this proposal was made and agreed to become honorary chorus master. Fred Rawlins also subsequently confirmed that he would take on the role as accompanist if he could find the time; he was then very busy as he was about to get married. At the committee meeting of 22 May 1952 the secretary, Margaret Robertson, confirmed three points: that Clarence Raybould would conduct orchestral concerts and help with the choral concerts; that the Musical Society would use St Paul's church for two concerts a year; and that the Local Education Authority would allow the free use of a hall, though the hall might not be available on Monday evenings. In fact, St Peter's hall, was made available for use on Mondays for rehearsals.

The ramifications of these changes were dealt with at the annual general meeting and at the committee meeting that followed in July 1952. The changes included a reduction of the Arts Council grant, which had been based on Clarence Raybould

57 *The Bedfordshire Times and Bedfordshire Standard*, 29 February 1952, p. 7. There is an interesting report on the same page as the review. Mrs R. E. Small, formerly closely associated with the Bedford Musical Society, sang in the Niteroi Choir at the Memorial Service to the late King at Christ Church, Rio de Janerio, on 15 February.

58 *Minute Book 1951–61*, July 1952, BLARS X817/1/9.

59 Mr Clark was the manager of Lloyds Bank in Bedford High Street. From 1951, Mr Symonds, also of Lloyds Bank, was treasurer of the Musical Society. Tom Winter, who was appointed secretary when Margaret Robertson stood down, worked at the same branch of Lloyds Bank, and was appointed treasurer in the 1960s.

60 In 1947, Fred Rawlins was a colleague of Margaret Robertson on the staff at the Harpur Secondary Modern School.

conducting three concerts a year. The Arts Council now offered ten per cent of concert takings (with a maximum payable of thirty pounds) with a bonus of one hundred pounds per annum. The forthcoming season's programmes were radically revised to be financially self-sufficient, which included using only an organ accompaniment. Freddie Stevens had a major part in planning this. He also took over the conducting of most of the choral concerts for which he had prepared the chorus.

Freddie Stevens was born in May 1912 and grew up in Vauxhall, South London.[61] His father was an engineer who, in the 1920s, worked on the manufacture of tooling for making the parts for early crystal-set wirelesses. Freddie Stevens showed an aptitude for music from a young age and was a competent pianist by the age of nine. He gained a place as a chorister at St Stephen's church, Walbrook, in the City of London. As he could read music, he was subsequently 'loaned' from time to time to other churches, notably St Alban's, Holborn (London) and St Barnabas's, Brighton. He won a scholarship to Dulwich College, and then an organ scholarship to St Catharine's College, Cambridge, though his first degree was in modern languages. His tutors at Cambridge included professor Edward Dent and Cyril Rootham, and Freddie Stevens also knew and studied under Boris Ord. At Cambridge, he played a lot of organ and piano solos, as well as chamber music. He also took part in the Footlights performances of 1934 and 1935. Although a gifted player, he did not wish to become a professional musician, so after Cambridge he went into teaching. He first taught at Giggleswick School (near Settle, North West Yorkshire). Then in 1938, shortly before the outbreak of war, he moved to Aldenham School, near Radlett. He was duly called up and before long was drafted into the Intelligence Service (21st Army Division), spending some time in the latter part of the war in Belgium, and then in Germany after VE Day. During the war, Freddie Stevens married Alice, the young widow of the Rev. Denzil Laborde, a friend of his from his Cambridge days. Alice's first husband had been a naval chaplain on HMS Westmoreland, which was sunk by the Japanese on Easter Sunday 1942. Alice came originally from Switzerland and already had two small children.

Freddie Stevens returned to Aldenham after the war, but left teaching (partly for financial reasons) in 1947 when he was appointed by Bedfordshire County Council as the first county adviser of music and drama. Soon afterwards, he was appointed conductor of the Biggleswade Choral Society, a post he did not hold for very long. He was co-opted onto the committee of the Musical Society in February 1948.[62] He and Alice became good friends with Clarence Raybould and his wife, as Clarence could speak *Suisse a Deutsche*, Alice's native tongue.

In his first few years in Bedford, Freddie Stevens gave regular solo piano recitals, promoted by the Bedfordshire Rural Music School.[63] This extract is from the review of a recital he gave on 27 February 1951: 'Free of the mannerisms that sometimes divest an audience's attention to the player and prevent full concentration on the

61 From 2000–08, the author was a close neighbour to Freddie Stevens in Felmersham. This biography is the result of regular discussions with him.

62 References in the minutes can be confusing as there was another Mr Stevens (D. J.) on the committee at the time. They are not always differentiated.

63 Bedfordshire Rural Music School was founded in 1929. For a number of years was it was largely responsible for musical education in the state school system. For details see *Bedford Music – A Year Book*, pp. 33–4.

music played, Mr. Frederick Stevens, County Music Organiser, interpreted pianoforte music of Bach, Haydn and Chopin to an almost full house … A selection of Chopins's *Mazurkas* and his *Fantasie in F minor* were played with sensitive feeling and sure touch.'[64]

In 1952, Freddie Stevens was appointed assistant director of education. His responsibilities included overseeing the eleven-plus examinations in the county, managing special educational needs and overall responsibility for the school meals service. Later, as a deputy director, he was involved in planning and establishing the three-tier system of education in Bedfordshire. He was appointed chorus master of the Musical Society in 1952 and remained in post until 1964.

The change in emphasis in 1952 was forced upon the Society by the financial situation, but it enabled Freddie Stevens to focus the chorus on *a capella* renaissance music and baroque music, especially Bach. For concerts at this time, the Musical Society had either to engage professional orchestras or to rely on organ accompaniment because the standard of the Bedford Symphony Orchestra was not sufficient.[65] Freddie Stevens was not prepared to conduct choral concerts with an orchestra even if the Musical Society had wished him to do so. As he put it to the author, the Society had to accept him on his own terms, or look elsewhere, which they were in no financial position to do. He made a virtue from economic necessity. He believed that including unaccompanied works in some concerts was very good training for the choir.

Concerts 1952–58

Of the fourteen Musical Society concerts that Freddie Stevens conducted over the six year period 1952–58, seven were performances of large scale works, five of which were works by Bach. Only two Bach works were actually performed, *St Matthew Passion* (performed three times, in May 1954, March 1956 and March 1957), and *Christmas Oratorio* (performed twice, in December 1952 and in December 1955). The two other large scale works were Brahms's *German Requiem* (performed in December 1957) and Handel's *Messiah* (performed in December 1958).[66] The remaining concerts, seven in all, included shorter works notably Palestrina's *Missa Papæ Marcelli*. All fourteen concerts were held in St Paul's church, Bedford, and all, apart from one, had organ, rather than orchestral accompaniment. The exception was the January 1957 concert at which a brass instrumental group accompanied the choir and performed separately.

The first of the concerts conducted by Freddie Stevens was a performance of Bach's *Christmas Oratorio*. This work is made up of six cantatas, three for the first three days of Christmas and three for the period of New Year's Day, New Year's Sunday and Epiphany. Only the first three cantatas were performed at the December 1952 concert. The organist was Dr George Thalben-Ball, the very well-known organist at the Temple Church in London, and subsequently Birmingham

64 *The Bedfordshire Times and Bedfordshire Standard,* 2 March 1951, p. 6. See also reviews of 24 February1948, p. 8 (a lecture-recital) and 9 May 1952, p. 7, for which the headline reads, 'Bedfordshire Rural Music School'.

65 This was Freddie Stevens's view. It is presumed that Clarence Raybould would have concurred.

66 This is technically outside the period covered by this chapter, as Clarence Raybould had left by this time, but it fits better here.

City organist.[67] Freddie Stevens had studied organ under him in the 1920s. The soloists should have included Stanley Riley, who sang with the Society in 1943, but he was not able to sing, so Arthur Reckless sang in his place at short notice. Anne Wood, who had sung in *Elijah* a couple of years earlier, was another of the soloists. The reviewer, E. L. N., had been somewhat critical of her then, but for her performance at this concert he complimented her, 'purity of tone and faultless intonation'.[68] He is also complimentary about the chorus and about Mr Stevens.[69]

The Boyd Neel Orchestra, which should have played at the next orchestral concert on 19 February, made a mistake in their booking arrangements, so the concert was held a month later, with a section of the London Symphony Orchestra playing instead. The booking fee for the London Symphony Orchestra was £122 plus fares and music, as against a fee of £136 12s 6d that the Boyd Neel Orchestra would have charged. There was also a muddle because the orchestral parts provided were not the ones that Clarence Raybould had intended to use, but, according to the minutes, it was an enjoyable concert.[70]

On 28 May, just over a week before the coronation of Queen Elizabeth II, Freddie Stevens conducted a second choral concert with organ accompaniment in St Paul's church. The reviewer, J.H.M.S., is uncomplimentary: 'The choral concert ... brought a new facet to Bedford's Coronation decorations – the ivory tower ... in an erudite programme, mainly of musicians' work for the appreciation of musicians, paid no concession to the warm, perhaps carefree, unbuttoned mood in which most Coronation musical tributes have been cast.'[71] He continues: 'Considered as a scholar's choice of music for musical *cognoscenti*, the concert fully achieved its aim. The singing in the Bach reached at times an ethereal purity reminiscent of the Three Choirs' Festival at its best.'[72] The programme also included Handel's *Zadok the Priest* and Vaughan Williams's *Benedicite*.

At the annual general meeting in July, Margaret Robertson paid tribute to J. Arnold Whitchurch. He had been president since the Musical Society's reformation in 1941, and had died in February 1953.[73] She recalled that:

> he had given twelve devoted years of service as President. He knew, she said, every facet of their work – financial, musical and personal. He had given practical help, encouraging words, and inspired everyone with powers of determination and endurance. It was his strength, she added, that had kept the Society going.[74]

67 George Thalben-Ball was also the BBC musical advisor on religious broadcasting during the Second World War and was based in Bedford, broadcasting from St Paul's church or in studios rigged up in an old church hall. *Picture Post*, 17 February 1945, p. 24.

68 *The Bedfordshire Times and Bedfordshire Standard*, 26 December 1952, p. 8.

69 'The singing of the choir was excellent for the most part, although the opening chorus found the sopranos a little afraid of the high notes ... The chorals were beautifully done with sensitive feeling for phrasing and awareness of the religious significance of the words. The ensemble throughout owed much to the calm leadership of Mr. Stevens, who guided his singers with economy of gesture and clear beat.' Ibid.

70 *Minute Book 1951–62*, meetings of 19 February and 25 March 1953, BLARS X817/1/9.

71 *The Bedfordshire Times and Bedfordshire Standard*, 5 June 1953, p. 9.

72 Ibid.

73 There is a very full obituary to J. Arnold Whitchurch in *The Bedfordshire Times and Bedfordshire Standard*, 27 February 1953, p. 7.

74 *The Bedfordshire Times and Bedfordshire Standard*, 31 July 1953, p. 8. J. Arnold Whitchurch had

Alderman Richard Turner was appointed chairman in March 1953: 'Following the Society's tradition of choosing a Chairman who is a member of the Borough council.'[75] He was elected president at the 1953 annual general meeting, where he presided.[76]

The next orchestral concert, once more with the Boyd Neel Orchestra, was held later than usual, on 25 November. Max Rostal, the soloist, played Bach's Violin Concerto in E. He was originally from Austria, but settled in England in 1934. As well as being a notable violinist, he was a professor at the Guildhall School of Music 1944–58.

The choral concert that followed was on 10 December and consisted of two works, Palestrina's *Missa Papæ Marcelli* and Schutz's *Christmas Story*. The organ accompanist was Fred Rawlins, and according to the review there was also a small orchestra – presumably four or five instrumentalists – for the Schutz. The reviewer, E.L.N., is more sympathetic to early music than J.H.M.S. and writes of the performance of *Missa Papæ Marcelli* that it was: 'a fine example of the writing of this great contrapuntalist, and under the scholarly direction of Mr. Stevens, members of the choir must have found the rehearsal and performance of the work of rewarding interest. They sang with confidence and understanding on this occasion and intonation and tone quality were usually good.'[77] He did not think that the *Christmas Story* was sung as well as the Palestrina Mass.

For the second time, there was a problem with the booking arrangements for the orchestral concert. For the concert of February 1954 a section of the London Symphony Orchestra was to have played, but the orchestra requested a release from the contract as the concert was due in the middle of a tour that they had been offered. The Boyd Neel Orchestra was engaged instead. The concert was poorly attended, despite a seemingly attractive programme.

At the end of May, the performance of Bach's *St Matthew Passion* – the second under Freddie Stevens – was very well supported. The reviewer, J.H.M.S., wrote: 'It was fitting that this great musical occasion should receive the tribute of a full church: every seat in every pew was taken.'[78] In the short programme note, Hans Freyhan comments on the immense emotional range of the work, and this is theme is developed by the reviewer: 'Mr. Stevens, who conducted, gave us an impeccable rendering, and in this he was assisted by a team of soloists and choral singers who – together with the organist (Dr. George Thalben-Ball) – were completely at one

been vice-president and then, from the late 1920s, president of the Bedford Choral Society, so he had a much longer involvement with choral music in Bedford than is suggested by Margaret Robertson at the 1953 annual general meeting.

75 General committee meetings during this period were usually held in the committee room at the Town Hall. Other committees often met at Margaret Robertson's home (School House, Oakley) until she stood down as secretary.

76 Hans Freyhan spoke very highly of Richard Turner and said he had a beneficial influence on the Musical Society when he was chairman.

77 *The Bedfordshire Times and Bedfordshire Standard*, 18 December 1953, p. 9. Bill Knight told the author the following story. While the choir were rehearsing the Kyrie of the *Missa Papæ Marcelli*, a Mr Field from Stevington, a committed Baptist, protested about singing in Latin, and said that he was leaving. Freddie Stevens said he was sorry that Mr Field felt like that, as that they were actually singing in Greek. Mr Field still walked out.

78 *The Bedfordshire Times and Bedfordshire Standard*, 4 June 1954, p. 9.

in the superb musicanship they displayed.'[79] He heaps praise on the soloists and on the Musical Society's chorus: 'who sang better than we have ever heard them sing before. At no time did the usual amateur choral faults obtrude.'[80] A slightly shortened version of *St Matthew Passion* was used and the performance lasted two hours.

The October orchestral concert, again with the Boyd Neel Orchestra, was not well supported. The concert included the *Concertino for Piano and Strings* by Walter Leigh, a British composer, who was killed in action in the Second World War.[81]

The programme for the final choral concert of the year, held in December 1954, was ambitious, with the performance of three substantial choral works. These were Palestrina's *Stabat Mater* (a motet for double chorus); Vaughan Williams's Mass in G Minor (also for double chorus, but with soloists); and Bach's cantata *Sleepers Awake!* for which the organ accompaniment was played by Geraint Jones. The first two works were sung unaccompanied. The reviewer, J.H.M.S., wrote: 'For an amateur chorus to prepare three major choral works, all requiring the highest degree of musical skill, for a single concert is an achievement which reflects the greatest possible credit on the singers and even greater credit on their conductor, Mr. F. E. Stevens.'[82] Later on in the review he was more critical: 'The performance gave us the impression of a detached, scholarly perfection, rather than of a thrilling experience.'[83] But at the end, he warmly congratulates the Musical Society. Despite the serious nature of the music being performed, there was a very full congregation (to use the reviewer's term).

The Boyd Neel Orchestra gave another orchestral concert six weeks later. This concert was again poorly supported. The soloist in Gordon Jacob's Concerto for Violin and Strings was Frederick Grinke. He was leader of the Boyd Neel Orchestra 1937–47 and began teaching at the Royal Academy of Music in 1939, where he was particularly influential.[84] He left the Boyd Neel Orchestra in 1947 to pursue a solo career and spend more time teaching. J.H.M.S. writes very favourably of the concerto in the review: 'The whole work gave us a musical experience we would not have missed and we owe thanks to the Musical Society for making it possible.'[85]

Unusually, Clarence Raybould conducted the next choral concert, a performance of Handel's *Samson*, in May. It is not clear why, though the fact that the Society's finances were in better shape may have had something to do with it. *Samson* had been proposed a year earlier by the programme planning sub-committee, but there was no suggestion then that it would be with orchestra. However, at the annual general meeting a few months after the programme planning sub-committee, the treasurer, Mr R. E. Brooks, was congratulated because the financial position was strong. This was the only time that Clarence Raybould conducted a major choral work without including other orchestral works after the 1952 'watershed'. The

79 Ibid.
80 Ibid. See also *Minute Book 1951–62*, 3 December 1953, BLARS X817/1/9.
81 This was presumably a transcription of Leigh's *Concertino for Harpsichord and Strings*. This work was performed again at one of the Musical Society's concerts in December 1965, this time with harpsichord.
82 *The Bedfordshire Times and Bedfordshire Standard*, 17 December 1954, p. 13.
83 Ibid.
84 During this time the Boyd Neel Orchestra gave the first performance of Britten's *Variations on a Theme of Frank Bridge* at the Salzburg Festival in 1937, with Frederick Grinke as leader.
85 *The Bedfordshire Times and Bedfordshire Standard*, 4 February 1955, p. 10.

critic, J.H.M.S., who had done credit to himself in reviews of the previous two concerts, did himself a disservice in his review of *Samson*: 'The only feature of the whole evening toward which a critical voice might be directed was the choice of programme. In all musical epochs the giants among the composers are remembered by their outstanding works, and the test of time has meant that their lesser *opera* are rightly relegated to the shelves of the musicologists.'[86] He goes on to list a number of Handel's oratorios, *Joshua*, *Jephtha*, *Deborah*, *Esther* and *Samson*, which, in his view, are best forgotten. He thinks it follows that the sparsity of the audience, which must have been very disappointing to the Musical Society, proves his point. He is, however, very complimentary about the performance.[87]

Margaret Robertson announced that she intended to resign as secretary at the committee meeting held in February 1955 and she made the formal announcement at the annual general meeting in July. By this time she had been secretary for twelve years. *The Bedfordshire Times and Bedfordshire Standard* is quite restrained in its comment: 'Tribute was paid to Miss Robertson who retired after fourteen years [*sic*].'[88] Fulsome appreciation of the work that she had done is recorded in the minutes in the *Minute Book*: 'Mr. Turner spoke a few words and expressed the wish that the Society's appreciation of Miss Robertson as Secretary of the Society for 14 years be placed on record. Mrs. Cooper seconded & stressed the value of the work done and asked her to continue to act as liaison with agents. Miss Robertson suitably replied.'[89]

In addition to her work with the Musical Society, Margaret Robertson was a leading member of the Arts Council for the East of England – Eastern Arts. Freddie Stevens remembers attending Arts Council meetings with her. In his view, her involvement enhanced the Musical Society's reputation, influence and prestige, and led to greater funding than would have otherwise been available. She remained very active in the Musical Society and on the committee.

Tom Winter succeeded Margaret Robertson as secretary. He was not a performing member of the Society, but his wife, Mollie, was. Tom Winter worked for Lloyd's Bank, which had offered him promotion to a post in Bedford, resulting in a move from Nottingham in the 1930s. Mollie Winter was a very good soprano singer, and had been a friend of the English mezzo-soprano, Constance Shacklock. At one time Mollie Winter had considered becoming a professional herself, but with a young family that was impossible. In the 1940s and early 1950s, she sang with Ethel Budd's choir, whose primary focus was taking part in music competitions. This choir had considerable success and Mollie Winter was one of their leading singers and main soloists. Tom Winter became involved with the Musical Society when he stood in at committee meetings for Mr R. E. Brooks, who was the treas-

86 *The Bedfordshire Times and Bedfordshire Standard*, 27 May 1955, p. 13.

87 'The choir, trained by Mr. F. E. Stevens, were in excellent form and, in spite of a preponderance of women's voices, nevertheless gave us a balanced force of sound ... The Boyd Neel Orchestra, augmented for the occasion by the necessary brass and woodwind, were as efficient as always … the four soloists … were in every respect agreeable to hear … Clarence Raybould … welded this not inconsiderable force of musicians into one very harmonious whole with something more than routine leadership – indeed with inspiration.' *The Bedfordshire Times and Bedfordshire Standard*, 27 May 1955, p. 13.

88 *Minute Book 1951–62*, 16 February 1955, BLARS X817/1/9.

89 *Minute Book 1951–62*, 18 July 1955, BLARS X817/1/9. See also *The Bedfordshire Times and Bedfordshire Standard*, 22 July 1955, p. 7.

urer for a number of years.[90] He was approached about becoming secretary soon after Margaret Robertson announced her intention to resign and his appointment was confirmed at the annual general meeting in July; he remained secretary for ten years.[91] He wrote the minutes for the 1955 annual general meeting and the minutes for committee meetings from then on. His minutes are full, florid almost, but not so lucid and succinct as those of Margaret Robertson.

At the February 1955 programme planning sub-committee, Margaret Robertson, who was then still the secretary, stated that Bedford was tired of string orchestras and the public wanted large orchestras.[92] The result was that the Musical Society engaged the Royal Philharmonic Orchestra for the first concert of the season on 24 November. This was to be the only concert during the 1955/56 season that Clarence Raybould conducted. The programme included Schumann's Piano Concerto in A Minor and Dvořák's Symphony No. 2 in D Minor, now known as his Symphony No. 7.[93] The reviewer calls the programme, 'unadventurous but none the less satisfying', and notes the flawless playing from all departments of the orchestra.[94] There was a good audience, though some thirty to forty seats were reported as unfilled. A photograph appears above the review showing Tom Winter, Margaret Robertson, Clarence Raybould, Miss Thorunn Tryggvason (the piano soloist) and Arthur Leavins (leader of the orchestra) before the start of the concert.[95]

Two weeks later the Musical Society chorus gave a second performance of Bach's *Christmas Oratorio*. As in 1952, only the first three cantatas were performed. The organist this time was Dr Peasgood. Despite the very cold weather, there was good audience. According to J.H.M.S., there was some difference of opinion between Dr Peasgood and the conductor, Freddie Stevens: 'At the start of this set of cantatas … Dr. Peasgood showed clearly that he intended to give us a virile performance. But the scholarly beat of Mr. F. E. Stevens slowed him up: and the same studious, exact, and careful Bach checked the chorus in its stride and made it not the vigorous forceful instrument it has been in the past … and in consequence lacking in the ability to drive the climaxes to that tension which the one thousand-and-fifty-five-year-old [*sic*] drama demands … The soloists, however, were in no way fettered by the prevailing *mistral*: no fog of unmanning caution hampered their voices as they sang.'[96]

At the committee meeting held towards the end of January 1956, *The Bedfordshire Times and Bedfordshire Standard's* adverse review of the concert was discussed.

[90] Mr R. E. Brooks later became county treasurer, so was probably working for Bedfordshire County Council at this time.

[91] Tom Winter was subsequently appointed treasurer, and after that continued to help at concerts, selling tickets at the door until the late 1980s or early 1990s.

[92] *Minute Book 1951–62*, 16 February 1955, BLARS X817/1/9.

[93] The programme confirms this. Dvořák's first four symphonies were originally seen as immature works and not counted as part of his canon, so the last five symphonies were numbered 1–5. This numbering system lasted until the 1960s.

[94] *The Bedfordshire Times and Bedfordshire Standard*, 2 December 1955, p. 10.

[95] Thorunn Tryggvason (also known as Thorunn Johannsdottir) married Vladimir Ashkenazy in 1961. Who's Who 2015 (London 2014), p. 72. Hans Freyhan recalled the 1955 performance in his review of the February 1985 concert, when the Ashkenazys' son, Vovka Ashkenazy, also played the Schumann Piano Concerto at a Musical Society concert before the choir sang Brahms's Requeim, *Bedfordshire Times,* 28 February 1985, p. 12.

[96] *The Bedfordshire Times and Bedfordshire Standard*, 9 December 1955, p. 9.

Chorus members were upset and it was felt that the report was very unfair to Freddie Stevens. The paper had published a letter of protest, but the chairman, Richard Turner, said that he would make a diplomatic approach to the editor. At the subsequent meeting, he reported that future reviews would be watched, as there had been other complaints.

Bach's *St Matthew Passion* was performed in March for the second time, ten days before Easter, a little less than two years after the first performance. The reviewer, R.B.P., noted that Freddie Stevens conducted: 'with the minimum of effort but obtained the maximum of effect.'[97] The organist for this concert was Charles Spinks, another well-known musician, who was the resident organist for the BBC.[98] It was after trying out the organ in St Paul's church before the rehearsal – probably for this performance – that Charles Spinks told Freddie Stevens that he would probably not be able to play because the organ was underpowered and the pressure too low. After an anxious discussion, he said he would be able to play if it was possible to obtain a couple of twelve volt batteries. So Freddie Stevens went along to his garage, Kennings, on the corner of Bromham Road and Union Street, and talked to the manager, Percy Bonnett, who did have some batteries available and charged two as required. Percy Bonnett was very sympathetic; he was churchwarden at Stagsden where the vicar was the Rev. Noel A. Bonavia-Hunt, a well-known authority on organ construction and in particular on the voicing of organ pipes.[99] Freddie Stevens returned to St Paul's with the batteries, they were wired up and the concert was able to go ahead. The St Paul's organist, Fred Rawlins, commented when he next played the organ that it sounded much better than it had done for some time![100]

The male soloists on this occasion, as for the other two performances of *St Matthew Passion*, were Eric Greene (tenor) and Hervey Allen (bass). The reviewer, R.B.P., writes of this performance: 'In recitative after recitative these two artists held our attention by their dramatic presentation of the narrative of the Passion.'[101] The soprano and contralto, for this performance and the subsequent performance in 1957 (though not for the first performance in 1954) were Pauline Brockless (soprano) and Celia Moran (contralto), whose voices blended very well, according to R.B.P.

The final concert of the season was a choral and instrumental concert again conducted by Freddie Stevens.[102] The instrumental works were performed by Hans Freyhan (piano) and Kate and Hans Freyhan's two sons – then in their teens – Peter (cello) and Michael (violin). The three of them played Mozart's Piano Trio in E Flat,

97 *The Bedfordshire Times and Bedfordshire Standard*, 30 March 1956, p. 7. R.B.P. were the initials of Robert Payne. He was a music teacher at Silver Jubilee School and organist of St Peter's church, Bedford. He was very supportive of the Musical Society.

98 Personal interview with Freddie Stevens by the author. Freddie Stevens also stated that 'Charlie' Spinks was a friend of Sam Wisdom, who in turn was a friend of his. Sam Wisdom was a performing member of the Musical Society, so Charlie Spinks was happy to come and play.

99 See *Irons in the Fire: The Bonavia-Hunt Memoirs* (London, 1959) pp. 101–2, the autobiography of the Rev. Noel A Bonavia-Hunt published by London Musical Opinion Ltd. In this book he writes that Percy Bonnett was a very good vicar's warden at Stagsden.

100 Personal interview with Freddie Stevens by the author.

101 *The Bedfordshire Times and Bedfordshire Standard*, 30 March 1956, p. 7.

102 R.B.P. writes: 'The choir, under his direction has acquired a great flexibility of expression. Their fortissimos are strong and rich, their pianissimos have a delicate and ethereal quality. The choral works included Stanford's eight-part Magnificat in B flat, and Kodály's *Jesus and the Traders*.' *The Bedfordshire Times and Bedfordshire Standard*, 25 May 1956, p. 9.

and Michael and Peter also played the allegro from Beethoven's Duo in C.[103] By this stage, Michael Freyhan was leader of the National Youth Orchestra and Peter Freyhan was leader of the cello section.[104] Freddie Stevens opened and closed the concert with, respectively, Bach's Prelude and Fugue in E Flat and one of Rheinberger's organ sonatas – an organ prologue and epilogue.

The new season opened rather disastrously. Instead of an orchestral concert, the October concert was given by the London Instrumental Players and included works by Mozart, Roussel and Damase.[105] It was very poorly supported. J.H.M.S. counted sixty-three people in the audience. According to the minutes of the next committee meeting, there were only one hundred people there. Bedford Music Club had also objected to the Musical Society putting on a chamber music concert on the grounds that this was their territory.

The Royal Philharmonic Orchestra returned to Bedford at the end of November. The main work was Brahms's Symphony No. 4, but the concert also included Elgar's *Scenes from the Bavarian Highlands* with the Musical Society's chorus joining the orchestra. The reviewer felt that Freddie Stevens had brought the chorus, 'very nearly to perfection', spoiled only by some shrillness in the sopranos.[106] This was the last time that Clarence Raybould conducted the chorus.

Freddie Stevens conducted the next concert at the end of January 1957. This mainly comprised renaissance music, Palestrina, Sweelinck and Monteverdi. There was a brass interlude with Locke's *Music for His Majesty's Sagbutts and Cornetts*, and the concert finished with two 'Hymns to the Trinity' by Tchaikovsky. The review by R.B.P. was very complimentary, first because of a stirring performance of the Sweelinck motet, but especially because of the Monteverdi.[107] The audience only occupied about a third of St Paul's church for this concert, which R.B.P. felt was a poor reflection on lovers of music in Bedford.

The last concert of the season a couple of months later, Bach's *St Matthew Passion*, conducted by Freddie Stevens, was performed by the Society under him for the third time. The soloists and the organist who had performed a year earlier returned for this performance. On this occasion, however, the Musical Society's chorus was augmented by members of Bedford Modern School choir. There was a larger audience for this concert than for the previous concert.

103 This was originally written for clarinet and bassoon (Wo027).

104 Both Peter and Michael Freyhan went on to become professional musicians. Peter was, for many years, a cellist in the BBC Symphony Orchestra, until his retirement in 2001. Michael is a freelance musician with a special interest in chamber music.

105 The players were: Trevor Williams, violin; Bernard Davis, viola; Ambrose Gauntlett, cello; John Francis, flute; and Enid Simon, harp. The programme planning committee had originally suggested a concert using local talent, but had decided to engage the London Instrumental Players instead as local talent concert could not be used to support an Arts Council grant. *Minute Book 1951–62*, 19 April 1956, BLARS X817/1/9.

106 *The Bedfordshire Times and Bedfordshire Standard*, 7 December 1956, p. 11. Above the review, there is a photograph of Clarence Raybould, Tom Winter and Arthur Leavins (leader of the Royal Philharmonic Orchestra) (Plate 11).

107 'The peak of the evening was reached, however, in Monteverdi's magnificent setting of the *Mass*. Here the singers, under the steady and unobtrusive direction of Mr. Stevens gave us a musical and spiritual experience to be remembered. They sang gloriously. The climaxes at the end of the Sanctus and Benedictus and the delicate pianissimo of the Agnus Dei, were perhaps the most telling moments of the whole evening.' *The Bedfordshire Times and Bedfordshire Standard*, 8 February 1957, p. 8.

The 1957/58 season opened with an orchestral concert conducted by Clarence Raybould. The reviewer, J.H.M.S., sets the scene for the concert: 'This was the occasion we had been awaiting for so long. A great orchestra in the Corn Exchange, a famous conductor, a young soloist (another Kreisler? another Menuhin?), every seat taken.'[108] The soloist in the Brahms Violin Concerto was the twenty-year-old Ralph Holmes, who had made his London debut in 1951. He was a leading violin soloist of his day. J.H.M.S., who could be idiosyncratic, was not that impressed, however. The other main work of the evening was Sibelius's Symphony No. 7.

In the review, there is a reference to Clarence Raybould being a friend of Sibelius, one of the greatest twentieth century composers, and a noted interpreter of his works. This concert must have been a poignant occasion for him, as Sibelius had died just over two weeks earlier, aged ninety-one. Hans Freyhan wrote in the programme notes: 'This great work had been included in tonight's programme before the composer's death on September 20th. Its performance will now be received as a memorial tribute to the Finnish master whose standing in this country was equalled only by that in his native land.'[109] There follows a brilliant analysis of the symphony in Hans Freyhan's distinctive style. This was the last of the Musical Society's concerts that Clarence Raybould conducted. He announced his resignation later on in the season.

Brahms's *German Requiem* followed early in December. The organist was again Charles Spinks. After writing how difficult a work it is for a local musical society to perform, the reviewer, R.B.P., writes: 'Bedford Musical Society, under its conductor, Mr. F. E. Stevens, gave a magnificent performance of the work. It was an evening to be remembered.'[110] This is one of the most complimentary reviews of any of the Musical Society's performances.

In his opening paragraph of the March 1958 concert review, R.B.P. refers to the high standard of the Brahms – a standard which he had come to expect from the Society, 'Last week's concert was no exception', he added.[111] The concert included two coronation anthems, Handel's *Zadok the Priest* and Parry's 'I was Glad', which were conducted by Kate Freyhan, assistant chorus master. Freddie Stevens seems to have played the organ for these and also gave solo performances of Bach and Scarlatti on the piano.

At the start of the Musical Society's committee meeting in April 1958, Richard Turner reported that Michael Blackledge (who was involved with the Bedford Society) had been in touch and wished to assist in promoting a series of orchestral concerts and that he had been invited to address the meeting. At the meeting, Michael Blackledge suggested that a series of orchestral concerts should be put on in Bedford each season. He put his various proposals to members of the committee. There was not really a meeting of minds. Members of the committee pointed out that the Musical Society did not have sufficient financial backing to engage on a project

108 *The Bedfordshire Times and Bedfordshire Standard*, 11 October 1957, p. 11.

109 *Concert Programme*, Tuesday 8 October 1957, BLARS X817/3/84.

110 *The Bedfordshire Times and Bedfordshire Standard*, 13 December 1957, p. 13. And he continues: 'We especially remember the latter part of the second chorus "and the ransomed of the Lord shall return again and come with singing unto Zion ... and sorrow and sighing shall flee away." Mr Stevens obtained a thrilling climax in the chorus "For we have here no abiding city".'

111 *The Bedfordshire Times and Bedfordshire Standard*, 28 March 1958, p. 22.

of the type proposed and no further discussions were arranged. The promotion of orchestral concerts was taken on, in due course, by Michael Blackledge under the umbrella of the Bedford Society, and there were regular concerts by leading orchestras in Bedford 1971–92.

The concert at the end of May, the last of the season, was described by the reviewer, J.H.M.S., as: 'being of a Third Programme type – and, we hasten to add, none the worse for that: but the relatively small audience was fortunately rather more than could have been expected for so rarified a programme.'[112]

Three choirs took part in this concert, the Lyric Singers and the Bedford Musical Society chorus who were conducted by Freddie Stevens, and the Elizabethan Singers, who were conducted by Paul Paviour.[113] Paul Paviour was born in Bedford and became a master at Bedford School. He was also organist at St Martin's church in Clapham Road, Bedford, at this time. He formed the Elizabethan Singers in the early 1950s and they were active until the mid-1960s when he emigrated to Australia. They took part in the St Martin's Festival in November 1953 when two of Paul Paviour's own compositions were performed. *The Bedfordshire Times and Bedfordshire Standard's* report referred to Paul Paviour as, 'a kapelmeister in our midst'.[114] The most ambitious work that the Elizabethan Singers performed in the May concert, according to the reviewer, was Bliss's *Aubade for Coronation Morning*. J.H.M.S. was very complimentary about them: 'the whole performance of this group of singers and their talented chorus-master was of the highest possible order.'[115]

J.H.M.S. was, perhaps unfairly, not so complimentary about the Lyric Singers and their madrigal-type songs, under Freddie Stevens.[116] He stated, incorrectly, that the songs were from the fourteenth and fifteenth centuries – they were in fact from the late sixteenth and early seventeenth centuries. He described the Musical Society's contribution: 'Always they sang unexceptionably, but Mr. Stevens's academic approach tended to rob, for example "One morning in the month of May" … of its true uninhibited gaiety. Careful rhythm is no substitute for lilt.'[117]

In May 1958, a few days before the 'Three Choirs' concert, an emergency committee meeting was called because Clarence Raybould had reluctantly tendered his resignation. This was partly the result of pressure from other engagements. By now he was well over seventy. At the annual general meeting in late July, members paid tribute to his, 'amiable personality and fine musicianship'. Hans Freyhan noted

112 *The Bedfordshire Times and Bedfordshire Standard*, 6 June 1958, p. 13. The BBC Radio Third Programme began broadcasting in September 1946; it was finally incorporated into BBC Radio 3 in April 1970.

113 Paul Paviour did some work on the history of the Musical Society, and it was he who gathered together many of the programmes from the 1880s, 1890s and early part of the twentieth century. He handed the programmes and other material that he had to Hans and Kate Freyhan who passed them to the author. The materials were deposited in 1994 in the Musical Society's archive in the Bedfordshire and Luton Archives and Records Service. When the author first talked to Kate and Hans Freyhan about the history of the Musical Society, they suggested trying to contact Paul Paviour. The author subsequently got in touch and found that he is still musically very active in Australia, although now in his 80s.

114 *The Bedfordshire Times and Bedfordshire Standard*, 13 November 1953, p. 8.

115 *The Bedfordshire Times and Bedfordshire Standard*, 6 June 1958, p. 13.

116 'The singing was always careful and musicianly and intensely interesting in a scholarly fashion; it did not stir the pulses or stiffen the sinews.' Ibid.

117 Ibid.

that working in Bedford had been difficult for him: 'Rehearsal time had been inadequate and it had usually been impossible to rehearse the choir at all.'[118]

Following Clarence Raybould's retirement, the Musical Society gave up promoting orchestral concerts played by professional orchestras, instead focusing on choral music. Richard Turner also announced at this committee meeting that he intended to stand down as president. He strongly recommended that Clarence Raybould be elected president, which duly happened at the annual general meeting. Clarence Raybould remained conductor of the National Youth Orchestra of Wales until 1966 when the orchestra celebrated its twenty-first birthday and he himself celebrated his eightieth birthday. He died in 1972.

The December 1958 concert, held before David Willcocks took up his appointment as conductor of the Musical Society, was conducted by Freddie Stevens – a performance of *Messiah*, in St Paul's church. The headline of the review sums up the performance, 'The "Messiah" In Its Full Version.' J.H.M.S. then explains why he was not impressed: 'It is a pity that Mr. F. E. Stevens, who conducted the "Messiah" on Thursday evening last, made the whole evening a test of endurance ... The oratorio loses, rather than gains by bringing in some of the arias and choruses which are now always omitted.'[119] The performance lasted three hours: 'without any sort of interval in wintry weather and with the church only barely warm.'[120] That said, J.H.M.S. had nothing but praise for all four soloists, especially the tenor, David Galliver, and for the organist, Richard Popplewell. He reserves his criticism for Freddie Stevens – his usual criticism – that he was too scholarly and accurate but not exultant: 'when it came to the great choruses, like "Lift up your heads, O ye gates", we felt a sense of restraint which marred the pleasure of hearing so fine a body of experienced singers.'[121]

Following this performance, Freddie Stevens continued to be chorus master and to take rehearsals, but did not conduct any concerts over the next two or three years.

118 *The Bedfordshire Times and Bedfordshire Standard*, 1 August 1958, p. 11. The report of the 1958 annual general meeting concentrated on Clarence Raybould's resignation.

119 *Bedford Record & Circular*, 9 December 1958, p. 11.

120 Ibid.

121 Ibid. There was a letter in the following week's *Bedford Record & Circular*, 9 December 1958, p. 13 from a member of the choir, a Miss Hooper, criticising the reviewer for not appreciating *Messiah* in full, and referring him to John Tobin's annual performances of *Messiah* in full in the Royal Festival Hall, London.

Chapter Ten

'You've never had it so good', 1959–91

'Indeed, let us be frank about it – most of our people have never had it so good.'[1]

The period 1959–91 was a very good one for the Musical Society. David Willcocks (he was not knighted until 1977) conducted many of the concerts from March 1959 until November 1987. In addition, in 1972, Michael Rose was appointed county music advisor in succession to Roy Rimmer, and he also regularly conducted the Musical Society's concerts from that period.[2]

Following the announcement of Clarence Raybould's resignation at an emergency committee meeting in May 1958, Thurston Dart was booked to conduct Bach's *St John Passion* with Philomusica, on 10 March 1959. Philomusica could not keep the engagement and asked for the booking to be changed to 11 March. However, this was not possible. It was a decision that was to have momentous consequences. At the 23 July committee meeting, it was reported that approaches had been made to David Willcocks about conducting the *St John Passion* and providing a small orchestra. He subsequently agreed, and arranged for the Jacques Orchestra to play.[3] The arrangements were confirmed at the 19 November committee meeting and the concert was duly held.

The review of the concert, by J.H.M.S., was very enthusiastic: 'The performance … was a *tour de force* for Mr. William Herbert, the tenor soloist, and for the Society's chorus … Stimulated by the clear and forceful leadership of Mr. David Willcocks who conducted, they made of the chorales delicate traceries of sound which could not be bettered.'[4]

The Musical Society was incredibly lucky to have been able to engage David Willcocks. He conducted the Musical Society when he was at his peak – as director of music at King's College, Cambridge, as principal of the Royal College of Music, and while he was conductor of the Bach Choir.

1 Harold Macmillan, the prime minister, speaking in Bedford. This is what he actually said although it is popularly abbreviated to 'You've never had it so good.' He was addressing a crowd of 2–3,000 people at Bedford Town Association Football Club, to mark twenty-five years' service by Mr Lennox-Boyd, the colonial secretary, as MP for Mid-Bedfordshire. *The Daily Telegraph*, 20 July 1957, p. 1. Two years later, in October 1959, the Conservatives had a resounding election victory, and the election slogan 'Life's better under the Conservatives' matched Harold Macmillan's own remark, said publicly only once, in Bedford.

2 At the time of writing (January 2015) he still does.

3 The fees were 40gns for David Willcocks and £152 plus travelling expenses for the Jacques Orchestra with twenty-four players.

4 *The Bedfordshire Times and Bedfordshire Standard*, 13 March 1959, p. 13.

David Willcocks (1919–2015)

David Willcocks was born in Newquay, Cornwall, where his father was the manager of Barclays Bank.[5] His parents were not particularly musical, though his father had sung in a church choir. David Willcocks' exceptional voice was recognised early, and his parents were advised that he should audition for Westminster Abbey choir; he sang in that choir for four years.[6] His voice broke early at the age of twelve. He was quite apologetic to Ernest Bullock, then organist and master of choristers, but Ernest Bullock saw it as something positive: it meant that he could now teach him to play the Westminster Abbey organ.

In due course, David Willcocks was awarded a music scholarship to Clifton College, Bristol. The music master at Clifton was Douglas Fox, a very fine musician, who unfortunately had to have his arm amputated to prevent gangrene spreading following an injury in the battle of the Somme. The music scholarship was followed by an organ scholarship at King's College, Cambridge, and he started there on 3 September 1939, the day that the Second World War broke out; he was called up a few weeks later.[7] In November 1944, David Willcocks was awarded the Military Cross for his part in the capture of Hill 112 in July 1944.[8]

He left the army in November 1945, and returned to Cambridge to study for a BA in history and economics at King's College, graduating in 1947. Soon afterwards he was offered the post of organist and choirmaster at Salisbury Cathedral in succession to Walter Alcock, the eighty-five year-old organist, who had just died. There is a note about this appointment in the Musical Society's *Minute Book* as David Willcocks had been proposed as accompanist, but could no longer be considered due to the Salisbury appointment.

After three years at Salisbury, Sir Adrian Boult made a recommendation to David Willcocks: that he should move to Worcester Cathedral following the retirement of the organist, Ivor Atkins, who had been there since 1897, and was by then in his eighties. Not only was the Three Choirs Festival held at Worcester, with artists from London coming to take part, but the City of Birmingham Choir was also looking for a new conductor. Adrian Boult thought that David Willcocks would stand a very good chance of being given that role if he secured the post of organist.

David Willcocks was at Worcester for seven years.[9] Then, in 1957, he was appointed organist at King's College, Cambridge, in succession to Boris Ord whose health was failing rapidly. David Willcocks was awarded a fellowship at King's and

5 Personal interview with David Willcocks by the author. For more information see Owen, *A Life in Music – Conversations with Sir David Willcocks and Friends*.

6 He had a very good ear and the choir master used to ask him to hum the starting note at rehearsals rather than playing it on the piano. If the men sitting behind him were singing a G natural rather than a G sharp (for example) he would tell them so. The men took it in good part.

7 He had hoped to be able to work in submarines as he could tell a lot about a submarine's speed and performance from the tone of the engine. However this kind of human knowledge had been superseded by radar, and he went into the Army instead.

8 Owen, *A Life in Music – Conversations with Sir David Willcocks and Friends*, p.57. There is a photograph of Field Marshall Montgomery presenting the Military Cross to him on p. 59.

9 David and Rachel Willcocks moved and came to enjoy Worcester, as they had enjoyed Salisbury. They had a house near the cathedral that overlooked the cricket ground on the other side of the river. All four of their children were born there. David Willcocks enjoyed visiting St Michael's College, Tenbury, and playing the very fine Father Willis organ in the church at St Michael's. He was appointed a Fellow of the College in 1953.

a university lectureship, he also became associated with the Cambridge University Musical Society and the University Orchestra, and with the Cambridge Inter-village Choral Society. Among the organ scholars that studied under him were Simon Preston and Andrew Davis.

It was quite soon after he started at King's that he produced, with Reginald Jacques, the first of the *Carols for Choirs* books, which were published by the Oxford University Press. At that stage Reginald Jacques was conductor of the London Bach Choir; David Willcocks took over from him in 1960. *Carols for Choirs* proved so successful that ten years later Oxford University Press asked for a further fifty carols for another book.[10]

David Willcocks was at King's College for sixteen years, moving to the Royal College of Music in 1973. After his move to the Royal College, he usually brought a student orchestra to play in concerts in Bedford. The players liked that as they were paid. When he was rehearsing the choir in Bedford, he would sometimes put a handkerchief or something on his head to test whether people were watching.

At the committee meeting a month after the first concert that David Willcocks conducted, the draft programme for the 1959/60 season was put forward, and it was stated that David Willcocks would conduct all three concerts. He does not seem to have been formally appointed conductor of the Musical Society. The second concert he conducted was a choral and orchestral concert in December 1959. Although it had a very strong Christmas flavour, it was not promoted as a Christmas concert.

The Musical Society performed another big Bach work in the spring of 1960, the Mass in B Minor, on the Tuesday of Holy Week. The reviewer, R.B.P., was full of praise: 'The whole performance was a great achievement and a triumph for the Society. Mr. David Willcocks conducted with great skill. There was a certainty in his control of the chorus and orchestra which inspired the singers and players to give their utmost in chorus after chorus.'[11] The Jacques Orchestra provided the orchestral accompaniment. The soloists included Pauline Brockless and Helen Watts, 'whose voices blended beautifully'.[12] There was recognition of the hard work that went on behind the scenes towards the end of the review: 'One important thing must not be forgotten. It is the great contribution given by Mr. F. E. Stevens, who trained the chorus during what must have been weeks of diligent rehearsal.'[13] A photograph of prominent people involved with the performance, including David Willcocks, Margaret Robertson, Alderman Richard Turner and Brian Dunn (from the Arts Council) appeared above *The Bedfordshire Times and Bedfordshire Standard's* review of the concert.

The last concert of the season was given a month later. This was largely an orchestral concert with the Cambridge University Musical Society orchestra. Philip Ledger, then a student at King's College – he subsequently succeeded David Will-

[10] As Reginald Jacques had died, David Willcocks suggested that John Rutter should work with him on the second book. David Willcocks told the Oxford University Press: 'I know an undergraduate here at Cambridge who is the most gifted composer that I've seen pass through the university. He is not only very able but quick, neat and you won't find any mistakes at all in his manuscripts.' Owen, *A Life in Music – Conversations with Sir David Willcocks and Friends*. p. 142.

[11] *The Bedfordshire Times and Bedfordshire Standard*, 15 April 1960, p. 20.

[12] Ibid.

[13] Ibid.

cocks as musical director there in 1974 – was the soloist in Grieg's Piano Concerto in A Minor. And 'our own' (in the words of the reviewer, J.H.M.S.) Michael Freyhan was the soloist in Bach's Violin Concerto in E. The chorus only joined in for Fauré's *Pavane* and Borodin's *Polovtsian Dances*.

Tragedy struck the chorus master, Freddie Stevens, in August that year. His wife, Alice, was killed in a road accident and his two sons were injured, one very seriously.[14] As a result, he did not rehearse the choir for the December 1960 concert; this was undertaken by Kate Freyhan instead. The concert comprised the first three cantatas of Bach's *Christmas Oratorio* and eleven carols. The Jacques Orchestra provided the accompaniment. The reviewer, J.H.M.S., was enthusiastic, pointing out that the Corn Exchange was full, with every seat taken, and that there were people standing in the gallery. He also emphasized that the chorus was well-balanced and well-rehearsed.[15]

Following the review, David Willcocks wrote to *The Bedfordshire Times and Bedfordshire Standard* as a friend had brought the review to his attention: 'I am anxious that your readers should know that the credit for the work of the chorus described as "well-balanced" and "well rehearsed" should be given to Mrs. Kate Freyhan (a member of the Bedford Musical Society) who undertook all but two of the chorus rehearsals in preparation for this concert.'[16] Kate Freyhan remembered this thoughtful gesture with great pleasure when she talked to the author over thirty years later.

At the beginning of the season, it was suggested that Freddie Stevens would not be able to rehearse or conduct any concerts during the 1960/61 season. He did, however, conduct the first of the two concerts that the Musical Society gave in March 1961, on 2 March. For the second time, he conducted Palestrina's *Missa Papæ Marcelli*. On this occasion, the other works performed included organ solos played by David Willcocks.

The main work of the 14 March concert was Beethoven's Symphony No. 9, the 'Choral' Symphony; David Willcocks conducted. The first half of the concert had been conducted by twenty-one year-old Michael Freyhan, and included Bruch's Violin Concerto in G Minor. The soloist was a young scientist from Cambridge University, Colin Gough. Michael Freyhan also led the Cambridge University Musical Society orchestra in the performance of the Beethoven, joined by the Musical Society chorus in the last movement. The Cambridge University Musical Society orchestra were happy to play for the Musical Society on this occasion as it was a run through for a concert they were giving in Cambridge, which included the 'Choral' Symphony. The reviewer was very impressed with the standard of the

14 *The Bedfordshire Times and Bedfordshire Standard*, 12 August 1960, p. 16. The accident occurred the day before, on 11 August.

15 He then goes on: 'The marvellously clear directions given by Mr. Willcocks must have helped very greatly to bring out the very best in every singer.' The audience joined the chorus and orchestra in singing the carols in the second half of the concert. David Willcocks remarked during the carols that it was a pity that there was no audience to applaud the audience. *The Bedfordshire Times and Bedfordshire Standard*, 16 December 1960, p. 13.

16 *The Bedfordshire Times and Bedfordshire Standard*, 6 January 1961, p. 11.

young players: 'Under Mr. David Willcocks, (with the chorus having been trained by Mr. F. E. Stevens) the orchestra was soon swept up into the clouds of glory.'[17]

The soloists included Heather Harper (soprano) and Marjorie Thomas (contralto). Two years later Heather Harper sang, at very short notice, in the first performance of Britten's *War Requiem* in Coventry Cathedral. Britten wrote the soprano solo part for Galina Vishnevskaya (the wife of the cellist Mstislav Rostropovich), but she was not able to get a visa to leave Russia and take part in the performance. Marjorie Thomas was at the height of her career by the time of the Bedford concert. She sang regularly in oratorios, often conducted by Sir Malcolm Sargent, and did a number of recordings with him, including a series of Gilbert and Sullivan operas. This second March concert was the last concert of the Musical Society's season.

The first concert of the 1961/62 season was not held until just before Christmas. In the first half there was a performance of Mozart's Requiem. Vaughan Williams's *Serenade to Music* opened the second half, and was followed by carols in which the audience joined. David Willcocks conducted and the Jacques Orchestra played. Among the soloists was Robert Tear, who had been a choral scholar at King's College under David Willcocks, but by this time was a lay vicar at St Paul's Cathedral and also working with the Ambrosian Singers. He was to make his operatic debut in 1963.[18]

J.H.M.S., who reviewed the concert, was obscurely uncomplimentary about the performance of Mozart's Requiem, and he made no comment about Robert Tear or the other soloists. He was more complimentary about the Vaughan Williams, and obviously enjoyed the carols.[19]

The Musical Society performed another big Bach work, the *St Matthew Passion,* during Holy Week. This concert was the last in the season. It was requested in the programme that in view of the sacred nature of the work there should be no applause. The baritone soloist was John Shirley-Quirk, another young singer whom David Willcocks brought to Bedford early in his career. He was to go on to become an outstanding interpreter of Elgar, Tippett and Britten.[20]

The financial loss during the 1961/62 season was nearly £600. It had only been possible for the Musical Society to bring orchestras to Bedford because of Arts Council funding and financial support from Bedford Corporation and Bedfordshire County Council, a point made at the annual general meeting in September 1962. Clarence Raybould stood down as president at this meeting, finally severing his connection with the Society. He wished to relinquish the post because of his move to Bideford in Devon. It was agreed at the meeting to approach Sir Thomas Armstrong about the president's position. He subsequently accepted the post, which he held for over twenty years.

[17] *The Bedfordshire Times and Bedfordshire Standard*, 14 March 1961, p. 15.

[18] When Sir David Willcocks talked to the author in November 2011 he specifically mentioned Robert Tear: 'Bob seemed to anticipate exactly the conductor's every suggestion about how a particular work should be sung.' Robert Tear was equally complimentary about David Willcocks in his very humorous contribution to Owen, *A Life in Music – Conversations with Sir David Willcocks and Friends*, pp. 180–1.

[19] 'He rehearsed us and touched us up and made us do single lines until we had got them perfect, or thereabouts. On the whole, we were not bad.' *The Bedfordshire Times and Bedfordshire Standard*, 22 December 1961, p. 9.

[20] Kennedy, *Oxford Dictionary of Music*, p. 660.

The Jacques Orchestra played twice during the 1962/63 season, in December and in April. Robert Tear returned to Bedford to take part in the first part of Handel's *Messiah* in December. J.H.M.S. gave him nodding approval: 'Mr. Robert Tear adequately fulfilled the tenor role.'[21] He was less complimentary about the chorus's singing.[22] The reviewer was much more enthusiastic about the carol singing in which the audience took part: 'In fact, Mr. Willcocks at one stage asked those who had been present at the equivalent concert last year to raise their hands and a forest of hands flew up. "I thought so", he said. "You have improved very much, and perhaps next year you should be on the platform and the choir in the hall". He spoke more presciently than he intended.'[23]

The spring 1963 concert with the Jacques Orchestra, held two weeks before Easter, was again conducted by David Willcocks. Unlike concerts performed at this time over previous years, the programme was secular. It opened with Purcell's 'semi-opera' *The Masque of Dioclesian* and ended with Lambert's *The Rio Grande,* with Philip Ledger returning to Bedford as the piano soloist.[24] The reviewer, R.B.P., compliments Hans Freyhan on his admirable programme notes.[25]

The May and December concerts both consisted of a number of shorter works, which may be one reason why neither concert was reviewed, perhaps even the inclusion of carols in the December concert in which the audience joined in, could not persuade J.H.M.S. to attend.[26]

The Musical Society repeated Bach's *St John Passion* in March 1964, the first work they had sung under David Willcocks. The bass soloist was John Carol Case, who three years later sang in the well-known recording that King's College Choir, Cambridge, made of Fauré's Requiem.[27] The contralto soloist concert was Margaret Cable; the reviewer was particularly complimentary about her performance.[28] The Jacques Orchestra played, as they had in the March 1959 performance. Freddie Stevens, still chorus master, played the continuo on the piano.

Freddie Stevens had indicated that he wished to resign as chorus master at the end of the season, and he was not involved in the May 1964 concert.[29] This was rehearsed and conducted by Kate Freyhan. The reviewer, R.B.P., notes that the

21 *The Bedfordshire Times and Bedfordshire Standard*, 28 December 1962, p. 4.

22 'As it was, even David Willcocks, the Director of Music at King's College, Cambridge, could not make anything more of them, as they sauntered through ... than a disjoined collection of voices.' Ibid.

23 Ibid.

24 *The Masque of Dioclesian* was originally incidental music for Thomas Betterton's play *The Prophetess,* or *The History of Dioclesian.*

25 Hans Freyhan quotes the poet Dryden who wrote, referring to the *The Masque of Dioclesian*, that although Purcell was only just over thirty, his greatness was fully recognised by his contemporaries: 'the excellent composition of Mr. Purcell in whose person we have at length found an Englishman equal to the best abroad.' *The Bedfordshire Times and Bedfordshire Standard*, 5 April 1963, p. 28.

26 Alternatively, the lack of a review may have been because the concert was held on a Wednesday and the review would not have appeared until after Christmas by which time it would be 'old news'.

27 The New Philharmonia Orchestra accompanied and David Willcocks conducted. Robert Chilcott was the boy treble soloist. See Owen, *A Life in Music – Conversations with Sir David Willcocks and Friends*, p. 172 and p.176.

28 'Miss Cable's voice, in particular, charmed us with its hint of Kathleen Ferrier in the *air* "Chains of bondage that I wrought me".' *The Bedfordshire Times and Bedfordshire Standard*, 20 March 1964, p. 10.

29 Freddie Stevens finally stood down at the end of the 1964/65 season. He was presented with a gift token at the end of the concert on 24 March 1965. He used the token to buy *The Oxford Companion to Music* – a book that he valued very much.

Freyhan family was well represented at the concert, although he missed Hans Freyhan's programme notes. Michael Freyhan (on viola), then in his mid-twenties, and two other young performers, played the Mozart Divertimento in E Flat for violin, viola and cello.

For the Christmas concert on 2 December, the Musical Society was joined by Dame Alice Harpur School Choir, Silver Jubilee Girls' School Choir and the Jacques Orchestra for a performance, in the second half, of Britten's *St Nicolas*. David Willcocks conducted and Robert Tear again sang with the Society. According the programme, the chorus master was Brian Lane.

There seems to have been some confusion during the autumn about who actually was the chorus master. According to the minutes, Dr John Seddon was originally to have taken the rehearsals for the December 1964 and March 1965 concerts.[30] However, Brian Lane took the rehearsals for the December concert.[31] Despite his announcement earlier in the year, Freddie Stevens was confirmed as chorus master at the November committee meeting, and conducted the February 1965 concert. At the March 1965 committee meeting it was proposed that Brian Lane, the county music adviser, be asked to be the chorus master for the next season. He accepted the appointment.

The February 1965 concert, like the concerts that Freddie Stevens conducted in the 1950s, was held in St Paul's church, with organ accompaniment by Brian Lane.[32] John Seddon 'reappears' as chorus master for the March 1965 concert. This concert was, once more, conducted by David Willcocks. In the first half there were two of Handel's coronation anthems, *Zadok the Priest* and *The King shall Rejoice*, and a concerto grosso, also by Handel. In the concerto grosso, Freddie Stevens played the continuo part on the piano as he had done a year earlier. The reviewer, A. R. le F. (Antony le Fleming), thought it was quite unsuitable: 'Surely a society which employs the Jacques Orchestra and Mr. Willcocks ought to use a harpsichord for a concert in which baroque music plays so large a part?'[33] A.R. le F. probably had a valid point. He was complimentary about other parts of the concert, but felt that more rehearsal time was required.[34] Anthony le Fleming was the son of the composer Christopher le Fleming, whose works included choral works and songs. He held many posts in school musical education.[35]

There was a long gap until the next concert, which was the Christmas concert, held on 8 December. This opened with Wiren's *Serenade for Strings*, which had

30 *Minute Book 1962–69*, 6 May 1965, BLARS X817/1/10.

31 *Minute Book 1962–69*, 17 June 1965, BLARS X817/1/10.

32 In the first half, there was a Bach Cantata (No. 21). The second half opened with the Vivaldi Concerto in D Minor, transcribed by J. S. Bach for organ. Two movements from *L'Ascension* by Messiaen followed. The final work was Holst's Psalm 148. In the programme notes, Hans Freyhan tells how W. F. Bach claimed the transcription as his own – a fraud only unmasked in the twentieth century.

33 *Bedfordshire Times*, 26 March 1965, p. 27.

34 He commented on Haydn's 'Nelson Mass' (No.9 in D Minor), and highlighted the singing by the sopranos: 'The best singing of the evening came in "Quoniam Tu Solus" when the sopranos, in particular, sang with great distinction.' He continued: 'Perhaps the amount of work put into this venture deserves at least one combined rehearsal of chorus and orchestra.' Unfortunately, this would have increased the concerts costs, possibly making it too expensive. Ibid.

35 Of his son Anthony he wrote: 'In the early spring of 1941, our third son Antony was born: he lost no time in giving intimations of becoming a great musician.' Christopher le Fleming, *Journey into Music by the Slow Train* (Bristol, 1982), p. 123.

previously been performed by the Society in 1948, 1949 and 1954. Leigh's *Concertino for Harpsichord and Strings* followed. Antony le Fleming, who had criticised the use of the piano for the continuo in the review of the March concert, was the harpsichord soloist. Vivaldi's *Gloria*, revived in 1939 and by 1965 a firm favourite - according to Hans Freyhan in the programme notes – concluded the first part of the concert. The second half was devoted to carols, with audience participation.

The first concert of 1966 was a performance of Verdi's Requiem. This took place on 2 March, a week earlier than originally intended so as not to clash with the Bedford Competitive Music Festival. David Willcocks conducted; the Cambridge University Musical Society orchestra played, and among the soloists was the tenor Kenneth Bowen. J.H.M.S.'s review was very favourable: 'We salute you, O Musical Society, for your greatest achievement yet.'[36] He is somewhat pretentious and does not say very much about the actual performance. He does, however, note that the Corn Exchange was packed and that the applause was very loud. This was his last review for the *Bedfordshire Times*.

Brian Lane's brief tenure as chorus master came to an end following the March committee meeting. The chorus secretary, Wendy Steele, said that there had been problems between Brian Lane and herself over the arrangements for the Verdi concert. Other members of the committee also expressed their dissatisfaction; Brian Lane was present at the meeting to hear the criticism.[37] At the April committee meeting, there was a letter from him, which to all intents and purposes offered his resignation. It was taken as such by the committee and accepted. His musicianship was never in question, but some people had not found him easy to work with.

As a result, the proposed concert for 9 June, which was to have included Lambert's *The Rio Grande*, Vaughan Williams's *Serenade to Music* and Borodin's *Polovtsian Dances* had to be completely rearranged. The Albany Consort, conducted by Mrs Pat Laslett, took part. Fred Rawlins conducted the Musical Society chorus. Because of the changes to the programme and the performers, the Society did not call on contingency funding available from the Bedford Corporation for Charter Year events, despite the fact that there was a loss on the concert. This concert was listed in the booklet published by the Bedford Corporation, *Bedford 1166–1966: A Record of the Charter Year*.[38]

There is a short chapter in this booklet on music by J.H.M.S., focused on the BBC Symphony Orchestra and the other BBC orchestras and bands that had been, or still were, based in the town. J.H.M.S. also refers to the local Operatic Society, the Marionettes, and to schools' music. Of the Musical Society he says not a word, which must have been quite hurtful to members of the Society, as he had reviewed their concerts as the *Bedfordshire Times's* music correspondent for over twenty years. There is, however, a very brief reference in the booklet in the opening chapter, 'This Ancient Borough', to the Society as one of the first cultural amenities, alongside the Scientific Institute and General Library and the Archaeological and Architectural Societies.

36 *Bedfordshire Times*, 4 March 1966, p. 29.
37 *Minute Book 1962–69*, 24 March 1966, BLARS X/817/1/10.
38 Bedford Corporation, *Bedford 1166–1966: A Record of the Charter Year* (Bedford, 1966), p. 66.

Despite problems with the June concert, the 1965/66 season as a whole was financially successful. Following Brian Lane's resignation, Antony le Fleming was appointed chorus master. At the 1966 annual general meeting at the start of October, Robert 'Bob' Atkins, who was to play a very prominent part in the Society's affairs during the 1970s and 1980s, was elected to the committee.

The main work in the first half of the December concert, conducted once more by David Willcocks, with the Jacques Orchestra accompanying, was one of Handel's 'Chandos Anthems'. Christopher le Fleming's *Five Psalms* was also performed. This was originally composed, and first performed, as a song cycle for tenor and piano. A revised version for soprano solo, chorus and full orchestra was performed at the Three Choirs Festival in Gloucester in 1947.[39] R.B.P.'s review simply states: 'This work is ingeniously written and falls pleasantly on the ear. We would like to hear a repeat performance.'[40] The review ends: 'At the end of the concert, Mr. David Willcocks paid tribute to Mr. Antony le Fleming, the Chorus Master, for inspiring the chorus and for much diligent rehearsal.'[41]

Antony le Fleming conducted the June 1967 concert. The headline of the review read, 'Concert is an evening of musical enjoyment.'[42] At this concert, the new Bedford Symphony Orchestra was launched. It comprised some sixty members. The review states: 'It was Mr. Antony le Fleming's evening without doubt. He has done a great deal for music in Bedford and it is with regret that we learn he will shortly be leaving us. He has a musicianly approach to everything he performs ... The accompaniment of the orchestra (to Mozart's concert aria *A questo seno*, K.374) under Mr. le Fleming's meticulous direction showed his love of Mozart and an appreciation of all that was required.'[43] The programme also included Bernstein's *Chichester Psalms* – heard twice during the concert – and Elgar's *Scenes from the Bavarian Highlands*. Of the Bernstein, the generally reliable reviewer, R.B.P. commented: 'we felt at the end that its discordance added little to the psalms'.[44]

When Antony le Fleming notified the chairman of his forthcoming move to Abingdon and consequent resignation as chorus master, he suggested that Roy Rimmer, who had replaced Brian Lane as the county music adviser, should be approached about taking on the role. Roy Rimmer was duly interviewed and appointed.

Before taking up his post in Bedfordshire, Roy Rimmer had been music master at the Queen Elizabeth Grammar School in Blackburn. Brian Kemball-Cook, then headmaster of Bedford Modern School, and also on the committee of the Musical Society, had also come from Blackburn and had known Roy Rimmer there, so was happy to endorse his appointment.[45]

Roy Rimmer rehearsed the choir from September 1967 for the Christmas concert at which the main choral work was Bach's cantata 'Sleepers, Awake!'. David Will-

39 From the programme notes, written by the composer, BLARS X817/3/97. See also Christopher le Fleming's autobiography *Journey into Music by the Slow Train*, p. 192.
40 *Bedfordshire Times*, 13 December 1966, p. 12. The work has never been repeated in Bedford.
41 Ibid.
42 *Bedfordshire Times*, 13 June 1967, p. 11.
43 Ibid.
44 Ibid.
45 Personal interview with Freddie Stevens by the author.

cocks conducted and the Jacques Orchestra accompanied. The soloists included Sally le Sage, the soprano who had had to drop out from the summer concert at short notice, and Brian Kay. This was shortly before the King Singers, of which he was a founder member, were formed.[46]

Elgar's wonderful work, *The Dream of Gerontius,* was performed in Bedford on Wednesday 28 February 1968 with the Cambridge University Musical Society orchestra conducted by David Willcocks. The Musical Society chorus was augmented by members of Cambridge University Musical Society chorus. The concert was repeated in Ely Cathedral on 2 March. The minutes of the committee meeting that followed a few days later note succinctly that: 'the concert had been well worth the effort'.[47]

The newly formed Bedfordshire Symphony Orchestra performed for the first time at one of the Musical Society's concerts in June 1968. It was also the first time that Roy Rimmer conducted. Four solo pianists accompanied – two for the Bach Concerto in C and two for Stravinsky's *Symphony of Psalms*. Freddie Stevens was one of the soloists in the Bach, and John Porter was one of the soloists in the Stravinsky. This latter work was performed twice during the concert, before the interval and after it, as the Bernstein's *Chichester Psalms* had been a year earlier.[48]

The London Gabrieli Brass Ensemble played at the December 1968 concert. The first half of the concert was quite serious for a Christmas concert, and included choral and instrumental music by several early composers, including Locke, Gabrieli and Purcell, and by two modern composers, Poulenc and Hindemith. The second half consisted of carols. The committee were not happy with the programme for the first half and felt that it was too 'bitty'.[49]

Roy Rimmer conducted the Musical Society again in May 1969 for a performance of Mendelssohn's *Elijah*. The Bedfordshire Symphony Orchestra, of which Roy Rimmer was also the conductor, accompanied the choir once more. The semi-choruses were sung by the Bedford Singers under their chorus master, Brian Lane (the Musical Society's former chorus master). The review in the *Bedfordshire Times* was the first review of one of the Society's concerts written by Hans Freyhan, who continued to write concert reviews for the paper until 1996, the year that he died. The *Elijah* review is much longer and more thorough than his later reviews were.[50] It is beautifully balanced, saying something of the work itself and Mendelssohn's genius, something about the overall performance and the performers and finishing with an overall assessment. The review noted that *Elijah* had not been performed

[46] The King Singers are a British *a cappella* vocal ensemble and take their name from King's College, Cambridge, where the group was founded in 1968 by six choral scholars. They were particularly popular in the 1970s and 1980s in the UK. Now they have widened their appeal and appear abroad a great deal, especially in the United States where they have featured regularly on television. None of the original six founding members now sing with the group. They have usually been all male, with two counter-tenors, but occasionally women have joined the group, including Felicity Palmer who stood in during 1969. Brian Kay was their bass for a number of years.

[47] *Minute Book 1962–69*, 12 March 1968, BLARS X817/1/10.

[48] The programme notes read: 'At this point, following the now common practice of giving a second hearing as an aid to critical appraisal, the *Symphony of Psalms* will be repeated.' *Concert Programme*, 30 May 1968, p. 4, BLARS X 817/3/99.

[49] David Willcocks agreed to some reconsideration of the programme for future concerts.

[50] Hans Freyhan's later reviews may have been shorter because they were more aggressively sub-edited.

by the Musical Society for a long time, twenty years in fact, and was very complimentary about Roy Rimmer and the achievement of all concerned.[51]

For the December 1969 concert, the Philip Jones Brass Ensemble played. The players included Philip Jones himself and Elgar Howarth on trumpet. Elgar Howarth subsequently became guest conductor of the London Sinfonietta, and has become well-known as a composer and arranger for brass band. There were only three 'serious' pieces, slotted in among the carols that otherwise occupied both the first and second halves of the concert. The major serious work was Gabrieli's Magnificat, which came second in the programme, after the carol, 'O Come, All Ye faithful'.

Brahms's *German Requiem* was the main work in the March 1970 concert. It was sung in English, something that the majority of chorus members preferred, and it occupied the first half of the concert. David Willcocks conducted and the Jacques Orchestra accompanied.[52] Beethoven's *Coriolan Overture* opened the second half, to celebrate the bi-centenary of his birth. The final work of the concert was Parry's setting of Milton's poem *Blest Pair of Sirens*.

Instead of conducting the 1970 Christmas concert, David Willcocks conducted a concert at the end of November.[53] This included Bach's Cantata No. 147, *Herz und Mund und Tat und Leben*; the programme unhelpfully does not give the English translation ('Heart and Mouth and Deed and Life'). In the review, written by Hans Freyhan, as were the programme notes, he says: 'The choir, singing in the original German words, coped well with the contrapuntal complexities and produced a beautiful balance in the choral.'[54] The concluding choral fantasia of this cantata is, under its English title, "Jesu, Joy of Man's Desiring".

Shortly before the Musical Society's own Christmas concert, the annual pre-Christmas performance of *Messiah* by the Bedford Messiah Choir took place. Hans Freyhan notes in his review that there had been an unbroken run for thirty years up to 1967. After the Bromham Road Methodist church had closed, performances took place for some years in St Paul's Methodist church (where Bedford Central Library, completed in 1972, now stands). St Paul's Methodist church closed in 1970, and the performance of *Messiah* that year took place in the Bunyan Meeting church. Performances are still given there.[55] The conductor in 1970 was Donald McCanlis.

51 Of the chorus he wrote: 'the masterly score stimulated [them] to their very best. Roy Rimmer, the conductor, was in obvious sympathy with the music and gave the climaxes their full due, without neglecting the quieter passages.' He was similarly complimentary about the Bedfordshire Symphony Orchestra. After highlighting the problems for an orchestra in providing the instrumental background for chorus and soloist, he writes: 'Our young county orchestra coped valiantly and with a commendable measure of success with some exquisite trumpet and oboe playing into the bargain.' He also complimented the organist: 'John Porter added weighty organ sounds to the voluminous textures.' Summing up, Hans Freyhan wrote: 'All in all, an ambitious enterprise which gave the audience the exhilarating experience they had come for.' The Musical Society was fortunate to have such a generous, but very knowledgeable, reviewer over a long period. *Bedfordshire Times*, 9 May 1969, p. 12.

52 In his review, Hans Freyhan noted: 'The choir sang with confidence throughout, exploring its wide dynamic range and producing strong and brilliant climaxes.' *Bedfordshire Times*, 27 March 1970, p. 17.

53 This arrangement of concerts had been proposed by Roy Rimmer. *Minute Book 1962–69*, 10 December 1969, BLARS X817/1/10.

54 *Bedfordshire Times*, 4 December 1970, p. 11.

55 The review is very informative about the history of the Messiah Choir. The first conductor, who conducted for many years, was Mr W. G. Poole. He died in 1970. Other conductors were Mr J. Mould, Mr W. L. Wooodward, Mr J. B. Westcombe, Donald McCanlis and subsequently, Brian Caves. Mr H. Kenneth Woollard, who played the organ in the 1970 performance, had missed only two performances

He was a relative of Audrey Armstrong, who was one of the main organisers of the Bedford Competitive Music Festival for many years.[56]

The Messiah Choir's 1970 performance was particularly significant because the tenor soloist was the twenty year-old Bonaventura Bottone, singing in Bedford for the first time. Of him, Hans Freyhan wrote: 'Among the soloists, the tenor, Bonaventura Bottone, was outstanding. Endowed with splendid material, he showed remarkable breath control and dynamic versatility.'[57] Bonaventura Bottone moved to Bedford in 1973 and lived in Bower Street. He and his wife, Jennifer Dakin, were to sing as soloists with the Musical Society on a number of occasions.[58]

The Musical Society performed *Messiah* three months later, in March 1971, to a sell-out audience.[59] The programme for this concert, held a month after the introduction of decimal currency in the United Kingdom, was seven and a half pence – one shilling and sixpence in 'old' money. This was the cost of programmes before decimalisation.

In October 1971, following the annual general meeting, Robert Atkins took over as secretary. Minutes of committee meetings were subsequently typed and pasted into the *Minute Book*. This practice continued until May 1977 when the *Minute Book* was full. From then on the minutes were filed. Robert Atkins's minutes were written in a very different style to the handwritten minutes of Tom Winter and his predecessors.

The main works in the November 1971 concert were Fauré's Requiem and, in the second half, Haydn's Mass in B Flat, the 'Harmoniemesse', his last large-scale work. What is striking about this concert was the size of the choir. The headline of the review was, 'Willcocks inspires 180-strong chorus.'[60] This was more than double the size of the chorus when David Willcocks began conducting in 1959.[61] The orchestra consisted mainly of Cambridge undergraduates and John Porter played the chamber organ. Hans Freyhan was particularly complimentary towards the four soloists: 'The solo quartet ... produced a remarkable feast of vocal sound.

since 1937, and the choir included two members who took part in the original performance. Local soloists Patricia Laslett (contralto) and Cyril Parker (tenor) sang with the Messiah Choir many times. For the origins of the Messiah Choir, see chapter six.

56 Audrey Armstrong wrote to *The Bedfordshire Times and Bedfordshire Standard* advocating the revival of the Bedfordshire Music Festival. Her letter was included in an article by the reviewer J. H. M. S. under the headline 'Bravo, Mrs. Armstrong', 23 November 1945, p. 8. She later took on the role of secretary (*Bedfordshire Times*, 26 March 1965, p. 3). She remained a key figure in the running of the Music Festival until her death in the late 1980s. She and her husband, Donald, lived for many years in Waterloo Road, Bedford.

57 *Bedfordshire Times*, 11 December 1970, p. 11.

58 As their daughter, Rebecca Bottone, has subsequently done.

59 Hans Freyhan wrote: 'A largish string orchestra of Cambridge students succeeded in holding its own against this huge choir, not only in those choruses where it was reinforced by trumpet and timpani ... David Willcocks who conducted, brings to Handel not only an aversion against dragging tempi but above all, a light touch which excludes all stodginess. He brushes the patina off the score and lays bare Handel's textures in all their lucid transparency.' *Bedfordshire Times*, 19 March 1971, p. 13.

60 *Bedfordshire Times*, 3 December 1971, p. 14.

61 At the committee meeting of 15 July 1970, Roy Rimmer had proposed a membership drive to bring the membership up to 200. By January 1971 it was reported that there were 191 members of the chorus and this was likely to cause seating problems at concerts.

The standard of their ensemble was comparable to that of a good string quartet – and that is saying a great deal!'[62]

In March 1972, the Musical Society joined with the Ely Choral Society and Cambridgeshire Village College Choirs for a performance of Verdi's Requiem (as they had in 1968 for a performance of *The Dream of Gerontius*). The orchestra was that of the Cambridge University Musical Society. John Handley, a member of the choir, remembered the day well, especially the cold:

> It started snowing in the morning on the way to Ely. It was very cold rehearsing, in spite of having pyjamas on under our clothes. My parents arrived from Peterborough during the rehearsal. After the rehearsal the four of us were so cold that we got into the car and drove out to find somewhere to get warm. We found a pub out in the Fens. It was only 5.00p.m. and a sign outside said 'Only open to Bona Fide travellers'. Our plight was so obvious to the landlord that he took us in, fed us and we listened to the BBC programme 'Sports Report' as we thawed out. Sadly my parents were too cold to stay for the performance.[63]

Another member of the choir, Deirdre Knight, remembered it being so cold in the cathedral that she wore an overcoat during the rehearsal. She was asked by David Willcocks to remove it but refused.[64] The performance was repeated in the Corn Exchange, Bedford, on Friday 21 April with the same orchestra and soloists, but without the Cambridgeshire Village College Choirs or Ely Choral Society.

Roy Rimmer announced in January 1972 that he would be leaving Bedford in April. He was moving to become a music adviser in Western Australia. The last rehearsal he attended – for the Bedford performance of Verdi's Requiem – was that held on 10 April. John Porter, the Society's accompanist, left Bedford at the end of March to become assistant organist and choirmaster at the Chapel Royal, Windsor, where Christopher Robinson was the organist.[65] Deirdre Edwards was appointed as his successor.[66] Fred Rawlins agreed to conduct the concert on 16 May, due to be held in St Paul's church.

Michael Rose was appointed county music adviser in succession to Roy Rimmer. He expressed interest in becoming conductor of the Musical Society, but was not happy about preparing concerts that he would not be conducting for David Willcocks.

In May, Peter Kneale was appointed chorus master, and undertook to prepare the chorus for the 7 November concert, which David Willcocks was due to conduct, and to prepare and conduct the Christmas concert in December. Peter Kneale was a lecturer at the College of Education in Bedford (the teacher training college). He is remembered for his brightly coloured T-shirts by those who sang and rehearsed under him. He prepared the chorus for the 7 November concert well according to the review in the *Bedfordshire Times*. The choral works were Bach's Cantata No. 10 and Schubert's Mass in G. Hans Freyhan considered the Schubert to be the lesser work,

62 *Bedfordshire Times*, 3 December 1971, p. 14.
63 Personal interview with John Handley by the author.
64 Personal interview with Deidre Knight by the author.
65 Sadly, John Porter took his own life a few years later while he was still at Windsor.
66 At this meeting members congratulated Margaret Robertson on being awarded an MBE for services to music. *Minute Book 1969–77*, 13 January 1972, BLARS X/817/1/11.

but to be the highlight of the evening. The tenor soloist was Philip Langridge, who was one of the world's most distinguished singers at the time, and was in demand on the operatic and concert platforms of Europe, America and Japan. He appeared regularly with many of the world's leading opera companies. [67] The bass soloist was Brian Rayner Cook.

The first concert that Peter Kneale conducted was the Christmas 1972 concert. The pattern of this concert was similar to the Christmas concerts that David Willcocks had conducted until three years earlier; a serious first half and carols and audience participation in the second half.[68] The first half featured a work by Michael Rose, *Winter Music*, which the choir did not find easy, and which Peter Kneale had some problems rehearsing. The programme note was written by Michael Rose and reads: 'I wrote this piece in 1966 for Roy Rimmer who was teaching at a school in Blackburn. By the time of its first performance in Blackburn Cathedral, Roy Rimmer had left for Bedford. It is a strange coincidence that the Musical Society, whose chorus master he was, should now be singing this piece this evening.'[69] The accompaniment is for two pianists and two percussionists, and in this performance one of the pianists was Deirdre Edwards, official accompanist for the Musical Society's chorus and soon to be appointed assistant chorus master. Mary Bainbridge, who would be involved in local music for many years to come, latterly with the Concord Singers, was the soprano soloist.

Michael Rose (1934–)

Michael Rose, the new county music adviser, was born in Norfolk, shortly before three of England's major composers, Elgar, Holst and Delius died.[70]At the age of sixteen, he entered the Royal Academy of Music, with piano and violin as joint main studies.[71] At the Royal Academy he began conducting and also set up a small choir, the Sine Nomine Singers. The choir is still going strong. He also began composing. On leaving the Royal Academy, he was called up for National Service, and was assigned to the Scots' Guards Band. He signed on for three years, which enabled him to stay in London, and survived army life by involving himself in musical activity, including taking part in the Edinburgh Tattoo. On leaving the army he taught – music, history, English and cricket – at his old school, John Lyon School in Harrow, for six years. He followed this by becoming a music adviser, first in Middlesex, and following local government reorganisation, for three London boroughs.

During this time, he also developed his conducting skills, and became a friend of George Hurst, director of the famous Canford Summer School of Music.[72] He became George Hurst's assistant on the course and an 'apprentice' conductor with

67 Bach Cantatas website, http://www.bach-cantatas.com/Bio/Langridge-Philip.htm, accessed March 2015.

68 The choir sang two carols by the twenty-seven year old John Rutter, the 'Shepherd's Pipe' carol and 'Quem Pastores Laudarere'. Both these are included in *Carols for Choirs. 2.: Fifty Carols for Christmas and Advent* (London, 1970), which he edited with David Willcocks.

69 *Concert Programme*, 20 December 1972, p. 1, BLARS X817/3/115.

70 Elgar died on 23 February 1934, Holst died three months later on 25 May and Delius died less than a month later on 10 June.

71 The biographical information comes from an article by Mrs Catherine Rose that appeared in the programme for Michael Rose's seventy-fifth birthday celebration concert in January 2009.

72 George Hurst died in September 2012, aged eighty-six.

the BBC Northern Symphony Orchestra. William Glock then invited Michael Rose to take up a new post as assistant-in-charge of the BBC Training Orchestra in Bristol. Here he worked with many distinguished conductors, including Sir Adrian Boult, Norman del Mar, Louis Fremaux and Sir Colin Davis. The chief conductor of the BBC Training Orchestra was Meredith Davies.[73] Regular concerts with the orchestra enabled Michael Rose to acquire a wide knowledge of the orchestral repertoire and of orchestral training techniques.

The BBC made savage cuts to its orchestral programmes in 1972, and this made it possible for Michael Rose to return to education. Roy Rimmer, who had met him a few years earlier at the Canford Summer School of Music, told him that he was leaving Bedfordshire and suggested that he apply for his job as Bedfordshire music adviser. Michael Rose was duly appointed and set about creating an extraordinary system of instrumental education using the foundations laid by his predecessor. By the time Michael Rose took early retirement in 1990, there were four youth orchestras, three bands, a jazz band, a choir and youth opera, as well as five Saturday music schools; Bedfordshire was one of the best counties for musical education in the United Kingdom.

Michael Rose was appointed conductor of the Bedfordshire Symphony Orchestra on his arrival in the county, and in the mid-1970s he founded the Bedford Sinfonia. He first conducted the Musical Society in April 1973 and has continued to conduct the Society, normally once a year, ever since. Following his retirement, he has also continued to conduct Bedfordshire Symphony Orchestra and Bedford Sinfonia concerts, and the County Youth Orchestra. He was chairman of the National Association of Youth Orchestras for fifteen years and an examiner for the Associated Board of the Royal Schools of Music for a similar period, travelling to many parts of the world on its behalf.

In January 2009, Michael Rose conducted a special concert to celebrate his seventy-fifth birthday. Ian Smith, the Musical Society's current musical director, who originally proposed the idea, wrote in the programme:

> The orchestra would be no 'ordinary' orchestra but could be made up of players who had been conducted by Michael in the more than thirty five years that he has been conducting the Bedfordshire County Youth Orchestra. So many players who have entered the music profession have spent their formative musical years under the direction of one of the best orchestral trainers in the country. I felt sure that many of them would be delighted to return to play in a concert for Michael … We are delighted that so many players have been able to come together to form this truly unique orchestra for what, we hope, will be a very special occasion.[74]

This illustrates the beneficial and lasting effect Michael Rose's appointment as county music adviser had and still has. He was awarded the OBE in 1990.

[73] Meredith Davies was organist of Hereford Cathedral while the author was at the Cathedral School, and went on to have a successful career as an operatic conductor.

[74] The names and current occupations of those playing in the orchestra were included in the programme. Fifty-six former players in the Bedfordshire County Youth Orchestra at the time of the concert were professional musicians. Author's collection.

In the first half of the April 1973 concert, conducted by Michael Rose, the choir sang *Zadok the Priest* and Vaughan Williams's *Serenade to Music*. One of the soloists, John Noble, sang Mahler's *Songs of a Wayfarer*. Walton's *Belshazzar's Feast* was performed in the second half of the concert. Hans Freyhan noted how Michael Rose had stirred up everyone's – the choir's and the orchestra's – enthusiasm for the work: 'As a result, the performance was marked by tremendous self-confidence and security of all participants … no mean achievement. But what mattered more: the essential force and tenseness of the music was never allowed to slacken.'[75] The review ends with a real vote of confidence: 'The concert was a real occasion for both choir and orchestra, but above all for the conductor whose great capacity it revealed to the full.'[76] The Bedfordshire Symphony Orchestra was incorrectly called the Bedford Symphony Orchestra on the front of the programme.

Michael Rose conducted the Musical Society's next concert in November, and the Bedford Sinfonia played for the first time with the Society. The organist was Michael Ashcroft, who was to conduct the Musical Society a few years later. The main choral work in the first half was Britten's *Rejoice in the Lamb*, an appropriate choice as Britten's sixtieth birthday was a few days after the concert. For this work, Britten had selected passages from a poem of the eighteenth century poet, Christopher Smart. In the review, Hans Freyhan comments: 'The weird atmosphere of the music, which responds to Christopher Smart's strange poetry, was well conveyed, and the striking originality of Britten's setting made its full impact.'[77]

Rejoice in the Lamb was commissioned in 1943 for the fiftieth anniversary of the consecration of St Matthew's church, Northampton. The vicar was the Rev. Walter Hussey, who was the son of the first vicar, Canon John Rowden Hussey. As well as commissioning this work by Britten, Walter Hussey also commissioned works by Gerald Finzi and Edmund Rubbra for the church. He also commissioned a number of works of art, a Madonna by Henry Moore (inscribed 1944) and paintings by Graham Sutherland and John Piper. After eighteen years at St Matthew's, Walter Hussey was appointed Dean of Chichester Cathedral. His most well-known commissions while there are Bernstein's *Chichester Psalms* and John Piper's large tapestry in the cathedral.[78]

At the start of 1974, David Willcocks left King's College, Cambridge, following his appointment as director to the Royal College of Music. The Musical Society was very fortunate that he continued to conduct its concerts at least once a year until 1987. After his appointment, he regularly brought a student orchestra from the Royal College to accompany the Society. He told the author that the students enjoyed coming to Bedford as it gave them valuable experience of playing at concerts, and they were also able to earn a little money. The Musical Society benefited from working with some very talented young performers.

The first concert he conducted after moving to the Royal College of Music was Bach's Mass in B Minor, at the end of March 1974.[79] He had previously conducted

75 *Bedfordshire Times*, 27 April 1973, p.13.
76 Ibid.
77 *Bedfordshire Times*, 16 November 1973, p. 7.
78 Walter Hussey's own collection is housed at the Pallant House Gallery, Chichester.
79 *Minute Book 1969–77*, 30 September 1974, BLARS X/817/1/11.

this work in Bedford in April 1960. There was a large and enthusiastic choir; 188 of the 208 members of the chorus took part. Of the orchestra, Hans Freyhan wrote: 'these young players proved a tremendous asset as their technical attainment was matched by an enthusiasm which cannot always be taken for granted with an orchestra of older professionals.'[80] He was hugely impressed by some of the individual continuo and obbligato players who are named in the programme.

The next concert (referred to as the 'spring concert'), was held on 8 June in St Paul's church and included Benjamin Britten's *St Nicolas*. This cantata, written for the centenary celebrations of Lancing College in 1948, has three treble soloists. Pilgrim School Choir, of which Michael Ashcroft was in charge, sang in the performance. Michael Rose conducted.

Peter Kneale stood down as chorus master towards the end of the 1973/74 season.[81] The position was offered to Deirdre Edwards, soon to remarry and be known as Mrs Deirdre Knight. She accepted the invitation, but proposed that Michael Ashcroft should prepare and conduct the December 1974 concert. At the subsequent annual general meeting, Michael Ashcroft, David Willcocks and Michael Rose, were all appointed as conductors of the Musical Society.

The November concert, conducted by Michael Rose, included Walton's coronation anthem and Verdi's *Four Sacred Pieces*; it should also have included Holst's *The Hymn of Jesus*, but this was postponed and replaced with orchestral works by Delius and Vaughan Williams, and by Elgar's 'Land of Hope and Glory'. Details of Holst's *Hymn of Jesus* were included in the printed programme, but it was omitted because Michael Rose felt that the chorus was not up to standard and needed more rehearsal time. Holst's *Choral Fantasia* was included instead to commemorate the centenary of his birth in September 1874 and the fortieth anniversary of his death.

The 1974 Christmas concert was a more serious affair than those of the past few years. A 'scratch' orchestra, the Bedford Camerata, accompanied the Musical Society's chorus, which Michael Ashcroft conducted. The first half was largely taken up with a sequence of *Carols for Instruments and Voices* by Charpentier and sung by the choir. The main work in the second half was Vaughan Williams's last work, which he did not quite complete, *The First Nowell*. This work was originally intended as a masque, but was subsequently arranged for concert performance, limited to settings of carols and Bach's 'How Brightly Shines the Morning Star'. John Handley wrote to the committee afterwards to say that the first part of the concert had been too long and that it was boring for children, with no opportunity for them to sing.

David Willcocks conducted a sell-out performance of Bach's *St Matthew Passion* in March 1975. The soloists included Ann Murray, Ian Partridge and Stephen Varcoe. Ann Murray had made her stage debut in 1974 in Gluck's *Alceste* at the Snape Maltings, Aldeburgh, and concentrated primarily on opera. Ian Partridge focused on oratorio and solo performance. Stephen Varcoe had sung in King's College Choir, Cambridge, and went on to make a career in both opera and oratorio. Hans Freyhan was very complimentary to all the main performers in his review.[82] Pilgrim School Semichorus took part in the performance.

80 *Bedfordshire Times*, 5 April 1974, p.18.
81 *Minute Book 1969–77*, 6 June 1974, BLARS X/817/1/11.
82 He thought that Ann Murray's main aria, 'Have Mercy, Lord', was one of the evening's most

Michael Rose conducted the performance of Brahms's *German Requiem* on Remembrance Sunday in the Corn Exchange. The choir was accompanied by the Bedfordshire Symphony Orchestra. Hans Freyhan notes in his quite brief review that, 'The choir was in good shape'.[83]

Deirdre Knight, chorus master since mid-1974, conducted the annual Christmas concert in December 1975. John Handley's criticism of the previous year's carol concert seems to have been taken on board, for there were lots of carols for the audience to join in with. The only 'unknown' items were the three pieces from Scheidt's *Battle Suite*, composed in 1621 and played by Brio Brass. Terry Hext was the director of this brass group, and his teenage son, Michael, was one of the trombonists. Michael was subsequently the winner of the first BBC Young Musician of the Year award in 1978.

The first concert of 1976 was Handel's *Israel in Egypt*, which David Willcocks conducted towards the end of March. The fourth concert of the season was conducted by Michael Ashcroft, which meant that each of the four concerts in the season had been conducted by a different conductor. This last concert was given in May in All Saint's church, Queen's Park, Bedford.

Early in the 1975/76 season, the secretary, Robert Atkins, contacted Philip Ledger about the possibility of his conducting the Musical Society, accompanied by the Cambridge University Musical Society orchestra. Philip Ledger had succeeded David Willcocks as director of music at King's College in 1974. He responded by saying that he would put it to the Cambridge University Musical Society committee and report back on its decision. The final outcome is expressed somewhat tersely in the Musical Society's minutes of the 12 March 1976: 'The Secretary had heard from Mr. Philip Ledger. It was unlikely that the Society would within the immediate future be able to hold concerts with Mr. Ledger and the Cambridge University Musical Society orchestra.'[84]

At the following annual general meeting, Sir Thomas Armstrong indicated that he wished to stand down as president because of advancing age. He was subsequently elected as a vice-president. The secretary then invited David Willcocks to become president, an invitation that he said that he would be happy to accept at an appropriate time. By 'appropriate time' he meant when he was no longer working for, and being paid by, the Society. So, for more than ten years the position of president remained 'in abeyance'.[85]

The first concert of the 1976/77 season was a performance, with orchestra, of Duruflé's Requiem, conducted by David Willcocks. The bass-baritone soloist was to have been Paul Wilson, who came to live in Bedford at about this time. As Paul

memorable events. Of the choir he wrote: 'The Society's large choir, thoroughly prepared by their new Chorus Master, Deirdre Knight, responded with alertness and enthusiasm to David Willcocks's superb direction.' *Bedfordshire Times*, 28 March 1975, p. 12.

83 *Bedfordshire Times*, 14 November 1975, p. 14.

84 *Minute Book 1969–77*, 12 March 1976, BLARS X817/1/11.

85 *Minute Book 1969–77*, 31 October 1975, BLARS X817/1/11. By the time that David Willcocks retired from conducting the Musical Society in 1987, Robert Atkins and other members of the committee felt that he had too many other commitments to be interested in the Society, and by then he was not very enthusiastic about the idea, so the proposal was shelved.

Wilson was unavailable, Jacek Strauch, a student at the Royal College of Music, sang the baritone part.

In the spring of 1977, Michael Rose conducted not only the Musical Society's own concert, but also the first of the Bedfordshire Choirs and County Youth Orchestra concerts in the Royal Albert Hall, London.

The Musical Society's concert was held on 20 March, and was a commemoration of Beethoven's death 150 years earlier. The concert included Mozart's Requiem and Beethoven's *Equali* for four trombones.[86] It also included Mozart's Piano Concerto in E Flat, described by Alfred Einstein in his famous biography of Mozart as 'Mozart's Eroica'. The soloist was Michael Freyhan, Hans Freyhan's son. The review in the *Bedfordshire Times* was mistakenly headed 'Mozartian Tribute'.[87] For obvious reasons the review of the piano concerto was not written by Hans Freyhan. It is signed J.A.I., who was probably John Ireland, then a lecturer at Mander College, Bedford. He wrote: 'Michael Freyhan gave a refined, classical performance … it was good to see a performer playing down the massive instrument at his disposal, and with the minimum of affectation – he looked good at the piano.'[88]

The Royal Albert Hall concert took place on 23 April 1977, and the main choral work was Walton's *Belshazzar's Feast*. The concert was in aid of the Vellore Trust for the Christian Medical College and Hospital in South India. The committee noted that: 'Belshazzar's Feast … had been very exciting and of excellent standard. Sec. had written to Michael Rose to express the Society's delight, and Michael Rose had replied indicating his appreciation of the Society's contribution. The Vellore Trust had indicated that they intended to invite Bedfordshire again in 1981.'[89]

A Grand Silver Jubilee concert followed in June. Hans Freyhan's review was headed, 'Crowning end to season', and after a short introductory paragraph he wrote: 'Under Michael Ashcroft's assured guidance, the Society's chorus enjoyed itself and delighted the audience in the well-known coronation pieces by Stanford (Te Deum), Parry (I was glad) and Handel (The King shall rejoice, and Zadok the Priest).'[90] Paul Edwards, one of Deirdre Knight's sons, was the alto soloist.[91] Howard Chalkley, a long-standing member of the choir, was the bass soloist.[92] Michael Ashcroft conducted the Musical Society for the last time, as he was leaving Bedford.

The committee meeting of 27 May was the last for which the minutes were kept in a *Minute Book*. At that meeting, Brian Caves' offer to hold auditions was accepted. He had recently been appointed the Society's accompanist, and the deci-

[86] As Hans Freyhan explained: 'Beethoven wrote these brief solemn movements in 1812, for All Souls' Day at Linz. After his death on March 26th 1827, an arrangement of these pieces for male voice chorus was sung as his body was taken from his last residence in Vienna while an immense crowd paid their last tribute. During the next few days, several Memorial Services were held, and at one of these, at the *Augustinerkirche*, Mozart's *Requiem* was sung.' *Bedfordshire Times*, 25 March 1976, p. 19.

[87] Unless it was intended to mean 'A Mozartian tribute to Beethoven'.

[88] *Bedfordshire Times*, 25 March 1977, p. 19.

[89] This committee meeting is notable as Kate Freyhan reported that she had a great many of the Musical Society's old programmes. She subsequently passed them to the author, and he later gave them to the Bedfordshire and Luton Archives and Record Service. They now form a significant part of the Musical Society's Archive.

[90] *Minute Book 1969–77*, 27 April 1977, BLARS X817/1/11.

[91] Paul Edwards has subsequently composed a number of short choral works.

[92] In 2015, Howard Chalkley was still singing with the choir.

sion to hold auditions was a new one. It was agreed that he should be assisted by a panel, and that auditioning of newcomers should start at the beginning of the new season, in September.[93] One of the reasons for holding auditions was to advise singers as to which part they should sing.

The Christmas concert was held on 14 December; Deirdre Knight conducted for the third and last time. Hans Freyhan was very complimentary.[94] Photographs of members of the choir and orchestra were taken before and during the rehearsal. Deirdre Knight had been reluctant to conduct this concert, and stood down as chorus master at the end of the season.[95]

Just over a week later, members of the Musical Society joined other choirs from Bedfordshire, the County Youth Orchestra and conductor Michael Rose for a performance of Handel's *Messiah* in the Royal Albert Hall. Massed rehearsals had previously been held at Redborne Upper School, Ampthill.

David Willcocks, who had been given a knighthood in the Queen's Silver Jubilee Honours List in June 1977, conducted the Musical Society in a performance of Haydn's *Creation* at the end of February 1978. He came to Bedford for a rehearsal on 13 February. This rehearsal was held at Newnham School, Bedford, rather than at Pilgrim School where rehearsals were normally held. Tragically, Margaret Robertson, who had done so much for the Musical Society, was killed in a car accident near Pilgrim School, where she had probably gone to redirect anyone who had arrived there by mistake.[96] She died on 23 March.

Tom Winter spoke at the 3 May committee meeting of her service to the Musical Society over many years, and said that she had been instrumental in bringing it to its present flourishing state as one of the leading choral societies in the country. He commented that she had always advocated that the Society should be bold and forward looking, and noted her work on the executive council of the National Federation of Music Societies. Her work there, for the past five years, with the attendant advantage it gave to the Musical Society, was widely appreciated. The committee expressed its deep gratitude for the commitment of Miss Robertson and stood in silence in her memory. Her influence extended beyond Bedfordshire, as John Handley recalled:

> Throughout the period 1958–93, and especially in the 1970s and 1980s, Bedford had an enviable reputation nationally in amateur music making. Bedford Musical Society as it still was, Bedford Music Club, Bedford Sinfonia, Bedfordshire Symphony Orchestra, the County Youth Orchestras and the annual Competitive Festival contributed to this reputation. The Musical Society played a very important role, with Margaret Robertson, Chairman of the Society, elected to

93 The author was among the very first people to be auditioned. The auditions took place while members of the choir were having a social and collecting their music for the next concert. The chorus master, Deirdre Knight, and the chorus secretary, Margaret Harden, joined Brian Caves to undertake auditions. Potential choir members were asked to recognise intervals and notes within a chord and to choose a hymn to sing. Margaret Harden died in March 2015.

94 'Her confident direction produced a splendid security of ensemble, and her choice of tempi, guided by deep-rooted understanding of Bach's requirements, left nothing to desire … the chorales were unhurried and thus not deprived of their dignity, while the wonderful Sinfonia was not allowed to drag.' *Bedfordshire Times*, 23 December 1977, p. 9.

95 *Minute Book* 1969–77, 27 April 1977, BLARS X817/1/11.

96 Personal interview with John Handley by the author.

> the National Executive of the National Federation of Music Societies. One of the major responsibilities of the National Federation of Music Societies was the allocation of the Arts Council funding to amateur music making societies throughout the country and advising how to make best use of this funding. Being on the Executive gave Margaret an insight into standards around the country and the criteria on which the funding decisions were made. I followed in Margaret's footsteps onto the National Executive as the Society's NFMS Representative.[97]

Before her accident, Margaret Robertson had had a preliminary interview with Michael Smedley, one of the shortlisted candidates to take over as chorus master for the 1978/79 season. He was subsequently appointed after having successfully taken a rehearsal in May, two days after the Society's performance of *The Dream of Gerontius*, conducted by Michael Rose. The review of the concert is quite short. Hans Freyhan opens with a reference to the *Minute Book* of 1902 where it stated that Dr Harding had proposed that the Society should perform *The Dream of Gerontius* during the forthcoming season. Hans Freyhan refers to this in the programme notes, assuming that the performance had taken place. As is now known, *The Dream of Gerontius* was not actually performed by the Society until 1910. Hans Freyhan reviewed the 1978 performance very favourably.[98]

The Musical Society contributed to the Tercentenary of the publication of John Bunyan's *The Pilgrim's Progress* by performing Vaughan Williams's cantata, *The Pilgrim's Journey*, in the opening concert of the 1978/79 season. Vaughan Williams had been interested in Bunyan from quite a young age, but he did not complete the opera *The Pilgrim's Progress* until 1949. It was premiered a couple of years later. After Vaughan Williams's death in 1958, excerpts from the opera were selected to make up the cantata. It was first performed in 1963. David Willcocks conducted the Bedford performance, and the Royal College of Music Chamber Orchestra accompanied the choir. The rehearsals were taken by the new chorus master, Michael Smedley. The full programme included other works by Vaughan Williams, *The Wasps* overture, *Serenade to Music* and *Toward the Unknown Region*. Hans Freyhan wrote in the review: 'In the Bunyan cantata, Pilgrim's Journey, choir and orchestra dealt successfully with the composer's considerable demands and the conductor steered them safely through the cliffs of the Vanity Fair scene.'[99] The reference to 'considerable demands' suggests that the choir found this work difficult, and they did. This is alluded to in the minutes of the committee meeting held a few days after the concert: 'Following a doubtful rehearsal, the choir had achieved a good performance, and both Sir David Willcocks and Mrs [*sic*] Ursula Vaughan Williams

[97] Personal interview with John Handley by the author. John Handley was instrumental in bringing the National Federation of Music Societies (NFMS) Annual Conference to Bedfordshire in 1981 when it was held in what is now Cranfield University. He was one of the '3 J's Team', which included Jo Churchill, who was later to become chairman of NFMS. Jo Churchill produced *The Way Ahead*, a critical review of the NFMS organisational structure, which led in due course to funding links with British Telecom and the name-change to Making Music. At this stage, Bedford was seen to be a shining light in the field of amateur music making, setting standards in quality of performance and imaginative initiatives.

[98] 'Under Michael Rose's accomplished direction, Elgar's large-scale structures were well defined and the contrasts and climaxes given full scope. The Society's chorus provided the conductor with a fervent response, which made its contribution a tower of strength throughout the evening.' Unusually, he was a little critical of one of the soloists because of his, 'occasional operatic mannerism'. *Bedfordshire Times*, 19 May 1978, p. 17.

[99] *Bedfordshire Times*, 10 November 1978, p. 21.

had expressed their pleasure.'[100] The Musical Society was obviously very pleased that Lady Ursula Vaughan Williams was able to come to the concert as the guest of honour.[101]

Michael Smedley conducted the Christmas concert on 13 December, the first of the Musical Society's concerts that he conducted. The programme included John Rutter's *Gloria*, but consisted otherwise of carols. A social event was held after the concert in St Peter's church hall.

Early in January 1979, in a very cold spell, the choir began rehearsals for the two April performances of Verdi's Requiem, which was to be performed with the Bedfordshire County Youth Orchestra. The first two rehearsals were held in the old hall of Bedford School with its wood panelled walls. Less than two months after these rehearsals, on Saturday 3 March, the hall was burnt down. It turned out to be arson – a burglar had started the fire.[102] Fortunately no one was killed or injured as the building was not used as living quarters by the school. Verdi's Requiem was performed first on 12 April, Maundy Thursday, and then on Sunday 29 April. Hans Freyhan, was fulsome in his praise, 'It was an exhilarating performance.'[103]

Michael Smedley conducted the June 1979 concert and was reappointed as chorus master 1979/80. He rehearsed the choir for Mendelssohn's *Elijah,* which David Willcocks conducted at the start of November. Trombonist Michael Hext was one of the players with the Royal College of Music orchestra, which played at the performance.

The Christmas concert, also conducted by Michael Smedley, included familiar carols with some audience participation. The 'choir-only' work was Bernstein's *Chichester Psalms* with organ, harp and percussion accompaniment. The organist was Brian Caves, still the Musical Society's accompanist. The work was very challenging. Hans Freyhan does not seem to have noticed the difficulties for he wrote: 'Michael Smedley propelled these (attractive modern) rhythms with unflagging vitality, obtaining a convincing response from the chorus who coped successfully with the tricky score.'[104]

100 *Committee Minutes*, 14 November 1978, BLARS X817/1/12.

101 John Handley remembers a totally unplanned *finale* to Lady Ursula's visit: 'After the concert, I took Lady Ursula to Bedford station for the last train to London. The station was deserted except for the person in the ticket office whom I recognised and to whom I introduced Lady Ursula. For the next five minutes they held an animated non-stop conversation, ending as Lady Ursula stepped into the train exclaiming: "I have never enjoyed myself so much at a railway station!" The person in the ticket office was the young Paul Edwards, Deirdre Knight's son. By working for British Rail, he could freely indulge his musical passion and organ playing talents, and was able to visit all the Three Choirs cathedrals and Festivals … He was particularly enthusiastic about Vaughan Williams's work.' Personal interview with John Handley by the author.

102 According to the *Bedfordshire Times*, 27 July 1979, pp. 1 & 5, Ian Ludman of Church Lane, Goldington, was found guilty of arson following his trial at Bedford Crown Court. He was sentenced to a long term of imprisonment. He set fire to the premises to destroy the evidence of his having broken into the building. He was traced as he had committed arson on two previous occasions.

103 'As the subdued supplication which opens Verdi's *Requiem*, came across the Corn Exchange … it set the atmosphere for a memorable performance which fulfilled the promise of those initial bars … The choir was in top form. Nowhere was this more evident than in the security and clear articulation which enhanced Verdi's brilliant fugal writing in the *Sanctus* and *Libera Me*. Both fugues were taken at very speedy tempo but showed no signs of strain … The Youth Orchestra lived up to expectations. The strings' precise attack in the unison passages of the *Dies Irae* was quite amazing.' *Bedfordshire Times*, 20 April 1979, p. 7.

104 *Bedfordshire Times*, 21 December 1979, p. 12.

Michael Rose conducted the first concert of 1980, Mozart's Solemn Vespers and Rossini's *Stabat Mater* – which Hans Freyhan refers to in his very brief review as 'two worthwhile additions to our local repertoire'.[105] The review may have been short because it was included in a review of a number of concerts, or because Hans Freyhan was not overly impressed with the performance. The National Federation of Music Societies observers at the concert thought that the standard of the performance was disappointingly low. Michael Rose agreed. Rehearsals for the Royal Albert Hall concert seemed to have got in the way.[106]

The Royal Albert Hall concert, on 17 April, celebrated the tenth anniversary of the first concert of the Bedfordshire County Youth Orchestra, and was given in aid of the British National Committee for the Prevention of Blindness. The main work was Beethoven's 'Choral' Symphony and the concert also included Borodin's *Polovtsian Dances*. Among the violinists listed were Susan Parry, now a successful soprano soloist, and Andrew Manze, now well-known as a soloist, conductor and broadcaster and an authority on Baroque music. Michael Hext was once more one of the trombonists.

A report of the Royal Albert Hall concert appeared in the following week's *Bedfordshire Times* of 25 April. This was written by one of the paper's feature writers, Doug Bowker, rather than by Hans Freyhan, which accounts for the references to 'Mike' rather than Michael Rose. In his relatively long report, Doug Bowker described what went on in rehearsal: 'The rapport between conductor, players and singers is vital. Mike Rose manages to keep music "fun", yet retains discipline, no small part of his remarkable make up.'[107] He did not attempt to review the concert itself, and his report ends as the concert began.

Michael Smedley conducted the June 1980 concert, and was to return to conduct the June 1981 concert. But Andrew Morris, director of music at Bedford School, was invited to be chorus master for the 1981/82 season. No reason is stated in the minutes for the change of chorus master, but it may have been to do with the payment of expenses. Michael Smedley came from Oxford – over fifty miles away – while Andrew Morris was local, well-qualified and available.

Andrew Morris was a boy chorister at Westminster Abbey under Sir William McKie. He gained a music scholarship to Bembridge School on the Isle of Wight, entered the Royal Academy of Music in 1967 and subsequently studied at the University of London before postgraduate research at Pembroke College, Cambridge. He was director of music at St Bartholomew the Great, London, 1972–79. During 1979–2011 he was director of music at Bedford School. During that time he developed the music school so that it was, in the words of a reporting inspector, 'one of the best non-specialist music schools in the country'.[108]

105 *Bedfordshire Times*, 4 April 1980, p. 11.
106 Notes of a special meeting between Michael Rose and Robert Atkins, 27 May 1980, BLARS X817/1/12.
107 *Bedfordshire Times*, 25 April 1980, p.16.
108 Andrew Morris has conducted most of the standard orchestral and choral repertoire and a large number of first performances of new works. He has worked with a number of well-known soloists, including Andrew Manze, Catherine Wyn-Rogers, Benjamin Luxon and James Bowman. He is a keyboard continuo player and has forty years' experience as an organist and harpsichordist. He has been president of the Music Masters' and Mistresses' Association and is currently on the Court of the Worshipful Company of Musicians, and is vice-chairman of the Friends of the Musicians' Chapel at

Andrew Morris' first task in his new role was to prepare the choir for Bach's *St John Passion,* which David Willcocks conducted in November 1980. Of this performance, Hans Freyhan was complimentary; the committee also felt that there had been an improvement in the standard of performance. Andrew Morris also played the harpsichord continuo.

As in 1980, Michael Rose conducted the Musical Society's concert at the end of March 1981, and another Royal Albert Hall concert at the end of April, this time in aid of the Christian Medical College and Hospital at Vellore, South India. In the first half of the concert, the orchestra performed Tchaikovsky's spectacular '1812 Overture'; the one work in the second half was equally spectacular, Berlioz's *Grande Messe des Morts*. Berlioz had been commissioned to write this Requiem in 1837 to commemorate the death of about twenty victims during the assassination attempt on Louis-Philippe, led by Fieschi, in 1835. Berlioz completed the work in three months, and it was first performed at Les Invalides in Paris at the end of 1837. The work calls for a very large orchestra with four additional brass bands performing off-stage in some movements. It also requires a large choir: the 750 voice Bedfordshire choir was ideally suited to such a work in the vast Royal Albert Hall. Hans Freyhan's brief review in the *Bedfordshire Times* stated: 'Michael Rose's unperturbed strategy ensure successful co-ordination between these large forces, as they produced the works super-climaxes … Admittedly not every problem was solved: there were a few shortcomings in intonation, and the male voices were a little tentative at times.'[109]

Michael Smedley conducted the Musical Society for the last time in June 1981. The work performed was Handel's *Acis and Galatea*, described by Hans Freyhan in the programme notes as a secular oratorio, but it has also been described as a serenata, a pastoral opera and a masque (it premiered as a masque in 1718). The part of Damon (a shepherd, like Acis) can be sung by a soprano, as happened at the original performance, or by a tenor. This confusion is reflected in the programme for the Bedford concert. It shows the names of two tenors, but where the four characters are listed, Damon is shown as a soprano. Two tenor soloists actually sang in the Bedford performance, both of them local, Reginald Searle and Bonaventura Bottone. Hans Freyhan wrote in his review: 'As Acis, Bonaventura Bottone struck the right medium between the hero's metal timbre and the gentle lover's *bel* canto, while not neglecting the demands of drama in the death scene. The lover's duet (with Helen Walker) was delightfully blended.'[110] Only seventy-six members of the choir sang in the concert. There were only about two hundred people in the audience.

On 29 July 1981, Prince Charles married Lady Diana Spencer in Westminster Abbey. David Willcocks was asked to conduct the Bach Choir during the signing of the register.[111] In the middle of November, David Willcocks once again returned to Bedford to conduct the Musical Society. The first half of the concert was rather

the National Musicians' Church of St Sepulchre, Holborn, London. http://www.andrewmorrisconductor.com/, accessed January 2015.

109 *Bedfordshire Times*, 1 May 1981, p. 17.

110 *Bedfordshire Times*, 18 June 1981, p. 15.

111 See Owen, *A Life in Music – Conversations with Sir David Willcocks and Friends,*pp. 201–3.

special, as Hans Freyhan noted in his review: 'To watch Sir David Willcocks conduct two of Handel's Coronation Anthems at the Corn Exchange brought back vivid memories of this year's Royal Wedding when we all saw him on our screens, in action at St. Paul's Cathedral. A great Handelian, he transmitted in Bedford, too, his bouncing energy to the choir and orchestra, casting his spell over them … The choir's famous entry in *Zadok the Priest* was quite overwhelming.'[112]

The main work was Mozart's Mass in C Minor. Bonaventura Bottone took over as tenor soloist (from Charles Daniels) at very short notice and, according to Hans Freyhan, he: 'proved himself as splendidly as he had done as Jose in the recent production of Carmen at the Corn Exchange.'[113]

The spring 1982 concert took place in late February when one of Elgar's large scale works, *The Kingdom*, was performed.[114] This was the first concert that Andrew Morris conducted, although he had been chorus master since September 1980. Hans Freyhan was very complimentary about him in his review of the concert.[115] He was also very complimentary about the soprano soloist, Wendy Eathorne: 'The soprano's top notes had a real splendour, and she made Mary's extended solo "The Sun Goeth Down" one of the evening's greatest experiences.'[116] The committee noted that: 'the choir had achieved a very high standard. The Bedfordshire Symphony Orchestra was very large and very noisy but had sold a very small number of tickets.'[117]

The summer 1982 concert was one of a series of concerts given to celebrate the rebuilding of Bedford School hall, and included music by Kodály, Vaughan Williams, Walton and a new piece by Paul Patterson, *Canterbury Psalms*. The work was not linked to Chaucer's *Canterbury Tales*, but was named because Paul Patterson had been appointed as composer-in-residence at King's School, Canterbury.[118] It was written for the school and dedicated to Alan Ridout; the first performance took place in Canterbury Cathedral in March 1981. Pat Jones, a long-standing member of the Musical Society choir, recalled that the choir's first entry in the rehearsal had been tentative. Paul Patterson, who was present, thought that it had been very effective and said that he would like to change the score so that it always sounded like that. Hans Freyhan made very little comment about Patterson's work apart from stating that it had been enjoyed by performers and audience alike.

The Musical Society performed Dvořák's *Stabat Mater* on 6 November. David Willcocks conducted, and the Royal College of Music Chamber Orchestra accompanied the choir. Among the soloists was Catherine Wyn-Rogers. David Willcocks is very complimentary about her in his book: 'Among the contraltos (who sang with the Bach Choir), Dame Janet Baker was outstanding, as was Catherine Wyn-Rogers, some twenty-five years younger than Dame Janet and a former student at the Royal College.'[119]

[112] *Bedfordshire Times*, 19 November 1981, p. 17.
[113] Ibid.
[114] This was the first performance of *The Kingdom* in Bedford.
[115] '[He] not only succeeded in establishing safe co-ordination between these large forces (Bedford Musical Society's Chorus and the Bedfordshire Symphony Orchestra) but also in bringing his artistic vision to bear on them.' *Bedfordshire Times*, 25 February 1982, p. 15.
[116] Ibid.
[117] *Committee Minutes*, 30 March 1982, BLARS X817/1/12.
[118] Paul Patterson was subsequently composer in residence for a year at Bedford School.
[119] Owen, *A Life in Music – Conversations with Sir David Willcocks and Friends*, p. 201.

The Musical Society's programme for 1983 was dominated by English music, in March, Vaughan Williams's *Five Tudor Portraits*; in May, Britten's *St Nicolas* and Lambert's *Rio Grande*; in November, Willcocks's *Voices of Time*; and in December, Finzi's *In Terra Pax*. The March concert, which also included Poulenc's *Gloria*, was held in Bedford School Hall and was, to quote from the committee minutes, 'a success musically but a financial disaster.' No explanation is given for this, but the reason is implicit in the resolution that followed: 'That major expenditure on orchestra and soloists would in future be permitted only when the concert was likely to attract a large audience.'[120] The orchestra was from the Royal Academy of Music. Brian Kay's wife, Gillian Fisher, was the soprano soloist and Ian Caddy – this was early in his very successful career – was the baritone soloist.

Because the financial situation was so unsatisfactory, the May concert, conducted by Michael Rose, was held in St Paul's church instead of in the Corn Exchange as had originally been planned. Along with works by Britten and Lambert, Michael Rose's son, Stephen, and Andrew Manze were the soloists in Bach's Concerto for Two Violins. Hans Freyhan wrote that they: 'gave an accurate and musicianly account of the solo parts, refreshingly unsentimental in the famous Largo.'[121]

One of Bedford's leading businesses, Kilroy Estate Agents, sponsored the five concerts that made up the 1983/84 season. Special programmes were produced.[122] The first concert in the series was conducted by David Willcocks and his son, Jonathan, who conducted his own work *Voices of Time*. This work had been premiered in 1980. It is a setting of Biblical texts and English poetry reflecting the significance of time. Hans Freyhan wrote in his review that: 'The musical language is never extravagant and is well accessible to the ordinary listener: it is based on sound English choral traditions.'[123] He adds, naughtily: 'with a touch of Orff as a wholesome ingredient.'[124] And as a final comment: 'The sincere applause of the capacity audience proved that a contemporary composer can secure a spontaneous impact.'[125] However, Mozart's Clarinet Concerto and Handel's *Ode for St Cecilia's Day* also probably helped to attract the audience,. David Willcocks waived his fee because the Musical Society had performed Jonathan's work. The Musical Society commissioned another work from Jonathan Willcocks a few years later and this was given its premiere in 1986.[126]

The main musical events in 1984 were the performances of Monteverdi's Vespers. The first performance was in May in St Paul's church, and the second was three weeks later, on 2 June, in St Alban's Cathedral. This was the first time that the Musical Society had performed this major work, which had become such a firm favourite in the choral repertoire during the second half of the twentieth century. For the performance in St Paul's church, the choir sat in the north aisle and was joined by the choristers of St Alban's Cathedral.[127] Among the six soloists was Brian Kay,

120 *Committee Minutes*, 15 March 1983, BLARS X817/1/12.
121 *Bedfordshire Times*, 26 May 1983, p. 13.
122 Chris Kilroy subsequently sold the business to Taylor's Estate Agents.
123 *Bedfordshire Times*, 10 November 1983, p. 10.
124 Ibid.
125 Ibid.
126 *Committee Minutes,* 5 November 1983, BLARS X817/1/12.
127 Hans Freyhan wrote of the performance: 'The conductor, Andrew Morris, kept all his forces well

who had previously sung with the Musical Society in 1967. In January 1984 he had been appointed chorus master of Huddersfield Choral Society.[128]

At the September 1984 committee meeting it was decided not to renew Andrew Morris's engagement as chorus master. Instead, from September 1985, the position was offered to Ian Smith.

The first concert of the new season was not held until 1 December 1984, and included works by Holst, Elgar and Delius, commemorating the fiftieth anniversary of their deaths. The main work was Elgar's *The Music Makers*, last performed in 1944. Hans Freyhan described it as: 'immensely personal, laying bare much of the composer's innermost mind and feelings, partly by means of self-quotation from some of his main works.'[129] This is a generous interpretation by a critic who was often generous in his reviews.

The first performance of 1985 was Brahms's *German Requiem*, conducted by Michael Rose. This concert was given to celebrate the founding of the National Federation of Music Societies on 23 February (the day of the concert) fifty years previously. The choir sang in German. Hans Freyhan questioned whether this was a good idea because the Biblical texts chosen by Brahms: 'produce a greater emotional impact on English audiences when the music is linked to the familiar words of the English Authorised Version.'[130] He thought that the Society's chorus tackled the linguistic problem valiantly. But singing in German had caused issues according to the minutes of the committee meeting that followed the concert, and the following resolution was passed: 'Except in the case of Latin church music, the rehearsal and performance of a work in a language other than English requires the approval of the Programme Sub-Committee in collaboration with the conductor.'[131] The concert was well supported and, despite the language problem, the performance was considered to have been successful. The other work performed was Schumann's Piano Concerto in A Minor, in which the soloist was Vovka Ashkenazy, eldest son of Vladimir Ashkenazy.[132] Biographies of soloists were printed for the first time in the programmes for this concert.

Andrew Morris conducted the Musical Society for the last time in a performance of Handel's *Samson* in May. Beside Hans Freyhan's very favourable review in the *Bedfordshire Times* there is a photograph that includes three leading members of the Society, Alan Stevens, Paul Andrews and Gary Mudd.[133] They had represented

under control and ensured safe co-ordination. Above all, he gave full scope to Monteverdi's magnificent climaxes which often mark the end of choral movements. The Society's chorus gave him ardent support ... A team of highly competent soloists ... all tackled their very demanding parts with admirable technical assurance and stylish insight.' *Bedfordshire Times*, 17 May 1984, p. 8.

128 Later, after his time at the Huddersfield Choral Society, Brian Kay became a regular broadcaster and subsequently followed David Willcocks as principal conductor of the 'Really Big Chorus' series of concerts held in the Royal Albert Hall.

129 *Bedfordshire Times*, 13 December 1984, p. 18.

130 *Bedfordshire Times*, 28 February 1985, p. 12.

131 *Committee Minutes*, 3 April 1985, BLARS X817/1/12.

132 Hans Freyhan wrote in his review: 'I still have memories (and a programme) of another Bedford Musical Society concert, back in November 1955, when the same work was performed by the soloist's mother, the then Icelandic teenage pianist Thorunn Tryggvason (who later married Vladimir Ashkenazy), with the Royal Philharmonic Orchestra conducted by Clarence Raybould.' *Bedfordshire Times*, 28 February 1985, p. 12.

133 *Bedfordshire Times*, 16 May 1985, p. 13.

the Musical Society in the Bedford Music Club's annual quiz and had recently won the competition.

At the annual general meeting in July, it was confirmed that Richard Heyes, who had been appointed accompanist during the year, would continue to be accompanist for the coming season. Richard Heyes had been appointed to the staff of Bedford School in 1982, and was to remain the Musical Society's accompanist for twenty years. Susan Moody was elected chorus secretary in place of Paula Hakon.

Susan Moody, née Horwood, was born in Oxford, and moved to Bedford with her then husband, John Moody, in the 1970s. In 1984, she published the first of her Penny Wanawake series of detective novels, *Penny Black*. The amateur detective is a six-foot, beautiful, black photographer. Since then, Susan Moody has written over twenty novels. Perhaps the best-known is *Love Over Gold*, the novelisation of the Nescafe Gold Blend advertisements. Susan Moody was, for a time, the chairman of the Crime Writers' Association. She subsequently married Australian John Donaldson and became the step-mother-in-law of Frederick, Crown Prince of Denmark, when he married John Donaldson's daughter, Mary, in 2004.[134] Susan Moody was chorus secretary for one year.[135]

Rehearsals began in September 1985 with Ian Smith, the new chorus master. The work performed in November was Bach's Mass in B Minor with David Willcocks conducting. The performance, in the Great Hall of Bedford School, celebrated the tercentenary of Bach's birth in March 1685. There is a glowing report of the concert in the minutes of the subsequent committee meeting: 'Bach's B minor Mass … had been an outstanding success. The soloists had performed well, the orchestra had given Sir David Willcocks particular satisfaction, and Sir David considered that this was the best concert that the choir had given under his direction. All tickets had been sold and many members of the audience had expressed their appreciation of the choir's performance. Sir David had drawn attention to the splendid way in which Ian Smith had prepared the choir.'[136] The soloists were husband and wife team Kathleen Livingstone (soprano) and Neil Mackie (tenor), along with Margaret Cable (contralto) and Ian Caddy (bass).

Ian Smith (1951–)

Ian Smith was born in London and began learning the violin when he was six years old, studying at the Blackheath Conservatoire of Music under Penelope Howard. Whilst there he was encouraged by the principal, Robert Munns, and played for the Blackheath String Orchestra, becoming leader at the age of sixteen.[137] After leaving school he went to York University to study a combined music and maths degree. Graduating in 1972, he continued his studies at Cambridge University gaining a

134 *Bedfordshire on Sunday*, 19 October 2003, p. 3.

135 Susan Moody's brother, William Horwood, was, like Susan, an author. His works include the successful *Duncton Wood* chronicles.

136 *Committee Minutes*, 26 November 1985, BLARS X817/1/12. There was a detailed preview with a photograph of David Willcocks in the *Bedfordshire Times*, 21 November 1985, p. 12, the day before the concert.

137 The information that follows is from a personal communication with Ian Smith by the author.

postgraduate certificate in education. At Cambridge, he studied violin with Nicholas Dowding (then leader of the Fitzwilliam String Quartet) and also with Eta Cohen.

Ian Smith's first teaching post was as resident violin teacher at Cranleigh School in Surrey, whilst there he played regularly under Vernon Handley in the Guildford Philharmonic Orchestra and in other professional orchestras. He was also appointed assistant conductor of the Guildford Choral Society, his first conducting post, which he held for four years.[138] After two years at Cranleigh he moved to Milton Keynes as head of music at Stantonbury Campus. There, as well as teaching, he worked extensively as a player and conductor, and was actively involved with young people through the Saturday Morning Music Centre. He also led Milton Keynes Sinfonia for a number of years. In 1977 he took up the post as musical director of the Danesborough Chorus, a post which he still holds. In 1981 Ian Smith moved to teach in Bedford at Pilgrim School. He was appointed conductor of the Bedfordshire County Youth Second Orchestra in 1982, and became chorus master of the Musical Society in 1985.[139]

The first concert conducted by Ian Smith was the December 1985 carol concert, with orchestral accompaniment; this included Vivaldi's Magnificat. The tenor soloist was Peter Hoare, at the time working for Bedfordshire Education Authority teaching percussion. He went on to have a successful career as a tenor with the Welsh National Opera and subsequently at Glyndebourne, the Royal Opera House, Covent Garden and La Scala, Milan.

The final concert of the season, early in June 1986, was performed in St Paul's church, with organ accompaniment. Although there was a fall-off in attendance by members of the choir, and the audience was relatively small, this was the one concert of the season which did not make a loss. The choir sang two of Bruckner's motets unaccompanied. The programme also included Kodály's *Missa Brevis*, which was composed in Budapest during the Russian siege of 1944. By the 1980s it had become a firm favourite.

The November concert included one of Handel's 'Chandos Anthems' and Beethoven's Mass in C conducted by David Willcocks. Jonathan Willcocks conducted *The Riddle of the World*, which had been commissioned by the Musical Society. He also undertook the rehearsals for his work beginning a couple of weeks before the concert. According to the minutes of the committee meeting following the concert: 'Jonathan Willcocks had been delighted by the way in which the choir had performed his new work.'[140] Not so, David Willcocks: the minutes read: 'Sir David had been very dissatisfied with the choir's performance and this had originated at the rehearsal that he had held on Saturday 1st November, a week before the concert. This had been poorly attended and the choir sang badly. The concert had

138 Ian Smith still does some orchestral conducting, notably of the Milton Keynes City Orchestra. He is also leader of the Beverley String Quartet.

139 Ian Smith later became head of Bedfordshire Music, a post he held for eleven years. This was followed by a return to the classroom as director of music, head of expressive arts and assistant head teacher at Wootton Upper School. During this period he also regularly conducted the Bedfordshire County Youth Second Orchestra, which included conducting them several times at the Edinburgh Festival. Ian Smith has adjudicated at music festivals and has made a number of radio recordings and television appearances for both the BBC and ITV.

140 *Committee Minutes*, 25 November 1986, BLARS X817/1/12.

been reasonably well attended. The Corn Exchange had been extremely hot and the long rehearsal during the afternoon and the long concert had proved rather taxing. Ian Smith thanked the choir for its efforts but it was agreed that the programme had been too long for the rehearsal period.'[141] The tenor section was quite small at the time and struggled with the Handel anthem 'O Praise the Lord with One Consent'. Ian Smith explained later that one of the leading tenors, Frank Wilkinson, had not been able to be at the rehearsal and that the other tenors – there were only a few – found the music difficult without his strong leadership.[142]

The carol concert in December was recorded and broadcast twice by BBC Radio Bedfordshire, on the Sunday before Christmas (21 December) and on Christmas Eve.

The 1987 season opened with the Musical Society's first performance of Tippett's *A Child of Our Time*. This impressive and moving work was composed just before the start of the Second World War, when Tippett was still in his thirties, and was first performed in the Adelphi Theatre in London in March 1944, with Walter Goehr conducting. The choir of Morley College, South London, where Tippett was teaching, took part. Among the soloists in that first performance was Peter Pears, then a singer with Sadler's Wells opera.

For the Musical Society performance, the Bedford Sinfonia was conducted by Michael Rose. The soloists included Susan Parry (contralto), who was at the start of a promising musical career. The soprano soloist was Carol Lesley-Green who lived locally. Hans Freyhan wrote of Carol Lesley-Green that she: 'made a truly outstanding contribution, excelling in her glorious high tessitura and commanding a wide dynamic range.'[143] The orchestra also played Tippett's Concerto for Double String Orchestra.

At the 1987 annual general meeting, held early in September, the author was elected to the committee, and Alan Stevens was elected chairman. Robert Atkins had expected to be elected chairman, and Alan Steven's election resulted in Robert Atkins tendering his resignation. Fortunately a compromise was found before the meeting was reconvened a week later. Robert Atkins, who had worked indefatigably for the Society as general secretary since 1971, was elected chairman, but gave notice that he would stand down at the end of the season.

Shortly after the November 1986 concert, which had left David Willcocks so dissatisfied with the choir's performance, Robert Atkins had written to invite him to conduct the November 1987 concert. David Willcocks accepted, but with some reasonable stipulations, mainly about choir members' attendance at rehearsals. In a post script he wrote: 'I think that next year ought to be my last as I think I should make way for a younger person. Ian Smith is clearly doing very good work.'[144] So the November 1987 concert was the last to be conducted by David Willcocks. It included Haydn's second setting of his Te Deum and Mozart's Requiem and Oboe Concerto. Of the performance of the Requiem, as of the other works, Hans Freyhan was full of praise in his review: 'To Sir David's superb direction, choir and orchestra

141 Ibid.

142 Personal interview with Ian Smith by the author.

143 *Bedfordshire Times*, 2 April 1987, p. 12.

144 *Committee Minutes*, 25 November 1986, Letter from David Willcocks, BLARS X817/1/12.

made a magnificent response, highlighting the dramatic element of the score as much as its rhythmical power.'[145] It was a notable occasion. Hans Freyhan's review opened with a memorable headline over a worthy valedictory statement, 'CLASSIC END TO AN ERA'. He continued:

> A packed Corn Exchange witnessed the farewell concert of Sir David Willcocks with the chorus of the Musical Society. This was the end of an era of glorious music making in Bedford over a period of 28 years, in which one of our times' most outstanding choral conductors gave unforgettable performances of the main repertoire of the choral classics in our town.[146]

The March 1988 concert, the third of the season, was also special. It was Bach's *St Matthew Passion* conducted by Michael Rose. The Bedford Sinfonia was divided into two orchestras, the first led by Jan Kaznowski and the second by the Musical Society's chorus master, Ian Smith. The very fine team of soloists included Ian Partridge, one of Britain's leading lyric tenors singing the part of the Evangelist, and Ian Caddy, especially well-known for his opera performances and as a master of baroque singing, in the part of Christ. Susan Parry returned once more to Bedford as the contralto soloist. The following note was included in the programme: 'In view of the sacred nature of the work, it is requested that there should be NO APPLAUSE!'[147]

The final concert of this memorable season consisted of English music from the very end of the nineteenth century, *Hiawatha's Wedding Feast* by Coleridge-Taylor and *Sea Pictures* by Elgar, as well as Stanford's *Songs of the Fleet*, from the early twentieth century. This was the last concert that the Society sang as the Bedford Musical Society.

During the 1988 summer holiday period, some sixty members of the Musical Society took part in the Cambridge Festival's concert in Ely Cathedral. The main work was a performance of Berlioz's *Grande Messe du Morts* with Russell Keable conducting. On the coach going to Ely, John Watson told the author that he had agreed to stand as the new general secretary in succession to Robert Atkins, who was standing down after seventeen years. John Watson had been deputy county librarian for Bedfordshire Library Service for many years until his retirement in 1988. He was duly elected at the 1988 annual general meeting, which was held in September. At this meeting, Ian Smith was appointed as the Musical Society's conductor. He was the first official holder of the post since Clarence Raybould had resigned thirty years earlier.

For many years, Robert Atkins had expected that David Willcocks would accept the appointment as president when he gave up conducting the Society's concerts. However, in his final report to the annual general meeting, Robert Atkins wrote that David Willcocks was less enthusiastic about this than when he had been approached after the October 1975 concert.[148] The post had been unfilled since Sir Thomas

145 *Bedfordshire Times*, 19 November 1987, p. 22.
146 Ibid.
147 *Concert Programme*, 19 March 1988, p. 8, BLARS X817/3/120.
148 *Annual General Meeting Minutes*, 12 September 1988, Bedford Choral Society. In this final annual report he added: 'Even now, I can't explain why the Society has always mattered so much to me and why I have always been so willing to fight its battles. I am very grateful for the enormous satisfaction

Armstrong stood down in 1976 and, after 1987, remained unfilled until 1993. Alan Stevens, chairman at the 1989 annual general meeting reported that: 'the position of President was still vacant, but he was actively sounding out a suitable person.'[149]

An item under the heading 'Change of Name' was discussed originally at the 1987 annual general meeting: 'The Society considered that the name of the Society was no longer appropriate and agreed to submit suggestions which they preferred.'[150] Essentially, the Musical Society's 'function' as a choral society was not evident from its name. Of the forty or so suggestions for the new name submitted in time for the October committee meeting, thirty people very sensibly proposed the name 'Bedford Choral Society'. This was approved by the committee, and the name change was agreed at an extraordinary general meeting in May 1988.

The first concert given by the Society under its new name was Haydn's *Creation*, in November 1988. Ian Smith, now the Choral Society's appointed conductor, conducted the performance. Hans Freyhan was duly complimentary about him in a brief review: 'The evening's greatest merit lay with the conductor, whose interpretation carried real conviction and spontaneity, and demonstrated the towering greatness of Haydn's master work.'[151]

Early in 1989, some forty members of the Choral Society took part in *Highway*, ITV's religious alternative to BBC's *Songs of Praise*. The programme, from Olney, Buckinghamshire, was shown in March and celebrated the life and work of John Newton and William Cowper. Sir Harry Secombe introduced the programme. Members of the choir travelled by coach from Bedford to a recording studio near the old football stadium at Wembley on a weekday in February to record the hymns. The orchestral accompaniment, which had been pre-recorded, was played as the choir sang. The choir then had to be filmed singing with Harry Secombe, first in Olney parish church, and then, a couple of days later, in the Baptist church which is to the west of the Market Square. The hymns were 'Glorious Things of Thee are Spoken' by John Newton of Olney (to Haydn's fine tune) and 'Jesus, Where'er Thy People Meet' by William Cowper to the tune by William Knapp. The choir was not actually recorded when it sang in either church. In the second verse of 'Glorious Things of Thee are Spoken', Harry Secombe muddled his words and sang, 'we'll supply thy sons and daughters'. He had to stand for long periods for the technicians

and pleasure which my wife and I have been given in taking part. I shall watch the Society's progress with great interest and confidence.'

149 *Annual General Meeting Minutes*, 4 September 1989, Bedford Choral Society. Samuel Whitbread was unanimously elected president at the 1994 annual general meeting.

150 *Annual General Meeting Minutes*, 7 September 1987, Bedford Choral Society.

151 *Bedfordshire Times*, 17 November 1988, p. 21. In the programme notes, Hans Freyhan refers to one of the Society's early programmes: 'An old programme booklet shows that Bedford Musical Society gave a performance of Haydn's "Creation" on May 15 1888, at the Corn Exchange. (At that time, Brahms, Bruckner and Verdi were still alive and working on new masterpieces!). The concert was the second in the Society's 22nd season, and it was given by a Band and Chorus of nearly 200 performers.' There was what is called 'professional stiffening' for: 'The Band will be assisted by eminent performers from the London Orchestras' [names follow].The conductor was P. H. Diemer, R.A.M. who also contributed the programme notes. His concluding words well deserve quotation: 'Whatever the music of the future may be, it will be long before it can displace so great a work as Haydn's "Creation" from the hearts and affections of the English nation.' *Concert Programme*, author's collection.

to prepare for filming and he cracked little jokes while he waited. Members of the Choral Society were an enthusiastic audience.[152]

The March 1989 concert was devoted to the work of Vaughan Williams. The choral works performed were the *Serenade to Music* and the *Sea Symphony* (Symphony No. 1). BBC Radio Bedfordshire recorded the *Sea Symphony*, which was eventually broadcast on 12 August 1989.

Back in September 1961, the possibility of the Society celebrating its centenary was raised by Mr Hooper. The minutes from the period indicate that no one seemed to know when the centenary should actually be celebrated. Alderman Richard Turner agreed to look through the old records in Bedford Library, but did not have any success. The honorary secretary at the time, Tom Winter, found out the details some months later. The relevant minute from the meeting held in May 1962 reads: 'The Hon. Secretary reported that he had searched the old Minute Books of the Society in the Library and found that the Society was formed on 16th January 1867. The matter of the centenary celebrations was left in abeyance.'[153] The idea of celebrating the centenary was forgotten by 1967, and no celebrations were held. However, it was decided that the Choral Society should celebrate its 125th anniversary season, and in July 1989 the first special meeting was held to consider initial arrangements. It was thought that the Society had been founded in 1866, which some sources, for example Joyce Godber in her *History of Bedfordshire*, state.[154] The new general secretary, John Watson, and the committee accepted 1866 as the correct date, so plans for holding the anniversary in 1991 and making it a very special season went ahead. Provisional programmes for the three concerts were suggested, including a performance of Handel's *Messiah* in March. It was also agreed that the Choral Society should commission a fifteen to twenty minute long work.

The 1989/90 season, before the anniversary year, was more modest. The November and March concerts each comprised several shorter works. In November, the choral works were Bruckner's Mass in E Minor and Stravinsky's *Symphony of Psalms*. In March, the choral works were Britten's *Cantata Academica* and Dvořák's Te Deum, conducted by Michael Rose. In his report to the 1990 annual general meeting, the general secretary, John Watson wrote: 'The November and March concerts attracted disappointing audiences, partly due, one assumes, to the content of the programmes which included some modern music which is more difficult 'to sell' to our supporters.'[155] Only the Christmas 1989 concert made a surplus. This was because there was an organ rather than orchestral accompaniment, and the only soloist was the organist, Richard Heyes, the Choral Society's accompanist. *Elijah* was performed in June 1990. Although it was a well-known and popular work, ticket sales were disappointing – perhaps because some members of the choir and regular supporters were on holiday. The performance itself was very successful. Jeremy White sang the part of Elijah, bringing to the title part, as Hans Freyhan put it in the review: 'his powerful bass and the necessary authority'.[156]

152 Author's reminiscence.
153 *Minute Book 1951–62*, 2 May 1962, BLARS X817/1/9.
154 Joyce Godber, *History of Bedfordshire 1066–1888* (Bedford, 1969), p. 524.
155 *Annual General Meeting Minutes*, 3 September 1990, Bedford Choral Society.
156 *Bedfordshire Times*, 22 June 1990, p. 15.

The 1989/90 season was extended to include the December 1990 concert. This was not a Christmas carol concert. The programme included Nielsen's delightful *Springtime in Funen*. Funen (Fyn) is the island between the Danish mainland (Jutland) and Zealand, where Nielsen was born and grew up. The other larger work was John Dankworth's *The Diamond and the Goose*.

John Dankworth, better known as a jazz musician, began writing film scores in the early 1960s. A decade later, after establishing, with his wife Cleo Laine, the arts centre now known as The Stables, Wavendon (where they lived), he became more interested in a broad spectrum of music that included orchestral and choral works. *The Diamond and the Goose* was commissioned by the City of Birmingham Choir to celebrate its sixtieth anniversary in 1981. The work is a cantata based on one of Sherlock Holmes's short detective stories, *The Blue Carbuncle*. In the programme notes, Victor Bainbridge wrote: 'For the record, the choral writing is rather unusual. There is a preponderance of, almost an obsession with, syllabic writing, the chorus being, almost without exception, used as homophonic chord singing. In this role, they provide not only a Sullivanesque commentary on what's going on but a distinctly new-look one. Theirs is not an easy task.'[157] In his review following the concert, Hans Freyhan notes that: 'Choir, orchestra and conductor enjoyed themselves splendidly in their utterly attractive task … John Dankworth attended the concert and was given a tremendous ovation.'[158]

The year of 1991, in which the Choral Society celebrated its 125th anniversary, started with members of the choir joining many other Bedfordshire choral societies and school choirs at the Bedfordshire County Youth Orchestra's twenty-first birthday concert in the Royal Albert Hall, with, once more, Michael Rose conducting.[159] The programme included Dvořák's Te Deum and Mahler's Symphony No. 2 (the 'Resurrection' Symphony). The concert was a spectacular opening to the Choral Society's own anniversary year. The *Bedfordshire Times* two-page report concentrated on the orchestra.

There was only one more Royal Albert Hall concert at which the County Youth Orchestra was joined by massed choirs from Bedfordshire for major choral works. There were a number of reasons for this, including the fact that Michael Rose had retired as county music adviser. From then on, the Royal Albert Hall concerts were entirely for youth groups – orchestras of different levels, brass bands and smaller choirs.

The first of the Choral Society's own concerts during the anniversary year was a performance of *Messiah*, given in the middle of March. There was something new for this concert; the posters and programmes were redesigned. The programmes were A5 in size, with coloured covers and, notably, introduced the Choral Society's new logo. The general secretary, John Watson, had reported to the committee the previous September that a consultant, Tristan Wooston of Buckingham, would

157 *Concert Programme*, 1 December 1990, p. 5, Bedford Choral Society.

158 *Bedfordshire Times*, 14 December 1990, p.15. A special Sherlock Holmes exhibition was organised in Bedford Central Library in conjunction with this concert.

159 *Bedfordshire Times*, 11 January 1991, pp. 10–11. The report included information about the orchestral players, with a number of photographs. There is little about the choirs, however.

prepare a selection of designs. Subsequently, some of the designs were put to members of the committee, who selected the one that they preferred.

Michael Rose conducted *Messiah*, with the Milton Keynes Chamber Orchestra accompanying the choir. Hans Freyhan was hugely impressed by Michael Rose's interpretation: 'His supreme musicianship gave to Handel's vigorous rhythms the right vitality and incisiveness.'[160]

For the anniversary year, the programme covers and the details about the conductors and soloists were pre-printed. A photograph of a section of the choir and the brass section of the orchestra, with the tubas given prominence, enveloped the front and back of the covers. Only the centre four pages of the programmes (eight pages for the November concert) specifically related to each particular concert. As a result, it was reported at the March committee meeting that some members of the chorus and the audience had complained at the cost of programmes (£1–00). In subsequent years, only the covers and advertisements were pre-printed.

The June concert opened with Mozart's *Regina Coeli*, to commemorate his death two hundred years earlier. This was followed by Beethoven's Violin Concerto in D with Andrew Watkinson, leader of the renowned Endellion String Quartet, as the soloist. The choir's chief contribution was Cherubini's Requiem in C Minor.[161]

The main concert of the year was given on Saturday 9 November. A preview of the gala performance was published in the *Bedfordshire Times* shortly before.[162] The preview included a photograph of the choir in rehearsal at Pilgrim School. The author was interviewed about the Choral Society and its history by Malcolm Singer on BBC Radio Bedfordshire's arts programme *Tabs* on Sunday 3 November. The concert was sponsored by British Telecomm, and a note in the programme read: 'We're particularly happy to be supporting the 125th Anniversary Gala concert because, at BT, we always try to be in tune with people's needs.'[163] The Bedford Sinfonia accompanied the choir, and Ian Smith conducted the concert.

The Choral Society commissioned a special work, *Ode to Saint Cecilia*, for the occasion. The composer, Elis Pehkonen, was English-born, though his father was Finnish. The Society had paid for a work of approximately fifteen minutes, but Pehkonen generously wrote a work of seven movements that was more than double the length and did not ask for any additional fee.[164] He wrote the programme notes himself: 'I have made up my own libretto by arranging a sequence of texts and verses from Striggio (the author of Monteverdi's *Orfeo* texts), John Milton and Thomas

160 *Bedfordshire Times*, 22 March 1991, p. 13. The previous week's edition (15 March 1991, p. 13) included a report about the 125th anniversary, with a photograph of the choir rehearsing in Pilgrim School hall. Michael Rose, who was taking the rehearsal, is shown seated at the piano.

161 In style and mood, this is mid-way between the dramatic power of the Requiems of Berlioz and Verdi and the reticence of Fauré. Hans Freyhan wrote: 'Throughout the work, choir and orchestra contributed a disciplined and sympathetic response. The magnificent large fugue in the *Offertorium* became a veritable feast of concise contrapuntal singing and playing. Unusually, Cherubini's *C minor Requiem* does not have any solo parts.' *Bedfordshire Times*, 14 June 1991, p.12.

162 The preview used the author's article about the Choral Society's history published in *The Bedfordshire Magazine* at the beginning of December, as a basis for its information. Unfortunately, columns two and three of the preview were reversed, making the account somewhat garbled. *Bedfordshire Times*, 25 October 1991, p. 17.

163 *Concert Programme*, 9 November 1991, p. 12, Bedford Choral Society.

164 The *Ode to St Cecilia* was originally commissioned for fifteen minutes at £200 per minute. It actually lasted for forty-five minutes.

Campion. In addition there are the traditional lines associated with St. Cecilia Odes, one or two lines by the Jacobean poet Crashaw, and one or two lines of my own making.'[165] He then goes on to say a little about St Cecilia, about whom very little is known, and about Purcell's and Handel's odes: 'My own *Ode to St. Cecilia* is rather different, although it begins and ends in the same manner as the classical odes. In fact the interesting texts are really nothing to do specifically or literally with Cecilia, but, by virtue of "poetic licence" she is firmly characterised as a kind of female Orpheus, Queen of Arcadia, and a Saintly person all rolled into one.'[166] He ends by writing: 'It is not contemporary music, whatever that is: it is simply music and must stand or fall on its own merit. But I do hope that it gives pleasure to both listeners and performers.'[167] Hans Freyhan quotes the conclusion of the programme in a longer than usual *Bedfordshire Times* review of the concert, noting: 'The choir sang with much needed conviction. The audience extended to the composer its sincere welcome to his work.'[168] Ian Smith commented after the concert: 'this was not one of the better performances by the Chorus, but the increased length of *Ode to Cecilia* had been a factor in the standard of the performance.'[169]

The review included photographs of the choir and orchestra at the concert, one of John Watson with two choir members; The Mayor of North Bedfordshire, Janice Lennon; and Bob Randall of BT at the reception in the Harpur Centre after the concert. One of the choir members, Celia Wright, is shown cutting the cake made to mark the 125th anniversary. Guests for the concert included the chairman of the National Federation of Music Societies, Miss Jo Churchill, OBE.

The final concert for this memorable year was a family Christmas carol concert held on 14 December. The gala concert was broadcast on BBC Radio Bedfordshire on Sunday 22 December 1991 at 2.30p.m. It was a fitting end to an unforgettable year.

Happily, the Choral Society continues to thrive.

165 *Concert Programme*, 9 November 1991, p. 9, Bedford Choral Society.
166 Ibid.
167 Ibid
168 *Bedfordshire Times*, 15 November 1991, p. 8.
169 *Committee Minutes*, 12 November 1991, Bedford Choral Society.

Afterword
Bedford Choral Society, 1991–2015

Ian Smith

Since 1991, the Choral Society has continued to perform at least three concerts every year as well as regularly presenting a Christmas carol concert. In recent years there have also been many requests for small groups to perform at weddings and funerals. This has enabled members to sing in a smaller choir, as well as generating much needed income for the Society.

One of the features of the Choral Society has been the willingness to present new and unusual repertoire as part of a balanced programme over the course of a season. This has been maintained and remains one of the features of the Society today.

Following a successful year in 1991, the Society undertook, for the first time, what must be one of the most challenging works in the whole choral repertoire – Howells's *Hymnus Paradisi*. This work, by an undervalued English composer, presents huge challenges for the choir in learning it and huge challenges in performance as well. It requires a large orchestra, and so balance between choir and orchestra is a major consideration for the conductor. Members put in a vast amount of effort to learn the work and gave a very creditable performance in November 1992.

This was the beginning of three years of challenging works. It was also the beginning of a deliberate policy to present 'lighter' summer concerts. Definitions of 'lighter' vary enormously, but the Choral Society has never departed from its fundamental principle of presenting high-quality choral compositions.

Preceding the Howells, two major works of the choral repertoire were performed, namely Dvořák's Requiem and Bach's profound *St John Passion*. The Choral Society did not perform any major work by Bach until 1927. Since then it has performed the *St John Passion* five times. It does seem extraordinary that one of the composers now considered 'great' was missing from the choir's repertoire for the first sixty years of its existence.

Another great choral work only received its second outing in 1993 - the Vespers of 1610 by Monteverdi. It had first been sung by the choir in 1984 and has subsequently (in 2007) had a further airing. It is a challenging work that can be sung by large and small choirs alike, but it becomes a firm favourite of the singers once performed. In the 2007 performance the Choral Society used a period instrument orchestra, Fiori Musicale, for the accompaniment, which gave the concert added excitement. The 1993 season was one of fewer contrasts of period of music than many as the two previous concerts both contained twentieth-century works (Lambert, Tippett, Gershwin and Britten). However, the styles were varied with spirituals from *A Child of Our Time*, the more jazz inspired *Rio Grande* and excerpts from *Porgy and Bess*.

Two giants of the choral repertoire followed in 1994. The first was Beethoven's *Missa Solemnis* and the second Elgar's *The Apostles*. Both these works require huge stamina from a choir, with the Elgar also requiring a larger than normal number of soloists. It was at this time that concert costs were beginning to rise so the Society had to keep a close eye on finances. Fortunately the orchestral costs were kept to a minimum with the continued use of the Bedford Sinfonia as the accompanying orchestra for the Choral Society's concerts, and with the use of up and coming soloists, often from the Royal Colleges of Music, rather than established professionals who were much more expensive. This lead to opportunities for young singers at the start of their professional career and proved to be a very satisfactory development.

The following year was more musically balanced with performances of Bach's Mass in B Minor, Orff's *Carmina Burana* and Brahms' *German Requiem*. This was the fourth time the Society had performed the Bach and the second time it had performed the Orff (both were performed again in 2007 and 2006 respectively). The 1995 performance of *Carmina Burana* was given in the two piano version in the Great Hall at Bedford School, a venue rarely used by the choir.

The year 1996 was also one of contrasts. It began with an all-Mozart programme including the Mass in C Minor, a magnificent example of music of the classical period, and arguably one of Mozart's greatest works. There followed the first of three opera gala concerts (subsequent concerts being in 1999 and 2014). These were all programmed for June as 'lighter music' for the summer concert. They gave the choir a chance to sing new repertoire, which went down well with both the members and the audience. This sort of concert is, however, quite difficult to programme and rehearse as it is 'bitty', and expensive to hire all the orchestral parts. The final concert of 1996 was very challenging – Delius's *Sea Drift*. Like Vaughan Williams's compositions the music is much more difficult to sing than it looks. With the addition of Finzi's masterpiece, *Intimations of Immortality*, there was a very difficult programme for choir members to learn. However, both pieces are great works and the choir rose to the occasion very well.

The next year was slightly less challenging, but included a commissioned piece. Michael Rose, as well as being the guest conductor for the Choral Society each season, is a published composer. It seemed most appropriate, therefore, to invite him to write a new work for the choir. He obliged by writing *Sounds and Sweet Airs* for the summer concert. The choir enjoyed the challenge of performing a work especially written for them and also enjoyed the music.

This concert followed the ever popular piece sung in the March concert, Verdi's Requiem. This has to be one of the highlights of the choral repertoire and is always a great 'sing' for a choir – it has been sung six times by the Society (on two of those occasions twice, in close succession). The final concert of 1997 was an all-Beethoven programme with the Mass in C and *Choral Fantasia* (a programme that was repeated in 2013). Beethoven's Mass in C is the most chorally accessible of his vocal works and always a pleasure to perform.

Elgar's *The Dream of Gerontius* was performed in March 1998. First performed by the Choral Society in 1910, there have been six performances of this masterpiece by the choir. Elgar has been a regularly performed composer by the Choral Society over the years making an appearance on no less than thirty occasions. The remainder of the season consisted of Schubert, Rachmaninoff and Debussy. In 1999, works included Bach's *St Matthew Passion* and Tippett's *A Child of Our Time* as well as the opera gala evening.

The next year began with a work never before performed by the Society – Dyson's *The Canterbury Pilgrims*. This was very well received by audience and choir alike and deserves another performance in the future. This was followed by, what might be thought as, a slightly strange summer programme of Britten's *St Nicolas* and Faure's Requiem. The programme was, however, deliberately designed to draw an audience, as *St Nicolas* uses a children's choir – it was hoped that the children would be supported by close family and friends. It did have the desired effect and drew a larger than normal summer audience. The millennium was celebrated in the last concert of the year by Patterson's *Millennium Mass*. This was coupled with the old favourite - Gloria by Vivaldi. The Society once again featured a contemporary English composer in its programme as it felt it important to perform works by modern musicians.

A more contemporary feel pervaded the next year too. Walton's Gloria is a challenging twentieth-century work which is more harmonically complicated than *Belshazzar's Feast*. It provided a tough job for the choir, but coupled with Verdi's *Four Sacred Pieces* it made for a good programme in the March 2001 concert. The summer concert featured Nielsen's *Springtime in Funen*, and this was followed in November by Fanshawe's *African Sanctus*. David Fanshawe often attended concerts when this piece was being performed, and the Choral Society were privileged that he came to this performance. It is a piece that combines live singing and playing with additional extracts recorded when Fanshawe was researching music from Africa. These extracts are played alongside the live performance. This gives the conductor a challenge in coordinating all the recorded extracts with the live performers, but it is a challenge well worth attempting as the final performance is moving and unique.

The following year combined the Viennese School with English composers. Mozart and Haydn featured alongside Elgar and Rutter. The summer concert featured Haydn's 'Nelson Mass' (only the fourth time the Society had performed it) and Rutter's Magnificat. The previous concert had featured Mozart's Requiem (for the fifth time with a subsequent performance in 2010) and Handel's coronation anthems (which had only been performed complete on one previous occasion). In November, Elgar's *The Kingdom* completed the season.

Handel's *Messiah* started off 2003 – the work most frequently programmed by the Choral Society (featuring twenty-eight times). Always a favourite of audience and performers, it almost always sells out a concert. This was followed by another very popular work in the summer, Haydn's *The Creation* (for the twelfth time, with one more to come in 2012). This is one of the simpler choral works to learn and so is often programmed when there are a limited number of rehearsals. Generally there have been twelve rehearsals for a concert, but this has depended on the date of the concert, which in turn has depended on the availability of the venues.

The final concert of 2003 was not actually performed until January 2004. The reason for this was that it was to be accompanied by the County Youth Orchestra, which had accompanied the Choral Society on a number of occasions in the past, especially in the Royal Albert Hall. The concert had to be timed to fit with the Youth

Orchestra rehearsal schedule. As the Youth Orchestra only rehearses in the school holidays, the concert had to be performed in early January. The programme included Prokofiev's *Alexander Nevsky* and Kodály's *Psalmus Hungaricus*, the former of which the Choral Society had not performed before.

The next concert of 2004 was the Handel oratorio most frequently performed by the Society (after *Messiah*) – *Judas Maccabaeus*. This was the seventh time this work had been performed. Again, this was judicious programme planning as it contains fewer choruses than some of the other Handel oratorios and so, given that there were to be fewer rehearsals than normal, it allowed sufficient rehearsal time to learn the work. Following the success of Michael Rose's previous commissions the Society commissioned another work from him. This time it was *Songs of Innocence and Experience* based on settings of poems by William Blake. This was coupled with Bliss's *Pastoral: Lie Strewn the White Flocks*, a short piece for flute, chorus and orchestra. The timing of the next concert, being relatively close to Christmas, allowed the choir to sing Bach's *Christmas Oratorio* for the sixth time. This time it was sung complete, which was a lot of work for the choir, but well worth the effort.

Another twentieth-century masterwork began the following year, the *Sea Symphony* by Vaughan Williams, accompanied by the Bedford Sinfonia. This was only the second time the choir had sung this work, and they gave a very fine performance. Brahms's *German Requiem* made an appearance in November. Always a great favourite, it was sung, on this occasion, in English. A later performance in 2014 was, however, sung in German.

In the summer of 2006 there was a second performance Sir John Dankworth's *The Diamond and the Goose*, based on *The Blue Carbuncle* by Arthur Conan Doyle. This is a very enjoyable setting of the story and was thoroughly enjoyed by performers and audience, all the more so because Sir John Dankworth came to the concert and agreed to give an 'interview', in the form of a discussion, before the performance in the Corn Exchange. This event was eagerly attended by many audience and choir members, who were entertained by Sir John talking about his work.

This year also saw a new drive on recruitment. Approaching the 140th anniversary of the choir there was a serious attempt to increase the membership to 140 people. For years it had been hovering between 120–130 members, and so the looming anniversary seemed an ideal opportunity to try to boost the choir's numbers. In the end the choir reached 132 members, but nevertheless, with a constantly evolving group of people as participants, this was a good attempt.

Standards and new works featured again in 2007. In March there was a fifth performance of Bach's Mass in B Minor, and in June a fourth presentation of the Monteverdi Vespers. The 'new' was represented by Jenkins's *The Armed Man*. He was becoming increasingly admired as a composer who had crossed the boundary from popular music to classical music. This work was written to commemorate the millennium and is subtitled 'A mass for peace'. It draws on the old medieval melody *L'homme armé* and uses it to produce a powerful and very popular work.

The following year featured mostly English music. The sixth appearance of Verdi's Requiem began the year and was followed by Coleridge-Taylor's *Hiawatha's Wedding Feast* and Lambert's *Rio Grande*. The year was concluded with the second performance by the Society of Elgar's *King Olaf*. This oratorio, perhaps unjustly neglected, was very much enjoyed by all who heard it.

'Standards' featured strongly in 2009, Bach's *St John Passion* for the fifth time; Haydn's Mass in B Flat, 'Harmoniemesse', for the second time; and Mendelssohn's *Elijah* for the twenty-first time (the second most performed work by the Society in its history). However, the traditional was tempered by a performance in June, along with the Haydn, of a work commissioned by the choir in 1986; Willcocks's *Riddle of the World.*

In 2010 there was a commission to a local composer, Tim Grant-Jones, who had also been the accompanist of the Choral Society for some years. This was *The Human Race*, a work celebrating various aspects of human life prior to the 2012 Olympics in London. It was programmed in the summer, together with a concert performance of Gilbert and Sullivan's *HMS Pinafore* as a more accessible programme for the audience.

In the following four years many previously performed works were featured, with the exception of Jenkins's Requiem in 2013 and an enterprising concert in summer 2015 consisting of Alexander L'Estrange's *Zimbe!* and Will Todd's *Mass in Blue*. *Zimbe!* is a setting of African songs with jazz band and children's choir whilst *Mass in Blue* is a jazz setting of the mass. The concert was particularly well received by the audience, and was very different from the Society's standard repertoire. It was a good experience for members of the choir to try to get into the jazz style, and most enjoyed the challenge.

As well as the regular concerts, there is a further activity that has engaged about two thirds of the choir during the summer months – the Bedford 'Proms in the Park'. The first of these events was held in the early 1990s. In 1996, Bedford Choral Society was invited for the first time to provide the choir for some of the items in the concert. The music chosen has always very popular, and has often been the same from year to year, but it has provided the Society with exposure to a much larger audience than at its own concerts. These concerts continued until 2011 (the fifteenth time the choir had been involved). There was then a break in promotion, but when the concerts began again in 2015 the Society was once again invited to participate – an invitation which it accepted with enthusiasm.

So as the 150th anniversary of the Bedford Choral Society approaches in 2017, it can be seen to be robust and innovative, as well ready to meet new challenges and opportunities. The Society is still flourishing, still presenting a mixture of 'choral standards' and newer works, and still actively recruiting and attracting new members.

It has been a privilege and pleasure to be the musical director of this long-running Society, and I hope that it will continue to grow and prosper for many years into the future.

Appendix 1
Concerts and Works Performed 1867–2010, Bedford Musical/Choral Society

List of concerts and works performed by the Bedford Amateur Musical Society 1867–1880, which became the Bedford Musical Society 1880–1988 (closed 1933, revived 1941), which became the Bedford Choral Society 1988-date. The purely orchestral concert performances 1924–29 and 1946–58 are listed separately in appendices three and four respectively. After 1959 the list does not include purely orchestral works.

This list is not complete for the period up to c.1900 as information had to be extracted from newspaper reviews. The newspaper reviews do not necessarily include all the works performed. The list is more substantially complete after that date as more concert programmes survive and fewer short songs were performed.

Year	Date	Composer	Work	
1867	April	Mendelssohn	*Lauda Sion*	Bedford Amateur Musical Society's first concert
		Handel	'Ye Sons of Israel' (from *Joshua*)	
		Handel	'Deeper and Deeper Still' (from *Jephtha*)	
		Handel	'Waft her Angels, through the Skies' (from *Jephtha*)	
		Mendelssohn	'Morning Prayer'	
		Costa	'I Dreamt I was in Heaven' (from *Naaman*)	
		Rossini	'To Thee, Great Lord' (from *Moses in Egitto*)	
		Handel	'The Holy One of Israel' (from *Samson*)	
		Handel	'To Fame Immortal Go' (from *Samson*)	
		Handel	'Disdainful of Danger' (from *Judas Maccabaeus*)	
		Costa	'March of the Israelites' (from *Eli*)	
		Handel	'Hallelujah Chorus' (from *Messiah*)	
1867	June	Haydn	*The Tempest*	
		Locke	*Macbeth*	
		Rousseau	*Le Devin du Village* (Intermezzo)	
		Handel	'Shake the Dome' (from *Solomon*)	
		Sullivan	'Will He Come'	
		Mendelssohn	'Early Spring'	
		Beethoven	'Adelaide'	
		Traditional	'The Blue Bells of Scotland'	
		Traditional	'God Save the Queen'	

1867	October	van Bree Balfe Bishop Mendelssohn Handel	*St Cecilia's Day* Songs Songs 'Autumn Song' 'Shake the Dome' (from *Solomon*)	
1867	December	Handel	*Messiah*	
1868	April	Müller (attributed Mozart) Ouseley Bach Mendelssohn Beethoven	'Twelfth Mass' *The Martyrdom of St Polycarp* (march) *I Wrestle and Pray* *Elijah* (solos and choruses) 'Hallelujah' (from *The Mount of Olives*)	
1868	June	Romberg Barnett Mendelssohn Barnby	*Lay of the Bell* *The Ancient Mariner* (selection) 'Farewell to the Forest' 'Sweet and Low'	
1868	October	Allen Diemer	*Harvest Home* *Thoughts of Home* (overture)	 Conducted by composer
1868	December	Handel	*Judas Maccabaeus*	
1869	April	Mendelssohn Gounod Sterndale Bennett	*Lauda Sion* *By Babylon's Wave* *The Woman of Samaria* (selection)	
1869	June	Handel –	*Alexander's Feast* Miscellaneous programme	
1869	October	Haydn Haydn Diemer	Symphony No. 104 in D *The Tempest* *Ivry* (selection)	 Conducted by composer
1869	December	Mendelssohn	*Elijah*	
1870	April	Haydn	*The Creation*	
1870	June	Sterndale Bennett Haydn –	*The May Queen* Symphony No. 7 in D Songs (various)	

1870	October	Beethoven Beethoven Beethoven	*The Ruins of Athens* Symphony No. 1 in C *The Mount of Olives* (last chorus only)	Beethoven's birth centenary concert
1870	December	Handel	*Messiah*	
1871	April	– Mendelssohn Spohr	Selection, including 'As Pants the Hart', Psalm 42 *God, Thou Art Great*	
1871	June	Mendelssohn Beethoven Hullah	*The First Walpurgis Night* *The Ruins of Athens* (overture and one chorus) 'The Storm'	
1871	October	–	Miscellaneous concert	
1871	December	Mendelssohn	*St Paul*	
1872	April	Chipp Haydn	*Naomi* *The Creation* (selection)	Conducted by composer
1872	June	Macfarren Haydn Gounod Auber	*May Day* Symphony No. 7 in D *Faust* (selection) *Masaniello* (overture and selection)	
1872	October	Barnett Beethoven Mozart Smart	*The Ancient Mariner* *Men of Prometheus* (overture) 'Sweet Peace Descending' 'Good Night thou Glorious Sun'	
1872	December	Mendelssohn	*Elijah*	
1873	March	Handel Handel Gounod	Selection from various works 'Dettingen' Te Deum *By Babylon's Wave*	
1873	May	Sterndale Bennett –	*The May Queen* Miscellaneous choruses and madrigals	
1873	October	Koechel	*Sea Maidens* (for ladies voices)	
1873	December	Handel	*Judas Maccabaeus*	
1874	16 April (i)	Handel	*Messiah*	For opening of the Bedford Corn Exchange

1874	16 April (ii)	–	Miscellaneous concert	For opening of the Bedford Corn Exchange
1874	May	Haydn	*The Creation*	
1874	October	Haydn Haydn – –	Symphony No. 93 in D *Autumn* (from *The Seasons*) Selection of works by Mendelssohn, Rossini, Suppe, Weber and Gluck	
1874	December	Handel	*Samson*	
1875	April	Mendelssohn Horsley Rossini Costa Bach Beethoven	Symphony No. 2 in B Flat 'Hymn of Praise' 'The Lord is my Shepherd' 'Prayer' (from *Moses in Egitto*) 'I will Extol Thee' (from *Eli*) 'My Heart ever Faithful' Hallelujah Chorus (from *The Mount of Olives*)	
1875	June	Handel Moscheles –	*Acis and Galatea* Piano concerto Songs and choruses	
1875	October	–	Ballad concert	
1875	December	Mendelssohn	*Elijah*	
1876	May	Macfarren Richards	*St John the Baptist* 'God Bless the Prince of Wales'	
1876	June	Mendelssohn Mendelssohn Haydn Sullivan Diemer	*A Midsummer Night's Dream* (fairy scenes) *Loreley* (a fragment) 'O Ruddier than the Cherry' (from Acis and Galatea) 'Sweethearts' 'Dewdrops'	
1876	October	Handel Schumann Rossini Sullivan Haydn	*Water Music* *Gipsy Life* *Mira la Bianca* 'Tell me from my Heart' 'Hunting chorus' (from *The Seasons*)	
1876	December	Handel	*Messiah*	

1877	April	Rossini Mendelssohn Gounod Handel	*Stabat Mater* 'Lord, how Long?' Psalm 13 'Entreat me not to Leave Thee' ('Song of Ruth') Choruses	
1877	June	Sullivan Wagner	*On Shore and Sea* Three opera choruses	
1877	October	Benedict Beethoven Sullivan Sullivan	*Undine* Symphony No. 5 in C Minor (first movement) 'The Lost Chord' 'Oh Hush, my Babe'	Conducted by composer
1877	December	Mendelssohn	*St Paul*	
1878	March	Mendelssohn Schubert Ouseley Haydn	Symphony No. 2 in B Flat 'Hymn of Praise' *The Song of Miriam* *The Martyrdom of St Polycarp* (march) 'The Heavens are Telling' (from *The Creation*)	
1878	April	Handel	*Messiah*	
1878	June	Gade Mendelssohn	*Spring's Message* *The First Walpurgis Night*	
1878	October	– Mendelssohn	Miscellaneous concert *The First Walpurgis Night*	
1878	December	Handel	*Jephtha*	
1879	February	Haydn	*The Creation*	
1879	May	Sterndale Bennett Weber Gounod Diemer Molloy Mendelssohn Weber	*The May Queen* *Der Freischutz* *Faust* (waltz and chorus) Minuet and Trio 'Darby and Joan' 'Early Spring' *Jubilee Overture*	The Musical Society's 50th concert
1879	October	–	Miscellaneous concert	
1879	December	Mendelssohn	*Elijah*	

1880	April	Rossini	*Stabat Mater*	
		Sullivan	*The Prodigal Son*	
1880	May	Barnett	*The Ancient Mariner*	
		Flotow	*Stradella* (overture)	
		–	'Truant Love'	
		–	'A Pair of Lovers'	
		Wagner	'Bridal Chorus' (from *Lohengrin*)	
1880	October	Aguilar	*The Bridal of Triermain*	Conducted by composer
		Haydn	Symphony in C (unspecified, first movement)	
		Flotow	*Martha* (harp solo)	
		Verdi	'Rataplan' (from *The Force of Destiny*)	
1880	December	Handel	*Israel in Egypt*	
1880	December	Handel	*Messiah*	Extra concert
1881	March	Sterndale Bennett	*The Woman of Samaria*	
		Beethoven	Symphony No. 5 in C Minor (first movement)	
		Mendelssohn	'Hear my Prayer'	
		Stainer	'My Hope is in the Everlasting'	
		Gounod	'Nazareth'	
1881	May	–	Ballad concert	
1881	October	Barnett	*The Building of the Ship*	
		Popham	Overture	
		–	Songs	
1881	November	Diemer	*Bethany*	Conducted by composer
		Diemer	'Autumn'	
		Beethoven	Symphony No. 5 in C Minor	
		Wagner	*Tannhäuser* (march and chorus)	
1881	December	Handel	*Judas Maccabaeus*	
1882	February	Macfarren	*St John the Baptist*	
1882	May	Beethoven	Symphony No. 2 in D	
		Gade	*The Erl King's Daughter*	
		Faning	'The Song of the Vikings'	
		Diemer	*Tarentella*	Conducted by composer
		Gounod	'Trumpet Blow' (from *Irene*)	

1882	October	–	Ballad concert	
1882	December	Mendelssohn	*Elijah*	
1882	December	Handel	*Messiah*	Extra concert
1883	February	Gade Mendelssohn Gounod Moscheles Macfarren (W) Weber	*Spring's Message* *The First Walpurgis Night* *Funeral March of a Marionette* Piano Concerto in F (first movement) 'You Stole my Love' *Der Freischutz* (overture)	
1883	May	Gaul Gounod Mendelssohn Bach Gounod Rossini	*The Holy City* *By Babylon's Wave* *Atalie* (overture) 'My Heart Ever Faithful' 'Nazareth' 'Prayer' (from *Moses in Egitto*)	
1883	October	–	Miscellaneous concert	
1883	December	Spohr Mendelssohn	*The Last Judgment* 'Hear my Prayer'	
1883	December	Handel	*Messiah*	Extra concert
1884	February	Diemer Rossini	*Bethany* *Stabat Mater*	Conducted by composer
1884	May	Cowen	*The Rose Maiden*	
1884	October	–	Miscellaneous orchestral and choral concert	
1884	December	Mendelssohn	*St Paul*	
1885	February	– Handel –	Commemoration concert, including 'Hallelujah Chorus', 'Hailstone Chorus', 'Shake the Dome', 'The Lord is a Man of War'	Bi-centenary of Handel's birth
1885	May	– Bandey	Miscellaneous concert, including a Part-song	 Composed by the Society's accompanist
1885	October	Diemer –	*Alcestis* Miscellaneous selection	Conducted by composer

1885	December	Mozart Handel	Requiem *Messiah* (selection)	
1886	March	–	Ballad concert	
1886	May	Stainer	*The Daughter of Jairus*	
1886	October	Sullivan	*On Shore and Sea*	
1886	November	Mendelssohn	*Elijah*	
1887	March	Sullivan Gounod Gounod-Bach Parker Rossini	*The Martyr of Antioch* *By Babylon's Wave* 'Ave Maria' 'Jerusalem' 'To Thee, Great Lord' (from *Moses in Egitto*)	
1887	May	Stanford Handel Arne Diemer	*The Revenge* *Zadok the Priest* 'Rule Britannia' *Sing People, Sing*	Jubilee concert for Queen Victoria Conducted by composer
1887	October	– Popham	Ballad concert, including *Hymn to Peace*	 Conducted by composer
1887	December	Handel Handel	*Messiah* 'Dead March' (from *Saul*)	
1888	February	Sterndale Bennett Mendelssohn Gounod	*The May Queen* *Ruy Blas* (overture) *Funeral March of a Marionette*	
1888	May	Haydn	*The Creation*	
1888	October	Wallace Auber Holst Faning	*Maritana* *Le Cheval de Bronze* (overture) *Grande Concertante* 'The Miller's Wooing'	
1888	December	Sullivan	*The Light of the World*	
1889	February	Mendelssohn Handel	*Athalie* *Samson* (selection)	
1889	May	Gade	*The Crusaders*	

1889	October	Sullivan Schubert	*The Golden Legend* Symphony No. 8 in B Minor ‘Unfinished Symphony’	
1889	December	Handel	*Messiah*	
1890	February	Mendelssohn Benedict Handel – Mendelssohn Pinusuti Gounod	Symphony No. 2 in B Flat ‘Hymn of Praise’ ‘Evening by the Sea of Galilee’ (from *St Peter*) ‘Ye Sacred Priests’ and ‘Farewell, ye Limpid Streams’ (from *Jeptha*) ‘For the New Year’ ‘Lead, Kindly Light’ ‘O, that we two are Maying’	
1890	May	Berlioz	*The Damnation of Faust*	
1890	October	–	Ballad concert	
1890	December	Handel	*Judas Maccabaeus*	
1891	February	–	Ballad and operatic concert	
1891	May	Beethoven Sullivan Rossini	Grand symphony (unspecified) *The Golden Legend* *William Tell* (overture)	
1891	October	Stanford Sullivan Dvořák	*The Revenge* *Ivanhoe* (extracts) *Gypsy Songs*	
1891	December	Mendelssohn	*Elijah*	The Musical Society’s 100th concert
1892	February	–	Miscellaneous orchestral and choral concert	
1892	April	Gounod	*The Redemption*	
1892	October	–	Ballad concert	
1892	December	Handel	*Samson*	
1893	February	–	Concert of sacred music	
1893	May	Diemer Gounod	‘Brother, Thou Art Gone Before Us’ *Faust*	Conducted by composer and sung in memory of Dr Steinmetz

1893	October	– Parry Bandey Gilbert and Sullivan	Ballad concert, including *Blest Pair of Sirens* *Fishwife's Cradle Song* 'Poor Wandering One' (from *The Pirates of Penzance*)	Conducted by composer
1893	December	Mendelssohn	*St Paul*	
1894	March	Rossini Mendelssohn Handel – Spohr Sullivan	*Stabat Mater* *Athalie* (overture) 'Deeper and Deeper Still' (from *Jephtha*) 'Waft her Angels, through the Skies' (from *Jephtha*) 'As Pants the Hart', Psalm 42 'Bring Forth the Best Robe' (from *The Prodigal Son*)	
1894	May	MacCunn –	*Lord Ullin's Daughter* Miscellaneous works	
1894	October	–	Operatic and humorous concert	
1894	December	Costa	*Eli*	
1895	March	Sullivan	*The Prodigal Son*	
1895	May	Smart Weber (orch, Berlioz) – Sullivan Sullivan	*The Bride of Dunkerron* *L'invitation a la Valse* Miscellaneous songs and madrigals 'Let me Dream Again' *Henry VIII* (dance)	
1895	October	Wagner – –	Selection Miscellaneous songs and choruses by English composers	
1895	December	Mendelssohn	*Elijah*	
1896	March	Handel	*Messiah*	
1896	May	Barnett Barnby Leslie Mendelsohn Bizet	*The Ancient Mariner* 'Sweet and Low' 'The Flax Spinner' Violin Concerto in E Minor (two movements) 'Toreador' (from *Carmen*)	

1896	October	– Parry Vincent Sullivan Mozart	Miscellaneous concert, including *Blest Pair of Sirens* *Choral Fantasia on National Melodies* *Henry VIII* (selection) Concerto for Two Pianos	
1896	December	Sullivan	*The Golden Legend*	
1897	March	Gounod	*The Redemption*	
1897	May	–	Diamond Jubilee concert ('patriotic' music)	Queen Victoria's Diamond Jubilee
1897	October	– Weber Faning Beethoven	Miscellaneous concert, including *Der Freischutz* – overture 'Daybreak' Choral Fantasy	
1897	December	Handel	*Joshua*	
1898	March	Haydn	*The Creation*	
1898	May	Sterndale Bennett –	*The May Queen* Miscellaneous selection	
1898	November	– Gluck Chaminade White	Miscellaneous concert, including *Orfeo ed Euridice* (excerpt) 'The Silver Ring' 'When you Return'	Clara Butt concert
1898	December	Mendelssohn	*Elijah*	
1899	April	Mendelssohn MacCunn Mendelssohn	*Loreley* *Lord Ullin's Daughter* *The Midsummer Night's Dream* (incidental music)	
1899	October	MacCunn	*The Cameronian's Dream*	
1899	December	Handel	*Messiah*	
1900	March	– Mendelssohn Mendelssohn Haydn	Sacred music concert, including Symphony No. 2 in B Flat 'Hymn of Praise' 'Judge me, O Lord', Psalm 43 'The Heavens are Telling' (from *The Creation*)	

1900	October	–	Selection of music, including	Opening of the Corn Exchange organ
		–	Organ solos (played by Henry Rose)	
		Handel	‘O, Ruddier than the Cherry’ (from *Acis and Galatea*)	
		Mendelssohn	‘O, for the Wings of a Dove’	
1900	November	Mendelssohn	*Elijah*	
1901	February	Parry	*Blest Pair of Sirens*	
		Mendelssohn	Symphony No. 3 in A Minor	
		Wagner	‘Elsa’s Dream’ (from *Lonengrin*)	
		Godard	*Chanson de Florian*	
		–	*Qui donc vois a donne vos yeax?*	
		Lehmann	‘Love the Fowler’	
		Stanford	*The Last Post*	
1901	May	Sullivan	*The Golden Legend*	
1901	November	Elgar	*The Banner of St George*	
		Mendelssohn	Symphony No. 4 in A	
		Wagner	‘Hail, Bright Abode’ (from *Tannhäuser*)	
1902	February	Handel	*Acis and Galatea*	
		Elgar	*Pomp and Circumstance Military Marches*	
1902	May	Coleridge-Taylor	*The Blind Girl of Castél-Cuillé*	
		Godfrey	*Coronation March*	
		Dowland	‘Awake, Sweet Love’	
		Morley	‘Now is the Month of Maying’	
		Elgar	*Pomp and Circumstance Military Marches*	
1902	November	Mascagni	*Cavalleria Rusticana*	
		Elgar	*Coronation Ode*	
1903	February	Bridge	*The Forging of the Anchor*	Conducted by composer
		Beethoven	Symphony No. 6 in F, ‘Pastoral’ Symphony	
		Lehmann	‘The Cuckoo’	
1903	May	Mendelssohn	*St Paul*	
1903	November	Gounod	*Faust*	
1904	February	Schubert	Symphony No. 2 in B Flat	
		Tchaikovsky	*Nutcracker Suite*	
		Harding	*Mucius Scaevola*	Conducted by composer

1904	May	Coleridge-Taylor Beethoven	*Hiawatha's Wedding Feast* Symphony No. 5 in C Minor	
1904	November	Mackenzie Elgar	*The Dream of Jubal* *Pomp and Circumstance Military Marches*	
1905	February	Coleridge-Taylor Coleridge-Taylor	*Four Characteristic Waltzes* *Three Choral Ballads*	Conducted by composer
1905	May	Mendelssohn Moszkowski	Symphony No. 2 in B Flat 'Hymn of Praise' *Suite from Foreign Parts*	Presentation to Philip Diemer
1905	November	Elgar	*King Olaf*	
1906	February	Harding Haydn Stanford	*Mucius Scaevola* *The Creation* (selection) *Songs of the Sea*	
1906	May	Cowen Cowen Chaminade Bach, Mozart, Beethoven and Mendelssohn	*John Gilpin* 'For a Dream's Sake' and 'Snowflakes' 'The Silver Ring' - Orchestral selection	Conducted by composer
1906	November	Brahms Sullivan Rachmaninoff and Liszt –	*Song of Destiny* 'Evening Hymn' Solo piano works Violin solos	
1907	February	– Stanford	Miscellaneous concert, including *The Revenge*	
1907	May	Mendelssohn	*Elijah*	Presentation to Edward. E. Halfpenny, leader of orchestra
1907	November	Parry Sibelius	*The Pied Piper of Hamelin* *Finlandia*	
1908	February	Coleridge-Taylor Wagner Elgar	*The Death of Minnehaha* *Die Meistersinger* (overture) *Wand of Youth*	
1908	May	Handel	*Messiah*	

1908	November	– Brahms Brahms Parry Sibelius Bach, Chopin and Liszt	Miscellaneous concert, including 'In Silent Night' 'Love, Fare thee Well' *Blest Pair of Sirens* *Valse Triste* Solo piano works	
1909	February	Mendelssohn	Symphony No. 2 in B Flat 'Hymn of Praise'	Mendelssohn centenary concert
1909	May	Handel	*Israel in Egypt*	
1909	November	Gounod	*Faust*	
1910	February	Stanford Stanford Stanford Stanford Stanford Stanford	'The Fairy Lough' 'The Alarm' *Songs of the Sea* *Irish Rhapsody No. 1* 'When She Answered Me' 'Trotting to the Fair'	Conducted by composer
1910	June	Elgar	*The Dream of Gerontius*	
1910	November	Coleridge-Taylor Coleridge-Taylor	*Death of Minnehaha* *Hiawatha's Departure*	
1911	February	Stanford Macfarren Cowen Sullivan Rubinstein Weber Lidgey Berlioz Boëllmann Elgar	*Phaudrig Crohoore* 'You Stole my Love' 'Evening brings us Home' 'The Long Day Closes' Piano Concerto No. 4 in D Minor 'Ocean, thou Might Monster' (from *Oberon*) Roundelay *Le Captive* *Variations Symphoniques* for orchestra and cello 'Song of Autumn'	
1911	March	–	Miscellaneous concert	
1911	May	– Brahms	Orchestral selection *German Requiem*	
1911	November	– Bridge	Miscellaneous selection *A Song of the English*	 Conducted by composer

1912	February	Mendelssohn	*Elijah*	
1912	May	– Wagner	Miscellaneous selection Wagner (selection)	
1912	December	Coleridge-Taylor –	*A Tale of Old Japan* Miscellaneous selection	
1913	March	Gounod – Stanford	*Gallia* Miscellaneous selection *Songs of the Fleet*	
1913	December	Coleridge-Taylor –	*Kubla Khan* Miscellaneous selection	
1914	March	Mendelssohn	*St Paul*	
1914	November	Handel	*Messiah*	Three concerts performed for the troops
1915–18	–	–	–	No concerts performed
1919	July	Somervell Mendelssohn Handel	*Vanguard 1914* Symphony No. 2 in B Flat ‘Hymn of Praise’ ‘Hallelujah Chorus’	Peace celebration concert
1920	January	Coleridge-Taylor –	*A Tale of Old Japan* Miscellaneous selection	
1920	May	Mendelssohn	*Elijah*	
1920	December	Harding –	*Mucius Scaevola* Miscellaneous selection	Conducted by composer
1921	May	Elgar	*The Dream of Gerontius*	
1921	December	Coleridge-Taylor Elgar Parry	*Kubla Khan* *Sea Pictures* *Blest Pair of Sirens*	
1922	May	Elgar	*The Apostles*	
1922	December	Stanford –	*The Last Post* Miscellaneous selection	
1923	May	Elgar	*The Apostles*	

1923	December	Vaughan Williams –	*Towards the Unknown Region* Miscellaneous selection	Presentation to Harry Harding
1924	March	Dvořák	*The Spectre's Bride*	
1924	December	Elgar	*King Olaf*	
1925	May	Bantock Parry Elgar Brahms	*A Pageant of Human Life* *An English Suite* *The Snow* *Death of Trenar*	
1925	December	Bizet	*Carmen* (concert performance)	
1926	February	Elgar –	*The Black Knight* Miscellaneous selection	
1926	December	Sullivan Shaw	*The Golden Legend* 'The Crib'	
1927	March	Mendelssohn	*Elijah*	
1927	December	Bach	*Lobet den Herrn, alle Heiden*	
1928	March	Coleridge-Taylor	*A Tale of Old Japan*	
1928	November	Elgar Schubert	*The Music Makers* Miscellaneous selection	
1929	March	Brahms Stanford Vaughan Williams Bullock Bairstow Bach –	*German Requiem* 'To the Soul' 'The Call' 'The Hostel' 'I Love my God' ''Twas in the Cool of Eventide' (from *St Matthew Passion*)	
1929	November	Brahms	*German Requiem*	
1930	February	Bantock Mendelssohn	*The Pilgrim's Progress* Symphony No. 2 in B Flat 'Hymn of Praise'	
1930	November	Mendelssohn	*St Paul*	

1931	March	Coleridge-Taylor Coleridge-Taylor Coleridge-Taylor	*Hiawatha's Wedding Feast* *Death of Minnehaha* *Hiawatha's Departure*	Concert with Kempston Musical Society
1932–1941	–	–	–	No concerts performed
1942	March	Handel	*Judas Maccabaeus*	
1942	July	Vaughan Williams Bach Palmer Various	*Dona Nobis Pacem* 'Peasant' cantata 'The Conductor's Song' Songs	
1942	December	–	Carol concert	
1943	April	Handel	*Messiah*	
1943	October	Purcell	*King Arthur*	
1943	December	Bach –	*The Christmas Oratorio* (selection) Christmas carols	
1944	April	Brahms Parry Coleridge-Taylor	*Song of Destiny* *Blest Pair of Sirens* *Hiawatha's Wedding Feast*	
1944	July	–	Miscellaneous madrigals, songs, piano and orchestral pieces	
1944	November	Elgar Dyson Elgar	*Sea Pictures* *Songs of Courage* and *Songs of Praise* *The Music Makers*	
1945	March	di Lasso Moeran	Madrigals *Songs of Springtime*	
1945	July	di Lasso Vaughan Williams	Madrigals English folk songs	
1945	December	Bach Handel	'Jesus, Priceless Treasure' (*Jesu meine Freude*) *Messiah* (selection)	
1946	March	Mendelssohn	*Elijah*	
1946	November	–	Orchestral concert	
1946	December	Handel	*Messiah*	Kathleen Ferrier performed

1947	April	Brahms Brahms	*German Requiem* Symphony No. 2 in D	
1947	November	Handel	*Acis and Galatea*	
1947	December	Handel	*Messiah*	
1948	March	Kodály Vaughan Williams	*Psalmus Hungaricus* *Dona Nobis Pacem*	
1948	November	Bach Brahms Brahms	*Lobet den Herrn, alle Heiden* Four Trios for Female Voices, Harp and Two Horns *Liebeslieder* waltzes	
1949	March	Kodály Verdi	*Missa Brevis* Requiem	
1949	December	Mendelssohn	*Elijah*	
1950	February	Borodin Parry	*Polovtsian Dances* (from *Prince Igor*) *Blest Pair of Sirens*	
1950	March	Haydn	*The Creation*	
1950	December	Handel	*Messiah*	
1951	April	Elgar Fauré Holst Ireland, John	*The Dream of Gerontius* (prelude) Requiem *King Estmere* *These Things Shall Be*	
1951	December	Coleridge-Taylor Strauss (J. II)	*Hiawatha's Wedding Feast* *Tales from the Vienna Woods*	
1952	April	Bliss Handel	*Pastoral: Lie Strewn the White Flocks* 'Dettingen' Te Deum	
1952	December	Bach	*The Christmas Oratorio*	
1953	May	Elgar Franck Handel Handel Vaughan Williams	'Great is the Lord', Psalm 48 Psalm 150 *The King shall Rejoice* *Zadok the Priest* *Benedicite*	

1953	December	Palestrina Schutz, Heinrich	*Missa Papæ Marcelli* *Christmas Story*	
1954	May	Bach	*St Matthew Passion*	
1954	December	Vaughan Williams Palestrina Bach	Mass in G Minor *Stabat Mater* 'Sleepers Awake!', Cantata No. 140 (*Wachet auf*)	
1955	May	Handel	*Samson*	
1955	December	Bach	*The Christmas Oratorio*	
1956	March	Bach	*St Matthew Passion*	
1956	May	Bach Brahms Kodály Stanford	*St Matthew Passion* *Wherefore Now Hath Life* *Jesus and the Traders* Magnificat	
1956	December	Elgar	*Scenes from the Bavarian Highlands*	
1957	January	Palestrina Monteverdi Sweelinck Sweelinck Tchaikovsky	'O Bone Jesu' *Messa a Quattro voci da capella* *Laudate Dominum* Psalm 134 *Hymn to the Trinity*	
1957	March	Bach	*St Matthew Passion*	
1957	December	Brahms	*German Requiem*	
1958	March	Lasso Bach Handel Parry	*Douce Mémoire* 'Jesus, Priceless Treasure' (*Jesu meine Freude*) *Zadock the Priest* 'I was Glad'	
1958	May	Morley and Bennet Bliss Bennet, Marenzio and Vautor Brahms Dvořák Vaughan Williams	Four madrigals *Aubade for Coronation Morning* Four madrigals – Op.93a *Songs of Nature* Four English folk songs	

1958	December	Handel	*Messiah*	
1959	March	Bach	*St John Passion*	
1959	December	Bush (G) Finzi Vaughan Williams	*In Praise of Mary* *In Terra Pax* *Fantasia on Christmas Carols*	
1960	April	Bach	Mass in B Minor	
1960	May	Fauré Borodin	*Pavane* *Polovtsian Dances* (from *Prince Igor*)	
1960	December	Bach	*The Christmas Oratorio*	
1961	March	Berger Palestrina	*Brazilian Psalm* *Missa Papæ Marcelli*	
1961	March	Beethoven	Symphony No. 9 in D Minor 'Choral' Symphony	
1961	December	Mozart Vaughan Williams	Requiem *Serenade to Music*	
1962	March	Bruckner	Mass in E Minor	
1962	April	Bach	*St Matthew Passion*	
1962	December	Handel	*Messiah*	
1963	March	Purcell Lambert	*The Masque of Dioclesian* *The Rio Grande*	
1963	May	Bach Berger Parry Purcell Stanford	'Come, Jesu, Come' (*Komm, Jesu, Komm*) *Brazilian Psalm* *Blest Pair of Sirens* Funeral Sentences Magnificat	
1963	December	Britten Bush (A) Vaughan Williams	*A Ceremony of Carols* *The Winter Journey* *Fantasia on Christmas Carols*	
1964	March	Bach	*St John Passion*	
1964	December	Britten –	*St Nicolas* Carols	

1965	February	Handel Handel Bach	*Zadok the Priest* *The King shall Rejoice* ‘My Spirit was in Heaviness’, Cantata No. 21	
1965	March	Handel Haydn	Coronation anthems Mass in D Minor ‘Nelson Mass’	
1965	December	Vivaldi	Gloria	
1966	March	Verdi	Requiem	
1966	June	Britten Bruckner Holst Handel Kodály Vaughan Williams	*Rejoice in the Lamb* Motets Psalm 148 *Zadok the Priest* Psalm 121 *Valiant for Truth*	
1966	December	Handel Le Fleming –	*O Praise the Lord with One Consent* *Five Psalms* Carols	
1967	March	Haydn	*The Creation*	
1967	June	Bernstein Elgar	*Chichester Psalms* *Scenes from the Bavarian Highlands*	
1967	December	Bach	‘Sleepers Awake!’, Cantata No. 140 (*Wachet auf*)	
1968	February	Elgar	*The Dream of Gerontius*	
1968	June	Stravinsky	*Symphony of Psalms*	
1968	December	Purcell Bruckner Gabrielli Purcell	Funeral Sentences Motets *Hodie Christus Natus Est* Funeral Sentences	
1969	February	Britten Rossini	*Gloriana* (choral dances) *Petite Messe Solonelle*	
1969	May	Mendelssohn	*Elijah*	

1969	December	Gabrielli Sweelinck –	Magnificat *Hodie Christus Natus Est* Carols	
1970	March	Brahms Parry	*German Requiem* *Blest Pair of Sirens*	
1970	May	Bartók Borodin Kodály Lambert	*Four Slovak Songs* *Polovtsian Dances* (from *Prince Igor*) *Matra Pictures* *The Rio Grande*	
1970	November	Bach Beethoven	Cantata No. 147 *(Herz und Mund und Tat und Leben*) Mass in C	
1970	December	–	Carol concert	
1971	March	Handel	*Messiah*	
1971	May	Orff	*Carmina Burana*	
1971	November	Fauré Brahms Haydn	Requiem *Alto Rhapsody* Mass in B Flat,'Harmoniemesse'	
1971	December	–	Carol concert	
1972	March	Verdi	Requiem	
1972	April	Verdi	Requiem	
1972	November	Bach Schubert	'My Soul doth Magnify the Lord', Cantata No. 10 Mass in G	
1972	December	Gabrielli Monteverdi Rose –	*In Ecclesiis* *Christe, Te Adoremus* *Winter Music* Carols	
1973	April	Handel Vaughan Williams Mahler Walton	*Zadok the Priest* *Serenade to Music* *Songs of a Wayfarer* *Belshazzar's Feast*	

1973	November	Britten Bach Haydn	*Rejoice in the Lamb* 'Come, Jesu, Come' (*Komm, Jesu, Komm*) Mass in D Minor 'Nelson Mass'	
1973	December	Handel –	*Messiah* (choruses) Carols	
1974	March	Bach	Mass in B Minor	
1974	June	Britten Holst	*St Nicolas* *A Choral Fantasia*	
1974	November	Walton Verdi Holst	Coronation anthem *Four Sacred Pieces* *A Choral Fantasisa*	
1974	December	Charpentier Vaughan Williams	*Carols for Instruments and Voices* *The First Nowell*	
1975	March	Bach	*St Matthew Passion*	
1975	June	Kodály	*Missa Brevis*	
1975	November	Brahms	*German Requiem*	
1975	December	–	Carol concert	
1976	March	Handel	*Israel in Egypt*	
1976	May	Bruckner Holst	Mass in E Minor *Two Psalms*	
1976	November	Brahms Duruflé	*Song of Destiny* Requiem	
1977	March	Mozart	Requiem	
1977	April	Walton	*Belshazzar's Feast*	Concert at the Albert Hall
1977	June	Finzi Handel Handel Stanford Bourgeois Parry	*Ceremonial Ode for St Cecilia* *The King shall Rejoice* *Zadok the Priest* Te Deum *The Old Hundredth* *I was Glad*	

1977	December	Bach –	*The Christmas Oratorio* (part 1) Carols	
1978	February	Haydn	*The Creation*	
1978	May	Elgar	*The Dream of Gerontius*	
1978	November	Vaughan Williams Vaughan Williams Vaughan Williams	*The Pilgrim's Journey* *Serenade to Music* *Toward the Unknown Region*	
1978	December	Rutter –	*Gloria* Carols	
1979	April	Verdi	Requiem	
1979	June	Bach Handel	Magnificat *Zadok the Priest*	
1979	November	Mendelssohn	*Elijah*	
1979	December	Bernstein –	*Chichester Psalms* Carols	
1980	March	Mozart Rossini	Solemn Vespers *Stabat Mater*	
1980	April	Beethoven Borodin	Symphony No. 9 in D Minor 'Choral' Symphony *Polovtsian Dances* (from *Prince Igor*)	Concert at the Albert Hall
1980	June	Bliss Haydn	*Pastoral: Lie Strewn the White Flocks* Mass in D Minor 'Nelson Mass'	
1980	November	Bach	*St John Passion*	
1981	March	Haydn Honneger	'Spring' (from *The Seasons*) *King David*	
1981	April	Berlioz	*Grande Messe de Morts*	Concert at the Albert Hall
1981	June	Handel	*Acis and Galatea*	
1981	November	Handel Handel Mozart	*My Heart is Inditing* *Zadok the Priest* Mass in C Minor	
1982	February	Elgar	*The Kingdom*	

1982	June	Kodály Patterson Vaughan Williams Walton	*Psalmus Hungaricus* *Canterbury Psalms* *Five Mystical Songs* 'Coronation' Te Deum	
1982	November	Dvořák	*Stabat Mater*	
1982	December	Handel –	*Messiah* (part 1) Carols	
1983	March	Poulenc Vaughan Williams	*Gloria* *Five Tudor Portraits*	
1983	May	Britten Lambert	*St Nicolas* *The Rio Grande*	
1983	November	Handel Willcocks (J)	*Ode for St Cecilia's Day* *The Voices of Time*	 Conducted by composer
1983	December	Finzi Vaughan Williams –	*In Terra Pax* *Fantasia on Christmas Carols* Carols	
1984	February	Brahms Mozart	*German Requiem* *Regina Coeli*	
1984	May and June	Monteverdi	Vespers	June performance in St Albans cathedral
1984	December	Holst Howells Elgar	*The Hymn of Jesus* Te Deum in E Flat Collegium Regale *The Music Makers*	
1985	February	Brahms	*German Requiem*	
1985	May	Handel	*Samson*	
1985	November	Bach	Mass in B Minor	
1985	December	Vivaldi –	Magnificat Carols	
1986	March	Brahms Schubert	*Song of Destiny* Mass in A Flat	

1986	June	Bach Bruckner Kodály Stanford	*Singet dem Herrn* Motets *Missa Brevis* Magnificat	
1986	November	Beethoven Handel Willcocks (J)	Mass in C *O Praise the Lord with One Consent* *The Riddle of the World*	 Conducted by composer
1986	December	Rutter Sweelinck –	*Gloria* *Hodie Christus Natus Est* Carols	Concert broadcast by BBC Radio Bedfordshire
1987	March	Tippett	*A Child of our Time*	
1987	May	Bruckner Fauré	Te Deum Requiem	
1987	November	Haydn Mozart	Te Deum Requiem	
1987	December	Bizet –	Te Deum Carols	
1988	March	Bach	*St Matthew Passion*	
1988	June	Coleridge-Taylor Elgar Stanford	*Hiawatha's Wedding Feast* *Sea Pictures* *Songs of the Fleet*	
1988	November	Haydn	*The Creation*	
1989	March	Vaughan Williams Vaughan Williams	Symphony No. 1 *Sea Symphony* *Serenade to Music*	*Sea Symphony* broadcast by BBC Radio Bedfordshire
1989	June	Brahms Debussy Elgar	*Alto Rhapsody* *La Demoiselle Elue* *The Music Makers*	
1989	November	Bruckner Stravinsky	Mass in E Minor *Symphony of Psalms*	
1989	December	Holst –	*Christmas Day* Carols	

1990	March	Britten Dvořák	*Cantata Academica* Te Deum	
1990	June	Mendelssohn	*Elijah*	
1990	December	Dankworth Nielsen	*The Diamond and the Goose* *Springtime in Funen*	
1991	March	Handel	*Messiah*	
1991	June	Cherubini Mozart	Requiem *Regina Coeli*	
1991	November	Pehkonen Poulenc	*Ode to St Cecilia* *Gloria*	Commissioned from composer for Choral Society's 125th anniversary
1991	December	Poston	*The Nativity*	Concert broadcast by BBC Radio Bedfordshire
1992	March	Bach	*St John Passion*	
1992	June	Dvořák	Requiem	
1992	November	Haydn Howells	'Winter' (from *The Seasons*) *Hymnus Paradisi*	
1993	March	Vaughan Williams Britten	*Serenade to Music* *A Spring Symphony*	
1993	June	Lambert Gershwin Bernstein Tippett Borodin	*The Rio Grande* *Porgy and Bess* (songs) *West Side Story* (songs) *A Child of Our Time* (five spirituals) *Polovtsian Dances* (from *Prince Igor*)	
1993	November	Monteverdi	Vespers	
1993	December	–	Carol concert	
1994	March	Beethoven	*Missa Solemnis*	
1994	June	–	'A Night at the Opera' Opera choruses	Gala charity concert with Boneventura Bottone and Jennifer Dakin
1994	November	Elgar	*The Apostles*	
1995	March	Bach	Mass in B Minor	

1995	June	Orff	*Carmina Burana*	
1995	November	Brahms	*German Requiem*	
1996	March	Mozart Mozart Mozart	*Exsultate Jubilate* *Ave Verum Corpus* Mass in C Minor	
1996	June	Elgar Various	*Scenes from the Bavarian Highlands* Opera choruses	
1996	November	Delius Finzi	*Sea Drift* *Intimations of Immortality*	
1997	March	Verdi	Requiem	
1997	June	Rose Vaughan Williams	*Sounds and Sweet Airs* *Serenade to Music*	Commissioned from composer
1997	November	Beethoven Beethoven	*Choral Fantasia* Mass in C	
1997	December	–	Carol concert	
1998	March	Elgar	*The Dream of Gerontius*	
1998	June	Schubert Schubert	Magnificat Mass in A Flat	
1998	November	Debussy Rachmaninoff	*Nocturnes* *The Bells*	
1999	January	Verdi	Requiem	
1999	March	Bach	*St Matthew Passion*	
1999	June	–	Opera choruses	
1999	November	Tippett	*A Child of Our Time*	
1999	December	–	Carol concert	
2000	March	Dyson	*The Canterbury Pilgrims*	
2000	June	Britten Fauré	*St Nicolas* Requiem	
2000	November	Patterson Vivaldi	*Millennium Mass* Gloria	

2001	March	Verdi Walton	*Four Sacred Pieces* Gloria	
2001	June	Nielsen Rose	*Springtime in Funen* *Sounds and Sweet Airs*	
2001	November	Fanshawe	*African Sanctus*	
2001	December	–	Carol concert	
2002	March	Handel Handel Mozart	*The King shall Rejoice* *Zadok the Priest* Requiem	
2002	June	Rutter Haydn	Magnificat Mass in D Minor 'Nelson Mass'	
2002	November	Elgar	*The Kingdom*	
2003	March	Handel	*Messiah*	
2003	June	Haydn	*The Creation*	
2003	December	–	Carol concert	
2004	January	Borodin Kodály Prokofiev	*Polovtsian Dances* (from *Prince Igor*) *Psalmus Hungaricus* *Alexander Nevsky*	
2004	March	Handel	*Judas Maccabaeus*	
2004	June	Bliss Rose	*Pastoral: Lie Strewn the White Flocks* *Songs of Innocence and Experience*	 Commissioned from composer
2004	December	Bach	*The Christmas Oratorio*	
2005	March	Vaughan Williams Vaughan Williams	Symphony No. 1 *Sea Symphony* *Towards the Unknown Region*	
2005	June	Brahms Edwards Sullivan	*Liebeslieder* waltzes Te Deum *Trial by Jury*	
2005	November	Strauss (R) Brahms	*Four Last Songs* *German Requiem*	
2005	December	–	Carol concert	

2006	March	Bernstein Orff	*Chichester Psalms* *Carmina Burana*	
2006	June	Dankworth Elgar	*The Diamond and the Goose* *Scenes from the Bavarian Highlands*	
2006	November	Mozart Mozart	*Ave Verum Corpus* Mass in C Minor	
2007	March	Bach	Mass in B Minor	
2007	June	Monteverdi	Vespers	
2007	November	Ireland Jenkins	*These Things shall Be* *The Armed Man*	
2007	December	–	Carol concert	
2008	April	Verdi	Requiem	Two performances with other choirs and Bedfordshire Youth Orchestra to celebrate their 40th birthday
2008	June	Gershwin (arr.Evans) Coleridge-Taylor	*Porgy and Bess* (songs) *Hiawatha's Wedding Feast*	
2008	November	Elgar	*King Olaf*	
2009	March	Bach	*St John Passion*	
2009	June	Willcocks (J) Haydn	*The Riddle of the World* Mass in B Flat, 'Harmoniemesse'	
2009	November	Mendelssohn	*Elijah*	
2009	December	–	Carol concert	
2010	March	Bruckner Schubert Rossini	Motets Symphony No. 8 in B Minor 'Unfinished Symphony' *Stabat Mater*	
2010	June	Grant-Jones Sullivan	*The Human Race* *HMS Pinafore*	Commissioned from composer
2010	December	Haydn Mozart	*The Tempest* Requiem	é

Appendix 2
Choral Works Performed 1920–33, Bedford Free Church Choral Union/Choral Society

Bedford Free Church Choral Union changed its name to Bedford Choral Society in 1924.

Year	Date	Composer	Work
1920	April	Handel	*Messiah*
1920	December	Handel	*Judas Maccabaeus*
1921	March	Handel	*Messiah*
1921	May	Coleridge-Taylor Coleridge-Taylor Coleridge-Taylor	*Hiawatha's Wedding Feast* *Death of Minnehaha* *Hiawatha's Departure*
1921	October	Handel	*Judas Maccabaeus* (excerpts)[1]
1921	December	Handel	*Samson*
1922	April	Handel	*Messiah*
1922	November	Handel	*Israel in Egypt*
1923	March	Coleridge-Taylor Coleridge-Taylor Coleridge-Taylor	*Hiawatha's Wedding Feast* *Death of Minnehaha* *Hiawatha's Departure*
1923	November	–	*Miscellaneous Concert*
1924	February	Mendelssohn	*Elijah*[2]
1925	April	Handel	*Acis and Galatea*
1925	December	Handel	*Messiah*
1926	February	Mendelssohn	*St Paul*
1926	May	Brewer	*Summer Sports*
1926	December	Handel	*Messiah*
1927	February	Coleridge-Taylor Coleridge-Taylor Coleridge-Taylor	*Hiawatha's Wedding Feast* *Death of Minnehaha* *Hiawatha's Departure*

1927	December	Handel	*Messiah*
1928	February	Haydn	*The Creation*
1928	December	Handel	*Messiah*
1929	February	Handel	*Belshazzar's Feast*
1929	December	Handel	*Messiah*
1930	February	Mendelssohn	*Elijah*
1930	December	Handel	*Messiah*
1931	March	Handel	*Samson*
1931	December	Handel	*Messiah*
1932	February	Handel	*Judas Maccabaeus*
1932	November	Coleridge-Taylor	*A Tale of Old Japan*
1932	December	Handel	*Messiah*
1933	February	Haydn	*The Creation*

1 The October 1921 performance of *Judas Maccabaeus* was an extra concert performed on a Sunday in aid of Bedford County Hospital.
2 The February 1924 performance of *Elijah* was given by Bedford Free Church Choral Union and Luton Choirs United. Concerts took place in both Luton and Bedford.

Appendix 3
Orchestral Works Performed 1924–29, Bedford Musical Society

Under its conductor, Herbert Coulson, the Musical Society gave a number of orchestral as well as choral concerts.

Year	Date	Composer	Work	
1924	November	Dvořák	Symphony No. 9 in E Minor ‘New World’ Symphony	Then known as Symphony No. 5.
1925	February	Elgar Grieg Beethoven	*Pomp and Circumstance* March No. 4 *Peer Gynt Suite* Symphony No. 5 in C Minor	This concert also included songs sung by Frank Phillips.
1925	November	Bach Dvořák	Double Violin Concerto Symphony No. 9 in E Minor ‘New World’ Symphony	
1927	February	Schumann Tchaikovsky	Piano Concerto in A Minor Symphony No. 6 in B Minor *Pathétique* Symphony	This concert also included songs sung by Mercy Collisson accompanied on the organ by Mrs F. Partridge.
1928	February	Massenet Sibelius Handel arr. Elgar Wagner Bruch Bantock	*Le Cid* *Finlandia* Overture in D Minor *Die Meistersinger* (overture) Violin Concerto in G Minor ‘O Praise the Lord’	The contralto soloist in the Bantock work was Edith Furmidge. She also sang some songs with piano and with flute accompaniment.
1929	February	Mendelssohn Schubert	Violin Concerto in E Minor Symphony No. 8 in B Minor ‘Unfinished’ Symphony	

Appendix 4
Orchestral Works Performed 1946–57, Bedford Musical Society

While Norman Frost was conductor of the Musical Society, three orchestral concerts were given in the 1947/48 season. Two of these were conducted by Norman Frost and the third, in February 1947, was conducted by Alec Sherman. Clarence Raybould succeeded Norman Frost as conductor in 1947, and he conducted all the Society's concerts until 1952 and all the orchestral concerts until 1958. After this, the Musical Society gave up promoting orchestral concerts.

Year	Date	Composer	Work	
1946	October	Bach	Brandenburg Concerto No. 3.	London Symphony Orchestra
		Rachmaninoff	Piano Concerto No. 2	
		Schubert	Symphony No. 8 in B Minor 'Unfinished' Symphony	
		Brahms	*Variations on a Theme of Haydn*	
1946	November	Grieg	*Holberg Suite*	Jacques Orchestra
		Britten	*Simple Symphony*	
		Elgar	*Introduction and Allegro for Strings*	
		Vaughan Williams	Oboe Concerto	Soloist, Leon Goossens
		Vaughan Williams	Symphony No. 3 *Pastoral* Symphony	
1947	February	Beethoven	Symphony No. 1 in C	New London Orchestra
			Violin Concerto	
			Symphony No. 8 in F	
1947	September	Delius	*Brigg Fair*	Boyd Neel Orchestra
		Vaughan Williams	*The Wasps*	
		Elgar	'Enigma' Variations	
		Franck	Symphony in D Minor	
1948	February	Bach	Piano Concerto in F Minor	Riddick String Orchestra
		Elgar	*Introduction and Allegro for Strings*	
		Turina	*Rapsodia Sinfonica*	
		Bloch	*Concerto Grosso*	
		Wiren	*Serenade for Strings*	
		Suk	*Serenade for Strings*	

1948	October	Dvořák Sibelius Rimsky-Korsakov	*Carnival* Overture Symphony No. 2 in D *Scheherazade*	London Philharmonic Orchestra
1949	February	Bach Pilati Thiman Wiren Saint-Saëns	Brandenburg Concerto No. 3 *Suite for Pianoforte and Strings* Variations on a Theme by Elgar *Serenade for Strings* Caprice for Piano and Strings	Riddick String Orchestra
1949	September	Weber Prokofiev Grieg Holst Vaughan Williams Britten	*Euryanthe* (overture) Symphony No.1 in D Piano Concerto in A Minor *The Perfect Fool* (ballet music) *Tallis Fantasia* *The Young Person's Guide to the Orchestra*	London Philharmonic Orchestra Soloist, Phyllis Sellick
1950	February	Sullivan Tchaikovsky Parry Sibelius Borodin	*Overture di Ballo* *The Nutcracker Suite* *Blest Pair of Sirens* (with choir) Symphony No. 5 in E Flat *Polovtsian Dances* (with choir)	Philharmonia Orchestra
1950	October	Debussy Brahms Vaughan Williams Dohnanyi	*L'Apres Midi d'un Faune* *Academic Festival Overture* Symphony No. 6 in E Minor Suite in F Sharp Minor	London Symphony Orchestra
1951	February	Bach Respighi Mozart Turina Bloch	Concerto in D Minor *Antiche Danze ed Arie* *Eine Kleine Nachtmusik* *Rapsodia Sinfonica* *Concerto Grosso*	Boyd Neel Orchestra Soloist, Ronald Smith
1951	October	Wagner Dvořák Prokofiev Sibelius Elgar	Die Meistersinger (three orchestral pieces) *The Noonday Witch* *Peter and the Wolf* *En Saga* (Symphonic poem) 'Enigma' Variations	

1952	February	Mozart Grieg Haydn Haydn Sibelius Schubert	Divertimento No. 11 in D (K. 251) *Holberg Suite* Trumpet Concerto Symphony No. 85 in B Flat *Romance in C* Symphony No. 5 in B Flat	Boyd Neel Orchestra Soloist, George Eskdale
1953	March	Haydn Bach Beethoven Rameau Bloch	Symphony No. 92 in G 'Jesu, Joy of Man's Desiring' Piano Concerto in B Flat *Castor and Pollux* *Concerto Grosso*	London Symphony Orchestra Soloist, Irene Kohler
1953	November	Schubert Lalo Bach Kodály Wagner Bach	Symphony No. 5 in B Flat Two Aubades Violin Concerto in E *Summer Evening* *Siegfried Idyll* Two chorales	Boyd Neel Orchestra Soloist, Max Rostal
1954	February	Purcell (arr. Rootham) Elgar Mozart Sibelius Massenet Haydn	*The Fairy Queen* (dances) *Chanson du Matin* and *Chanson de Nuit* Piano Concerto in A (K. 488) *Pelleas and Melisande* *The Last Sleep of the Virgin* Symphony No. 85 in B Flat	Boyd Neel Orchestra Soloist, Nina Milkina
1954	October	Mozart Leigh Haydn Mozart Wiren	Divertimento No. 11 in D (K. 251) *Concertino for Piano and Strings* Symphony No. 43 in E Flat 'The Mercury'[1] Piano Concerto in E Flat (K. 449) *Serenade for Strings*	Boyd Neel Orchestra Soloist, Robin Wood

[1] The advertisement states that Haydn's Symphony No. 6 in D was to be played.

1955	January	Handel Barber Suk Jacob Bach	*Concerto Grosso* *Adagio for Strings* *Serenade for Strings* Concerto for Violin and Strings Brandenburg Concerto No. 3	Boyd Neel Orchestra
1955	November	Beethoven Schumann Tchaikovsky Dvořák	*Fidelio* (overture) Piano Concerto in A Minor *Theme and Variations* from Suite No. 3 for Orchestra Symphony No. 2 in D Minor (now No. 7)	Royal Philharmonic Orchestra Soloist, Thorunn Tryggvason
1956	October	Mozart Damase Schubert Roussel	Quartet for Flute, Violin Viola and Cello (K.285) Trio for Harp, Flute and Cello Nocturne[2] Serenade for Flute, Violin, Viola, Cello and Harp	London Instrumental Players
1956	December	Weber Prokofiev Elgar Brahms	Der Freischütz (overture) Symphony No. 1 in D *Scenes from the Bavarian Highlands* (with chorus) Symphony No. 4 in E Minor	Royal Philharmonic Orchestra
1957	October	Dvořák Brahms Sibelius Elgar	*My Homeland* (overture) Violin Concerto in D Symphony No. 7 in C 'Enigma' Variations	London Philharmonic Orchestra Soloist, Ralph Holmes

2 This is Schubert's arrangement of a Nocturne by Wenzel Matiegka for Flute, Viola and Guitar. Schubert added a 'cello part, written for his father. A harp often replaces the guitar.

Bibliography

Archives

Bedford Modern School Archives
Application for musical director, Norman Frost, 12 February 1949
Letter of H. W. Liddle, headmaster of Bedford Modern School, 7 December 1944
Letter of Rev. H. Spence, undated, in response to a letter dated 25 February 1949

Bedfordshire and Luton Archives and Records Service
BP 43/44 and BP 43/6 Bedfordshire County Press
Li/LibB1/1/3 Bedford Literary and Scientific Institute and General Library
MO Archives of the Bedford Moravian Congregation in Bedford St Peter's
X274 Bedford Harmonic Society
X817 Bedford Choral Society
Z50/21/27 Copy print collection
Z160/932 Gifts of Richard Wildman

Newspapers and magazines

Bedford and County Record
The Bedford Bee
Bedford Record
The Bedford Record and Circular
Bedford Times
Bedford Times and Bedfordshire Independent
Bedfordshire Times
The Bedfordshire Times and Bedfordshire Standard
Bedfordshire Times & Citizen
Bedfordshire Times and Independent
The Daily Telegraph
The Guardian
Huddersfield Examiner
Picture Post
The Radio Times
The Sidmouth Journal & Directory
Sidmouth Observer
The Times
Times & Citizen
Woburn Reporter

Websites

http://en.wikipedia.org/wiki/Alfred_Rouse Wikipedia
http://www.andrewmorrisconductor.com Andrew Morris

http://www.bach-cantatas.com Bach Cantatas
http://www.bbc.co.uk/proms/events/performers BBC Proms
http://www.oxfordmusiconline.com Grove Music Online

Primary sources

Benson, Michael, 'Diary' (unpublished)
Palmer, H. Marshall, 'Memoirs' (unpublished)
Pinnock, Joe, 'Reminiscences', 4 November 1989 (unpublished)
Smart, Richard, ed., *The Bousfield Diaries: A Middle-class Family in Late Victorian Bedford*, BHRS, vol. 86 (Bedford 2007)

Secondary sources

Baker, A. E. and N. C. Wilde, *Bedford in Times Past* (Chorley, 1980)
Baker, Austin, *The Library Story: Bedford Public Library and its Forerunners 1700–1958* (Bedford, 1989)
Bayes, George E., *These Years Have Told: The Story of Park Road Baptist Church, Rushden* (Rushden, 1951)
Bedford, James John Russell, Duke of, *A Silver-plated Spoon; The Story of the Dukes of Bedford, including the Author's own Life* (London, 1959)
Bedford Corporation, *Bedford 1166–1966: A Record of the Charter Year* (Bedford, 1966)
Bedford Modern School, 'The Staff', *The Eagle*, vol. 27, no. 3 (Summer 1949), pp. 166–7
Bedford Music - A Year Book 1947 (Bedford, 1947)
Benson, Mike, 'Bedford Corn Exchanges', *The Bedfordshire Magazine*, vol. 25, no. 194 (Autumn 1995), pp. 58–64
Benson, Mike, 'Bedford Choral Society', *The Bedfordshire Magazine*, vol. 23, no 179 (Winter 1991), pp. 100–4
Bevan, Elinor, *A Bedford Childhood: The Early Life (from 1908–1925) of Francis Charles Victor Brightman (1904 -2004)* (Edinburgh, 2006)
Bonavia-Hunt, Rev. Noel A. *Irons in the Fire: The Bonavia-Hunt Memoirs* (London, 1959)
Boult, Adrian, *My Own Trumpet* (London, 1973)
Brown, James D. and Stephen S. Stratton, *British Musical Biography: A Dictionary of Musical Artists, Authors, and Composers born in Britain and its Colonies* (New York, 1971)
Burrows, Donald, *Handel* (New York, 2012), The Master Musicians; Master Musicians Series
Carrodus, J. T., *How to Play the Violin: Chats with Violinists* (London, 1895)
Coleridge, Samuel Taylor, *The Works of Samuel Taylor Coleridge* (Ware, 1994)
Coombs, James, *Recollections Personal and Political: As Read before the Bedford Liberal Club the President Alderman Hawkins JP Mayor in the Chair April 4 1889* (Bedford, 1889)
Dibble, Jeremy, *C. Hubert H. Parry: His Life and Music* (Oxford, 1992)
Dibble, Jeremy, *Charles Villiers Stanford: Man and Musician* (Oxford, 2002)
Dibble, Jeremy, *John Stainer: A Life in Music* (Woodbridge, 2007)
Edwards, R. A., *And the Glory – A History in Commemoration of the 150th of Huddersfield Choral Society 1836–1986* (Leeds, 1985)
Fitzpatrick, Richard W., *Memorials of R. W. Fitzpatrick* (London, 1878)
Fuller Maitland, J. A., ed., *Grove's Dictionary of Music and Musicians*, (London, 1904–10, repr. 1921) 5 vols

Godber, Joyce, *The Harpur Trust, 1552–1973* (Bedford, 1973)
Godber, Joyce, *History of Bedfordshire 1066–1888* (Bedford, 1969)
Graves, Robert, *The Greek Myths* (London, 1955), 2 vols
Grubert, Halina, 'Cecil Higgins – Collector Extraordinary I', *The Bedfordshire Magazine*, vol. 18, no. 143 (Winter 1982), pp. 269–74
Grubert, Halina, 'Cecil Higgins – Collector Extraordinary II', *The Bedfordshire Magazine*, vol. 18, no. 144 (Spring 1983), pp. 334–40
Harding, Harry Alfred, *Analysis of Form: As Displayed in Beethoven's Thirty-two Pianoforte Sonatas* (London, n.d.)
Harding, Harry Alfred, *Bedford School Songs* (Bedford, 1929)
Harding, Harry Alfred, *5000 Scale and Arpeggio Tests Arranged in Irregular Order in Every Key* (unknown)
Harding, Harry Alfred, *Musical Ornaments with Questions and Exercises* (London, c.1912)
Harding, Harry Alfred, *Score Reading Exercises Written Specially for Candidates Preparing for the Royal College of Organists' Examinations, etc.* (London, c.1912)
'Harry Alfred Harding', *The Musical Times*, vol. 71, no. 1054 (December 1930), pp. 1084–5
Hurd, Michael, *Rutland Boughton and the Glastonbury Festivals* (Oxford, 1993)
Kelly, E. R., ed., *Post Office Directory of Northamptonshire, Huntingdonshire, Bedfordshire, Buckinghamshire, Berkshire and Oxfordshire 1869* (London, 1869)
Kennedy, Michael, *The Oxford Dictionary of Music* (Oxford, 1985)
Kennedy, Michael, *The Works of Ralph Vaughan Williams* (London, 1964)
Kenyon, Nicholas, *The BBC Symphony Orchestra: The First Fifty Years 1930–1980* (London, 1981)
le Fleming, Christopher, *Journey into Music by the Slow Train* (Bristol, 1982)
McGregor, Margaret, 'Music in Bedfordshire I', *Bedfordshire Magazine*, vol. 17, no. 129 (Summer 1979), pp. 3–8
McGregor, Margaret, 'Music in Bedfordshire II', *Bedfordshire Magazine*, vol. 17, no. 130 (Autumn 1979), pp. 56–60
Mitchell, Martin and David Bernstein, eds, *Well Remembered Fields*: *The Story of One School's Evacuation 1939–1945* (unknown, 2003)
Musgrave, Michael, *The Musical Life of the Crystal Palace* (Cambridge, 1995)
The New Grove Dictionary of Music and Musicians (London, 2001), 20 vols
Northrop Moore, Jerrold, *Edward Elgar: A Creative Life* (Oxford, 1984)
Owen, William, ed., *A Life in Music: Conversations with Sir David Willcocks and Friends* (Oxford, 2008)
Oxford Dictionary of National Biography (Oxford, 2004), 60 vols
Plunket Greene, Harry, *Interpretation in Song* (London, 1912)
The Poetical Works of Longfellow (London, undated)
Rutherford, Mark, *Catharine Furze* (London, 1893), 2 vols
Salter, Lionel, ed., *More Romantic Pieces for the Piano* (London, 1990)
Scholes, Percy A., *The Oxford Companion to Music*, 8th ed. (Oxford, 1950)
Scholes, Percy A., *The Oxford Companion to Music*, 9th ed. (Oxford, 1956)
A Short History of the Festival (Bedford, c.1980)
Slonimsky, Nicolas, *Baker's Biographical Dictionary of Musicians* (Oxford, 1984)
Steinmetz, H., *A History of Modern Europe from the Invasion of the Barbarians to the Present Day (AD 375–1869): A Hand-book for Schools* (London, 1869)
Sutton, Anna, *A Story of Sidmouth* (Sidmouth, 1953)
Wesley, Mary, *The Camomile Lawn* (London, 1984)
Westaway, K. M., ed., *A History of Bedford High School* (Bedford, 1932)
Weston, Stephen J. *The Organ and Organists of Bedford High School 1898–1998* (Bedford, 1998)

Who's Who 2015 (London 2014)
Wildman, Richard, *Bedford* (Stroud, 1995), Britain in Old Photographs
Wildman, Richard, 'The Bedford Flood, 1947', *The Bedfordshire Magazine*, vol. 26, no. 201 (Summer 1997), pp. 11–15
Willcocks, David and John Rutter, eds, *Carols for Choirs. 2: Fifty Carols for Christmas and Advent* (London, 1970)

Index of Musical Works

A reference may occur more than once on a page.
n after arabic numbers refers to a footnote on that page.

Index of Personal Names

Dates of birth and death (where known) relate only to well-known composers.
A reference may occur more than once on a page.
n after arabic numbers refers to a footnote on that page.

Subject Index

A reference may occur more than once on a page.
n after arabic numbers refers to a footnote on that page.